Democracy for the Few

Fifth Edition

692-4297

Case #6242
Appeal
WLB III
915-673-5278

Democracy for the Few

Fifth Edition

Michael Parenti

St. Martin's Press
New York

Library of Congress Catalog Card Number: 87-060558

Manufactured in the United States of America.
21098
fedc

For information, write:
St. Martin's Press, Inc.
175 Fifth Avenue
New York, NY 10010

cover design: Darby Downey
cover illustration: Eldon C. Doty

ISBN: 0-312-19366-1

ACKNOWLEDGMENTS

Page 11: Tony Auth in *The Philadelphia Inquirer.* **Page 18:** Mike Konopacki, *IUE News*, International Union of Electronic Workers. **Page 27:** Fred Wright/*UE News*. **Page 40:** Drawing by Donald Reilly; © 1974 The New Yorker Magazine, Inc. **Page 85:** From *Herblock Through the Looking Glass* (W. W. Norton, 1984). **Page 93:** By permission of Johnny Hart and News American Syndicate. **Page 102:** By permission of Johnny Hart and News American Syndicate. **Page 118:** From *Herblock Through the Looking Glass* (W. W. Norton, 1984). **Page 125:** By permission of Johnny Hart and News American Syndicate. **Page 132:** Copyright 1977 Jules Feiffer. Reprinted with permission of Universal Press Syndicate. All rights reserved. **Page 146:** Copyright 1976 by Herblock in the *Washington Post*. **Page 190:** *Dunagin's People* by Ralph Dunagin © Field Enterprises, Inc., 1980, by permission of North American Syndicate, Inc. **Page 198:** Drawing by Dana Fradon; © 1974 The New Yorker Magazine, Inc. **Page 215:** From *Herblock Through the Looking Glass* (W. W. Norton, 1984). **Page 235:** Reprinted by permission: Tribune Media Services. **Page 258:** From *Herblock Through the Looking Glass* (W. W. Norton, 1984). **Page 278:** Drawing by Dana Fradon; © 1973 The New Yorker Magazine, Inc. **Page 316:** Vadillo in *El Sol de Mexico*/Rothco Cartoons.

For my son, Christian

Preface to the Fifth Edition

The study of politics is itself a political act, containing little that is neutral. True, we can all agree on certain neutral facts about the structure of government and the like. However, the book that does not venture much beyond these minimal descriptions will offend few readers but also will interest few. Any determined pursuit of how and why things happen draws us into highly controversial areas. Most textbooks pretend to a neutrality they do not really possess. While claiming to be objective, they are merely conventional. They depict the status quo in implicitly accepting terms, propagating fairly orthodox notions about American politics.

For decades, mainstream political scientists and other apologists for the existing social order have tried to transform practically every deficiency in our political system into a strength. They would have us believe that the millions who are nonvoters are content with present social conditions, that high-powered lobbyists are nothing to worry about because they perform an information function vital to representative government, and that the growing concentration of executive power is a good thing because the president is democratically responsive to broad national interests. The apologists have argued that the exclusion of third parties is really for the best because too many parties (that is, more than two) would fractionalize and destabilize our political system, and besides, the major parties eventually incorporate into their platforms the positions raised by minor parties (which is news to a number of socialist parties whose views have remained unincorporated throughout this entire century).

Reacting to the mainstream tendency to turn every vice into a virtue, left critics of the status quo have felt compelled to turn every virtue into a vice. Thus they have argued that electoral struggle is meaningless, that our civil liberties are a charade, that federal programs for the needy are next to worthless, that reforms are mostly sops to the oppressed, and labor unions are all complacent, corrupt, and conservative. The left critics have been a much needed antidote to the happy pluralists who painted a silver lining around every murky cloud. But they were wrong in seeing no victories, no "real" progress in the democratic struggles fought and won. *Democracy for the Few* tries to strike a balance; it tries to explain how democracy is incongruous with modern-day capitalism and is consistently violated by a capitalist social order, and yet how democracy refuses to die and continues to fight back and even make gains despite the great odds against popular forces.

Democracy for the Few offers an interpretation that students are not likely to get in elementary school, high school, or most of their college courses, nor in the mass media or mainstream political literature. There are political scientists who for thirty years have written about American government, the presidency, and public policy without ever once mentioning capitalism, a feat of omission that would be judged extraordinary were it not so commonplace. In this book I talk about that forbidden subject, capitalism, so better to comprehend the underpinnings of the political system we are studying. It may come as a surprise to some academics, but there is a marked relationship between economic power and political power.

I have attempted to blend several approaches. Attention is given to traditional political *institutions* such as the Congress, the presidency, the bureaucracy, the Supreme Court, political parties, elections, and the law-enforcement system. But these institutional, formalistic features of American government are placed in an overall framework that relates them to the realities of class power and interest.

In addition, the book devotes attention to the *foundations and historical development* of American politics, particularly in regard to the making of the Constitution, the growing role of government, and the political culture. The major eras of reform are investigated with the intent of developing a more critical understanding of the class dimension in American politics, the struggle waged by democratic forces, and the difficulties of reform.

Herein we will give critical attention not only to the existing practices and institutional arrangements of the American political system (who governs, what governs, and how?), but also to the outputs of the system (who gets what?). Thus a major emphasis is placed on the *political-economic aspects of public policy*. The significance of government, after all, lies not in its abstracted structure as such, but in what it does, what policies it produces, and how these policies affect people at home and abroad. I have included a good deal of public-policy information of a kind not ordinarily found in the standard texts, first, because students tend to be poorly informed about politico-economic issues, and second, because it makes little sense to talk about the "policy process" as something abstracted from actual issues and content, divorced from questions of power and interest. This descriptive information, however, is presented with the intent of drawing the reader to an analysis and an overall synthesis of American political reality.

Every chapter and almost every page of this edition have been revised, not only for the purpose of updating but also in an attempt to refine the analysis. This is especially so in regard to the chapters on Congress, the Supreme Court, the bureaucracy, and the media. My hope is that this new edition proves as useful to students and lay readers as were the earlier ones.

I wish to thank Dr. William Fierman, University of Tennessee, Knoxville; Dr. Peter Remender, University of Wisconsin—Oshkosh; Dr. James Klonoski, Department of Political Science, University of Oregon, Eugene; Dr. Benjamin Marquez, Department of Political Science, University of Utah; and Dr. Edward I. Sidlow, Northwestern University, for the criticisms they offered. A special word of appreciation goes to Philip Green of Smith College who provided a superb and commanding critique of both the large and small questions treated herein.

I once more benefited from the conscientious assistance of the staff at St. Martin's Press, especially my editor Larry Swanson, who both prodded and supported me right down to the finish line, and Patricia Mansfield, senior project editor. An expression of gratitude goes to Simon Gerson, the political writer, activist, and friend who supplied me with materials and conversations that proved useful for this book, and to another friend, Barbara Tillman, who provided emergency support during the crucial deadline days.

Acknowledgment is due to the late Samuel Hendel, a friend and former teacher of mine to whom the previous four editions of this book were dedicated. Sam Hendel gave to several generations of appreciative students the encouragement and guidance we needed. Unlike so many others, he resisted the temptations of conformist cold-war scholarship and understood that democratic principles were meaningless if divested of social and economic content. I miss him greatly.

This fifth edition is dedicated to Christian Parenti because no father could wish for a better son.

Michael Parenti

Contents

1

Politics and "The System"

How does the American political system work and for what purpose? What are the major forces shaping political life and how do they operate? Who governs in the United States? Who gets what, when, how, and why? Who pays and in what ways? These are the central questions investigated in this book. Many of us were taught a somewhat idealized textbook version of American government, which might be summarized as follows:

1. The United States was founded by persons dedicated to building a nation for the good of all its citizens. A Constitution was fashioned to limit political authority and check abuses of power. Over the generations it has proven to be a "living document," which, through reinterpretation and amendment, has served us well.
2. The nation's political leaders, the president and the Congress, are for the most part responsive to the popular will. The people's desires are registered through periodic elections and the operations of political parties and a free press. Decisions are made by small groups of persons within the various circles of government, but these decisionmakers are kept in check by each other's power and by their need to satisfy the electorate in order to remain in office. The people do not rule but they select those who do. Thus, government decisions are grounded in majority rule—subject to the restraints imposed by the Constitution for the protection of minority rights.
3. The United States is a nation of many different social, economic, ethnic, and regional groups, which make varied and competing demands on public officeholders. The role of government is to act as a mediator of these conflicting demands, formulating policies that bene-

fit the public. Although most decisions are compromises that seldom satisfy all interested parties, they usually allow for a working consensus; hence, every group has a say and no one chronically dominates.

4. These institutional arrangements have given us a government of laws and not of individuals, which, while far from perfect, allows for a fairly high degree of popular participation. Our political system is part of our free and prosperous society, a society that is the envy of peoples throughout the world.

THE POLITICO-ECONOMIC SYSTEM

This view of the United States as a happy, pluralistic polity says little about the actual outputs of the system. It assumes that existing social, economic, and political institutions operate with benign effect, that interests are fairly accommodated even if not perfectly so, that elections and leaders operate with democratic effect, that power is not highly concentrated nor heavily skewed toward those who control vast wealth, that capitalism is not to be treated as of critical concern when discussing American government, and that the state is a neutral entity with no special class relationship to those who own the land, technology, resources, and capital of this and other societies. These enormous assumptions will be challenged in the pages ahead.

With the persistence of poverty; unemployment; recessions; inflation; overseas military interventions; gargantuan defense budgets; crises in our transportation, health, educational, and welfare systems; environmental devastation; deficient consumer and worker protection; arduous and unfairly distributed taxes; a national debt that is growing at an ever increasing rate; and widespread crime in the streets and in high places, many persons find it difficult to believe that the best interests of the American people are being served by the existing state of affairs.

The central theme of this book is that our government often represents the privileged few rather than the needy many, and that participating in elections and the activities of political parties and exercising the right to speak out are insufficient measures against the influences of corporate wealth. The laws of our polity operate chiefly with undemocratic effect because they are written principally to advance the interests of the haves at the expense of the have-nots and because, even if equitable as written, they usually are enforced in highly discriminatory ways. Furthermore, it will be argued that this "democracy for the few" is not a product of the venality of particular officeholders but a reflection of the entire politico-economic system, the way the resources of power are distributed within it, and the interests that are served by it.

However, the American people have not been merely the passive victims to all this (nor usually the willing accomplices). The democratic forces of society—that is, the mass of ordinary working people, oppressed minorities, women, and persons from other social groups—have fought for and won important gains in political rights and in economic and social betterment, forcing—often after long and bitter struggles that went beyond the electoral process—important concessions from the politico-economic hierarchy. This democratic struggle is an important part of the story, and it will be given more attention in the pages ahead.

This book takes a holistic approach in that it recognizes, rather than denies, the linkages between various components of the whole politico-economic system. When we study any part of that system, be it the media, lobbying, criminal justice, overseas intervention, or environmental policy, we will see how that part reflects the nature of the whole and how in its particular way it serves, for the most part, to maintain the larger system—especially the system's overriding class interests. We will see that issues and problems are not isolated and unrelated, even though they are treated that way by various academics and news commentators. Rather, they are interrelated in direct and indirect ways. This will become more evident as we investigate the actual components of the political system in some detail.

By the "political system," I mean the various branches of government along with the political parties, laws, lobbyists, and private interest groups that affect public policy. One of my conclusions is that the distinction between "public" and "private" is often an artificial one. Government agencies are heavily influenced by private interest groups, and some private interest groups, such as some defense companies, depend completely on the public treasure for their profits and survival.

The decisions made by government are what I mean by "public policy." One characteristic of policy decisions is that they are seldom neutral. They almost always benefit some interests more than others, entailing social costs that are rarely equally distributed. The shaping of a budget, the passage of a piece of legislation, and the development of an administrative program are all policy decisions, all *political* decisions, and there is no way to execute them with neutral effect. If the wants of all persons could be automatically satisfied, there would be no need to set priorities and give some interests precedence over others; indeed, there would be no need for policies or politics as the words have just been used.

Politics extends even beyond the actions of state. Decisions that keep certain matters within "private" systems of power—such as leaving rental costs or health care to the private market—are highly political even if seldom recognized as such. Power in the private realm is generally inequitable and undemocratic and is often the source of struggles that spill over into the public arena (e.g., management-labor disputes, race and sex discrimination). In this book, we will focus principally on the public realm and how it fosters and responds to private power.

Someone once defined a politician as a person who receives votes from the poor and money from the rich on the promise of protecting each from the other. And President Jimmy Carter observed: "Politics is the world's second oldest profession, closely related to the first." Many people share this view. For them, politics is little more than the art of manipulating appearances in order to sell oneself, with the politician as a more subtle and less honest kind of prostitute. While not denying the large measure of truth in such observations, I take a broader view of politics; it is more than just something politicians do. Politics is the process of struggle over conflicting interests carried into the public arena; it may also involve the process of muting and suppressing conflicting interests. Politics involves the setting of public priorities, the choosing of certain interests and goals, and the denial of others.

Politics involves not only the competition among groups within the present system but also the struggle to change the entire system, not only the desire to achieve predefined ends but the struggle to redefine ends and to pose alternatives to the existing politico-economic structure.

Along with discussing the political system as such, I frequently refer to "the politico-economic system." Politics today covers every kind of issue, from abortion to school prayers, but *the bulk of public policy is concerned with economic matters*. The most important document the government produces each year is the budget. Probably the most vital functions of government are taxing and spending. Certainly they are necessary conditions for everything else it does, from delivering the mail to making war. The very organization of the federal government reflects its close involvement with the economy: thus, one finds the departments of Commerce, Labor, Agriculture, Interior, Transportation, and Treasury, and the Federal Trade Commission, the National Labor Relations Board, the Interstate Commerce Commission, the Federal Communications Commission, and the Securities and Exchange Commission all involved in regulating economic activity. Most of the committees in Congress can be identified according to their economic functions, the most important having to do with taxation and appropriations.

If much of this book seems concerned with economic matters, it's because that's what government is mostly about. Nor should this relationship be surprising. Politics and economics are but two sides of the same coin. Economics is concerned with the allocation of scarce resources for competing ends, involving conflicts between social classes and among groups and individuals within classes. Much of politics is a carryover of this struggle. Both politics and economics deal with the material survival, prosperity, and well-being of millions of people; both deal with the first conditions of social life itself.

This close relationship between politics and economics is neither neutral nor coincidental. Large governments evolve through history in order to protect large accumulations of property and wealth. In nomadic and hunting societies, where there is little surplus wealth, government is rudimentary and usually communal. In societies where wealth and property are controlled by a select class of persons, a state develops to protect the interests of the haves from the have-nots. As wrote John Locke in 1689: "The great and chief end . . . of Men's uniting into Commonwealths, and putting themselves under Government, is the Preservation of their Property." And Adam Smith, who is above suspicion in his dedication to capitalism, wrote in 1776: "The necessity of civil government grows up with the acquisition of valuable property." And "Till there be property there can be no government, the very end of which is to secure wealth, and to defend the rich from the poor."[1]

Many political scientists have managed to ignore the relationship between government and wealth, treating the corporate giants, if at all, as if they were but one of a number of interest groups. Most often this evasion is accomplished by labeling any approach that links class, wealth, and capitalism to politics as "Marxist." To be sure, Karl Marx saw such a relationship, but so did more conservative theorists like Thomas Hobbes, John Locke, Adam Smith and, in America, Alexander Hamilton and James Madison. Indeed, just about every theorist and practitioner of politics in the seventeenth, eighteenth, and early nineteenth centuries saw the linkage between political organization and economic interest, and between state and class, as not only important but *desirable* and essential to the well-being of the polity. "The people who own the country ought to govern it," declared John Jay. A permanent check over the populace should be exercised by "the rich and the well-born," urged Alexander Hamilton.

Unlike most of the theorists before him, Marx was one of the first in the modern era to see the existing relationship between property and power as *un*desirable, and this was his unforgivable sin. Marx wrote during the mid-to-late nineteenth century, when people increasingly criticized the abuses of industrial capitalism and when those who owned the wealth of society preferred to draw attention away from the relationship between private wealth and public power and toward more "respectable" subjects. The

---

1. John Locke, *Treatise of Civil Government* (New York: Appleton-Century-Croft, 1937), p. 82. Adam Smith, *An Inquiry into the Nature and Causes of the Wealth of Nations* (Chicago: Encyclopaedia Britannica, 1952), pp. 309 and 311.

tendency to avoid critical analysis of American capitalism persists to this day among business people, journalists, lawyers, and academics.[2]

Many economists pay no heed to politics and many political scientists give but a passing thought to economic forces. Yet there exists in the real world a close interrelationship between political power and economic wealth, between state and class. As the sociologist Robert Lynd once noted, power is no less political because it is economic. By "power," I mean the ability to get what one wants, either by having one's interests prevail in conflicts with others or by preventing others from raising conflicting demands. Power presumes the ability to control the actions and beliefs of others through favor, fear, fraud, or force and to manipulate the social environment to one's advantage. Power belongs to those who possess the resources that enable them to control the behavior of others, such as jobs, organization, technology, publicity, media, social legitimacy, expertise, essential goods and services, and—the ingredient that often determines the availability of these things—money.

UNDERSTANDING "THE SYSTEM"

We hear a great deal of talk about "the system." What is often lacking is any precise investigation of what the system is and what it does or doesn't do. Instead, some people will attack the system and others will defend it. Some say it does not work and should be changed or overthrown; others say it does work or, in any case, we can't fight it and should work within it. Some argue that the existing system is "the only one we have" and imply that it is the only one we ever *could* have. Hence, some people fear that a breakdown in this system's social order would mean a breakdown in all social order, an end to society itself or, in any case, a creation of something monstrously worse than the status quo. These fearful notions keep many people not only from entertaining ideas about new social arrangements but also from taking a critical look at existing ones.

Sometimes the complaint is made: "You're good at criticizing the system, but what would you put in its place?" the implication being that unless you have a finished blueprint for a better society, you should refrain from pointing out existing deficiencies and injustices. But this book is predicated on the notion that it is desirable and necessary for human

---

2. See William Appleman Williams, *The Great Evasion* (Chicago: Quadrangle Books, 1964) for an analysis of the way Marxist thought has been stigmatized or ignored by American intellectuals and those who pay their salaries. Also Sidney Fine, *Laissez-Faire and the General-Welfare State* (Ann Arbor: University of Michigan Press, 1964) for a description of capitalist, anti-Marxist orthodoxy in the United States in the late nineteenth century and its control over business, law, economics, university teaching, and religion.

beings to examine the society in which they live, possibly as a step toward making fundamental improvements. The purpose here is to understand what *is* and not to present a detailed, speculative study of what could be. It is unreasonable to demand that we refrain from making a diagnosis of an illness until we have perfected a cure. Such a method of solving problems, medical or social, would be futile. (In any case, suggestions for fundamental changes are offered in the closing chapter.)

Political life is replete with deceit, corruption, and plunder. Small wonder that many people seek to remove themselves from it. But whether we like it or not, politics and government play a crucial role in determining the conditions of our lives. Readers might go "do their own thing," pretending that they have removed themselves from the world of politics and power. They can leave political life alone, but it will not leave them alone. They can escape its noise and its pretensions but not some of its worst effects. One ignores the doings of the state only at one's own risk.

If the picture that emerges in the pages ahead is not pretty, this should not be taken as an attack on the United States, for this country and the American people are greater than the abuses perpetrated upon them by those who live for power and profit. To expose these abuses is not to denigrate the nation that is a victim of them. The greatness of a country is to be measured by something more than its rulers, its military budget, its instruments of dominance and destruction, and its profiteering giant corporations. A nation's greatness can be measured by its ability to create a society free of poverty, racism, and sexism and free of domestic and overseas exploitation and social and environmental devastation. Albert Camus once said, "I would like to love my country and justice too." In fact, there is no better way to love one's country, no better way to strive for the fulfillment of its greatness, than to entertain critical ideas and engage in the pursuit of social justice at home and abroad.

2

Wealth and Want in the United States

Most scholars and journalists who write about the American political system never mention capitalism. But the capitalist economy creates imperatives that bear urgently upon political life. If politics is concerned with who gets what, then we might begin by considering who's already got what? How is wealth distributed and used in the United States?

WEALTH AND CLASS

One should distinguish between those who own the wealth of the society, specifically the very rich families and individuals whom we might call "the owning class," and those who are dependent on that class for their employment, "the working class." The latter includes not only blue-collar workers but just about everyone else who is not independently wealthy. The distinction between owners and employees is blurred somewhat by the range of wealth within the owning and working classes. Thus, although "owners" include both the wealthy stockholders of giant corporations and the proprietors of small stores, the latter control a relatively small portion of the wealth and hardly qualify as part of the *corporate* owning class. While glorified as the purveyors of the entrepreneurial spirit, small businesses are really just so many squirrels dancing among the elephants. Small owners usually devote much of their own labor to their enterprises, are dependent on larger contractors for their existence, and are easily stamped out when markets decline or bigger competitors move in.[1]

1. The casualty rate for small and medium-sized businesses is increasing. In 1979, there were 7,564 business bankruptcies in the United States; by 1983, there were 31,334, or an

Likewise, among the employee class are professionals and middle-level executives who in income, education, and life-style tend to be identified as "middle class." Then there are some entertainment and sports figures, lawyers, doctors, and executives who earn such lavish incomes that they become in part, or eventually in whole, members of the owning class by investing their surplus wealth and living mostly off the profits of their investments.

You are a member of the owning class when your income is very large and comes mostly from the labor of other people—that is, when others work for you, either in a company you own, or by creating the wealth that allows your money and realty investments to increase in value. Hard work seldom makes anyone rich. *The secret to wealth is to have others work hard for you.* This explains why workers who spend their lives toiling in factories or offices retire with little or no wealth to speak of, while the owners of these businesses, who do not work in them at all, can amass riches from such enterprises.

Wealth is created by the labor power of workers. As Adam Smith noted, "Labor . . . is alone the ultimate and real standard by which the value of all commodities can at all times and places be estimated and compared. It is their real price; money is their nominal price only."[2] What transforms an unmarketable tree into a profitable commodity such as paper or furniture is the labor that goes into harvesting the timber, cutting the lumber, and manufacturing, shipping, advertising, and selling the commodity (along with the labor that goes into making the tools, trucks, and whatever else is needed in the production process). For their efforts, workers are paid wages that represent only a portion of the wealth created by labor. The unpaid portion is expropriated by the owners for their personal consumption and for further investment.

Workers suffer an exploitation of their labor as certainly as did slaves and serfs. The difference is that with wage labor, the portion taken from the worker is not visible. All one sees is five days' pay for five days' work. Under feudalism, when serfs worked three days for themselves and three days for the lord, the expropriation was readily apparent; so with sharecroppers who must give, say, half their crop to the landowner. If wages did represent the total wealth created, there would be no surplus wealth, no profits for the owner, no great fortunes for those who do not labor.

But don't managers and executives make a contribution to production for which they should be compensated? Yes, if they are performing useful

---

average of 602 a week: *Washington Post*, March 5, 1984; also S. N. Nadel, *Contemporary Capitalism and the Middle Classes* (New York: International Publishers, 1983).

2. Adam Smith, *An Inquiry into the Nature and Causes of the Wealth of Nations* (New York: Modern Library, 1937), p. 33.

labor for the enterprise, and usually they are paid very well, indeed. But income from ownership is apart from salary and apart from labor; it is money you are paid *when not working*. The author of a book, for instance, does not make "profits" on his book; he *earns* an income from the labor of writing it, proportionately much less than the sum going to those who own the publishing house and who do none of the writing, editing, printing, and marketing of books. The sum going to the owners is profits; it is *unearned* income.

While the corporations are often called the "producer" interests, the truth is that they produce nothing. They are organizational devices for the expropriation of labor and for the accumulation of capital. The real producers are those who apply their brawn, brains, and talents to the creation of goods and services. The primacy of labor was noted years ago by a Republican president. In his first annual message to Congress, Abraham Lincoln stated: "Labor is prior to and independent of capital. Capital is only the fruit of labor and could not have existed had not labor first existed. Labor is the superior of capital and deserves much the higher consideration." Lincoln's words went largely unheeded. The dominance of capital over labor remains the essence of the American economic system, bringing ever greater concentrations of wealth and power into the hands of a small moneyed class.

WHO OWNS AMERICA?

Contrary to a widely propagated myth, this country's wealth does not belong to a broad middle class. The top 10 percent of American households own over 86 percent of the stocks, bonds, savings, property, and other financial assets. The top 0.5 percent owns more than 45 percent of the privately held wealth, while 90 percent of the American people have little or no net financial assets. The single greatest source of individual wealth is inheritance.[3] (In other words, if you are not rich, it is principally because you lacked the foresight and initiative to pick the right parents at birth.)

The recent trend has been toward still greater economic inequality. Since 1974, the share of the national income that goes to wages and salaries (adjusted for inflation) has declined by over 10 percent, while the share derived from interest, rents, and dividends has almost doubled, having become the fastest growing kind of personal income. In 1983, a year the U.S. economy actually shrank, the combined net worth of the richest 400 Americans jumped 28 percent, from $92 billion to $118 billion.

3. Stephen J. Rose, *The American Profile Poster: Who Owns What* (New York: Pantheon, 1986), p. 31; *New York Times*, September 23, 1986.

No fewer than 116 of these super-rich persons enjoyed at least a 50 percent increase in their fortunes.[4]

Less than 1 percent of all corporations control two-thirds of the corporate assets of the entire economy. Forty-nine of the biggest banks hold a controlling interest in the 500 largest corporations. Thus, ITT, Sears, American Express, IBM, BankAmerica, and Citicorp can all claim J. P. Morgan, Inc., as one of their top investors. J. P. Morgan is the nation's largest stockholder, with more than $15 billion invested in the stock market.[5] In the United States, as in most other industrial countries, finance capital dominates other forms of capital formation, including manufacturing.

4. *Washington Post*, July 8, 1985; John Cavanaugh, "It's a Rich Man's World," *The New Internationalist*, July 1984, pp. 1–3. "Corporate Profits Rise," *USA Today*, May 21, 1984. By 1985, profits were beginning to slump in what was supposed to be a "recovery": *New York Times*, August 12, 1985. Rose, *The American Profile Poster*, p. 31.

5. Report by the Joint Economic Committee, *The Concentration of Wealth in the United States*, Washington D.C., Government Printing Office, 1986; Lester Thurow, "The Leverage of Our Wealthiest 400," *New York Times*, October 11, 1984; *Forbes*, September 17, 1984; Erik Bert, "The Web of Corporate Capital," *Political Affairs*, November 1981, pp. 32–40, and December 1981, pp. 20–27.

The trend is toward greater concentrations of corporate wealth as giant companies are bought up by supergiants. Mobil Oil purchased Montgomery Ward; Philip Morris inhaled Miller Brewing, and Coca-Cola swallowed Paramount Pictures. In 1984, Texaco engulfed Getty Oil for $10.1 billion, the largest corporate merger to date. Nine of the ten largest corporate mergers in history occurred during the 1981–85 period. Some $100 billion of corporate cash resources have been spent on mergers at a great profit to company executives and big stockholders. Such takeovers absorb money that could have been spent on new technologies and new jobs. Rather than create new capital assets, mergers merely rearrange old ones for quick paper profits. Instead of enlarging the economic pie, corporate and financial elites cut bigger slices for themselves. This is why, despite repeated recessions and sluggish economic growth, profits doubled in the early 1980s.[6]

Americans are taught that the economy consists of a wide array of independent producers. We refer to "farmers" as an interest apart from businesspeople, at a time when the Bank of America has a multimillion-dollar stake in California farmlands, and Cal Pak and Safeway operate at every level from the field to the supermarket. The larger agribusiness firms now control over half of all the farmland in the United States. Just one percent of all food corporations control 80 percent of all the industry's assets and close to 90 percent of the profits, while totally monopolizing food advertising on television. Just three companies control 60 to 70 percent of all the country's dairy products. Six multinational firms handle 90 percent of all the grain shipped in the world market.[7]

This centralized food industry represents an American success story—for the big companies. Independent family farms are going deeper into debt or completely out of business.[8] By 1980, the total farm debt was $160 billion, *eight times net farm income*; by 1985, the farm debt climbed to over $235 billion.[9] With the growth of corporate agribusiness, regional self-sufficiency in food has virtually vanished. The Northeast, for instance, imports more than 70 percent of its food from other regions. For every $2 spent to grow food in the United States, another $1 is spent to move it.

---

6. Leslie Wayne, "The Corporate Raiders," *New York Times Magazine*, July 18, 1982, pp. 18, 47–51; Michael Pertschuk and Kenneth Davidson, "Whats Wrong with Conglomerate Mergers?" in Mark Green and Robert Massie, Jr. (eds.), *The Big Business Reader* (New York: Pilgrim Press, 1980).

7. Frances Moore Lappe and Joseph Collins, *World Hunger: Ten Myths*, 4th edition (San Francisco: Institute for Food and Development Policy, 1979), p. 15.

8. Ibid.; also Keith Schneider, "As More Family Farms Fail, Hired Managers Take Charge": *New York Times*, March 17, 1986.

9. Helvi Savola, "The Farm Crisis and the All People's Front," *Political Affairs*, May 1985, p. 37.

Giant agribusiness farms rely on intensive row crop farming and heavy use of chemical spraying and artificial fertilizers, all of which cause massive erosion and place a strain on water supplies. The nation's ability to feed itself is being jeopardized, as each year more and more land is eroded by large-scale, quick-profit commercial farming.[10]

Many corporations are owned by stockholders who, because of their scattered numbers, have little say over the management of their holdings. From this fact, it has been incorrectly inferred that control of most firms has passed into the hands of corporate managers who run their companies with a regard for the public interest that is not shared by their profit-hungry stockholders. Since 1932, when A. A. Berle and Gardner Means first portrayed the giant firms as developing "into a purely neutral technocracy," controlled by disinterested managers who allocated resources on the basis of public need "rather than private cupidity,"[11] many observers have come to treat this fantasy as a reality.

In fact, the separation of ownership from management is far from complete. Almost one-third of the top 500 corporations in the United States are controlled by one individual or family. Furthermore, the decline of family capitalism has not led to widespread ownership among the general public. *The diffusion of stock ownership has not cut across class lines but has occurred within the upper class itself.* In an earlier day, three families might have owned companies A, B, and C, respectively, whereas today all three have holdings in all three companies, thereby giving "the upper class an even greater community of interest than they had in the past."[12]

Some "family enterprises" are of colossal size. Indeed, a small number of the wealthiest families, such as the Mellons, Morgans, DuPonts, and Rockefellers, dominate the American economy. The DuPont family controls eight of the largest defense contractors and grossed over $15 billion in military contracts during the Vietnam War. The DuPonts control ten corporations that each have billions of dollars in assets, including General Motors, Coca-Cola, and United Brands, along with many smaller firms. The DuPonts serve as trustees of scores of colleges. They own about forty

---

10. Hundreds of millions of acres of topsoil are blown away each year, a result of "hard pan," a deadening and hardening of soil due to the use of insecticide and artificial fertilizer and to intensive commercial farming: *Washington Post*, November 18, 1981, and February 7 and 8, 1982; also the excellent documentary film, *September Wheat*, produced by Peter Krieg, New Times Films, New York, 1980.

11. A. A. Berle, Jr., and Gardner Means, *The Modern Corporation and Private Property* (New York: Harcourt, Brace, 1932), p. 356.

12. G. William Domhoff, *Who Rules America*? (Englewood Cliffs, N.J.: Prentice-Hall, 1967), p. 40; also Domhoff's *Who Rules America Now*? (New York: Simon and Schuster, 1983).

manorial estates and private museums in Delaware alone and have set up thirty-one tax-exempt foundations. The family is frequently the largest contributor to Republican presidential campaigns and has financed right-wing and antilabor causes.[13]

Another powerful family enterprise, that of the Rockefellers, extends into just about every industry in every state of the Union and every nation in the nonsocialist world. The Rockefellers control five of the twelve largest oil companies and four of the largest banks in the world. They finance universities, churches, "cultural centers," and youth organizations. At one time or another, they or their close associates have occupied the offices of the president, vice-president, secretaries of State, Commerce, Defense, and other cabinet posts, the Federal Reserve Board, the governorships of several states, key positions in the Central Intelligence Agency (CIA), the U.S. Senate and House, and the Council on Foreign Relations.[14]

In companies not directly under family control, the supposedly public-minded managers are large investors in corporate America. Managers award themselves stupendous salaries and other benefits. Thus, despite recessions and widespread layoffs in various industries, compensation for executives has been rising more than 13 percent annually. By 1986, most chief executive officers were making between $1 million and $2 million a year in salaries, bonuses, stock options, and other perks. Some do even better: in 1985, Victor Posner, chairman of DWG Corporation, reaped $12.7 million, while Lee Iacocca, head of Chrysler, took in $11.5 million. A few years before, Frederick Smith, chairman of Federal Express, pocketed $54 million, and Charles Lazarus, chairman of Toys 'Я' Us, raked in $44 million.[15] As Richard Munro, president of Time Inc., admitted: "Corporate managers lead just about the most privileged lives in our society."[16]

The executives of large corporations are almost always wealthy individuals who have a direct interest in corporate profits. Far from being neutral technocrats dedicated to the public welfare, they represent the more active element of a self-interested owning class. Their power does not rest in their holdings but in their corporate positions. "Not great fortunes, but great corporations are the important units of wealth, to which individuals of property are variously attached."[17]

---

13. Gerard Colby, *DuPont Dynasty: Behind the Nylon Curtain* (New York: Lyle Stuart, 1985).

14. Peter Collier and David Horowitz, *The Rockefellers* (New York: Holt, Rinehart and Winston, 1976).

15. Cleveland Amory, "What the Rich Earn," *Parade*, June 10, 1984; Lloyd Shearer, "Who Earned the Most?" *Parade*, August 3, 1986; "Insurance Execs Enjoy Big Salary Increases," *Public Citizen*, August 1986, p. 9.

16. *Washington Post*, February 11, 1982.

17. C. Wright Mills, *The Power Elite* (New York: Oxford University Press, 1956), p. 116.

THE DYNAMIC OF CAPITALISM

There is something more to capitalism than just the concentration of wealth. Vast fortunes existed in ancient Egypt, feudal Europe, and other pre-capitalist class societies. What is unique about capitalism is its perpetual dynamic of capital accumulation and expansion—and the dominant role this process plays in the economic order.

In a sense, capital is dead labor. Unless it can be invested in production—that is, mixed with living labor to create more capital—it has no function and no value. Capitalists like to say that they are "putting their money to work," but money as such cannot create more wealth. What capitalists really mean is that they are putting more human labor power to work for them, paying workers less in wages than they produce in value, thereby siphoning off more profit for themselves. That's how money "grows."[18] Of itself, capital cannot produce anything; it is the thing that is produced by labor.

Normally when we think of work, we think of the worker using the means of production (tools, machines, vehicles). But under capitalism, the means of production use the worker. The ultimate purpose of work under capitalism is not to produce goods, such as cars or breakfast cereals, or to perform services, such as insurance or banking, but to make more money for the investor. Money harnesses labor in order to convert itself into goods and services that will produce still more money. Capital annexes living labor in order to create more capital.[19]

Corporate profit is surplus wealth that must be either distributed to stockholders as dividends or reinvested by the corporation for more profits. As a corporation grows, it must find ways of continuing to grow. It faces the problem of constantly having to make more money, of finding new profitable areas of investment for its surplus earnings. Ecologists who worry about the way industry devastates the environment and who dream

---

18. Today the average employee works a little over two hours for herself and almost six hours for the boss. That latter portion is the "surplus value," which Marx described as the source of the owner's wealth. Sometimes the publicity that is designed to lure investments will acknowledge the existence of surplus value. Thus New York State boasts: "New York's manufacturing workers produce $4.25 in value over and above every dollar they get in wages." In other words, they produce four times more than what they are paid. Workers in Texas produce $5 in surplus value for every wage dollar. The percentage is vastly higher in most Third World nations: Gus Hall, *Karl Marx: Beacon for Our Times* (New York: International Publishers, 1983), pp. 24–25. Investments having no direct link to the employment of labor still indirectly rely on labor for their income. Money in the bank or invested in bonds earns interest only because borrowers can invest it—that is, use it to extract a profit from labor greater than the interest they must pay on the original bank loan.

19. For the great statement on the nature and function of capital, see Karl Marx, *Capital*, vol. 1, available in various editions.

of a "no-growth capitalism" as the solution seem not to realize that such a goal is unattainable, for a "no-growth capitalism" is a nonexpanding, noninvesting, nonprofit capitalism, a contradiction in terms, no capitalism at all.

The first law of capitalism is: accumulate profits or go out of business. "Profits provide the internal funds for expansion. Profits are the sinew and muscle of strength. . . . As such they become the immediate, unique, unifying, quantitative aim of corporate success."[20] The function of the corporation is not to perform public services or engage in philanthropy but to make as large a profit as possible. The social uses of the product and its effects upon human well-being and the natural environment win consideration in capitalist production, if at all, only to the extent that they do not violate the profit goals of the corporation. As David Roderick, the president of U.S. Steel (now USX) put it: "United States Steel Corporation is not in the business of making steel. We're in the business of making profits."[21]

This relentless pursuit of profit results from something more than just greed—although there is enough of that. Under capitalism, enterprises must expand in order to survive. To stand still amidst growth is to decline, not only relatively but absolutely. A slow-growth firm is less able to move into new markets, hold onto old ones, command investment capital, and control suppliers. A decline in the rate of production eventually cuts into profits and leads to a company's decline. Even the biggest corporations, enjoying a relatively secure oligopolistic control over markets, are beset by a ceaseless drive to expand, to find new ways of making money. Ultimately, the only certainty, even for the giants, is uncertainty. (Witness the near demise in recent years of General Dynamics, Lockheed, Chrysler, and Continental Illinois.) Larger size, greater reserves, and better organizational control might bring security were it not that all other companies are pursuing these same goals. So survival can never be taken for granted.

Recession and Stagnation

Business leaders admit that they could not survive if they tried to feed or house the poor, or invested in nonprofit projects for the environment, or in something so nebulous as a desire to "get the economy moving again." Nor can they invest simply to "create more jobs." In fact, most of their invest-

20. Paul Baran and Paul Sweezy, *Monopoly Capital* (New York: Monthly Review Press, 1968), pp. 39–40.

21. Quoted in Pat Barile, "Where Production Benefits Workers," *Daily World*, September 20, 1984, p. 4.

ments in new plants and in overseas areas are designed to cut labor costs by creating fewer jobs and lower wages.

By doing everything possible to hold down wages and increase profits, capitalists work against themselves, for they cut into the buying power of the very public that is supposed to consume their services and commodities. Every owner would prefer to pay employees as little as possible while selling goods to better-paid workers from other companies. "For the system as a whole, no such solution is possible; the dilemma is basic to capitalism. Wages, a cost of production, must be kept down; wages, a source of consumer spending, must be kept up."[22] This contradiction is a source of great instability, leading to chronic overproduction and a tendency toward stagnation.

When markets sag, production is cut back and layoffs and wage cuts are imposed by management. As workers lose their benefits and then their jobs, their buying power declines and sales drop further. Inventories accumulate; investment opportunities disappear; more cutbacks and speedups are imposed; and the stagnation deepens. Throughout the 1980s, the economy performed so sluggishly that the "recovery" of 1983–86 resembled a recession, with an investment growth rate of 1 to 2 percent (down from an 8.6 percent average for 1969–75), huge trade deficits, a continual decline in personal savings, and an unemployment level of 7 to 8 percent (higher than in the *recessions* of the 1960s and 1970s). Bank failures multiplied from ten a year in 1979–81 to about seventy a year in 1984–86. And small businesses were going bankrupt at a faster rate than at any time since the Great Depression of the 1930s.[23] Meanwhile, U.S. companies were investing abroad at twice the rate of domestic investment, attracted by the high profits to be made off the wretchedly low wages in Third World countries.[24]

For the big capitalists, recessions are not unmitigated gloom. Economic slumps keep labor from getting too aggressive in its wage demands and help weed out the weaker capitalists—to the benefit of the stronger. In boom times, with nearly full employment, workers are more ready to strike for better contracts. Other jobs are easy to get, and business finds it too costly to remain idle while markets are expanding. But with recession, the job market tightens, business is better able to resist labor demands. A reserve army of unemployed helps to deflate wages. Unions are weakened and often broken and profits rise faster than wages. Big business comes out

---

22. "Economy in Review," *Dollars and Sense*, March 1976, p. 3.

23. See the business pages of the *New York Times*, July 20 and August 12, 1986, and March 20, 1985; also John Culbertson, "Economic 'Miracle' or Illusion?" *New York Times*, March 27, 1986; Bertell Ollman, "Small Business Myths," *New York Times*, February 19, 1984; Russell Parker, "Doubts About the Recovery," *New York Times*, March 15, 1984.

24. Barry Bluestone, *The Deindustrialization of America* (New York: Basic Books, 1982).

ahead of the workers. "The general pattern reveals increased profits, decreased buying power, increased unemployment, higher labor productivity and decreased strike activity."[25]

Corporations draw subsidies from the public treasure; enter into monopolistic mergers; rig prices at artificially high levels; impose speedups, layoffs, and wage and benefit cuts; and move to cheaper overseas labor markets. In these ways, they are often able to increase profits amidst widespread want and unemployment. Business does fine; only the people suffer. In 1980–1982, a period of recession, firms like GE, AT&T, and Exxon reported record earnings. The idea that all Americans are in the same boat, experiencing good and bad times together, should be put to rest. Millions of working people suffer dearly during economic recession. But the very rich, enjoying vast reserves, endure few privations and may prosper all the more. In the recession years of 1974–75 and 1980–82, sales of jewelry, antiques, artwork, executive apartments, mansions, yachts, and luxury cars were booming among upper-class patrons. One top execu-

25. Ben Bedell in the *Guardian*, January 14, 1976, p. 4.

tive confessed, "The last two recessions have been poor man's recessions. People who have money have not suffered that much."[26]

Inflation

A common problem of modern capitalism is inflation. The 4 to 5 percent inflation rate that has regularly plagued our economy can, in a few years, substantially reduce the buying power of wage earners and persons on fixed incomes.[27] Corporation leaders maintain that inflation is caused by the wage demands of labor unions. In fact, wages have not kept pace with prices and profits. According to the *New York Times*, "Except for a few brief intervals, inflation has risen faster than wages for nearly two decades [1963–1982], leaving workers less well off."[28]

Hardest hit by inflation are the four essentials, which devour 70 percent of the average family income: food, fuel, housing, and health care. But in these necessities, the share of costs going to labor has been dropping. In the case of housing, high interest rates and real-estate speculations rather than wages have driven up prices. Labor costs in home construction have actually declined as construction unions have failed to win contracts and have been broken. Likewise, the rise in food prices cannot be ascribed to the wages paid farm workers who barely make enough to survive, nor to the independent farmers who are going broke, but to the higher land prices and higher rents caused by outside investors and the price fixing of agribusiness monopolies and supermarket chains.[29] And the astronomical costs of medical care cannot be blamed on the wages—among the lowest in the country—paid to hospital workers, but to the profits reaped by the hospital corporations, head doctors, and the drug industry.[30]

Over the past decade, labor has held back on wage demands, sometimes even taking cuts, yet prices continued to rise. In 1982, for instance, after workers at Ford and General Motors took $4 billion in wage and benefit cuts, the two companies promptly raised the prices of their cars

---

26. Gilbert Mauer of Hearst Corporation in *Business Week*, October 5, 1981; also "What Depression?" *Economic Notes*, May 1983, p. 3.

27. After inflation climbed to double-digit levels by 1982 and then returned to a 4 to 5 percent rate by 1984–86, the lower rate was no longer considered so inflationary. In fact, President Reagan was credited with having contained inflation even while it remained at the very same rate, 4 percent, that was considered a serious problem in the early 1970s.

28. *New York Times*, June 12, 1983.

29. In 1984 the federal government indicted three supermarket chains for fixing prices "at artificial and non-competitive levels": *New York Times*, June 10, 1984.

30. Gus Tyler, "Growth Without Inflation," *New Leader*, October 12, 1982, pp. 9–15.

and went on to enjoy record profits.[31] The "wage-price spiral" is more often a profit-price spiral, with the worker more the victim than the cause of inflation.

The major cause of higher prices is the grab for profits, a phenomenon inherent to the monopolistic structure of modern capitalism. As financial power is concentrated in fewer and fewer hands, supplies, markets—and prices—are more easily manipulated. "Ever-increasing prices for the same or less is the leading characteristic of monopoly pricing; it is also a major contribution to inflation."[32] In most industries, prices are fixed at artificially high levels. Instead of lowering prices when sales drop, the big firms often raise them to compensate for sales losses. The same with agribusiness: whether crops are poor as in the drought year of 1980 or plentiful as in 1981, food prices still climb.[33] The law of supply and demand is rewritten: the companies manipulate the supply; then they demand higher prices.

Prices are pushed upward also by limits on production—as when the oil companies repeatedly create artificial scarcities in oil supplies (1920, 1929, 1947, 1973, and 1977), which mysteriously disappear after the companies get big price increases, or when federal acreage-reduction programs award billions of dollars to agribusiness for producing nothing.

Other inflationary expenditures include the billions spent on the "social wage"—that is, unemployment payments and welfare expenditures to assist the poor, the jobless, and others who fall by the wayside under capitalism. There are also hundreds of thousands of able-bodied young and middle-aged adults who do not work but who consume a substantial portion of the surplus value because they are wealthy. While not all the rich are idle, practically all live parasitically, largely off their trust funds or other "private incomes."[34]

Massive military expenditures "happen to be a particularly inflation-

---

31. Joseph Budish, "The 'wage-price spiral' fraud," *Daily World*, July 20, 1984. Between 1979 and 1983, the portion of GM's production costs going to wages declined by 15 percent, while the share going to salaries for the corporate brass rose 25 percent, and interest payments to bankers increased 200 percent: Victor Perlo's report in the *Daily World*, July 21, 1983.

32. Douglas Dowd, "The Heart of the Matter," *Monthly Review*, December 1982, p. 53.

33. *Wall Street Journal*, October 1, 1981. During recessions, small competitive companies often must lower their prices when market demand falls. Not so the monopolies; they can maintain and even raise their prices in the face of declining markets. In every recession since 1953, prices in the monopoly sector have risen: Howard Sherman, "Inflation, Unemployment and Monopoly Capital," *Monthly Review*, March 1976, pp. 34–35.

34. Of IRS tax returns listing over $1 million in adjusted gross income (i.e., income after deductions), only 16 percent of the income was derived from wages and salaries; the rest was from ownership of capital: Benjamin Page, *Who Gets What from Government* (Berkeley: University of California Press, 1983), p. 15.

producing type of federal spending," admits the *Wall Street Journal*.[35] The Civil War, the First and Second World Wars, the Korean War, and the Vietnam War all produced periods of extreme inflation. Aggregate demand—mostly government demand for military goods and payments to military personnel—far exceed supply during wartime and are not usually covered by increased taxes. Even during "peacetime," assuming that's what we have today, huge defense outlays help create inflationary scarcities, as the military consumes vast amounts of labor power and material resources. (For instance, it is the largest single consumer of fuel in the United States.) The resulting excess of demand over supply generates an upward pressure on prices, especially since the defense budget is funded mostly through deficit spending—that is, by the government's spending more than it collects in taxes.[36]

Finally, wage and benefit struggles won by workers are a problem for the capitalist in that they cut into profits, and represent costs that are often passed along to the consumer. But as already noted, wage increases usually lag behind price-profit growth, and labor's share of the value produced either remains the same or is proportionately reduced.[37]

PRODUCTIVITY AND HUMAN NEEDS

Those who insist that private enterprise can answer our needs seem to overlook the fact that private enterprise has no such interest, its function being to produce the biggest profits possible for the owners. People may *need* food, but they offer no market until their need (or want) is coupled with buying power to become a market *demand*. When asked by the Citizens Board what they were doing about the widespread hunger in the United States, food manufacturers responded that the hungry poor were not their responsibility. As one company noted: "If we saw evidence of profitability, we might look into this."[38]

The difference between *need* and *demand* shows up on the international market also. When buying power rather than human need determines how resources are used, poor nations feed rich ones. Much of the beef, fish, and other protein products consumed by North Americans (and

---

35. *Wall Street Journal*, August 30, 1978.

36. Victor Perlo, "Militarism and Inflation," *Political Affairs*, July 1982, pp. 2–8.

37. Another example: While Chrysler's prices and profits climbed in the 1980s, Chrysler workers' share of the value they produced fell from 54 percent in 1980 to 29 percent in 1984: *Economic Notes*, September 1985, pp. 1–2. Comparisons of wages and profits almost always deal with wages *before* taxes and profits *after* taxes, thereby exaggerating the portion going to wages.

38. Quoted in *Hunger, U.S.A.*, a report by the Citizens Board of Inquiry into Hunger and Malnutrition in the United States (Boston: Beacon Press, 1968), p. 46.

their livestock and domestic pets) comes from Peru, Mexico, Panama, India, and other countries where grave protein shortages exist. These foods find their way to profitable United States markets rather than being used to feed the children in these countries who suffer from protein deficiencies. In Guatemala alone, 55,000 children die before the age of five each year because of illnesses connected to malnutrition. Yet, the dairy farmers of countries like Guatemala and Costa Rica are converting to more profitable beef cattle for the United States market. The children *need* milk, but they lack the money, hence, there is no market. Under capitalism, money is invested only where money is to be made.

Capitalism's defenders claim that the pursuit of profit is ultimately beneficial to all since corporate productivity creates prosperity. This argument overlooks several things: high productivity frequently *detracts* from the common prosperity even while making fortunes for the few, and it not only fails to answer to certain social needs but may generate new ones. The coal-mining companies in Appalachia, for example, not only failed to mitigate the miseries of the people in that area; they *created* many miseries, swindling the Appalachians out of their land, underpaying them, forcing them to work under dangerous conditions, destroying their countryside, and refusing to pay for any of the resulting social costs.

Furthermore, an increase in productivity, as measured by a gross national product (GNP) of more than $2 trillion a year, may mean *less* efficient use of social resources and more waste. The GNP, the total value of all goods and services produced in a given year, contains some hidden values in its measurements. Important nonmarket services like housework and child rearing go uncounted, while many things of negative social value are tabulated. Thus, highway accidents, which lead to increased insurance, hospital, and police costs, add quite a bit to the GNP but take a lot out of life.

The *human* value of productivity rests in its social purpose. Is the purpose to plunder the environment without regard to ecological needs, fabricate endless consumer desires, produce shoddy goods designed to wear out quickly, create wasteful, high-priced forms of consumption and service, pander to snobbism and acquisitiveness, squeeze as much compulsive toil as possible out of workers while paying them as little as possible, create artificial scarcities in order to jack up prices—all in order to grab as big a profit as one can? Or is productivity geared to satisfying the communal needs of the populace in an equitable manner? Is it organized to serve essential needs first and superfluous wants last, to care for the natural environment and the health and safety of citizens and workers? Is it organized to maximize the capabilities, responsibilities, and participation of its people?

Capitalist productivity-for-profit gives little consideration to the latter set of goals. What is called productivity, as measured by quantitative indices, may actually represent a decline in the quality of life—hence, the relationship between the increasing quantity of automotive and industrial usage and the decreasing quality of our environment. Under capitalism, there is a glut of nonessential goods and services for those with money and a shortage of essential ones for those without money. Stores groan with unsold items while millions of people are ill-housed and ill-fed.

It is argued that the accumulation of great fortunes is a necessary condition for economic growth, for only the wealthy can provide the huge sums needed for the capitalization of new enterprises. Yet in many industries, from railroads to atomic energy, much of the funding has come from the government—that is, from the taxpayer—and most of the growth has come from increased sales to the public—from the pockets of consumers and from the wealth created by the labor power of workers. It is one thing to say that large-scale production requires capital accumulation but something else to presume that the source of accumulation must be the purses of the rich.

It is also argued that the concentration of corporate wealth is a necessary condition for progress because only big companies are capable of carrying out modern technological innovations. Actually, giant companies leave a good deal of the pioneering research to smaller businesses and individual entrepreneurs. The inventiveness record of the biggest oil companies, Exxon and Shell, is strikingly undistinguished. Referring to electric appliances, one General Electric vice-president noted: "I know of no original product invention, not even electric shavers or heating pads, made by any of the giant laboratories or corporations. . . . The record of the giants is one of moving in, buying out, and absorbing the small creators."[39]

Defenders of the present system claim that big production units are more efficient than smaller ones. In fact, huge firms tend to become less efficient and more bureaucratized with size, and after a certain point in growth there is a diminishing return in productivity. Moreover, bigness is less the result of technological advance than of profit growth. When the same corporation has holdings in manufacturing, insurance, utilities, amusement parks, and publishing, it becomes clear that giantism is not a technological necessity that brings greater efficiency but the outcome of capital concentration. The search is not for more efficient production but for new areas of investment.

The concern is not to maintain the well-being of the industry as such, but to extract as large a profit as possible. One need only recall how

39. Quoted in Baran and Sweezy, *Monopoly Capital*, p. 49.

railroads, shipping lines, mines, factories, and housing complexes have been bought and sold like so many game pieces for the sole purpose of extracting as much profit as possible, often with little regard for maintaining their functional capacity.[40] The long-term survival of an enterprise is of less concern to the investor than the margin of profit. If firms sometimes totter on the edge of ruin, to be rescued only by generous infusions of government funds, it is after stockholders have collected millions in high profits. Thus, during the years 1967 to 1971, the "depressed" aerospace industry, plagued by climbing costs and layoffs and repeatedly rescued from the brink of insolvency by fat government subsidies, netted for its investors $3 billion in after-tax profits.

During boom times, corporate representatives are full of self-congratulations. During economic slumps, however, they are inclined to blame "low worker productivity"—which supposedly can only be corrected with speedups and cutbacks in the work force. If we are to believe management, workers must learn to work harder for less. But studies show that American workers are far more productive than workers in most other capitalist nations. On an average, six workers in the United States produce as much as ten in Japan, and eight American workers turn out as much as ten in Germany—to mention the two countries whose productivity allegedly surpasses ours.[41]

Actually, the low productivity is among U.S. *managers*, most of whom are paid too much for too little work. In 1980, business administrative costs exceeded $800 billion, of which $500 billion went to executives and corporate professionals. Factory-worker productivity soared 80 percent in the last decade, while white-collar productivity rose only 4 percent. One study estimates that as little as one-fourth of a manager's time is actually spent working, that is, developing, analyzing, or executing company policies.[42]

Another cause of low productivity is overcapitalization, which means idle machines and a relatively low output for the existing plant. Technological obsolescence is another factor. Big companies are unwilling to spend their own money to modernize their plants. Corporations cry poverty and call for federal funds to finance technological renovations ("reindustrialization"), supposedly to help them compete against foreign firms.

40. Matthew Josephson, *The Robber Barons* (New York: Harcourt, Brace, 1934), pp. 19, 203.

41. Gus Tyler, "The Politics of Productivity," *New Leader*, March 22, 1982, p. 9; also *Economic Notes*, May/June 1985, p. 15.

42. Josh Martin, "Managers Are the Main Reason for Poor Productivity," *In These Times*, October 14–20, 1981, p. 17, and the study conducted by management consultants referred to therein; also Warren Brown, "Silver Lining for Automakers," *Washington Post*, January 23, 1983.

Yet, these same companies then produce huge cash reserves, which they use to buy up other companies in multibillion-dollar mergers. One example says a lot: after laying off 20,000 workers, refusing to modernize its aging plants, and milking the government of hundreds of millions of dollars in subsidies and tax write-offs, U.S. Steel came up with $6.2 billion to purchase Marathon Oil in 1981.

Productivity is adversely affected by the continual shift of industry from one location to another, in search of cheaper labor markets, usually in the Third World. The export of millions of jobs and the abandonment of perfectly good plant sites and labor forces have a disastrous effect on communities, generating serious social costs that do not show up on the corporate balance sheet. At other times, perfectly sound factories belonging to larger firms are milked and plundered by their own managements and then closed. This is a quick way to amass capital for future takeovers and concentrate on units that produce the very highest profits. These maneuvers bring a loss of jobs and a decline in productive enterprise.[43]

Unemployment

In capitalist societies, unlike socialist ones, people have no guaranteed right to employment. If they cannot find work, that's their tough luck. No capitalist economy has ever attained full employment. Nor is full employment the most desirable thing from the boss's perspective. Without a reserve army of unemployed to compete for jobs, labor would become "too expensive" and cut too deeply into profits. So some unemployment is functional to capitalism. In the United States, during the "boom times" of the 1920s, 1950s, and 1960s, there were—even by official statistics—always at least several million people in need of jobs.

In recent years unemployment has ranged as high as 7 to 12 percent, and this official figure does not count the 2.5 million who since 1983 have given up looking for work, nor the many who have exhausted their unemployment compensation and have left the rolls. Neither does it include the 6.5 million part-time or reduced-time workers who want full-time jobs, nor the persons forced into early retirement, nor those who have found new jobs but at substantially reduced pay, nor the youths who have joined the armed forces because they could not find work. (Persons in the armed forces are now tallied as among the employed!) In sum, an official unem-

43. David Moberg, "Shutdowns Inflict Massive Social Cost," *In These Times*, April 30–May 6, 1980, p. 2; Barry Bluestone and Bennett Harrison, "Why Corporations Close Profitable Plants" *Working Papers* May/June 1980, pp. 15–23; Dotson Rader, "Can The Little Guys Win?" *Parade Magazine*, December 12, 1982, pp. 6–9.

ployment rate of 7 percent may represent a *real* rate of over 16 percent, more than double the official count.[44]

If we are to believe Ronald Reagan, there are plenty of jobs but people are just lazy. In a January 1982 press conference, he said he found pages of help-wanted ads in the Sunday newspapers. A more systematic survey of unemployment ads throughout New York State found that 85 percent of the positions required college training or special skills. For the remaining 1,305 "entry-level" openings, 29,316 people applied. In Chester, Pennsylvania, almost 3,000 people stood all day in the freezing rain for thirty job openings in a refinery. In Kansas City, over 9,000 people showed up for sixty letter-sorting jobs. And in Tacoma, Washington, 1,575 people applied for six part-time bus-driver jobs.[45] Certainly, there are individuals in almost every society who evade gainful employment. But when unemployment jumped 2.3 million in 1981–1982, was it because a mass of people suddenly found work too irksome and preferred to lose their income, homes, cars, medical coverage, and pensions?[46]

Another myth is that union-scale wages cause unemployment by "pricing workers out of the market." Actually, in states where labor unions are weak and wages low, like North Carolina, Georgia, Mississippi, and Alabama, unemployment rates are among the highest in the nation.[47] For the country as a whole, the decline in unions and union-scale wages during the 1970s and 1980s has been accompanied by a higher, not a lower, rate of unemployment.

The groups hardest hit by unemployment are racial minorities, youths, women, and unskilled workers. Official figures for jobless Black youths exceed 40 percent, while actual figures may be much higher. Unemployment among Blacks in general is more than twice that of Whites and the Black-White income gap continues to widen.[48]

---

44. Only persons who actively sought work during the month are counted as in the labor force. Anyone who worked as little as one hour during the survey week is counted as employed: *New York Times*, February 26, 1986, and August 24, 1984; *Washington Post*, December 9, 1982. Another 2 million or so are counted as employed but are on unpaid (and usually involuntary) leave: Victor Perlo "Reaganism—Hooverism for the '80s," *Political Affairs*, March 1984, p. 5; also John Howley, "Calculating Unemployment," *Economic Notes*, November 1984, p. 4.

45. *Washington Post*, January 24, 1983; *Workers World*, April 9, 1982.

46. Opinion surveys indicate that people want jobs, not welfare. See the study of low-income youths reported in the *Washington Post*, May 3, 1983; also the survey, "Basic Work Ethic Found to Endure," *Los Angeles Times*, April 20, 1981.

47. *Daily World*, June 4, 1982.

48. *New York Times*, April 21, 1983; U.S. Bureau of Labor Statistics report, January 1982. Women, especially Black and Latino females, are concentrated in the low-paid employment market. Women who move into the better-paying professional and corporate jobs are mostly from higher-income families, the well-to-do wives and daughters of fairly affluent families: "Women at Work," *Wall Street Journal*, September 8, 1978. As a whole, women earn less than sixty cents for every dollar earned by men; *Washington Post*, September 1981.

THE PLIGHT OF THE MIDDLE AMERICAN

Even when regularly employed, many workers do not earn enough to support themselves and their families in any comfort or security. They work for a living but not for a living wage. A Census Bureau survey of 51 urban areas found that more than 60 percent of all *employed* workers in the inner city could not make enough to maintain a decent standard of living and 30 percent were earning wages below the poverty level.[49] Most of the poor in America have jobs. It is not laziness that keeps them in poverty but the low wages their bosses pay them and the high prices, rents, and taxes they have to pay others.

One hears many references to the "affluent workers" of America, of construction workers who make more than doctors, and sanitation workers who earn more than college professors. Such stories are unfounded. First, it is not clear why sanitation workers should not be paid more than college professors, since they work harder and at more unpleasant, unhealthy tasks. Second, as a matter of fact, sanitation workers usually make substantially less. Even well-paid construction workers, assuming they can find work at all, average less per year after decades on the job than the young college graduate who enters a management trainee program for industry. In any case, discussions on "how good labor has it" always focus on these better-paying jobs and ignore the 50 million or more people who earn subsistence wages and who face high injury rates, job insecurity, and chronic indebtedness. To make ends meet, millions of workers are obliged to hold down two jobs. Millions more are compelled by their employers to work involuntary overtime for extended periods. Owners prefer to impose overtime hours on the work force they have rather than hire more help, thereby saving on the benefits that must be paid to additional employees. And from New York to Los Angeles, growing numbers of workers toil in unsafe and unhealthy sweatshop conditions, sometimes ten to twelve hours a day for less than the minimum wage and without medical coverage, sick pay, or other benefits.[50]

Corporate and political leaders often boast of the millions of new jobs that have been created over the years. But, aside from the fact that there still are not enough of them, an unusually high number of new jobs are poor paying. Since 1973, the average number of jobs per family grew by 20 percent, yet earnings declined an astonishing 14.3 percent (after accounting for inflation), with most of the decline coming in the Reagan years. Today, there are 14 million U.S. workers toiling at or near the minimum wage. Keep in mind that the minimum wage, $3.35 an hour, has not been increased since Reagan was inaugurated in 1981, while the cost-of-living index has risen 26 percent. Thus the real income of the millions whose wages are fixed by the minimum has been reduced by one-fourth.[51]

---

49. William Spring, Bennett Harrison, and Thomas Vietorisz, "Crisis of the *Under-employed*," *New York Magazine*, November 5, 1972.

50. Jay Mazur, "Back to the Sweatshop," *New York Times*, September 6, 1986; William Serrin, "After Years of Decline, Sweatshops Are Back," *New York Times*, October 12, 1983.

51. Stephen Greenhouse, "The Average Guy Takes It on the Chin," *New York Times*, July 23, 1986; also *New York Times*, May 20 and June 8, 1984; and John Hess, "Our Horn of Plenty Is Running Out," *Washington Post*, July 20, 1986. In the 1980s, more than 5 percent of

Generally, it is becoming increasingly difficult for American employees to procure jobs that pay them middle-class wages. What we are witnessing is a slippage in living standards from parents to children. Today a 30-year-old male head of household earns about 10 percent less in real buying power than his father did at the same age. In 1970 three out of four American families could afford to buy an average-priced house; today, less than one in three could do so, with the average new home costing over $100,000. And mortgage delinquencies were higher during 1981–86 than at any time since the Great Depression.[52]

By 1985 over 80 percent of American families were in debt, up dramatically from 54 percent nine years earlier. A majority indicated they had borrowed money not for luxuries but for necessities. By 1986 Americans owed $664 billion for consumer, home improvement, and college education loans (up $164 billion from six years earlier), and they owed $1.4 trillion for housing (three times higher than a decade before).[53] Even if most middle Americans earn a sufficient income to make ends meet, they have little security against layoffs, prolonged illness, and the drop in earning power that comes with old age. They have virtually no wealth—in a society where wealth is the only certain measure of economic security.

In sum, the pursuit of profits enriches the few at the expense of the many. Productivity, efficiency, and technological innovation are retarded or advanced, depending on how they best serve capitalism's supreme consideration, to accumulate the largest amount of capital at the fastest rate possible.

The power of the business class is not total, "but as near as it may be said of any human power in modern times, the large businessman controls the exigencies of life under which the community lives."[54] The giant corporations control the rate of technological development and the terms of production; they fix prices and determine the availability of livelihoods; they decide which labor markets to explore and which to abandon; they create new standards of consumption; they divide earnings among labor, management, and stockholders; they transform the environment, devour its resources, and poison the land, water, and air; they command an enormous surplus wealth while helping to create and perpetuate conditions of scarcity for millions of people at home and abroad; they exercise trustee power over religious, recreational, cultural, medical, and charita-

---

those of middle-class income descended into low-budget status or actual poverty. The middle class has been shrinking while the rich get still richer; see Rose, *The American Profile Poster*.

52. *New York Times*, February 3, 1986, and June 25, 1985; also "Mortgage Defaults," *Economic Notes*, October 1985, p. 10.

53. Peter Behr, "A Nation of Debtors," *Washington Post*, January 12, 1986.

54. Thorstein Veblen, *The Theory of the Business Enterprise* (New York: New American Library Edition, n.d., originally published in 1904), p. 8.

ble institutions and over much of the media and the educational system; and they enjoy a powerful voice in the highest councils of federal, state, and local governments—as we shall see.

POVERTY AND MISERY

Americans have been taught to believe that they have it so much better than people in other countries. The truth is, in life expectancy, 20-year-old American males rank 36th among the world's nations, and 20-year-old American females rank 21st. The infant mortality rate in the United States is worse than in twenty other western nations, and twice as bad for Black infants as for White ones, because of poverty and the relative inaccessibility of prenatal and postnatal medical care. In eleven countries women have a better chance to live through childbirth than in the United States. According to the Bureau of Labor Statistics, the number of people who live below the poverty level climbed from 24 million in 1977 to about 35 million in 1986, making the poor the fastest growing demographic group in the United States. An additional 40 million or more live on incomes estimated as below a "low standard adequacy" by the Department of Labor.[55]

One out of every five American adults is functionally illiterate.[56] One out of four Americans lives in substandard housing without adequate plumbing, heat, or other facilities. Housing is the largest single expenditure for most families. The scarcity of decent dwellings allows landlords to charge exorbitant rents. In some places, landlords take ownership of a building for a minimum down payment, milk it ruthlessly, neglect to provide fuel and maintenance, and eventually abandon it in a ruined condition, making off with gains far in excess of their initial investment. For almost all renters, especially lower-income people, housing costs are rising faster than the ability to pay. Due to fast-buck plunder, investment speculation, condominium conversions, underemployment, and the like, more and more people are being priced out of the market. According to

---

55. *Washington Post*, September 2, 1986, and November 18, 1984; *New York Times*, March 20, 1985; *Los Angeles Times*, August 21, 1981. In 1984, the "poverty index" was set by the federal government at $10,609 for a family of four. Official tabulations of poverty are based on a national census that undercounts transients, homeless people, and those living in poor rural and inner-city areas. Numerous cities complained of undercounting in the 1980 census. Most of the people below the poverty level are Whites, some 20 million; the remainder are Afro-American, Latino, and other minorities. But the minorities are statistically overrepresented; thus, while Blacks compose only 13 percent of the population, they number over 35 percent of those in poverty.

56. Jonathan Kozol, *Illiterate America* (New York: Anchor Press, 1985).

conservative estimates by the Department of Health and Human Services, some 2 million people are homeless, a high percentage of whom are single women and women with children. They sleep in emergency shelters, abandoned sites, wooded areas, hallways, and alleys. There is an additional homeless population of vast proportion living doubled up or tripled up with friends or relatives.[57]

In 1985 the Physicians Task Force on Hunger reported that at least twenty million Americans go hungry every month. Some 50 percent of children from the very poorest families grow to maturity with impaired learning ability, while 5 percent are born mentally retarded because of prenatal malnutrition.[58] Having studied malnourished four- and five-year olds, the psychologist Robert Coles observed:

> They ask themselves and others what they have done to be kept from the food they want or what they have done to deserve the pain they seem to feel. . . .
>
> All one has to do is ask some of these children in Appalachia who have gone north to Chicago and Detroit to draw pictures and see the way they will sometimes put food in the pictures. . . . All one has to do is ask them what they want, to confirm the desires for food and for some kind of medical care for the illnesses that plague them.[59]

A team of doctors investigating rural poverty found children plagued with diseases of the heart, lungs, and kidneys, and an array of other serious ailments that impaired a normal life and "that in other children would warrant immediate hospitalization."[60] Due to the Reagan administration's cutbacks in food programs, the number of malnourished children in America has increased during the 1980s.[61] "Hunger is a problem of epidemic proportions across the nation," reported the Physicians Task Force after extensive field studies conducted in four regions. The physicians found growing instances of lethargy, "stunting," "wasting," and kwashiorkor and

---

57. *New York Times*, June 22, 1986, and September 13, 1986; *Guardian*, January 18, 1984; Chester Hartman (ed.), *America's Housing Crisis: What Is to Be Done?* (Boston: Routledge and Kegan Paul, 1983); William Taab, *The Political Economy of the Black Ghetto* (New York: Norton, 1970). Capitalist economics makes arson profitable as buildings are put to the torch so that landlords can collect the insurance and drive out low-income tenants for condominium conversion: "Why It Pays to Burn," *Dollars and Sense*, January 1980, pp. 7–9.

58. *New York Times*, February 27, 1985, and November 2, 1983.

59. *Hunger USA: A Report by the Citizen's Board of Inquiry into Hunger and Malnutrition in the United States* (Boston: Beacon Press, 1968), pp. 31–32; also Loretta Schwartz-Nobel, *Starving in the Shadow of Plenty* (New York: McGraw-Hill, 1981).

60. *Hunger USA*, p. 13.

61. *New York Times*, July 7, 1985 and *Washington Post*, February 7, 1984, and June 3, 1984. Due to poverty and malnourishment, two of Cleveland's poorest neighborhoods now experience a higher infant mortality rate than Honduras: *Cleveland Plain Dealer*, April 20, 1984.

marasmus, "third world diseases of advanced malnutrition." [62] In places like New York, Washington, D.C., Chicago, St. Louis, Detroit, Philadelphia, Los Angeles, and many smaller towns and rural areas, there are people who pick their food out of garbage cans and town dumps. "If the president on his visit to China had witnessed Chinese peasants eating from garbage cans, he almost certainly would have cited it as proof that communism doesn't work. What does it prove when it happens in the capitalist success called America?"[63]

More than half of the Americans who live below the poverty level are elderly. A third of these have a daily intake of less than 1,000 calories—amounting to a slow starvation diet. Every winter hundreds of people, mostly the very old and very young, freeze to death in unheated apartments or perish in fires caused by gas stoves (used to compensate for heat cutoffs). Many elderly cannot afford medical and nursing care or decent housing and transportation that would allow them to maintain normal social relations. They face loneliness and isolation in a market society that treats old people like used cars.[64]

Even as the economy was said to be on an upswing in 1983–85 (as measured by investment and profits), the numbers of poor, hungry, and homeless were increasing, demonstrating the unjustly selective nature of the economic "recovery."[65] In any case, under capitalism, poverty has its functions. In disproportionate numbers, the poor serve in the army, in a kind of economic conscription that replaces the draft. The poor do the "dirty work" of society, performing most of the toughest, grimiest, mindless, lowest-paying tasks, and acting as servants, custodians, and cleaning people for the more affluent. The poor buy goods other people don't want, such as low-grade produce, day-old bread, and market-reject commodities. Poor communities are a source of real profit for price-gouging merchants and rent-gouging slumlords. Most important of all, the poor form a reserve army of labor, a ready supply of unemployed that helps deflate wage scales and keeps profits up.[66]

Economic want is not just a material condition; it affects every aspect of life. It is difficult for those who have never known serious economic adversity to imagine the stress, insecurity, and misery it can cause. Studies have found that even small rises in unemployment bring noticeable in-

---

62. *New York Times*, February 27, 1985; also Richard Margolis, "Hunger in the Eighties," *New Leader*, April 5, 1985, pp. 12–14.

63. William Raspberry, "Garbage Eaters," *Washington Post*, May 2, 1984.

64. Margolis, "Hunger in the Eighties"'; "How the Poor and Elderly Fare Under Reagan," correspondence in the *New York Times*, April 2, 1984.

65. *Washington Post*, April 20, 1985; *New York Times*, August 3, 1984.

66. Herbert Gans, *More Equality* (New York: Pantheon, 1973), p. 106; David Caplovitz, *The Poor Pay More* (New York: Free Press, 1967).

creases in illness, alcoholism, homicide, and suicide.[67] With anywhere from 23,000 to 24,000 killings a year, the United States homicide rate is one of the highest in the world. The suicide rate among young people has increased 300 percent since 1950, to become the third leading cause of death among U.S. youth. In all, about 25,000 to 27,000 Americans take their own lives each year.[68] The growing number of farm failures has been accompanied by increasing reports of suicides among farmers and of farmers seeking psychiatric counseling.[69]

About 30 percent of American households (some 24 to 25 million homes) experience a crime of violence or theft each year, with the highest crime rates found in the poorest neighborhoods. Over the last two decades, serious crimes almost doubled. And so did the prison population (now almost 700,000) and the funds spent for prisons.[70] Over ten million adults have serious alcohol problems and one in five (about 29 million) adults suffer from "psychiatric disorders ranging from mildly disabling anxiety to severe schizophrenia," with the least economically secure having the most problems.[71] Heroin and cocaine addiction currently plagues upwards of a million Americans. Millions of others are addicted to amphetamines, barbiturates, and other drugs. The pushers are mostly doctors; the suppliers are the drug industry; the profits are stupendous.[72]

The American divorce rate is the highest in the world, nearly double that of Sweden, the runner-up. Divorce among lower-income people is higher than among the more affluent. Loss of job often leads to worsening marital relations and divorce. Some 28 million women are beaten each year by men, with 4.7 million sustaining serious injury.[73] With growing unemployment, incidents of child abuse by jobless parents have increased dramatically. Nearly 2 million children, predominantly but not exclusively from low-income families, are brutalized, abused, abandoned, or neglected each year. Child abuse kills more children than leukemia, automobile accidents, and infectious diseases combined. Among the abandoned children are many "throwaway kids"—that is—"young people whose parents do not want them or cannot feed them or abuse them so

---

67. Maya Pines, "Recession Is Linked to Far-Reaching Psychological Harm," *New York Times*, April 6, 1982; also *Washington Post*, February 22, 1985.

68. That includes only suicides that are reported as such: *New York Times*, September 11, 1986; *Washington Post*, June 21, 1985. Suicide among young American males in particular is "now one of the highest, if not the highest in the world": *New York Times*, September 24, 1983.

69. *New York Times*, February 10, 1985.

70. *Washington Post*, July 14, 1986, September 11, 1985, and December 12, 1983.

71. *Los Angeles Times*, November 2, 1984; *Denver Post*, October 3, 1984.

72. *Washington Post*, January 13, 1980.

73. Pines, "Recession Is Linked to Far-Reaching Psychological Harm,"; also *New York Times*, March 25, 1986.

badly that they cannot go home."[74] Every year, of the 150,000 children reported missing, some 50,000 simply vanish. Perhaps half of the unidentified bodies buried annually in this country are missing children.[75]

One of ten elderly persons who live with a member of the family is subjected to serious abuse, such as forced confinement and beatings. With financial stress and unemployment, some families resent having to feed and care for an old person. The mistreatment of elderly parents is a problem that is growing dramatically as economic conditions worsen.[76] Certainly not all social pathology can be ascribed to economic want but much of it can be prevented or treated by a more equitable and humane social order, one that puts people before profits.

In sum, the story of the United States' great "affluence" is of people becoming increasingly entrapped in a high-priced, high-profit, high-pressured, highly unequal system. It is not enough to denounce the inequities that exist between the wealthy and the majority of the population; it is also necessary to understand the connection between them. For it is the way wealth is organized and used that creates most of the existing want and insecurity. By its very nature, the capitalist system is compelled to exploit the resources and labor of society for the purpose of maximizing profits. This systemic imperative creates the imbalances of investment, neglect of social needs, privation, wastage, and general economic oppression and inequality that bring so much wealth to a few and misery to so many.

---

74. *New York Times*, January 3, 1983, also January 4, 1984; "Work Problems May Lead to Child Abuse," *Daily World*, July 20, 1984.

75. *New York Times*, October 8, 1982.

76. Lewis Koch and Joanne Koch, "Parent Abuse—A New Plague," *Washington Post*, January 27, 1980; also *Washington Post*, February 7, 1985.

3

The Plutocratic Culture: Institutions, Values, and Ideologies

In trying to understand the American political system we would do well to look at the social context in which it operates. What can be said about the predominant social institutions, values, and ideologies and their relationship to the distribution of power within American society?

AMERICAN PLUTOCRACY

American capitalism represents more than just an economic system; it is an entire cultural and social order, a plutocracy—that is, a system of rule by and for the rich—for the most part. Most universities and colleges, publishing houses, mass circulation magazines, newspapers, television and radio stations, professional sports teams, foundations, churches, private museums, charity organizations, and hospitals are organized as corporations, ruled by boards of trustees (or directors or regents) composed overwhelmingly of affluent businesspeople. These boards exercise final judgment over all institutional matters.[1]

Consider the university: institutions of higher education are public or private corporations (e.g., the Harvard Corporation, the Yale Corpora-

1. My book *Power and the Powerless* (New York: St. Martin's Press, 1978) has a more detailed discussion of business power within social and cultural institutions.

tion) run by boards of trustees with authority over all matters of capital funding and budget; curriculum, scholarships, and tuition; hiring, firing, and promotion of faculty and staff; degree awards; student fees; and so on. Most of the tasks related to these activities have been delegated to administrators, but the power can be easily recalled by the trustees, and in times of controversy it usually is. These trustees are granted legal control of the property of the institution, not because they have claim to any academic experience but because as successful businesspeople they supposedly have proven themselves to be the responsible leaders of the community.[2]

This, then, is a feature of real significance in any understanding of political power in America: *almost all the social institutions existing in this society, along with the immense material and vocational resources they possess, are under plutocratic control, ruled by nonelected, self-selected, self-perpetuating groups of affluent corporate representatives who are answerable to no one but themselves.*

The rest of us make our way through these institutions as employees and clients. These institutions shape many of our everyday experiences and much of our social consciousness; yet we have no vote, no portion of the ownership, and no legal decision-making power within them. The power they exercise over us is hierarchical and nondemocratic.

The existing social order and culture are not independent of the business system. Nor are social institutions independent of each other, being controlled by the more active members of the business class in what amounts to a system of interlocking and often interchanging directorates. We can point to more than one business leader who not only presides over a bank or corporation but has served as a cabinet member in Washington, is a regent of a large university, a trustee of a civic art center, and at one time or another a member of the board of a major newspaper, foundation, church, or television network.

Through this institutional control, the business elites are able to exercise a good deal of influence over the flow of mainstream ideas and over the actions of broad constituencies. The ruling ideas, as Karl Marx once said, are the ideas of the ruling class. Those who control the material production of society are also able to control the mental production. What exactly are the dominant values of our society and how are they propagated?

---

2. Ibid., pp. 156–63; also David N. Smith, *Who Rules the Universities?* (New York: Monthly Review Press, 1974). Businesspeople who are trustees generally have no administrative or scholarly experience in higher education. They are more transient than the students, faculty, and staff, usually visiting the campus from out-of-town for monthly board meetings. They take none of the financial risks; their decisions are covered by insurance paid out of the university budget. On most fiduciary and technical problems, they rely on consultants, and

SOCIALIZATION INTO ORTHODOXY

The power of business does not stand naked before the public; it is enshrouded in a mystique of its own making. The agencies of ruling class culture, namely the media, the schools, the politicians, and others, associate the capitalist system with the symbols of patriotism, democracy, prosperity, and progress. Criticisms of the system are equated with un-Americanism. Capitalism is treated as an inherent part of democracy, although, in truth, capitalism also flourishes under the most brutally repressive regimes, and capitalist interests have supported the overthrow of democracies in Chile, Guatemala, and other Third World countries and the installment of right-wing dictators who make their lands safe for corporate investments. Capitalism is presented as the sole alternative to "communist tyranny." The private enterprise system, it is taught, creates equality of opportunity, rewards those who show ability and initiative, relegates the parasitic and slothful to the bottom of the ladder, provides a national prosperity that is the envy of other lands, and safeguards (through unspecified means) personal liberties and political freedom.

Among the institutions of plutocratic culture, our educational system looms as one of the more influential purveyors of dominant values. From the earliest school years, children are taught to compete individually rather than work cooperatively for common goals and mutual benefit. Grade-school students are fed stories of their nation's exploits that might be more valued for their inspirational nationalism than for their historical accuracy. Students are instructed to believe in America's global virtue and moral superiority and to fear and hate the Great Red Menace. They are taught to hold a rather uncritical view of American politico-economic institutions. One nationwide survey of 12,000 children (grades two to eight) found that most youngsters believe "the government and its representatives are wise, benevolent and infallible, that whatever the government does is for the best."

Teachers concentrate on the formal aspects of representative government and accord little attention to the influences that wealthy, powerful groups exercise over political life.[3] Teachers in primary and secondary schools who wish to introduce radical critiques of American politico-economic institutions do so often at the risk of jeopardizing their careers. High-school students who attempt to sponsor unpopular speakers and

---

accountants. The reason businesspeople are trustees, we might conclude is that they are there to exercise a class control function—which they do.

3. A Carnegie Institute three-year study reported in the *New York Times*, September 23, 1970.

explore dissident views in student newspapers have frequently been overruled by administrators and threatened with disciplinary action.[4]

School texts at the elementary, high-school, and even college levels seldom give but passing mention to the history of labor struggle and the role of American corporations in the exploitation and maldevelopment of the Third World. Almost nothing is said of the struggles of indentured servants, of Latino, Chinese, and European immigrant labor, and of small farmers. The history of resistance to slavery, racism, and U.S. expansionist wars is largely untaught in American schools at any level.[5] One learns that the Soviet Union is to blame for all cold-war tensions. Teaching about the "evils of communism" is required by law in many state education curricula, although little of any informational value is taught about the actual social realities of existing socialist societies.[6]

Schools are inundated with millions of dollars worth of printed materials, films, and tapes provided by the Pentagon and the giant corporations at no cost, to promote a glorified view of the military and to argue for tax subsidies to business and deregulation of industry. Pro-business propaganda on nutrition (boosting commercial junk foods), nuclear power, environmental issues, and the wonders of free enterprise are also widely distributed in schools and communities.[7]

Colleges and graduate and professional schools offer a more sophisticated extension of this same orthodox socialization. Over the last decade, conservative think tanks and academic centers have proliferated, along with conservative journals, conferences, and endowed chairs, all funded by tens of millions of dollars from corporations and right-wing foundations.[8] College faculty, and even students, have been subjected to discriminatory treatment because of their dissenting views and political activities,

---

4. Commission of Inquiry into High School Journalism, *Captive Voices: High School Journalism in America* (New York: Schocken Books, 1974). A survey of 500 high school newspapers found censorship to be widespread; see *Washington Post*, December 30, 1981. For an overall analysis of American schools, see Samuel Bowles and Herbert Gintis, *Schooling in Capitalist America* (New York: Basic Books, 1976).

5. Philip Meranto, Oneida Meranto, Matthew Lippman, *Guarding the Ivory Tower, Repression and Rebellion in Higher Education* (Denver: Lucha Publications, 1985); Frances FitzGerald, *America Revised* (New York: Random House, 1980).

6. For instance, Florida has no minimum math, science, or language requirements for a high school diploma, but it does require every student to complete a thirty-hour course called "Americanism vs. Communism." The Florida law dictates: "No teacher or textual material assigned in this course shall present Communism as preferable to the system of constitutional government and the free-enterprise, competitive economy indigenous to the U.S." *New York Times*, May 4, 1983.

7. Sheila Harty, *Hucksters in the Classroom: A Review of Industry Propaganda in Schools* (Washington, D.C.: Center for Study of Responsive Law, 1979); Betty Medsger, "The 'Free' Propaganda That Floods the Schools," *Progressive*, December 1976, p. 42.

8. Peter Stone, "Businesses Widen Role in Conservatives' 'War of Ideas,'" *Washington Post*, May 12, 1985.

suffering negative evaluations and loss of scholarships, research grants, and jobs. While sometimes portrayed as being above worldly partisan interests, the average American university performs a wide range of services—from advanced research to specialized personnel training and recruitment—which are essential to military and corporate interests. The "neutral" university also has a direct investment link to the corporate structure in the form of a substantial stock portfolio.[9]

Socialization into the orthodox values of American culture is achieved not only by indoctrination but also by economic sanctions designed to punish the dissident critics and reward the political conformists. This is true of the training and advancement of lawyers, doctors, journalists, engineers, managers, bureaucrats, and teachers. To get along in one's career, one learns to go along with things as they are and avoid the espousal of views that conflict with the dominant economic interests of one's profession, institution, and society.[10]

Another agent of political socialization is the government itself. Government officials prevent leaks of potentially embarrassing information but these same officials flood the public and the media with press releases and planted information supporting the viewpoints of government, industry, and the military. Hardly a day passes without the president or some White House official feeding us reassuring pronouncements about the economy and alarming assertions about communist threats from abroad.

Although we are often admonished to "think for ourselves," we might wonder if our socialization process allows us to do so. Ideological orthodoxy so permeates the plutocratic culture, masquerading as "pluralism," "democracy," and the "open society," that it is often not felt as indoctrination. The worst forms of tyranny are those so subtle, so deeply ingrained, so thoroughly controlling as not even to be consciously experienced. So, there are Americans who conform unswervingly to the capitalist orthodoxy, afraid to entertain contrary notions for fear of jeopardizing their jobs, but who think they are "free."

In a capitalist society, one is bombarded with inducements to maintain a life-style that promotes the plutocratic culture. Each year business spends billions to get people to consume as much as they can—and sometimes more than they can afford. Mass advertising offers not only commodities but a whole way of life, teaching us that the piling up of

---

9. Meranto et al., *Guarding the Ivory Tower.*

10. For studies of ideological orthodoxy and political repression in the United States, see William Preston, Jr., *Aliens and Dissenters* (Cambridge, Mass.: Harvard University Press, 1963); William Appleman Williams, *The Great Evasion* (Chicago: Quadrangle Books, 1964); Michael Parenti, *The Anti-Communist Impulse* (New York: Random House, 1969); Sidney Fine, *Laissez-Faire and the General-Welfare State* (Ann Arbor: University of Michigan Press, 1964); Meranto, *Guarding the Ivory Tower.*

"Religious freedom is my immediate goal, but my long-range plan is to go into real estate."

Drawing by Donald Reilly; © 1974 The New Yorker Magazine, Inc.

possessions is a life goal, a measure of one's accomplishment and proof of one's worth. As Philip Green noted, American capitalists spend billions of dollars in advertising to persuade us to expend all our incomes upon ourselves and our families: "Of the last hundred TV commercials any of us saw, it would be miraculous if more than one or two (or any) advocated devoting a significant portion of one's own economic resources to a public purpose."[11]

11. Philip Green, "Two Cheers for the State," *Nation*, April 14, 1979, p. 399.

In the plutocratic culture, the emphasis is on self-absorption: "do your own thing" and "look out for number one." We are taught to seek more possessions and more privacy: a private home, private car, private vacation place; and we often feel alienated and lonely when we get them. Born of a market economy, the capitalist culture is essentially a market culture, one that minimizes cooperative efforts and human interdependence and keeps us busily competing as workers and consumers. The ability or desire to work collectively with others is much retarded.[12]

We are admonished to "get ahead." Ahead of whom and what? Of others and of one's present material status. This kind of "individualism" is not to be mistaken for the freedom to choose deviant political and economic practices. Each person is expected to operate "individually" but in more or less similar ways and similar directions. Everyone competes against everyone else but for the same things. "Individualism" in the United States refers to *privatization* and the absence of social forms of ownership, consumption, and recreation. You are individualist in that you are expected to get what you can for yourself and not be too troubled by the problems faced by others. This attitude, considered inhuman in some societies, is labeled approvingly as "ambition" in our own and is treated as a quality of great social value.

Whether or not this "individualism" allows one to have control over one's own life is another story. The decisions about the quality of the food we eat, the goods we buy, the air we breathe, the prices we pay, the wages we earn, the way work tasks are divided, the opinions fed to us by the media—the controlling decisions concerning the realities of our lives—are usually made by people other than ourselves.

People who want to maintain or further their positions within the social hierarchy become committed to the hierarchy's preservation. They fear that they might be overtaken by those below, making all their toil and sacrifice count for naught.[13] The plutocratic culture teaches us that proximity to the poor is to be shunned, while wealth is something to be pursued and admired. Hence the road upward should be kept open, free of artificial impediments imposed by the government on those who can advance,

---

12. Philip Slater, *The Pursuit of Loneliness* (Boston: Beacon Press, 1970), p. 7; also Robert Bellah et al., *Habits of the Heart, Individualism and Commitment in American Life* (New York: Harper and Row, 1985).

13. According to one study, the higher their income and education, the less people believe that all groups should have equal political power. Low-income people and Blacks were the firmest supporters of equality; see William Form and Joan Rytina, "Ideological Beliefs on the Distribution of Power in the United States," *American Sociological Review*, 34 (February 1969), pp. 19–31.

while the road behind should not be provided with special conveyances for those who wish to catch up.

The insecurities of capitalism propagate a scarcity psychology even among affluent people. There is always more to get, and more to lose. The highly paid professional feels the pressure of "moreness," as does the lowly paid blue-collar worker. Economically deprived groups are seen as a threat because they want more, and more for the have-nots might mean less for the haves. The scarcity psychology, then, leaves some people with the feeling that the poor and the racial minorities (potential competitors) should be kept in their place.

Those possessed by a scarcity psychology will sometimes convince themselves of the inferiority of deprived groups. Unfortunately, the racism, sexism, and class bigotry thus activated militate against working people's understanding of their common interests and leave some of them inclined to exclude categories of people from competing for the desired things in life. So, bigots can convince themselves that the hardships endured by victimized minority groups are due to the groups' deficiencies. "Those people don't *want* to better themselves," say the bigots, who then become quite hostile when deprived groups take actions intended to better their lot.

Small hate groups like the American Nazi party and the Ku Klux Klan try to redirect the anger that working Americans might feel toward the financial class, by targeting irrelevant foes such as Blacks, Latinos, Jews, women, trade unionists, and radicals. The religious right, with organizations like the Moral Majority and various television preachers, often well-financed by moneyed persons and accorded generous publicity and media access, attempt to direct legitimate class grievances toward noneconomic issues such as school prayer, abortion, pornography, and gay rights, while warning us of the imminent dangers of communism and "secular humanism."[14]

The conservative Reagan administration picked up on many of these same themes, searching for issues that might blur economic alignments by splitting the public along racial and cultural lines, thus diverting attention from the growing economic inequality of the 1980s.[15]

A special word should be said about *class* bigotry, which, along with racism and sexism, is one of the widely held forms of prejudice in American society and the least challenged. In movies, on television, in school textbooks, and in popular fiction, the world is portrayed as a predominantly White upper-middle-class place. Working-class people are often

---

14. Flo Conway and Jim Siegelman, *Holy Terror: The Fundamentalist War on America's Freedom of Religion, Politics and Our Private Lives* (New York: Dell, 1986).

15. Roger Wilkins, "Smiling Racism," *Nation*, November 3, 1984.

presented as villainous characters or as uncouth, unintelligent, and generally undesirable persons.

The message we get is that material success is a measure of one's worth; thus the poor are not worth much and society's resources should not be squandered on them. If rich and poor get pretty much what they deserve, then it is self-evident that the poor are not very deserving.[16] As the American humorist Will Rogers once said: "It's no disgrace to be poor, but it might as well be."

It would be easy to fault Americans, who manifest these competitive, acquisitive traits, as people who lack some proper measure of humanity. But most such attitudes evolve as products of plutocratic class dominance. The emphasis placed on getting ahead and making money is not the outcome of some genetic flaw in the American character. Americans have their doubts about the rat race, and many who are able to, seek an alternative life-style, consuming less and working in less demanding jobs. But the economy does not always allow such a choice. With wage cutbacks, inflation, and growing tax burdens, most people must keep running on the treadmill just to stay in the same place. In a society where money is the overriding determinant of one's life chances, the competitive drive for material success is not merely a symptom of greed but a factor in one's very survival. Rather than grasping for fanciful luxuries, most Americans are still struggling to provide for basic necessities. If they need more money than was essential in earlier days, this is largely because essentials cost so much more.

Because human services are based on ability to pay, money becomes a matter of life and death. To have a low or modest income is to run a higher risk of illness, insufficient medical care, and job exploitation, and to have a lesser opportunity for education, leisure, travel, and comfort. The desire to "make it," even at the expense of others, is not merely a wrong-headed attitude but a reflection of the material conditions of capitalist society wherein no one is ever really economically secure except the super-rich.

For those who enjoy affluence, position, and the best of everything, or who anticipate attaining these things, the existing politico-economic system is a smashing success. For those who are its most hapless victims, or who are concerned about the well-being of all and not just themselves, the system is something of a failure. Those in between are not sure. They fear losing what they have and want more security. Dreading the decline in

---

16. James T. Patterson, *America's Struggle Against Poverty* (Cambridge, Mass.: Harvard University Press, 1981); Janet M. Fitchen, *Poverty in Rural America* (Boulder, Colo.: Westview, 1981). These books discuss the low esteem in which the poor are held, often by the poor themselves. See also Sidney Lens, "Blaming the Victims, 'Social Darwinism' Is Still the Name of the Game," *Progressive*, August 1980, pp. 27–28; and William Ryan, *Blaming the Victim* (New York: Random House, 1972).

earning power and living standards that comes with unemployment or an unprotected retirement, they are absorbed with the struggle to stay afloat. As one unemployed and downwardly mobile steel worker told President Carter at an "Energy Roundtable": "I don't feel much like talking about energy and foreign policy; I am concerned about how I'm going to survive."[17]

ARE AMERICANS CONSERVATIVE?

Bombarded daily by the ruling-class point of view, most Americans nevertheless have serious questions about our institutions and public policies. A 1984 Harris poll found that only 18 percent placed "great confidence" in corporate executives, down from 29 percent in 1973 and 55 percent in the mid-1960s. Confidence in religious, military, and other establishment elites also manifested sharp declines, as has support for capitalism as a system.[18] A majority of Americans believe that both the Democratic and Republican parties favor big business over the average worker. Majorities of more than 2 to 1 favor increased government efforts to assist the elderly and the poor; improve the quality of education, health care, transportation, and occupational safety; and protect the environment. By lopsided majorities, Americans believe the tax system favors the rich at the expense of the average person, and that too much money is going into military spending.[19]

Despite years of persistent propagandizing, President Ronald Reagan was seldom able to rally majority support for his militaristic, cold-war foreign policies. By more than 4 to 1 margins, Americans disapproved of Reagan's interventions in Lebanon and Central America, and the aid he gave to the counterrevolutionaries ("contras") to subvert the Nicaraguan government.[20] In marked contrast to the Reagan administration's stance, the American people, by 74 to 22 percent, want the elimination of all nuclear weapons by countries that possess them. Majorities of 89 and 96 percent reject nuclear confrontation and nuclear war as a viable policy.

---

17. Peter Carroll, *It Seemed Like Nothing Happened: The Tragedy and Promise of America in the 1970's* (New York: Holt, Rinehart and Winston, 1983).

18. *New York Times*, August 19, 1984; *Public Opinion*, December/January 1984; *Gallup Report*, October 1983, p. 4. Herbert McClosky and John Zaller, *The American Ethos, Public Attitudes Toward Capitalism and Democracy* (Cambridge, Mass.: Harvard University Press, 1985). Opinion polls are usually taken by telephone, which excludes from the sample the homeless and about 10 million poor households that are without telephones.

19. *Washington Post*, February 14, 1986, and May 15, 1985. When assistance for the poor is associated with "welfare," however, then opinion registers negative, welfare being thought of as a handout to laggards and chiselers.

20. *Washington Post*, March 8 and 17, 1986; January 20, 1984; *New York Times*, April 15, 1986.

And by 2 to 1 the public supports a negotiated arms limitation with the Soviets and opposes Reagan's plans to abandon the arms limitation agreements that exist between the United States and the USSR.[21]

Since the early 1960s, Americans have become more tolerant of cultural and political dissenters, more supportive of racial equality, less likely to be stampeded by fears of communism, and have remained supportive of legalized abortion.[22] In short, while the business-owned media keep talking about how the nation is in a "conservative mood," on almost every important issue, a majority of the public seems to hold positions contrary to those pursued by political and corporate elites.

Opinion polls are only part of the picture. There is a whole history of progressive democratic struggle in this country, of people confronting the repressive powers of the state, protesting overseas wars and militarism, and fighting against ethnic, racial, gender, and class exploitation. The fight against oppression and inequality continues to this present day, but as in years past, it is underplayed or misrepresented by those who disseminate most of the information and images of our society.

Political activism, supposedly a passing phenomenon of the 1960s, remained very much a reality across the nation through the 1970s and 1980s, with mass demonstrations, strikes, boycotts, civil-disobedience actions, and thousands of arrests—targeting such things as investments in South Africa, nuclear arms, nuclear reactors, Klan rallies, CIA campus recruitments, and U.S. involvement in Central America. The Selective Service System admitted that some 800,000 young men had defied the law and refused to register for the draft (the actual number was probably higher).[23]

Religious groups, including previously conservative ones like Roman Catholics and Southern Baptists, denounced nuclear arms as dangerous and immoral.[24] Religious organizations were active in the sanctuary move-

---

21. *Washington Post*, June 10, 1986 and September 7, 1984; Daniel Yankelovich and John Doble, "The Public Mood: Nuclear Weapons and the USSR," *Foreign Affairs*, 63, Fall 1984, pp. 33–34; *Bulletin of Atomic Scientists*, August/September 1982; *New York Times*, April 15, 1983.

22. Survey reported in the *New York Times*, January 13, 1982. A *New York Times*–CBS News poll showed no shift in 1981–85 to the right on a range of ideological questions: *New York Times*, January 28, 1986. An ABC opinion poll, January 22, 1985, found that 88 percent favored some kind of legalized abortion (a majority favored unrestricted abortion on demand); only 11 percent were categorically opposed.

23. *New York Times*, April 4, 1985; Patrick Coy, "Civil Disobedience: An American Tradition," *St. Louis Post-Dispatch*, February 22, 1985; Emily DeNitto "U.S. Peace Movement Toward the Summit," *Political Afairs*, November 1985, pp. 7–10; Stephen Kohn, *The History of American Draft Law Violations 1658–1985* (Westport, Conn.: Greenwood Press, 1986); *Guardian*, May 1, 1985, p. 6.

24. See the stance taken by the National Conference of Catholic Bishops and other Christian denominations: *Washington Post*, December 25, 1981.

ment to protect Salvadoran refugees from the U.S.-sponsored war in El Salvador. Antiwar organizations, civil-liberties, environmental, and women's-rights groups reported increases in membership and activities.

From 1984 to 1986 major strikes occurred at USX, LTV, Bath Iron, Chrysler, United Airlines, Pratt & Whitney, and Phelps Dodge. On any one day in early 1986, there were twenty strikes in progress, showing that labor militancy was not a thing of the past.[25] In the early 1980s, alliances formed between independent farmers and urban labor unions from Ohio to Colorado and up to the Dakotas against the companies and banks that profited so much from their labor.[26]

College students in the 1980s manifested a shift away from social concerns and toward more success-oriented and business-careerist goals. Given the cutbacks in scholarships, students are more than ever from upper-income families. In keeping with their class backgrounds and economic interests, they have been generally more pro-Reagan—and they have been more conservative on issues like capital punishment and abortion than were students in the late 1960s and early 1970s. In addition, campus conservatives have received a good deal of off-campus funding and media visibility. Yet, within an overall conservative trend, progressive movements have arisen on campuses throughout the nation, around all the abovementioned issues of war, peace, and social justice.[27]

Even the election in 1980 and reelection in 1984 of a right-wing president does not signal a mass conservative mood as such. In 1980 the vote for Ronald Reagan was a protest against the high inflation and high unemployment under Jimmy Carter. In 1984, only 6 percent of those who voted for Reagan said they did so because of his conservative philosophy. Most supported him because their real wages had improved somewhat in 1983–84 with the drop in inflation, and because of their mistaken perception of Reagan's "pro-people" politics, and their sense that he would give less to minority groups (who had been perceived as "getting everything") and eventually more to themselves. Whatever the case, Reagan's victories did not translate into across-the-board triumphs for Republican conservatives. Democrats retained control of the House, most of the governorships, big city mayoralties, and state legislatures, and in 1986, the Democrats regained control of the U.S. Senate.[28]

---

25. The best current coverage of labor's struggles can be found in *Economic Notes* and *People's Daily World*.

26. Andrew Malcolm, "Farm, Labor Alliance Grows," *Quad-City* (Iowa) *Times*, June 5, 1983.

27. *Chronicle of Higher Education*, February 5, 1986; *New York Times*, October 16, 1984; *Guardian*, November 28, 1984; *Christian Science Monitor*, February 6, 1984.

28. Gus Hall, "Reagan's 'Political Realignment' Didn't Show," *Political Affairs*, December 1984, pp. 2–13.

In sum, despite all the propaganda and indoctrination by plutocratic institutions, Americans have not been totally taken in. The disparities between what elites profess and what they practice remain glaringly apparent to large numbers of people. There is a limit to how effectively the sugar-coated orthodoxies of capitalist culture can keep Americans from tasting the bitter realities of economic life. This is not to deny that there remain millions of Americans who are racists, who detest the poor and who support conservative, repressive, authoritarian, and militaristic policies at home and abroad. But they are not the only Americans around, and on many issues they are outnumbered.

Furthermore, political socialization does not operate with perfectly conservative effect, there being unexpected and contradictory spin-offs. Thus, when opinion makers indoctrinate us with the notion that we are a free and prosperous people, we, in fact, begin to demand the right to be free and prosperous. The old trick of using democratic rhetoric to cloak an undemocratic class order will backfire if people begin to take the rhetoric seriously and translate it into democratic economic demands. Also, there are many people who love justice more than they love money or a narrow professional success, and who long not for more things for themselves but for a better quality of life for all. It is not that they are without self-interests, but that they define their interests in a way that conflicts with the interests of the privileged and the powerful. In general, Americans are hardly as conservative as we have been led to believe. If they were given more truthful information and if they could see a way to change things, they would be more likely to move in a progressive direction on most economic policies—and, indeed, they show signs of wanting to do just that. A conservative newspaper, the *Brooklyn Tablet*, ran an editorial on a senior-citizens conference that serves as a good description of working Americans of all ages.

> They all are concerned about the economy. They had worked hard all their lives and felt themselves entitled to freedom from money worries at this stage of their lives. They felt betrayed by inflation, government promises and the general lack of fairness in the way they were treated by society. . . .
>
> Yet once they began to articulate what they wanted from society it was also obvious that they were demanding deep social changes in our economic system.
>
> They wanted their income protected from inflation. They wanted their decreased income sheltered from taxation, and taxes shifted to those who had greater ability to pay them. They wanted corporate profits limited in order that adequate pensions could be paid workers. Yet it was a federalized program of income maintenance, social security, that they most trusted and respected. They felt that medical services and housing were rights they were entitled to and at government expense.
>
> They were not trying to write a socialistic charter. They would deny that

they were anything but conservative Americans. . . . Yet when they looked carefully at the social problems that they understood and wanted to help solve, they came up with some very radical solutions.[29]

CONSERVATIVES, LIBERALS, SOCIALISTS, AND DEMOCRACY

Political ideologies in the United States might be roughly categorized as conservative, liberal, and socialist. Each of these terms carries certain ambiguities and within each category there are variations and differences. Here we will try to draw the broad outlines of the three tendencies. The *conservative* ideology, held most firmly by corporate and political elites and by many—but not all—persons of high income and substantial property, supports the system of capitalism and defends the interests of business as the primary mainstays of the good society. Conservative leaders believe that most reforms should be resisted. They may recognize that there are some inequities in society, but these will either take care of themselves or, as with poverty, will always be with us. Conservatives believe that people are poor usually because, as Richard Nixon once noted, they are given to a "welfare ethic rather than a work ethic."

Conservatives are for strong or weak government depending on what interests are being served. They denounce as government "meddling" those policies that appear to move toward an equalization of life chances, income, and class, or that attempt to make business more accountable to public authority. But they usually advocate a strong government that will restrict dissent, intervene militarily in other countries, and regulate our private lives and personal morals.[30]

Conservatives say they are for reducing government spending and bureaucracy, but the cuts they make are selective, focusing on human services and aid to the needy, while ever greater sums go to the largest bureaucracy within the government: the Department of Defense. Far from being frugal, the conservative Reagan administration regularly produced record budget deficits, more than twice that of any liberal administration. When Reagan entered the White House in 1981, the national debt was $900 billion. By the time he departs in 1988, it will be thrice that, about $2.7 trillion or $2,700 billion. Conservatives decry all government "hand-

29. The *Tablet* editorial is quoted in Gus Hall, "The New Political Reality: Analysis and Perspective," *Political Affairs*, January 1981, pp. 2–3.

30. Amidst much talk about "getting government off the backs of the American people," conservatives on the Senate Judiciary Committee have proposed restricting the right of habeas corpus and ending the ban against court admission of illegally obtained evidence. *New York Times*, May 26, 1986.

outs" except defense contracts, corporate subsidies, and tax breaks for business and the well-to-do. They believe taxes reduce the freedom of people to spend their own money, so they prefer to shift the tax burden onto those with less money, presumably thereby taking away less freedom.

Conservatives argue that recessions occur because corporations do not have enough money to invest, and unemployment occurs because people prefer to live off welfare. So conservatives support tax cuts for the rich and cuts in assistance to the poor, in the belief that the rich must be given more money before they will work, while the poor must have money taken from them before they will work.

In sum, conservative leaders put their stock in individual acquisitiveness, the "free market" of capitalism, and other established values such as institutional authority and hierarchy, a strong police force, and a large military establishment. The conservative keystone to individual rights is the enjoyment of property rights, especially the right to make a profit off other people's labor. Not all conservatives are members of the corporate elite. People of rather modest means, who oppose big government because they do not see it doing anything for them, will call themselves conservatives, for want of an alternative.

There are differences among conservatives (as among liberals and socialists). Some dream of a mythic free enterprise in which business, once totally free of government restraints and taxes, will become so productive as to bring prosperity to all. More conventional corporate elites understand that government's true historic role is not to keep hands off business but to enhance business profits with subsidies, price supports, manipulated money supplies, market protections, and restrictions on labor. Differences also emerge in foreign policy; thus the corporate and financial elites, for profit's sake, show themselves willing to trade with, and lend money to, communist nations, while the New Rightist ideologues are more likely to call for embargos and holy-war confrontations against the communists.[31]

A *liberal*, like a conservative, accepts the basic structure and values of the capitalist system but believes that social problems should be rectified by a redirection of government spending and by better regulatory policies. Liberals do not usually see these problems as being interrelated and endemic to the present system. They believe that if the right persons finally

---

31. Many of the most hawkish conservatives, who support military actions in Lebanon, Central America, and elsewhere, did not do military service when the occasion presented itself during the Korean and Vietnam Wars, including such hardline interventionists as the editor Norman Podhoretz, the Senator Paul Trible, the Congressmen Dan Lungren and Fred Eckert, and the columnists Robert Novak and Emmet Tyrrell. These and other conservatives talk tough but wimp out when it comes time to serve their country, preferring to let the less educated and less wealthy fight and die for their conservative principles. See Jack Newfield, "The Rambo Coalition, War Wimps," *Village Voice*, July 23, 1985, pp. 15–17.

win office, and with the right combination of will, public awareness, and political push, the system will be able to take care of its major crises. Liberals generally support government intervention in the economy in the hope of curbing some of the worst abuses of the economic system and changing "our warped priorities" so that more money will be spent on needed public services and less on private privileges. Liberals call for cuts in "excessive" military spending and advocate protection of individual rights against government suppression and surveillance, and assistance for the poor and needy, but in the world of action some liberals in Congress vote for huge military budgets, support security and intelligence agencies, and make cuts in human services for the needy.

Some liberals are not overly fond of capitalism, but they like socialism even less. Socialism, in their minds, conjures up stereotyped images of "drabness" and "regimentation," of people waiting in line for shoddy goods wrapped in dull gray packages, and of Stalinist purges and labor camps. The liberal's concern seems to be that freedom would be lost or diminished under socialism. Some are also worried about the diminution of their own class and professional privileges and the loss of status they might suffer with the democratization of institutions advocated by American socialists. In this respect, they often resemble conservatives.

In matters of foreign policy, liberals generally have shown themselves as willing as conservatives to contain the spread of socialism in other lands and make the world safe for American corporate investments and markets. Since Vietnam, many liberals have come to think that we should not get involved in suppressing social revolutionary movements in other countries. But whatever their feelings about revolution abroad, most liberals have little tolerance for revolutionary struggle in the United States.

Only a small portion of Americans currently identify themselves as socialists (this is not surprising, because they have had no exposure to socialism as an alternative except through the capitalist schools and media). Yet many citizens adhere to views that are close to socialist principles. A *socialist* is someone who wants to replace the capitalist system with a system of public and communal ownership, an economy that is rationally planned around social and human needs. The socialist sees capitalism as a system that:

1. strikes hardest at those who are least able to protect themselves—the disabled, unemployed, aged, and indigent
2. has given us twenty-seven industrial depressions in 122 years
3. leaves millions without adequate housing while a third of the housing construction work force is looking for work
4. leaves millions hungry while agribusiness is paid billions in govern-

ment subsidies to put land out of production or store surplus production in warehouses

5. gives wealth and power to a small number of persons while millions live in want and desolation

6. organizes the land, labor, resources, and technology of society around no goal other than the accumulation of capital.[32]

Some socialists explicitly reject existing socialist societies as models for American socialism, pointing out that countries like the Soviet Union come from a different tradition and a history of poverty, foreign hostility, and invasion. Other socialists note that whatever the faults, past crimes, and social problems of socialist societies, their citizens do have a guaranteed right to a job; are free from hunger and homelessness; do not pay more than 7 percent of their income in rent; have free medical care and free education to the highest level of their ability; have paid vacations and adequate disability insurance; enjoy such things as subsidized utilities and subsidized transportation, an earlier retirement than people in capitalist societies (sixty for men, fifty-five for women), and a guaranteed pension after retirement (with the right to continue working at another job).[33]

Socialists are distinguished from liberal reformers in their belief that our social problems cannot be solved within the very system that is creating them. Socialists do not believe that every human problem at every level of existence is caused by capitalism but that many of the most important ones are and that capitalism propagates a kind of culture and social organization that destroys human potentials and guarantees the perpetuation of poverty, racism, sexism, and exploitative social relations at home and abroad.

Socialists believe that American corporate and military expansionism abroad is not the result of "wrong thinking" but the natural outgrowth of profit-oriented capitalism. To the socialist, American foreign policy is not beset by folly and irrationality but has been quite successful in maintaining the status quo and the interests of multinational corporations, crushing social change in many countries and establishing an American financial and military presence throughout much of the world.

---

32. See Harold Freeman, "Toward Socialism in America," *Monthly Review*, September 1979, pp. 21–29.

33. See Albert Szymanski, *Human Rights in the Soviet Union* (New York: Praeger, 1985). In our own country, American leftists score dramatically higher in support of civil liberties than conservatives; see Herbert McClosky and Alida Brill, *Dimensions in Tolerance: What Americans Believe About Civil Liberties* (New York: Russell Sage Foundation/Basic Books, c. 1983).

Democracy: Form and Substance

Conservatives, liberals, and socialists all profess a dedication to "democracy," but tend to mean different things by the term. In this book, democracy refers to a system of governance that represents in both *form* and *content* the interests of the ruled. Decisionmakers are not to govern for the privileged few but for the many. Their policies should be of *substantive benefit to the populace.* The people exercise a measure of control by electing their representatives and subjecting them to open criticism, the periodic check of elections, and, if necessary, recall and removal from office. Besides living without fear of political tyranny, a democratic people should be able to enjoy freedom from economic, as well as political, oppression. In a real democracy, the material conditions of people's lives should be humane and pretty much equal.

Some people have argued that democracy is simply a system of rules for playing the game, which allows some measure of mass participation and government accountability, and that the Constitution is a kind of rule book. One should not try to impose particular class relations, economic philosophies, or other substantive arrangements on this open-ended game. This argument certainly does reduce democracy to a game. It presumes that formal rules can exist in a meaningful way independently of substantive realities. But whether one is treated by the law as pariah or prince, depends largely on material realities that extend beyond a written constitution or other formal guarantees of law. The law in its majestic equality, Anatole France once observed, prohibits rich and poor alike from stealing bread and begging in the streets. And in so doing the law becomes something of a farce, a fiction that allows us to speak of "the rights of all" divorced from the class conditions that often place the rich above the law and the poor below it. In the absence of certain substantive conditions, formal rights are of little value to millions who lack the time, money, and opportunity to make a reality of their rights.

Take the "right of every citizen to be heard." In its majestic equality, the law allows both the rich and the poor to raise high their political voices: both are free to hire the best-placed lobbyists and Washington lawyers to pressure public officeholders; both are free to shape public opinion by owning a newspaper or television station; and both rich and poor have the right to engage in multimillion-dollar election campaigns in order to pick the right persons for office or win office themselves. But again, this formal political equality is something of a fiction, as we shall see in the pages ahead. Of what good are the rules for those millions who are excluded from the game?

Some people think that if you are free to say what you like, you are living in a democracy. But freedom of speech is not the sum total of democracy, only one of its necessary conditions. Too often we are free to *say* what we want, while those of wealth and power are free to *do* what they want regardless of what we say. Democracy is not a seminar but a system of power, like any other form of governance. Freedom of speech, like freedom of assembly and freedom of political organization, is meaningful only if it keeps those in power responsible to those over whom power is exercised.

Nor are elections and party competitions a sure test of democracy. Some two-party or multiparty systems are so thoroughly controlled by like-minded elites that they discourage broad participation and offer policies that serve establishment interests no matter who is elected. In contrast, a one-party system, especially in a newly emerging, social revolutionary country, might actually provide *more* democracy—that is, more popular participation, more meaningful policy debate within the party, and more accountability and responsiveness to the people than occurs between the parties in capitalist systems.

In the chapters ahead, we will take a critical look at our own political system and measure it not by its undoubted ability to hold elections but by its ability to serve democratic ends. It will be argued that whether a political system is democratic or not depends not only on its procedures but on the *substantive* outputs—that is, the actual material benefits and costs of policy and the kind of social justice or injustice it propagates. By this view, a government that pursues policies that by design or neglect are so inequitable as to deny people the very conditions of life is not democratic no matter how many elections it holds.

4

A Constitution for the Few

To help us understand the American political system, let us investigate its origins and its formal structure, the rules under which it operates, and the interests it represents, beginning with the Constitution and the men who wrote it. Why was a central government and a Constitution created? By whom? And for what purposes?

It is commonly taught that in the eighteenth and nineteenth centuries men of property preferred a laissez-faire government, one that kept its activities to a minimum. In actuality, while they wanted government to leave them free in all matters of trade and commerce, not for a moment did they desire a weak, inactive government. Rather, they strove to erect a civil authority that worked *for* rather than against the interests of wealth, and they frequently advocated an extension rather than a diminution of state power. They readily agreed with Adam Smith, who said that government was "instituted for the defense of the rich against the poor" and "grows up with the acquisition of valuable property."[1]

CLASS POWER AND CONFLICT IN EARLY AMERICA

During the period between the Revolution and the Constitutional Convention, the "rich and the wellborn" played a dominant role in public affairs.

> Their power was born of place, position, and fortune. They were located at or near the seats of government and they were in direct contact with legislatures and government officers. They influenced and often dominated the local

1. For citation and fuller quotation, see the discussion in chapter one.

> newspapers which voiced the ideas and interests of commerce and identified them with the good of the whole people, the state, and the nation. The published writings of the leaders of the period are almost without exception those of merchants, of their lawyers, or of politicians sympathetic with them.[2]

The United States of 1787 has been described as an "egalitarian" society free from the extremes of want and wealth that characterized the Old World, but there were landed estates and colonial mansions that bespoke an impressive munificence. From the earliest English settlements, men of influence had received vast land grants from the crown. By 1700, three-fourths of the acreage in New York belonged to fewer than a dozen persons. In the interior of Virginia, seven persons owned a total of 1,732,000 acres.[3] By 1760, fewer than 500 men in five colonial cities controlled most of the commerce, banking, mining, and manufacturing on the eastern seaboard and owned much of the land.[4]

As of 1787, property qualifications left perhaps more than a third of the White male population disfranchised.[5] Property qualifications for holding office were so steep as to prevent most voters from qualifying as candidates. Thus, a member of the New Jersey legislature had to be worth at least 1,000 pounds, while state senators in South Carolina were required to possess estates worth at least 7,000 pounds, clear of debt.[6] In addition, the practice of oral voting, rather than use of a secret ballot, and an "absence of a real choice among candidates and programs" led to "widespread apathy."[7] As a result, men of substance monopolized the important offices. Not long before the Constitutional Convention, the French *chargé d'affaires* wrote to his Foreign Minister:

> Although there are no nobles in America, there is a class of men denominated "gentlemen." . . . Almost all of them dread the efforts of the people to despoil

---

2. Merrill Jensen, *The New Nation* (New York: Random House, 1950), p.178.
3. Sidney H. Aronson, *Status and Kinship in the Higher Civil Service* (Cambridge, Mass.: Harvard University Press, 1964), p.35.
4. Ibid., p.41; see also the estimates in Jackson Turner Main, *The Social Structure of Revolutionary America* (Princeton, N.J.: Princeton University Press, 1965); Allan Kulikoff, "The Progress of Inequality in Revolutionary Boston," *William and Mary Quarterly* (1971), 28, pp.375–412.
5. This is Beard's estimate regarding New York. Charles A. Beard, *An Economic Interpretation of the Constitution of the United States* (New York: Macmillan, 1936), pp. 67–68. In a few states like Pennsylvania and Georgia, suffrage was more widespread; in others it was even more restricted than in New York; see Arthur Ekrich, Jr., *The American Democratic Tradition* (New York: Macmillan, 1963). For a pioneer work on this subject, see A. E. McKinley, *The Suffrage Franchise in the Thirteen English Colonies in America* (Philadelphia: B. Franklin, 1969, originally published 1905).
6. Beard, *An Economic Interpretation*, pp. 68, 70. Seven thousand pounds was equivalent to almost a million dollars today.
7. Aronson, *Status and Kinship*, p. 49.

> them of their possessions, and, moreover, they are creditors, and therefore interested in strengthening the government, and watching over the execution of the law. . . . The majority of them being merchants, it is for their interest to establish the credit of the United States in Europe on a solid foundation by the exact payment of debts, and to grant to Congress powers extensive enough to compel the people to contribute for this purpose.[8]

The Constitution was framed by financially successful planters, merchants, and creditors, many linked by kinship and marriage and by years of service in Congress, the military, or diplomatic service.[9] They congregated in Philadelphia in 1787 for the professed purpose of revising the Articles of Confederation and strengthening the powers of the central government. They were aware of the weaknesses of the United States in its commercial and diplomatic dealings with other nations. There were also problems among the thirteen states involving trade, customs duties, and currency differences, but these have been exaggerated and in fact, some reforms were being instituted under the Articles.[10]

Most troublesome to the framers of the Constitution was the increasingly insurgent spirit evidenced among the people. Fearing the popular takeover of state governments, the wealthy class looked to a national government as a means of protecting their interests. Even in states where they were inclined to avoid strong federation, the rich, once faced with the threat of popular rule "and realizing that a political alliance with conservatives from other states would be a safeguard if the radicals should capture the state government . . . gave up 'state rights' for 'nationalism' without hesitation."[11]

The nationalist conviction that arose so swiftly among men of wealth during the 1780s was not the product of inspiration; it was not a "dream of nation-building" that suddenly possessed them. (If so, they kept it a secret in their public and private communications.) Rather, their newly acquired nationalism was a practical response to material conditions affecting them in a most immediate way. Their like-minded commitment to federalism was born of a common class interest that transcended state boundaries.

The populace of that day has been portrayed as irresponsible and parochial spendthrifts who never paid their debts and who believed in

---

8. Quoted in Herbert Aptheker, *Early Years of the Republic* (New York: International Publishers, 1976), p. 41.

9. Even Forrest McDonald, a critic of Charles Beard's "economic interpretation" of the Constitution, documents the opulent background of fifty-three of the fifty-five delegates; see his *We, the People: The Economic Origins of the Constitution* (Chicago: University of Chicago Press, 1958), chapter two.

10. Aptheker, *Early Years of the Republic*, pp. 34–35.

11. Merrill Jensen, *The Articles of Confederation* (Madison: University of Wisconsin Press, 1948), p.30.

nothing more than timid state governments and inflated paper money. Most scholars say little about the actual plight of the common people, the great bulk of whom lived at a subsistence level. Most of the agrarian population consisted of poor freeholders, tenants, and indentured hands (the latter lived in conditions of servitude). Small farmers were burdened by heavy rents, ruinous taxes, and low incomes. To survive, they frequently had to borrow money at high interest rates. To meet their debts, they mortgaged their future crops and went still deeper into debt. Large numbers were caught in that cycle of rural indebtedness which is today still the common fate of agrarian peoples in many countries.[12]

Throughout this period, newspapers complained of the "increasing numbers of young beggars in the streets."[13] Economic prisoners crowded the jails. In 1786, one county jail in Massachusetts held eighty-eight persons of whom eighty-four were incarcerated for debts or nonpayment of taxes.[14] Among the people there grew the feeling that the revolution against the English crown had been fought for naught. Angry armed crowds in several states began blocking foreclosures and forcibly freeing debtors from jail. Disorders of a violent but organized kind occurred in a number of states. In the winter of 1787, debtor farmers in western Massachusetts led by Daniel Shays took up arms. But their rebellion was forcibly put down by the state militia after several skirmishes that left eleven men dead and scores wounded.[15]

CONTAINING THE SPREAD OF DEMOCRACY

The specter of Shays's Rebellion hovered over the delegates who gathered in Philadelphia three months later, confirming their worst fears. They were determined that persons of birth and fortune should control the

---

12. Ibid., pp. 9–10; also Beard, *An Economic Interpretation*, p. 28. The historian Richard B. Morris writes: "Unable to pay for seed and stock and tools, farmers were thrown into jail or sold out to service. Except for the clothes on the debtor's back, no property was exempt from seizure or execution. . . . But imprisonment for debt is only part of the story. The records disclose case after case of debtors sold off for sizable terms to work off their debts to their creditors—peonage lacking only the Mexican term"; quoted in Aptheker, *Early Years of the Republic*, p.33. Interest rates on debts ranged from 25 to 40 percent and taxation systems discriminated against those of modest means; Aptheker, p.36. Historians like Robert Brown who attack Beard's economic interpretation are able to assert that little or no poverty existed in post-Revolutionary America by ignoring the large debtor class, poorhouses, and debtor jails. They also ignore studies like Clifford Lindsey Alderman, *Colonists For Sale, The Story of Indentured Servants in America* (New York: Macmillan, 1975).

13. Aptheker, *Early Years of the Republic*, p. 137.

14. Ibid., pp.144–45.

15. David Szatmary, *Shays' Rebellion: The Making of an Agrarian Insurrection* (Amherst: University of Massachusetts Press, 1980).

affairs of the nation and check the "leveling impulses" of the propertyless multitude that composed "the majority faction." "To secure the public good and private rights against the danger of such a faction," wrote James Madison in *Federalist* No. 10, "and at the same time preserve the spirit and form of popular government is then the great object to which our inquiries are directed." Here Madison touched the heart of the matter: how to keep the *spirit* and *form* of popular government with only a minimum of the *substance*; how to construct a government that would win some popular support but would not tamper with the existing class structure, a government strong enough to service the growing needs of an entrepreneurial class while withstanding the democratic egalitarian demands of the popular class.

The framers of the Constitution could agree with Madison when he wrote in the same *Federalist* No. 10 that "the most common and durable source of faction has been the various and unequal distribution of property. Those who hold and those who are without property have ever formed distinct interests in society" and "the first object of government" is "the protection of different and unequal faculties of acquiring property." The framers were of the opinion that democracy was "the worst of all political evils," as Elbridge Gerry put it. Both he and Madison warned of "the danger of the leveling spirit." "The people," said Roger Sherman, "should have as little to do as may be about the Government." And according to Alexander Hamilton, "All communities divide themselves into the few and the many. The first are the rich and the well-born, the other the mass of the people. . . . The people are turbulent and changing; they seldom judge or determine right."[16]

The delegates spent many weeks debating their interests, but these were the differences of merchants, slave owners, and manufacturers, a debate of haves versus haves in which each group sought safeguards within the new Constitution for its particular concerns. Added to this were disagreements about how best to achieve agreed-upon ends. Questions of structure and authority occupied a good deal of the delegates' time: How much representation should the large and small states have? How might the legislature be organized? How should the executive be selected? What length of tenure should exist for the different officeholders? Yet questions of enormous significance, relating to the new government's ability to protect the interests of property, were agreed upon with surprisingly little

16. The comments by Gerry, Madison, Sherman, and Hamilton are from Max Farrand (ed.), *Records of the Federal Convention* (New Haven: Yale University Press, 1927), vol. 1, passim. For further testimony, see John C. Miller, *Origins of the American Revolution* (Boston: Little, Brown, 1943), pp. 491 ff. and Andrew C. McLaughlin, *A Constitutional History of the United States* (New York: Appleton-Century, 1935), pp. 141–44.

debate. On these issues, there were no dirt farmers or poor artisans attending the convention to proffer an opposing viewpoint. The debate between haves and have-nots never occurred. Thus Article I, Section 8 of the Constitution, which gives the federal government the power to support commerce and protect the interests of property, was adopted within a few days with little debate.[17] It empowered Congress to:

1. Regulate commerce among the states and with foreign nations and Indian tribes
2. Lay and collect taxes and impose duties and tariffs on imports but not on commercial exports
3. Establish a national currency and regulate its value
4. "Borrow Money on the credit of the United States"—a measure of special interest to creditors
5. Fix the standard of weights and measures necessary for trade
6. Protect the value of securities and currency against counterfeiting
7. Establish "uniform Laws on the subject of Bankruptcies throughout the United States"
8. "Pay the Debts and provide for the common Defence and general Welfare of the United States"

Congress was limited to powers specifically delegated to it by the Constitution or implied as "necessary and proper" for the performance of the delegated powers. Over the years, under this "implied power" clause, federal intervention in the private economy grew to an extraordinary magnitude.

Some of the delegates were land speculators who expressed a concern about western holdings. Accordingly, Congress was given the "Power to dispose of and make all needful Rules and Regulations respecting the Territory or other Property belonging to the United States." Some delegates speculated in highly inflated and nearly worthless Confederation securities. Under Article VI, all debts incurred by the Confederation were valid against the new government, a provision that allowed speculators to make enormous profits when their securities, bought for a trifling, were honored at face value.[18]

---

17. John Bach McMaster, *The Political Depravity of the Founding Fathers* (New York: Farrar, Straus, 1964), p. 137. Max Farrand refers to the consensus for a strong national government that emerged after the small states were given equal representation in the Senate. Much of the work that followed "was purely formal"; see his *The Framing of the Constitution of the United States* (New Haven: Yale University Press, 1913), pp. 134–35.

18. Beard, *An Economic Interpretation*, passim. The profits accrued to holders of public securities were in the millions.

By assuming this debt, the federal government—under the policies of the first Secretary of the Treasury, Alexander Hamilton—"monetarized" the economy, using the public treasury to create a vast amount of credit for a propertied class that could then invest further in commerce and industry. The eventual payment of this assumed debt would come out of the pockets of the general public. In effect, the government helped greatly to finance the early process of capital accumulation. In assuming the debt, Hamilton was using the federal power to bolster not only the special interests of speculators and creditors but also the overall interest of an emerging capitalist class.[19]

In the interest of merchants and creditors, the states were prohibited from issuing paper money or imposing duties on imports and exports or interfering with the payment of debts by passing any "Law impairing the Obligation of Contracts." The Constitution guaranteed "Full Faith and Credit" in each state "to the Acts, Records, and judicial Proceedings" of other states, thus allowing creditors to pursue their debtors across state lines.

Slavery—another form of property—was afforded special accommodation in the Constitution. Three-fifths of the slave population in each state were to be counted when calculating representation in the lower house. The importation of slaves was given constitutional protection for another twenty years. And slaves who escaped from one state to another had to be delivered up to the original owner upon claim, a provision that was unanimously adopted at the Convention.

The framers believed the states acted with insufficient force against popular uprisings, so Congress was given the task of "organizing, arming, and disciplining the Militia" and calling it forth, among other reasons, to "suppress Insurrections." The federal government was empowered to protect the states "against domestic Violence." Provision was made for "the Erection of Forts, Magazines, Arsenals, dock-Yards and other needful Buildings" and for the maintenance of an army and navy for both national defense and to establish an armed federal presence within the potentially insurrectionary states—a provision that was to prove a godsend to the industrial barons a century later when the army was used repeatedly to break strikes by miners and railroad and factory workers.

In keeping with their desire to contain the majority, the founders inserted "auxiliary precautions" *designed to fragment power without de-*

---

19. See Forrest McDonald, "The Constitution and Hamiltonian Capitalism," in Robert A. Goldwin and William A. Schambra (eds.), *How Capitalistic Is the Constitution?* (Washington, D.C.: American Enterprise Institute, 1982), pp. 49–74. The debt assumed by the newly established federal government consumed nearly 80 percent of the annual national revenue during the 1790s: see Aptheker, *Early Years of the Republic*, p. 114.

mocratizing it. By separating the executive, legislative, and judicial functions and then providing a system of checks and balances among the various branches, including staggered elections, executive veto, Senate confirmation of appointments and ratification of treaties, and a bicameral legislature, they hoped to dilute the impact of popular sentiments. They contrived an elaborate and difficult process for amending the Constitution, requiring proposal by two-thirds of both the Senate and the House, and ratification by three-fourths of the state legislatures.[20] (Such strictures operate with anti-majoritarian effect to this day. Thus, although national polls show a substantial majority of Americans supports the Equal Rights Amendment, the proposal failed to make its way through the constitutional labyrinth.) To the extent that it existed at all, the majoritarian principle was tightly locked into a system of minority vetoes, making swift and sweeping popular action less likely.

The propertyless majority, as Madison pointed out in *Federalist* No. 10, must not be allowed to concert in common cause against the established social order.[21] First, it was necessary to prevent a unity of public sentiment by enlarging the polity and then compartmentalizing it into geographically insulated political communities. The larger the nation, the greater the "variety of parties and interests" and the more difficult it would be for a majority to find itself and act in unison. As Madison argued, "A rage for paper money, for an abolition of debts, for an equal division of property, or for any other wicked project will be less apt to pervade the whole body of the Union than a particular member of it." An uprising of impoverished farmers may threaten Massachusetts at one time and Rhode Island at another, but a national government will be large and varied enough to contain each of these and insulate the rest of the nation from the contamination of rebellion.

Second, not only must the majority be prevented from finding horizontal cohesion, but its vertical force—that is, its upward thrust upon government—should be blunted by interjecting indirect forms of representation. Thus, the senators from each state were to be elected by their respective state legislatures. The chief executive was to be selected by an electoral college voted by the people but, as anticipated by the framers, composed of political leaders and men of substance who would gather in their various states and choose a president of their own liking. It was believed

20. Amendments could also be proposed through a constitutional convention called by Congress on application of two-thirds of the state legislatures and ratified by conventions in three-fourths of the states. This method has yet to be tried.

21. *Federalist* No. 10 can be found in any of the good editions of the *Federalist Papers*. It is one of the most significant essays on American politics. With clarity and economy of language it explains how government may preserve the existing undemocratic class structure under the legitimating cloak of democratic forms.

that they would usually be unable to muster a majority for any one candidate, and that the final selection would be left to the House, with each state delegation therein having only one vote.[22] The Supreme Court was to be elected by no one, its justices being appointed to life tenure by the president and confirmed by the Senate. In time, of course, the electoral college proved to be something of a rubber stamp, and the Seventeenth Amendment, adopted in 1913, provided for popular election of the Senate—demonstrating that the Constitution is modifiable in democratic directions, but only with great difficulty.

The only portion of government directly elected by the people was the House of Representatives. Many of the delegates would have preferred excluding the public entirely from direct representation: John Mercer observed that he found nothing in the proposed Constitution more objectionable than "the mode of election by the people. The people cannot know and judge of the characters of Candidates. The worst possible choice will be made." Others were concerned that demagogues would ride into office on a populist tide only to pillage the treasury and wreak havoc on all. "The time is not distant," warned Gouverneur Morris, "when this Country will abound with mechanics [artisans] and manufacturers [industrial workers] who will receive their bread from their employers. Will such men be the secure and faithful Guardians of liberty? . . . Children do not vote. Why? Because they want prudence, because they have no will of their own. The ignorant and dependent can be as little trusted with the public interest."[23]

When the delegates finally agreed to having "the people" elect the lower house, they were referring to a select portion of the population. Property qualifications disfranchised the poorest White males in various states. Half the adult population was denied suffrage because they were women. American Indians had no access to the ballot. About one-fourth, both men and women, had no vote because they were held in bondage, and even of the Blacks who had gained their legal freedom, in both the North and the South, none was allowed to vote until the passage of the Fourteenth Amendment, after the Civil War.

PLOTTERS OR PATRIOTS?

The question of whether the framers of the Constitution were motivated by financial or national interest has been debated ever since Charles Beard published *An Economic Interpretation of the Constitution* in 1913. Beard

---

22. The delegates did expect George Washington to be overwhelmingly elected the first president, but they anticipated that in subsequent elections the electoral college would seldom be able to decide on one person.

23. Farrand, *Records of the Federal Convention*, vol. 2, pp. 200ff.

believed that the "founding fathers" were guided by their class interests. Arguing against Beard are those who say that the framers were concerned with higher things than just lining their purses. True, they were moneyed men who profited directly from policies initiated under the new Constitution, but they were motivated by a concern for nation building that went beyond their particular class interests, the argument goes. To paraphrase Justice Holmes, these men invested their belief to make a nation; they did not make a nation because they had invested. "High-mindedness is not impossible to man," Holmes reminds us.

That is exactly the point: high-mindedness is a common attribute among people even when, or especially when, they are pursuing their personal and class interests. The fallacy is to presume that there is a dichotomy between the desire to build a strong nation and the desire to protect wealth and that the framers could not have been motivated by both. In fact, like most other people, they believed that what was good for themselves was ultimately good for the entire society. Their universal values and their class interests went hand in hand, and to discover the existence of the "higher" sentiment does not eliminate the self-interested one.

Most persons believe in their own virtue. The founders never doubted the nobility of their effort and its importance for the generations to come. Just as many of them could feel dedicated to the principle of "liberty for all" and at the same time own slaves, so could they serve both their nation and their estates. The point is not that they were devoid of the grander sentiments of nation building but that *there was nothing in their concept of nation that worked against their class interest and a great deal that worked for it*.

People tend to perceive issues in accordance with the position they occupy in the social structure; that position is largely—although not exclusively—determined by their class status. Even if we deny that the framers were motivated by the desire for personal gain that moves others, we cannot dismiss the existence of their class interest. They may not have been solely concerned with getting their own hands in the till, although enough of them did, but they were admittedly preoccupied with defending the wealthy few from the laboring many—for the ultimate benefit of all, as they understood it. "The Constitution," as Staughton Lynd noted, "was the settlement of a revolution. What was at stake for Hamilton, Livingston, and their opponents, was more than speculative windfalls in securities; it was the question, what kind of society would emerge from the revolution when the dust had settled, and on which class the political center of gravity would come to rest."[24]

24. Staughton Lynd, *Class Conflict, Slavery and the United States Constitution* (Indianapolis: Bobbs-Merrill, 1967). For discussions of the class interests behind the American

The small farmers and debtors, who opposed a central government that was even farther beyond their reach than the local and state governments, have been described as motivated by self-serving, parochial interests—unlike the supposedly higher-minded statesmen who journeyed to Philadelphia and others of their class who supported ratification.[25] How and why the wealthy became visionary nation-builders is never explained. Not too long before, many of them had been proponents of laissez-faire and had opposed a strong central merchantile government. In truth, it was not their minds that were so much broader but their economic interests. Their motives were neither higher nor lower than those of any other social group struggling for place and power in the United States of 1787. They pursued their material interests as might any small freeholder. But possessing more time, money, information, and organization, they enjoyed superior results.

How could they have acted otherwise? For them to have ignored the conditions of governance necessary for the maintenance of the social order that meant everything to them would have amounted to committing class suicide—and they were not about to do that. They were a rising bourgeoisie rallying around a central power in order to develop the kind of national powers that would (a) better provide for the growing needs of a national commercial economy, (b) protect their overseas trading and diplomatic interests, and (c) defend their class interests from the competing claims of other classes within their own society. Some of us are quite willing to accept the existence of such a material-based nationalism in the history of other countries, but not in our own.

Finally, those who argue that the founders were motivated primarily by high-minded objectives consistently overlook the fact that the delegates repeatedly stated their intention to erect a government strong enough to protect the haves from the have-nots. They gave voice to the crassest class prejudices and never found it necessary to disguise the fact—as have latter-day apologists—that their concern was to diminish popular control and resist all tendencies toward class equalization (or "leveling," as it was called). Their opposition to democracy and their dedication to moneyed interests were unabashedly and openly avowed. Their preoccupation with their class interests was so pronounced that one delegate, James Wilson of Pennsylvania, did finally complain of hearing too much about how the sole

---

Revolution, see Alfred F. Young (ed.), *The American Revolution: Explorations in the History of American Radicalism* (DeKalb, Ill.: Northern Illinois University Press, 1977); and Edward Countryman, *A People in Revolution* (Baltimore: Johns Hopkins Press, 1982).

25. See several of the essays in Robert Goldwin and William Schambra (eds.), *How Democratic Is the Constitution?* (Washington, D.C.: American Enterprise Institute, 1980); also David G. Smith, *The Convention and the Constitution* (New York: St. Martin's Press, 1965).

or primary object of government was property. The cultivation and improvement of the human mind, he maintained, was the most noble object—a fine sentiment that evoked no opposition from his colleagues as they continued about their business.

If the founders sought to "check power with power," they seemed chiefly concerned with restraining mass power, while assuring the perpetuation of their own class power. They supposedly had a "realistic" opinion of the rapacious nature of human beings—readily evidenced when they talked about the common people—yet they held a remarkably sanguine view of the self-interested impulses of their own class, which they saw as inhabited largely by virtuous men of "principle and property." According to Madison, wealthy men (the "minority faction") would be unable to sacrifice "the rights of other citizens" or mask their "violence under the forms of the Constitution."[26] They would never jeopardize the institution of property and wealth and the untrammeled uses thereof, which in the eyes of the framers constituted the essence of "liberty."

An Elitist Document

More important than to conjecture about the framers' motives is to look at the Constitution they fashioned, for it tells us a good deal about their objectives. The Constitution was consciously designed as a conservative document, elaborately equipped with a system of minority checks and vetoes, making it easier for entrenched interests to endure. It provided ample power to build the services and protections of state needed by a growing capitalist class but made difficult the transition of rule to a different class. The Constitution was a historically successful ruling-class undertaking whose effects are still very much with us—as we shall see in the chapters to come.

The Constitution championed the rights of property over the rights and liberties of persons. For the founders, liberty meant something different from and antithetical to democracy. It meant liberty to invest, speculate, trade, and accumulate wealth and to secure its possession without encroachment by sovereign or populace. The civil liberties designed to give all individuals the right to engage in public affairs won little support from the delegates. When Colonel Mason recommended that a committee be formed to draft "a Bill of Rights," a task he said could be accomplished "in a few hours," the other convention members offered little discussion on the motion and voted unanimously against it.

26. *Federalist* No. 10.

If the Constitution was so blatantly elitist, how did it manage to win ratification? Actually, it did not have a wide backing, initially being opposed in most of the states. But the same superiority of wealth, organization, and control of political office and the press that allowed the rich to monopolize the Philadelphia Convention enabled them to orchestrate a successful ratification campaign. The Federalists also used bribes, intimidation, and other discouragements against opponents of the Constitution.[27] What's more, *the Constitution never was submitted to a popular vote*. Ratification was by state convention composed of delegates drawn mostly from the same affluent strata as the framers. Those who voted for these delegates were themselves usually subjected to property qualifications.[28]

DEMOCRATIC CONCESSIONS

For all its undemocratic aspects, the Constitution was not without its historically progressive features.[29] Consider the following:

1. The very existence of a written constitution with specifically limited powers represented an advance over more autocratic forms of government.
2. No property qualifications were required for any federal officeholder, unlike in England and most of the states. And salaries were provided for all officials, thus rejecting the common practice of treating public office as a voluntary service, which only the rich could afford.
3. The president and all other officeholders were elected for limited terms. No one could claim a life tenure on any office.
4. Article VI reads: "no religious Test shall ever be required as a Qualification to any Office or public Trust under the United States," a feature that represented a distinct advance over a number of state constitutions that banned Catholics, Jews, and nonbelievers from holding office.
5. Bills of attainder, the practice of declaring by legislative fiat a specific person or group of people guilty of an offense, without benefit

27. Jackson Turner Main, *The Antifederalists* (Chapel Hill: University of North Carolina Press, 1961).

28. Even if two-thirds or more of the adult White males could vote for delegates, probably not more than 20 percent actually did; see the studies cited in Beard, *An Economic Interpretation*, pp. 242 ff.; McDonald agrees with this estimate in *We, the People*.

29. This section on the progressive features of the Constitution is drawn from Aptheker, *Early Years of the Republic*, p. 71 ff. and passim.

of a trial, were made unconstitutional. Also outlawed were ex post facto laws, the practice of declaring an act a crime and punishing those who had committed it *before* it had been unlawful.

6. As noted earlier, the framers showed no interest in a Bill of Rights, but supporters of the new Constitution soon recognized their tactical error and pledged the swift adoption of such a bill as a condition for ratification. So, in the first session of Congress, the first ten amendments were swiftly passed and then adopted by the states; these rights included freedom of speech and religion; freedom to assemble peaceably and to petition for redress of grievances; the right to keep arms; freedom from unreasonable searches and seizures, self-incrimination, double jeopardy, cruel and unusual punishment, and excessive bail and fines; the right to a fair and impartial trial; and other forms of due process.

7. The Constitution guarantees a republican form of government and explicitly repudiates monarchy and aristocracy; hence, Article I, Section 9 states: "No title of Nobility shall be granted by the United States. . . ." According to James McHenry, a delegate from Maryland, *at least twenty-one of the fifty-five delegates favored some form of monarchy.* Yet few dared venture in that direction out of fear of popular opposition. Furthermore, delegates like Madison believed that stability for their class order was best assured by a republican form of government. The time had come for the bourgeoisie to rule directly without the baneful intrusions of kings and nobles.

Time and again during the Philadelphia Convention, this assemblage of men who feared and loathed democracy found it necessary to show some regard for popular sentiment (as with the direct election of the lower house). If the Constitution was going to be accepted by the states and if the new government was to have any stability, it had to gain some measure of popular acceptance; hence, the founders felt compelled to leave something for the people. While the delegates and their class dominated the events of 1787–1789, they were far from omnipotent. The class system they sought to preserve was itself the cause of marked restiveness among the people.

Land seizures by the poor, food riots, and other violent disturbances occurred throughout the eighteenth century in just about every state and erstwhile colony.[30] This popular ferment spurred the framers in their effort to erect a strong central government *but it also set a limit on what they could do.* The delegates "gave" nothing to popular interests, rather—as with the Bill of Rights—they reluctantly made concessions under the

30. Howard Zinn, *A People's History of the United States* (New York: Harper and Row, 1980), chapter three.

threat of democratic rebellion. They kept what they could and grudgingly relinquished what they felt they had to, driven not by a love of democracy but by a fear of it, not by a love of the people but by a prudent desire to avoid popular uprisings. The Constitution, then, was a product not only of class privilege but of class struggle—a struggle that continued and intensified as the corporate economy and the government grew.

5

The Rise of the Corporate State

Although the decisions of government are made in the name of the entire society, they rarely benefit everyone. Some portion of the populace, frequently a majority, loses out. What is considered *national* policy is usually the policy of dominant groups strategically located within the political system. The standard textbook view is that American government manifests no consistent class bias. The political system is said to involve a give-and-take among many different groups, "a plurality of interests." What government supposedly does is act as a regulator of conflict, trying to limit the advantages of the strong and minimize the disadvantages of the weak.

I will argue for a very different notion—that the existing political system enjoys no special immunity to the way power resources are distributed in society. It responds primarily—although not exclusively—to the powers and needs of the corporate system. Thus, the rise of corporate society brought the rise of the corporate state.

SERVING BUSINESS: THE EARLY YEARS

The upper-class dominance of public life so characteristic of the founding fathers' generation continued throughout the nineteenth century. In the 1830s, the period of "Jacksonian democracy," supposedly an era of the common person, a financial aristocracy controlled "the economic life of the great northeastern cities" and exercised a "vast influence" over the nation, while "the common man appears to have gotten very little of whatever it was that counted for much."[1] President Andrew Jackson's key

1. Edward Pessen, *Riches, Class and Power Before the Civil War* (Lexington, Mass.: D.C. Heath, 1973), p. 278 and p. 304.

appointments were drawn overwhelmingly from the ranks of the rich, and his policies regarding trade, finances, and the use of government lands reflected the interests of that class.[2]

The poor and destitute comprised upwards of a third of the population, even more in the South and the immigrant-congested cities. Poverty and overcrowding in the northeastern urban areas brought the cholera and typhoid epidemics of 1832, 1837, and 1842, during which "the rich fled the cities, the poor stayed and died."[3] Working people struggled under horrendous conditions. The press carried articles about adolescent girls laboring from six in the morning until midnight for three dollars a week, of women who fainted beside their looms, of children as young as nine and ten toiling 14-hour shifts, falling asleep beside the machines they tended, suffering from malnutrition, sickness, and stunted growth.[4] In an address before "the Mechanics and Working Classes" in 1827, a worker lamented: "We find ourselves oppressed on every hand—we labor hard in producing all the comforts of life for the enjoyment of others, while we ourselves obtain but a scanty portion, and even that in the present state of society depends on the will of employers."[5]

As early as 1805, when eight shoemakers were indicted in Philadelphia for "a combination and conspiracy to raise wages," employers used the courts to brand labor unions as conspiracies against property and the Constitution. Similar charges were brought against workers throughout the first half of the nineteenth century.[6]

Contrary to the view that the nation was free of class conflict, the class struggles of nineteenth century America "were as fierce as any known in the industrial world."[7] After the sporadic uprisings and strikes of the early decades, there came the railroad strikes of the 1870s, followed by the farmers' rebellions and the industrial strikes of the 1880s and 1890s. Involving hundreds of thousands of people, these struggles were highly developed in organization, while militant and sometimes even revolutionary in political tone.

---

2. See Howard Zinn, *A People's History of the United States* (New York: Harper and Row, 1980), pp. 125–29, passim.
3. Ibid., p. 213.
4. Richard Boyer and Herbert Morais, *Labor's Untold Story* (New York: United Electrical, Radio and Machine Workers, 1972), p. 25 and passim; also John Spargo, *The Bitter Cry of the Children* (Chicago: Quadrangle, 1968) originally published in 1906.
5. Zinn, *A People's History*, p. 216.
6. Boyer and Morais, *Labor's Untold Story*, p. 16 *fn*.
7. The historian David Montgomery quoted in ibid., p. 221. The monumental study on the labor struggle is Philip Foner, *History of the Labor Movement in the United States*, vols. 1–6 (New York: International Publishers, 1947, 1955, 1964, 1965, 1980, 1981).

How did the state respond? When public authority intervened, it was almost invariably on the side of the wealthy element and against the laboring class. The hardships that beset working people failed to enlist the efforts of government, but civil authorities took energetic measures to crush strikes, using first the police and state militia and later federal troops. "The industrial barons made a habit of calling soldiers to their assistance; and armories were erected in the principal cities as measures of convenience."[8] Short of having the regular army permanently garrisoned in industrial areas, as was the desire of some owners, government officials took steps "to establish an effective antiradical National Guard."[9]

The high-ranking officials who applied force against workers often were themselves men of wealth. President Cleveland's attorney general, Richard Olney, a millionaire owner of railroad securities, used antitrust laws, court injunctions, mass arrests, labor spies, deputy marshals, and federal troops against workers and their unions. From the local sheriff and magistrate to the president and Supreme Court, the forces of "law and order" were utilized to suppress unions and to serve the defensive needs of large capitalist enterprises. The very statutes declared to be unworkable against the well-known monopolistic and collusive practices of business were now promptly and effectively invoked against "labor conspiracies."

The same federal government that remained immobilized while violence was perpetrated against abolitionists, and while slaves were imported into the United States in violation of the Constitution right until the Civil War, was able to comb the land with bands of federal marshals and troops to capture fugitive slaves and return them to their masters. The same government that could not find the constitutional means to prevent the distribution of contaminated foods and befouled water supplies could use federal troops to break strikes, shoot hundreds of workers, and slaughter thousands of Indians. The same government that had not a dollar for the indigent (poverty being a matter best left to private charity) gave 21 million acres of land and $51 million in government bonds to the few railroad financiers.[10]

While insisting that the free market worked for all, most businesspeople showed little inclination to deliver their own interests to the stern judgments of an untrammeled, competitive economy; instead they resorted to such things as tariffs, public subsidies, land grants, government

---

8. Matthew Josephson, *The Robber Barons* (New York: Harcourt, Brace, 1934), p. 365. Boyer and Morais, *Labor's Untold Story*. Hundreds of strikers and supporters were wounded, beaten, given long jail terms, or killed.

9. William Preston, Jr., *Aliens and Dissenters* (Cambridge, Mass.: Harvard University Press, 1963), p. 24.

10. Zinn, *A People's History*, p. 253.

loans, contracts, patents, trademarks, and other services and protections provided by civil authority.

Well before the Civil War, the common law was redone to fit the needs of capitalism. Through the law of "eminent domain" the government took land from farmers and gave it as subsidies to canal and railroad companies. The idea of a fair price for goods was replaced in the courts by the free-market notion of *caveat emptor* (let the buyer beware). Contract law was used to deny back pay to workers who wished to quit undesirable jobs, and to deny compensation to injured employees. Workers were killed or maimed because of blatantly unsafe conditions imposed by owners—without the latter being held liable. By the Civil War, "the legal system had been reshaped to the advantage of men of commerce and industry at the expense of farmers, workers, consumers, and other less powerful groups." The law promoted "a legal redistribution of wealth against the weakest groups in the society."[11]

In the late nineteenth century, the millions of dollars collected by the government "from the consuming population, and above all from the . . . poor wage earners and farmers," constituting an enormous budget surplus, was paid out to big investors in high-premium government bonds.[12] Likewise, a billion acres of land in the public domain, *almost half of the present area of the United States*, was given over to private hands. Matthew Josephson describes the government's endeavors to transform the common wealth into private wealth:

> This benevolent government handed over to its friends or to astute first comers, . . . all those treasures of coal and oil, of copper and gold and iron, the land grants, the terminal sites, the perpetual rights of way—an act of largesse which is still one of the wonders of history. The Tariff Act of 1864 was in itself a sheltering wall of subsidies; and to aid further the new heavy industries and manufactures, an Immigration Act allowing contract labor to be imported freely was quickly enacted; a national banking system was perfected.[13]

Though strenuously active on behalf of business, the government did exercise laissez-faire in regard to the needs of the common people, giving little attention to poverty, unemployment, unsafe work conditions, child labor, and the spoliation of natural resources.

Despite the power of ruling interests, and the largely one-sided role played by government, democratic struggle persisted throughout the nineteenth century. A women's suffrage movement gathered strength. Labor

11. Morton Horowitz, *The Transformation of American Law*, quoted in Zinn, *A People's History*, pp. 234–35.
12. Josephson, *The Robber Barons*, p. 395.
13. Ibid., p. 52.

unions repeatedly regrouped their shattered ranks to fight pitched battles against the industrial moguls. One important victory that came with the Civil War was the defeat of the Southern slavocracy and the abolition of slavery. The Reconstruction period that followed was one of the few times the power of the federal government—backed by troops and the participation of poor Whites and former slaves organized into leagues and self-defense militias—was used to decree equal rights, enfranchisement for all males, popular assemblies, fairer taxes, schools for the poor, and some very limited land reform. But once the Northern capitalists put an end to Reconstruction and allied themselves with the Southern oligarchs, better to face their struggles against labor and western farmers, most of the democratic gains in the former Confederate states were rolled back, not to be regained until well into the next century—if then.[14]

THE NOT-SO-PROGRESSIVE ERA

In the twentieth century, as in the centuries before, people of wealth looked to the central government to do for them what they could not do for themselves: to repress democratic forces, limit competition, regulate the market to their advantage, and in other ways bolster the process of capital accumulation.

Contrary to the view that the giant trusts controlled everything, price competition with smaller companies in 1900 was vigorous enough to cut into the profits of various industries.[15] Suffering from an inability to regulate prices, expand profits, and free themselves from the "vexatious" reformist laws of state and local governments, big business began demanding action by the national government. As the utilities magnate Samuel Insull said, it was better to "help shape the right kind of regulation than to have the wrong kind forced upon [us]."[16] During the 1900–1916 period, known as the Progressive Era, federal price and market regulations in meat packing, food and drugs, banking, timber, and mining were initiated at the insistence of the strongest companies within these industries. The overall effect was to raise prices and profits for the larger producers, tighten their control over markets, and weed out smaller competitors.

The individuals who occupied the presidency during the Progressive Era were faithful collaborators of big business. Teddy Roosevelt, for one,

14. James S. Allen, *Reconstruction: The Battle for Democracy, 1865–1876* (New York: International Publishers, 1937), an excellent study of this period.

15. Gabriel Kolko, *The Triumph of Conservatism* (Chicago: Quadrangle, 1967), chapters 1 and 2.

16. James Weinstein, *The Corporate Ideal in the Liberal State* (Boston: Beacon Press, 1968), p. 87.

was hailed as a "trust-buster" because of his occasional verbal attacks against the "malefactors of great wealth," yet his major proposals reflected corporate desires. He was hostile toward unionists and reformers, derisively dubbing the latter "muckrakers," and enjoyed close relations with business magnates, inviting them into his administration. Similarly, neither William Howard Taft nor Woodrow Wilson, the other two White House occupants of that period, "had a distinct consciousness of any fundamental conflict between their political goals and those of business."[17] Wilson railed against the corrupt political machines and the big trusts, but his campaign funds came from a few rich contributors, and he worked closely with associates of Morgan and Rockefeller, showing himself as responsive to business as any Republican.[18] "Progressivism was not the triumph of small business over the trusts, as has often been suggested, but the victory of big businesses in achieving the rationalization of the economy that only the federal government could provide."[19]

The period is called the Progressive Era because of the much publicized but largely ineffectual legislation to control monopolies; the Sixteenth Amendment, which allowed for a graduated income tax; the Seventeenth Amendment, which provided for the direct popular election of United States Senators; and such dubious electoral reforms as the long ballot, the referendum and recall, and the nonpartisan election. The era was "progressive" more in tone than substance. Yet some victories were won. By 1915, many states had passed laws limiting the length of the workday and providing worker's compensation for industrial accidents. By 1913, several states had passed minimum wage laws and thirty-eight states had enacted child labor laws restricting the age children could be employed and the hours they could work. And in a few industries, workers won an eight-hour day and time-and-a-half overtime pay.[20]

These enactments represented longstanding demands by American workers, in some cases going back over a century. They were wrested from fiercely resistant elites by democratic forces after bitter and sometimes bloody struggle. Even with these victories, the conditions of labor remained far from good. The American workers' "real wages—that is, their ability to buy back the goods and services they produced—were lower in 1914 than during the 1890s."[21] Millions worked 12- and 14-hour days, usually six or seven days a week, and 2 million children, according to government figures, were still forced to work in order to supplement the

17. Kolko, *The Triumph of Conservatism*, p. 281.
18. Frank Harris Blighton, *Woodrow Wilson and Co.* (New York: Fox Printing House, 1916).
19. Kolko, *The Triumph of Conservatism*, pp.283–84.
20. Boyer and Morais, *Labor's Untold Story*, p. 180; Zinn, *A People's History*, p. 341.
21. Boyer and Morais, *Labor's Untold Story*, p. 181.

family income. As is the case today, much of the reform legislation went unenforced.

World War I brought industry and government even closer. Sectors of the economy were converted to war production along lines proposed by business leaders—many of whom now headed the government agencies in charge of defense mobilization.[22] The war also gave authorities an opportunity to intensify the oppression against labor.

As of 1916, millions worked for wages that could not adequately feed a family. Each year 35,000 were killed on the job, mostly because of unsafe work conditions, while 700,000 suffered injury, illness, blindness, and other work-related disabilities.[23] The war helped quell class conflict at home by focusing people's attention on the menace of the "barbarian Huns" of Germany, who supposedly threatened Anglo-American civilization. Patriotic feelings ran high as Americans were exhorted to make sacrifices for the war effort. Strikes were now treated as seditious interference with war production. Federal troops raided and ransacked IWW (Industrial Workers of the World) headquarters and imprisoned large numbers of workers suspected of socialist sympathies.

Nor did things improve during the postwar "Red scare," as the government resorted to mass arrests, deportations, political trials, and congressional investigations to suppress labor unrest and anticapitalist ideas.[24] The public was treated to lurid headlines and alarming stories of how the Russian Communists ("Bolsheviks") were about to invade the United States, and how they were murdering anyone in their own country who could read or write or who wore a white collar.[25] The capitalist leaders of the world greeted the Russian Revolution of 1917 as a nightmare come true: the workers and peasants had overthrown not only the autocratic Czar but the capitalist class that owned the factories, mineral resources, and most of the lands of the Czarist empire. As Secretary of State Robert Lansing told President Woodrow Wilson, this revolution was a bad example to the common person in other nations, including the United States.[26] Along with England, France, and eleven other capitalist nations, the United States invaded Soviet Russia in 1919 in a bloody but unsuccessful attempt to overthrow the revolutionary Bolshevik government.

---

22. Paul A. C. Koistinen, "The 'Industrial-Military Complex' in Historical Perspective: The Inter War Years," *Journal of American History*, 56, March 1970, reprinted in Irwin Unger (ed.), *Beyond Liberalism: The New Left Views American History* (Waltham, Mass.: Xerox College Publishing, 1971), pp. 228–29.

23. Boyer and Morais, *Labor's Untold Story*, p. 184 and passim; see also Zinn, *A People's History*.

24. Preston, *Aliens and Dissenters*, passim.

25. Robert Murray, *Red Scare* (New York: McGraw-Hill, 1955), pp. 95–98.

26. William Appleman Williams, "American Intervention in Russia: 1917–20," in David Horowitz (ed.), *Containment and Revolution* (Boston: Beacon Press, 1967).

In the United States, during the "normalcy" of the 1920s, prosperity was supposedly within everyone's grasp; stock speculations and other get-rich-quick schemes abounded. Not since the Gilded Age of the robber barons had the more vulgar manifestations of capitalist culture enjoyed such an uncritical reception. But the bulk of the population still lived in conditions of want. In 1928, Congressman Fiorello La Guardia reported on his tour of the poorer districts of New York: "I confess I was not prepared for what I actually saw. It seemed almost incredible that such conditions of poverty could really exist."[27]

The stock market crash of 1929 brought years of extreme economic hardship. Millions of people who had remained untouched by the prosperity of the 1920s were soon joined by millions more.

THE NEW DEAL: HARD TIMES AND TOUGH REFORMS

Speaking about the Great Depression of the 1930s, banker Frank Vanderlip admitted: "Capital kept too much and labor did not have enough to buy its share of things."[28] Such candor was not characteristic of most members of the plutocracy, who treated economic misery as if it were a natural disaster, a product of "hard times." Others blamed the depression on its victims. Millionaire Henry Ford said the crisis came because "the average man won't really do a day's work. . . . There is plenty of work to do if people would do it." A few weeks later Ford laid off 75,000 workers.[29]

With a third of the nation ill-fed, ill-clothed, and ill-housed, and at least another third just managing to get by, a torrent of strikes swept the nation, involving hundreds of thousands of harbor workers, textile workers, autoworkers, and coal miners. Between 1936 and 1940, the newly formed Congress of Industrial Organizations (CIO) organized millions of workers on an industry-wide basis and won significant gains in wages and work conditions. These victories were achieved only after protracted struggles in which hundreds of thousands went on strike, dem-

---

27. Zinn, *A People's History*, p. 376. According to the figures of the Brookings Institution, in the 1920s almost 60 percent of United States families did not receive enough income to provide for "the basic necessities" of life. See Boyer and Morais, *Labor's Untold Story*, p. 237.

28. Boyer and Morais, *Labor's Untold Story*, p. 249. Senator Hugo Black (D-Ala.) observed in 1932: "Labor has been underpaid and capital overpaid. This is one of the chief contributing causes of the present depression. We need a return of purchasing power. You cannot starve men employed in industry and depend upon them to purchase." Quoted in Rhonda Levine, "Crisis and Intra-Capitalist Conflict: The Formulation of the National Industrial Recovery Act," paper presented at the American Political Science Association meeting, New York, September 1981.

29. Zinn, *A People's History*, p. 378.

onstrated, or occupied factories in sit-downs; thousands were locked out, fired, blacklisted, beaten, and arrested; and hundreds were wounded or killed by police, soldiers, and company thugs.[30] The gains were real but they came at a high cost in human suffering.

The first two terms of President Franklin D. Roosevelt's administration have been called the New Deal, an era commonly believed to have brought great transformations on behalf of "the forgotten man." Actually, the New Deal's central dedication was to business recovery rather than social reform. The first major attempt was the National Recovery Administration (NRA), which set up "code authorities," usually composed of the leading corporate representatives in each industry, to restrict production and set minimum price requirements—with results that were more beneficial to big corporations than to smaller competitors.[31] In attempting to spur production, the government funneled large sums from the public treasure into the hands of the moneyed few. In nine years the Reconstruction Finance Corporation alone lent $15 billion to big business.

Faced with mass unrest, the federal government created a relief program that eased some of the hunger and starvation and—more importantly from the perspective of business—limited the instances of violent protest and radicalization. But as the New Deal moved toward measures that threatened to compete with private enterprises and undermine low wage structures, business withdrew its support and became openly hostile. While infuriating Roosevelt, who saw himself as trying to rescue the capitalist system, business opposition probably enhanced his reformist image in the public mind.

The disparity between the New Deal's popular image and its actual accomplishments remains one of the unappreciated aspects of the Roosevelt era. To cite specifics: the Civilian Conservation Corps provided jobs at subsistence wages for 250,000 out of 15 million unemployed persons. At its peak, the Works Progress Administration (WPA) reached about one in four unemployed, often with work of unstable duration and wages below the already inadequate ones of private industry. Of the 12 million workers in interstate commerce who were earning less than forty cents an hour, only about a half-million were reached by the minimum wage law. The Social Security Act of 1935 made retirement benefits payable only in 1942 and thereafter, covering but half the population and providing no medical insurance and no protection against illness before retirement. Similarly,

30. Boyer and Morais, *Labor's Untold Story*; and Zinn, *A People's History*, provide numerous and vivid accounts. See also Irving Bernstein, *Turbulent Years, A History of the American Worker 1933–1941* (Boston: Houghton Mifflin, 1970).

31. Barton Bernstein, "The New Deal: The Conservative Achievements of Liberal Reform," in Barton Bernstein (ed.), *Toward a New Past* (New York: Pantheon, 1963), p. 269; Douglas Dowd, *The Twisted Dream* (Cambridge, Mass.: Winthrop, 1974), pp. 102–3.

old-age and unemployment insurance applied solely to those who had enjoyed sustained employment in select occupations. Implementation was left to the states, which were free to set whatever restrictive conditions they chose. And social-welfare programs were regressively funded through payroll deductions and sales taxes.[32]

The federal housing program stimulated private construction, with subsidies to construction firms and protection for mortgage bankers through the loan insurance program—all of little benefit to the many millions of ill-housed poor. Likewise, the New Deal's efforts in agriculture primarily benefited the large producers through a series of price supports and production cutbacks, while many tenant farmers and sharecroppers were evicted when federal acreage rental programs took land out of cultivation.[33]

Government programs were markedly inadequate for the needs of the destitute, but they achieved a high visibility and did much to dilute public discontent. Once the threat of political unrest and violence subsided, federal relief was drastically slashed, as in 1936–1937, reducing many families to a destitution worse than any they had known since the 1929 crash. "Large numbers of people were put off the rolls and thrust into a labor market still glutted with unemployed. But with stability restored, the continued suffering of these millions had little political force."[34]

Several laws were passed during this period giving labor the right to bargain collectively, most notably the Wagner Act of 1935. Such legislation was both a measure of organized labor's growing legitimacy and a support to that legitimacy. But legal guarantees did not bring automatic compliance by business or vigorous enforcement by government. Labor victories against the "open shop" came only through direct struggle at the workplace—and mostly on terms that soon proved functional to the corporate system. Most labor leaders were dedicated to maintaining the capitalist system. In 1935, John L. Lewis warned that "the dangerous state of affairs" might lead to "class consciousness" and "revolution as well"; he pledged that officials of his own union were "doing everything in their power to make the system work and thereby avoid [revolution]."[35]

---

32. Frances Fox Piven and Richard Cloward, *Regulating the Poor* (New York: Pantheon, 1971), chapters 2 and 3; Robert McElvaine, *America 1929–1941: The Great Depression* (New York: Times Books, 1984); Paul Conkin, *The New Deal* (New York: Crowell, 1967).

33. Piven and Cloward, *Regulating the Poor*, p. 76; see also Bernstein, "The New Deal . . ." pp. 269–70.

34. Piven and Cloward, *Regulating the Poor*, p. 46.

35. Quoted in Ronald Radosh, "The Corporate Ideology of American Labor Leaders from Gompers to Hillman," in Unger, *Beyond Liberalism*, p. 226. Union leaders were often pushed into more militant positions than they cared to take by the actions of their rank and file, as was true of the sit-down strikes of 1936–1937.

The Roosevelt administration's tax policies provide another instance of the disparity between image and performance. New Deal taxation was virtually a continuation of the Hoover administration's program. Business firms avoided many taxes during the depression by taking advantage of various loopholes. When taxes were increased to pay for military spending in World War II, the major burden was taken up by those of more modest means, who had never before been subjected to income taxes. "Thus, the ironic fact is that the extension of the income tax to middle- and low-income classes was the only original aspect of the New Deal tax policy."[36]

All this is not to deny that, in response to enormous popular pressure, the Roosevelt administration produced real democratic gains, including some long-overdue social-welfare legislation, an expansion of collective bargaining rights, a number of worthwhile conservation and public-works projects, a reduction in unemployment from 25 to 19 percent, a program to finance middle-class home buyers, and a Federal Deposit Insurance statute to protect small bank savings. Yet the New Deal era hardly adds up to a triumph for the people. They were ready to go a lot further than Roosevelt did, and probably would have accepted a nationalized banking system, a less begrudging and more massive job program, and a national health-care system.[37]

Of the New Deal's "three Rs"—relief, recovery, and reform—it can be said that *relief* was markedly insufficient for meeting the suffering of the times and, in any case, was rather harshly curtailed after the 1936 electoral victory; *recovery* focused on business and achieved little until the advent of war spending; and *reform*, of the kind that might have ended the maldistribution and class abuses of the capitalist political economy, was rarely attempted.

As with class reform, so with race reform. In regard to school desegregation, open housing, fair employment practices, voting rights for Blacks, and antilynch laws, the New Deal did nothing. Blacks were excluded from jobs in the Civilian Conservation Corps, received less than their proportional share of public assistance, and under the NRA were frequently paid wages below the legal minimum.[38]

By 1940, the last year of peace, the number of ill-clothed, ill-fed, and ill-housed Americans showed no substantial decrease. Unemployment continued as a major problem. And the level of consumption and national income was lower than in 1929.

---

36. Gabriel Kolko, *Wealth and Power in America* (New York: Praeger, 1962), p. 31; also Conkin *The New Deal*, p. 67.

37. McElvaine, *America 1929–1941* . . .

38. Bernstein, "The New Deal . . ." pp. 278–79.

> The New Deal failed to solve the problem of depression, it failed to raise the impoverished, it failed to redistribute income, it failed to extend equality and generally countenanced racial discrimination and segregation. It failed generally to make business more responsible to the social welfare or to threaten business's pre-eminent political power. In this sense, the New Deal, despite the shifts in tone and spirit from the earlier decade, was profoundly conservative and continuous with the 1920s.[39]

Only by entering the war and *remaining thereafter on a permanent war economy* was the United States able to maintain a shaky "prosperity" and significantly lower the Depression era unemployment.

To comment on some of the points raised in this chapter: It is commonly taught that the United States government has been a neutral arbiter presiding over an American polity free of the class antagonisms that beset other societies. The truth is, our history has been marked by intense and often violent class struggles, and government has played a partisan, repressive role in these conflicts. Government has responded to the existing power formation, mostly to the business interests of society, which predominate in the control of money, resources, labor, cultural institutions, and established ideology. When divisions have arisen *within* the business class, as between large and small competitors, not surprisingly, government usually has resolved matters to the satisfaction of the more powerful.

Government's growing involvement in economic affairs was not at the contrivance of meddling Washington bureaucrats, but was a response to the increasing concentration of production, wealth, and labor. Along with the many small local labor conflicts, handled by small local government, there developed large-scale class struggle—which had to be contained by a large state. The centralization and growth of the powers of the federal government, a process initiated by the framers of the Constitution to secure the class interests of property, continued at an accelerated pace through the nineteenth and twentieth centuries. Government provided the regulations, protections, subsidies, and services that business could not provide for itself. The corporate society needed a corporate state.

While the populace won formal rights to participate as voters, the state with its judges, courts, police, army, and officialdom remained mostly at the disposal of the wealthy class. The law was cut loose from its ancient moorings and rewritten and reinterpreted to better serve capital and limit the ability of labor to fight back. However, working people were not without resources of their own, specifically the ability to disrupt and threaten the process of capital accumulation by withholding their labor through strikes, and by engaging in other acts of protest and resistance.

---

39. Ibid., pp. 264–65.

The concessions wrested from the owning class and the state brought some real material gains for the better organized segments of the working class but fell far short of any all-out attack on capitalism. By giving a little to keep a lot, the corporate state sought to contain the class struggle. Nonetheless, the minimum-wage reform, the eight-hour workday, the right to organize, and the Social Security and unemployment compensation legislation won by labor-led coalitions of the 1930s were stepping stones that put working people on higher ground from which to continue struggling.

6

Politics: Who Gets What?

With the advent of World War II, business and government became ever more intertwined. Occupying top government positions, business leaders were able to set the terms of war production; wages were frozen, prices leaped upward, and profits soared.[1] The large corporations picked up the lion's share of government war contracts, thereby accelerating the trend toward greater concentrations of wealth. The war demonstrated to business and political leaders that the most advantageous way to avoid severe economic depression and a breakdown in the business system was to use the immense borrowing, taxing, and spending powers of government to sustain private capital accumulation. Since the Second World War, successive Democratic and Republican administrations have dedicated themselves to that endeavor; first, through an elaborate system of corporate subsidies and services; second, through a massive military program, which transformed the United States into a permanent war economy.

WELFARE FOR THE RICH

After the war, the Eisenhower administration sought to undo the "creeping socialism" of the New Deal by handing over to private corporations vast offshore oil reserves, government-owned synthetic rubber factories, public lands, public power, and atomic installations, some $50 billion worth of

1. Richard Boyer and Herbert Morais, *Labor's Untold Story* (New York: United Electrical, Radio and Machine Workers, 1972), pp. 331–32, 339, for an account of how business extorted enormous profits during World War II.

resources and enterprises.[2] Nor were things much different by the 1980s, when the Reagan administration sold or leased—at fees of 1 to 10 percent of true market value—billions of dollars worth of coal and oil reserves, grazing and timber lands, and mineral reserves. In any given year, the federal government hands out more than $100 billion to big business in price supports, loan guarantees, payments in kind, research and development, export subsidies, subsidized insurance rates, promotion and marketing services, irrigation and reclamation programs, and new plants and equipment.[3] In recent times, the government has provided billions to bail out such giant companies as Chrysler and Lockheed—while small independent businesses are left to sink or swim on their own. In 1984, when one of the nation's largest banks, Continental Illinois, was on the brink of failure, it received $7.5 *billion* in federal aid.[4]

Probably the most outrageous case of compensation involves corporations such as DuPont, Ford, and ITT, which owned factories in Germany during World War II that produced tanks, bombers, synthetic fuels, and other such things for the Nazi war effort. After the war, rather than being prosecuted for aiding and abetting the enemy, ITT collected $27 million from the United States government for war damages inflicted on its German plants by Allied bombings. General Motors collected more than $33 million in compensation for damages to its enemy war plants.[5]

Under corporate-state capitalism the ordinary citizen pays twice for most things—first as a taxpayer who provides the subsidies and supports, then as a consumer who buys the high-priced commodities and services.[6] The government distributes billions of dollars in research-and-development grants, mostly to corporations that are permitted to keep the patents and market the product for profits. Whole new technologies are developed at public expense, as with nuclear energy, electronics, synthetics, space communications, mineral exploration, and computer systems, only to be handed over to industry for private gain. Thus, AT&T managed to have the entire satellite communications system put under its control in 1962—after U.S. taxpayers had put up the initial $20 billion to develop it. And in 1982, two corporations began building a huge synthetic fuel plant for

2. Ibid.

3. Public Citizen newsletter (Washington, D.C.), January 1986; *New York Times*, February 26 and November 17, 1985; Congressional Budget Office, *Federal Support of U.S. Business* (Washington, D.C.: Government Printing Office, 1984). Federal crop subsidies benefit mostly agribusiness and affluent big farmers, with relatively little going to small farmers; see *Washington Post*, July 13, 1985.

4. *New York Times*, May 18, 1984; *Washington Post*, September 15, 1983.

5. Charles Higham, *Trading with the Enemy* (New York: Dell, 1983).

6. Federal support for the nuclear industry, for instance, absorbs more than half of all nuclear production costs. *The Kindest Cuts of All: Cutting Business Subsidies in Fiscal Year 1982*, a report by Public Citizen Congress Watch (Washington, D.C., 1982), p. 6.

$4.5 billion, under a federal program that picked up 98 percent of the cost.[7]

Sometimes the state forces the public to pay for the capital investments of a private corporation because no one else will. In 1981, the oil and gas companies pushed for the construction of a natural-gas pipeline from Alaska to California and Illinois, costing an estimated $59 billion. The venture was rejected as too risky and too costly by the banks, so the Reagan administration sponsored, and Congress passed, a bill that pre-charges to hundreds of millions of consumers—through their monthly gas bills—the expense of the pipeline, even if it is never completed. The charge is as much as $200 per family each year and will continue for some twenty years. So business and government use the law to force consumers and workers to provide all the risk capital with no possibility of gain for themselves, while the big companies risk nothing and reap the profits for their wealthy stockholders.[8]

The government pays out many billions in unnecessarily high interest rates, and permits billions of government dollars to remain on deposit in banks without collecting interest. It tolerates overcharging by firms with whom it does business. It awards highly favorable contracts to large firms, along with long-term credits, tariff protections, and lowered tax assessments amounting to many billions of dollars yearly. Government makes available to defense industries billions of dollars worth of government-owned land, buildings, machinery, and materials, thereby in part saving them the job of financing their own investments; and it applies the anti-trust laws in ways that seldom hurt corporate America's interests.

MILITARY SPENDING: BUTTERING THE GUNS

Another way the state keeps the corporate economy afloat is through defense spending. While the military budget is the most costly and socially unproductive means of creating capital accumulation, it is also the most profitable and least troublesome for the big companies, since most of the costs and risks are assumed by the government.

The Department of Defense (known also as the Pentagon) is the largest, richest unit of government. The total expenses of the legislative and judiciary branches and all the regulatory commissions combined constitute little more than half of 1 percent of what the Pentagon spends in any given year. The military budget (over $300 billion for fiscal 1987) continues to grow in leaps, regardless of whether there is war or peace. After only eight years in

7. *Washington Post*, January 27, 1982. On the AT&T deal see Steve Babson and Nancy Brigham, "Why Do We Spend So Much Money?" *Liberation*, September/October 1973, p. 19.

8. Colman McCarthy in the *Washington Post*, November 28, 1981.

office, President Reagan will have spent over $2 trillion ($2,000 billion) on defense, eighty times the cost of the Vietnam War and more than was expended in all the years since World War II. Some $70 billion of the 1986 budget was allocated for nuclear weapons alone. During the Reagan era, defense production grew at three times the clip of U.S. industry as a whole. Over 30,000 companies are now engaged in military production. And military-related government agencies sign 52,000 contracts *each day*, or more than 15 million a year.[9]

9. Report by the Center for Defense Information, *New York Times*, September 14, 1986; SANE newsletter (Washington, D.C.) March 1985; Georgi Tsagolov, *War Is Their Business* (Chicago: Progress Publishers, 1985); Tom Gervasi, *Arsenal of Democracy* (New York: Grove, rev. ed. 1981); *Washington Post*, April 1, 1985.

For over forty years the Pentagon has conjured up the specter of Soviet military supremacy in order to maintain its hold over the public purse. In 1956, Americans were alerted to a dangerous "bomber gap"; in 1960, it was a "missile gap"; in 1967, an "antiballistic missile gap"; in 1975, a "multiple-warhead missile gap." From 1977 through 1981, scare reports described how the Soviets had moved ahead in conventional arms. And in the 1980s, the Reagan administration repeatedly warned of a "military-spending gap" that threatened to put us fatally behind the Soviets. In each instance it was discovered that no such weakness existed and that U.S. and NATO capabilities in nuclear and conventional forces were equal or superior to those of the Soviet Union and the Warsaw Pact nations.[10] But Congress, ever concerned that it not appear "soft-on-the Russians," has continued to vote record military budgets (while trimming a little off White House requests). The image propagated by our leaders and the press is of a Soviet "adversary" who is ready to pounce on us—with nuclear arms—at the first sign of weakness.

Actually, in recent years the Soviets unilaterally stopped underground nuclear tests and asked Washington to do the same; called for another strategic arms limitation treaty between the United States and the USSR; proposed a 50-percent cut in long-range nuclear missiles and the eventual elimination of all nuclear weapons by the year 2000; signed a no first-use pledge regarding nuclear weapons; supported a ban on all weapons in outer space; unilaterally stopped all tests on antisatellite weapons; called for mutual cuts in East and West conventional forces in Europe and an eventual disbanding of both NATO and the Warsaw Pact; proposed a nuclear-free Europe; and endorsed a bilateral, verifiable nuclear freeze. In each instance, the Reagan administration either did not respond or denounced the proposals and actions as "propaganda ploys."[11]

Instead, Reagan continued to escalate military spending, announced his intention to scrap the SALT II treaty, and embarked upon a concerted effort to put arms in outer space, under the so-called Strategic Defense Initiative (SDI) or "Star Wars." Devouring huge amounts of our scientific talent and costing over a trillion dollars, SDI will violate the antiballistic missile treaty and the treaty ban on atmospheric testing. It could never defend us from an all-out attack from 10,000 Soviet missiles, but it is designed to minimize a feeble retaliatory response from the Soviets after they are hit first and most of their missiles are destroyed. It is part of the U.S. first-strike arsenal even though paraded as a "defense shield." Oppo-

---

10. Fred Kaplan, *Dubious Specter: A Skeptical Look at the Soviet Nuclear Threat* (Washington, D.C.: Institute for Policy Studies, 1980); Franklyn D. Holzman, "A Gap? Another? " *New York Times*, March 9, 1983.

11. See Tom Wicker's columns, *New York Times*, February 28 and August 22, 1986.

nents of this push for first-strike nuclear superiority by Washington argue that it will succeed only in drawing Moscow into a dramatic new escalation of the nuclear arms race, thus destabilizing the deterrence balance between the two nations, and bringing both closer to a hair-trigger confrontation.[12]

Profitable Waste

The Pentagon procurement program is rife with waste, duplication, and profiteering. Senior military officers and civilian Pentagon officials, who favor certain companies when handing out the billions of dollars in contracts, are then rewarded with posh jobs in those very same companies.[13] The General Accounting Office (GAO), an investigative arm of Congress, revealed that the defense budget was regularly padded by billions of dollars to ensure against congressional cuts. The GAO found thousands of duplicate bills written out by corporate contractors, resulting in huge overpayments by the Defense Department. On one occasion, the Pentagon was unable to locate where half its procurement budget, a sum of $20 billion, was being spent, the money having gone to corporate subcontractors about whom no records were kept. It was also discovered that Pentagon officials had lost track of $30 billion in weapons and other military equipment intended for foreign orders. David Stockman, when serving as Reagan's Director of the Office of Management and Budget, described the Department of Defense as a "swamp of waste" containing up to $30 billion in fat that could be cut with no risks to U.S. military capacity.[14]

The Defense Department is unable to spend its money as fast as it gets it. From 1980 to 1985, the Pentagon's backlog of funds increased from $92 billion to $244 billion. This was not a result of thrift, for no one can throw money around like the Pentagon. The Air Force wasted up to $3 billion

---

12. Robert Aldridge, *First Strike! The Pentagon's Strategy for Nuclear War* (Boston: South End Press, 1983); Union of Concerned Scientists, *The Fallacy of Star Wars* (New York: Vintage, 1984); *Washington Post*, June 8, 1986; *New York Times*, May 27, 1986. In conjunction with Star Wars, Reagan also lent his support to a space shuttle project that will cost over $10 billion and will do very little to advance U.S. high-technological and manufacturing industry, according to David Sanger in the *New York Times*, January 30, 1986.

13. *New York Times* editorial, September 6, 1986; *Wall Street Journal*, January 8, 1985; Gordan Adams, *The Iron Triangle: The Politics of Defense Contracting* (New York: Council on Economic Priorities, 1981).

14. Gordon Adams, "The Department of Defense and the Military-Industrial Establishment," in Frank Fischer and Carmen Sirianni (eds.), *Critical Studies in Organization and Bureaucracy* (Philadelphia: Temple University Press, 1984), p. 324; Harvey Rosenfeld, "Fraudulent Billing Costs," *Public Citizen*, February 1986, p. 20; *Business Week*, July 24, 1978; *New York Times*, May 23, 1977. The Pentagon admits that it loses or misplaces more than $1 billion of weaponry each year: *New York Times*, September 29, 1985.

developing a radar jammer while working on a similar jammer with the Navy. The Army allocated $1.5 billion to develop a heavy-lift helicopter, even though it already had such helicopters and the Navy was building an almost identical one. The U.S. military has *four* tactical air forces, one each for the Army, Navy, Air Force, and Marines, paid for by the taxpayers. Each flies different aircraft, which means thirty different production lines and hundreds of thousands of different contracts.[15]

On many defense projects, private companies contract for one price but end up charging another. The C5A transport plane had a $4 *billion* cost overrun (and its wings kept falling off). A Navy antisubmarine weapon system almost doubled in cost from $3.6 billion to $7 billion. A Brookings Institution study estimated that virtually all large military contracts have cost overruns from 300 to 700 percent.[16] The corporate contractors pilfer the public purse on small items too. The military paid $511 for light bulbs that cost ninety cents, $640 for toilet seats that cost $12, $7,600 for coffee makers, and $900 for a plastic cap to place under the leg of a navigator's stool. After paying Boeing Aircraft $5,096 for two pliers, the tough Pentagon procurers renegotiated the price down to $1,496—a real bargain.[17]

Armaments and the Economy

Along with condemning excessive and wasteful military spending, we might also try to understand its function in capitalist society. Propelled by images of a "Soviet Menace," military spending is a way to build both U.S. global domination and high profits. For millions of taxpayers, deprived of domestic services because the military budget devours such a large chunk of the public treasure, defense spending is wasteful. But for the financial

15. Kai Bird and Max Holland, "Pentagon Bulimia," *Nation*, June 21, 1986; *Washington Post*, January 31, 1985 and April 24, 1986; *St. Louis Post-Dispatch*, April 7, 1985.

16. *Washington Post*, March 3, 1981; Sidney Lens, *The Military-Industrial Complex* (Philadelphia: United Church Press, 1970), chapter 1; also *Washington Post*, May 25, 1985. In one decade, at least sixty-eight weapon systems were scrapped as unworkable. As weapons become more complex (and more profitable to produce), they also become less functional and more prone to breakdowns, needing excessively elaborate maintenance and highly trained personnel: Adams, *The Iron Triangle*; Chris Robinson, "Arms Buildup: Expensive, Elaborate and Useless," *Guardian*, February 1, 1984. One senior Defense Department official charged that the cost of many military products was 50 percent higher than necessary because contractors failed to make things right the first time: *New York Times*, June 26, 1983.

17. *Washington Post*, February 24, March 30, and July 11, 1985, and August 21, 1983; *New York Times*, November 20, 1983.

and industrial plutocrats who have grown still richer, defense spending is wonderful. Consider the following:

1. The taxpayers' money covers all the risks of weapons development and sales. Unlike automobile manufacturers, who must worry about selling the cars they produce, the weapons dealer has a contracted market, complete with cost-overrun guarantees.
2. The government picks up most of the costs of production, including research, technology, buildings, and lands. Thus, at first glance, sales profits may be 10 percent for a defense contractor, but since the company puts up only, say, 20 percent of the equity and gets to keep all the profits, then the return on the private investment is more like 50 percent (or 78 percent in the case of Chrysler's contract on the M-1 tank). Companies like Boeing, Litton, Tenneco, and RCA enjoy a return on their military assets that is easily two or three times higher than on their commercial investments.[18]
3. Almost all contracts are awarded without competitive bidding, at just about whatever price a corporation names, ensuring high costs, fat profits, low productivity, and inflation.
4. The overproduction of consumer products leads to a glutted market and a falling rate of profit, a chronic tendency under capitalism. The armaments market provides a whole new area of demand and capital investment that does not compete with the consumer market and is virtually limitless. Not long after one generation of armaments comes off the assembly line, it becomes technologically obsolete, to be replaced by more expensive weapons.

Taking into account the multiplier effect of a dollar spent and the network of subsidiary services that feed indirectly off the defense dollar, possibly a fifth of all economic activity in the United States is dependent on military expenditures. U.S. leaders have acknowledged that the arms budget is dictated in part by the needs of the corporate economy rather than by defense needs. Thus, Defense Secretary Caspar Weinberger described the massive military spending of the 1980s as "the second half of the administration's program to revitalize America."[19] True, defense spending creates jobs. So do pornography and prostitution. But there are many more socially useful, less wasteful things that might command our

18. *New York Times*, July 3, 1986; *Washington Post*, April 1, 1985; James Cypher, "The Basic Economics of 'Rearming America,'" *Monthly Review*, November 1981, pp. 11–27.
19. Cypher, "The Basic Economics of 'Rearming America,'" p. 15.

labor and resources. In any case, arms spending provides fewer jobs than any other government expenditure except the space program, and thousands of defense workers have lost their jobs in recent years despite the escalation in military expenditures. A report by the Congressional Budget Office shows that for every $1 billion of military spending, at least 4,000 more jobs could be created by the same investment in civilian sector production.[20]

Yet military spending is preferred by the business community to other forms of government spending as a way of maintaining effective demand and absorbing capital surplus. Government funds invested in public works, public transportation, medical research, schools, scholarships, fire fighting, environmental protection, drug rehabilitation centers, and other human services expand the public sector of the economy and redistribute income in a way favorable to ordinary citizens, shifting demand to not-for-profit public pursuits and away from the private-profit market. But a weapons order is just like an order from a private customer; it pumps public money right back into the private-profit sector, and redistributes income in an upward direction.

To get a better idea of how much we spend on the military, consider the following: The cost of only three B-1 bombers would finance a year's Medicaid for all pregnant women and children living below the poverty level, or buy school lunches for four million children for an entire school year. Every American child could be lifted out of poverty for less than half of the 1986 *increase* in military spending. What the people of Cleveland have to spend on armaments in two weeks would be enough to wipe out Cleveland's debt and end its financial crisis. The money spent annually on pensions for the military brass (about $17 billion), financed exclusively by U.S. taxpayers (millions of whom have no pension programs for themselves), amounts to more than the total costs of the federal welfare program, the school lunch program, and all other child nutrition programs *combined*. The $300 million that Reagan saved in 1981 by denying food aid to 700,000 undernourished infants, older children, and pregnant women is equivalent to what the Pentagon spends in *ten hours*.[21]

---

20. Cited in *The Witness*, September 1986, p. 6; also "The Military Economy," *In These Times*, March 21–27, 1984; and studies by Employment Research Associates and Council of Economic Priorities summarized in *Washington Post*, January 13, 1982.

21. Report by the Children's Defense Fund, cited in the *Washington Post*, March 21, 1985; Seymour Melman, "The Butter That's Traded Off for Guns," *New York Times*, April 22, 1985; also *New York Times*, July 26, 1981. The bulk of military pensions goes to senior officers "who are comfortably ensconced in the wealthiest one-fifth of our society": *Washington Post*, March 10, 1985.

The Military Culture

The leading beneficiaries of defense buildup, the giant corporations, help propagate the military's cause with skillful lobbying, campaign contributions, and mass advertising that stresses the importance of keeping America on its arms-spending binge. The Pentagon itself spends many millions a year on exhibitions, films, publications, and recruitment tours to schools and a flood of press releases, planted as "news reports" in the media, to propagate the military's view of the world.[22] Increasingly, high schools are offering military programs through Junior Reserve Officers Training Corps. At the college level, the Reagan administration has cut student scholarships while increasing the number of ROTC scholarships, thereby making it financially harder to graduate as a civilian and easier to graduate as an officer. Meanwhile, war toys, television programs, and Hollywood films like *Rambo* do their share to bolster a violent cold-war, militaristic climate.

Pentagon-financed research has increased greatly over the years, absorbing upwards of a half of all the academic and commercial scientific talent in the country, accompanied by increasing Pentagon controls over how the money is spent. Two-thirds of federally funded research and development for fiscal year 1987 went for military projects.[23] As one researcher at MIT noted: "Our job is not to advance knowledge but to advance the military."[24] Many social scientists have joined programs financed by the military. In hundreds of conferences and in thousands of brochures, articles, and books written by members of the academic community who are in the pay of the government, military propaganda is lent an aura of academic objectivity. Casting a shadow on their own integrity as scholars and teachers, such intellectuals transmit to an unsuspecting public the military view of reality and the Pentagon's sense of its own indispensability.

---

22. Ernest Drucker, "Military Recruitment in Our High Schools," *Intervention*, Winter 1985, pp. 16–20; Patricia Morrisroe, "Largest Filmmaking Machine in the World," *Parade*, May 10, 1981, pp. 16–17; William Fulbright, *The Pentagon Propaganda Machine* (New York: Vintage, 1971). That it happens to be a federal offense to use taxpayers' money to propagandize the public seems not to have deterred the military.

23. *New York Times*, February 6, 1986 and June 26, 1983; *Washington Post*, December 1, 1985. The government spends about twice as much research money on military goals as on all other social goals combined. The patent rights of most publicly funded research end up in the hands of big business. Thus, the only legal mechanism for transferring scientific knowledge to the public is through the private-profit market: David Dickson, *The New Politics of Science* (New York: Pantheon, 1984).

24. Quoted in Bert Cochran, *The War System* (New York: Macmillan, 1965), p. 307.

If we define "military state" as any polity that devotes the major portion of its public resources to purposes of war, then the United States is a military state, the biggest in history. A civilian constitutional government is as capable of becoming a militarist power as is a dictatorship. The political system of a nation is of less importance in determining its military capacity than is the need to bolster capital accumulation and corporate profits, the need to guard against real or imagined foreign enemies, and the need to expand and defend overseas investment areas.

ECONOMIC IMPERIALISM

In their never-ending search for profits, U.S. industries and banks invest increasingly larger portions of their wealth abroad, attracted by the underpaid labor in Third World countries, the high investment return, and the near absence of taxes, environmental protections, and occupational safety restrictions. Rather than discouraging the flight of industry and jobs from the United States, the federal government performs two major functions for U.S. capitalism overseas, roughly the same ones it performs at home: first, it subsidizes and finances corporate foreign investments with many billions of dollars yearly; and second, it provides a military force to protect private capital in its conflicts with labor in other countries. Consider each of these in turn:

The U.S. government compensates corporations and banks for high-risk overseas ventures, as with the $8.4 billion funneled through the International Monetary Fund to save the big banks from their reckless investments abroad—one of the biggest bail-outs in financial history. The government also compensates firms for losses due to war, revolution, insurrection, or confiscation by a foreign government, and refuses aid to any country that nationalizes, without compensation, assets owned by American firms.[25]

U.S. investments to Third World countries do very little to advance the economies of those countries, being designed mostly to extract a country's natural resources and exploit its underpaid labor. If anything, the corporations push out local businesses and buy up the best land for cash export crops leaving less land for homegrown foods to feed the indigenous populations. Thus, poor countries feed and support the corporate interests of rich countries, exporting meats, fish, fruits, vegetables, coffee, cocoa, sugar,

25. James Petras, "U.S. Business and Foreign Policy," in Michael Parenti (ed.), *Trends and Tragedies in American Foreign Policy* (Boston: Little, Brown, 1971).

tin, timber, and a vast array of other products, while their own peoples are increasingly undernourished and ill-housed.[26]

While U.S. investments to poorer countries have grown during the 1980s, real wages in the Third World have declined about 15 to 20 percent, unemployment in poorer countries is higher than ever, and Third World debts have accumulated to the point where debt payments to U.S. banks absorb almost all of the poorer countries' export earnings. The land, labor, and resources of poorer nations are mobilized to fit the interests of U.S. banks and corporations rather than the needs of the populace. The result is low wages, high illiteracy, and chronic poverty. In Chile alone over the last several decades, U.S. copper companies extracted $3.8 billion in profits, leaving in their wake devastated mining lands and impoverished communities.

The U.S. government spends from $12 billion to $16 billion yearly on foreign-aid programs, ostensibly to help poorer nations help themselves, but these funds actually buttress the rule of wealthy Third World oligarchs who are friendly to U.S. investors and U.S. policies. Most of the aid goes directly to the military leaders of these various countries to help them keep their impoverished populations in line, and to allow the generals to live in a manner to which they are accustomed. Large amounts of aid finds its way into the hands of the big landowners and top government officials of

---

26. *Economic Notes*, December 1983; Harry Magdoff, *Imperialism: From the Colonial Age to the Present* (New York: Monthly Review Press, 1978).

the recipient nations.[27] Thus, before he was deposed, the Philippines' President Ferdinand Marcos siphoned off billions of dollars from the Filipino public treasure, much of it compliments of the American taxpayer.

U.S. economic "aid" comes with strings attached: the recipient nations must allow the American companies to repatriate profits made in the poorer lands; they must give tax breaks and guarantee low wages and make no attempt to protect local businesses. And they must make efforts to transfer their public assets (such as publicly owned mines, mills, and utilities) into the hands of private (U.S.) corporations. To qualify for bank loans, the poor nations usually must agree to cut back on services to their people, consume less, and export more, in order to earn more to pay to the banks.[28]

The growth of American capitalism from a weak domestic position to a dominant international one has been accompanied by a similar growth in American military interventionism. Sometimes the sword has rushed in to protect the dollar, and sometimes the dollar has rushed in to enjoy the advantages won by the sword. To make the world safe for capitalism, the United States government has embarked on a global counterrevolutionary strategy, suppressing insurgent peasant and worker movements throughout Asia, Africa, and Latin America. But the interests of the corporate elites never stand naked; rather they are wrapped in the flag and coated with patriotic appearances. Knowing that the American people would never agree to sending their sons and daughters to fight wars in far-off lands in order to protect the profits of Chase Manhattan and General Motors,[29] the corporate elites and their political spokespersons play upon popular fears, telling us that our "national security" necessitates American intervention wherever a colonial order is threatened by a popular uprising seeking to establish a socialist economic system.

From 1979 onward, after a decade of détente between the United States and the Soviet Union, the Carter and Reagan administrations revived the cold war anti-Soviet rhetoric of the 1950s, sounding alarms about the imminent threat of Soviet aggression. Moscow's intervention into Afghanistan and Soviet pressures on Poland were treated as certain evidence that the USSR was bent on world conquest and was planning nuclear dominance and aggression against the United States. Every popular insurgency against reactionary dictatorships, from Africa to Central

---

27. Frances Moore Lappe, Joseph Collins, and David Kinley, *Aid as Obstacle* (San Francisco: Institute for Food and Development Policy, 1980); *Washington Post*, February 2, 1984.

28. *New York Times*, February 20, 1984; James Petras, *Critical Perspectives on Imperialism and Social Class in the Third World* (New York: Monthly Review, 1978).

29. Opinion polls from 1981 through 1986 showed overwhelming opposition to American military involvement in Lebanon and Central America. See chapter two.

America, was depicted as Soviet inspired—as if the indigenous peoples of these countries fought not for their own interests but because the Kremlin commanded them to do so. This view of the world was instrumental in winning ever fatter military budgets at home and buttressing U.S. intervention to protect corporate investments abroad.[30]

To justify U.S. interventionism in other countries, our policymakers also claim they are defending democracy from communism. But closer examination shows they are defending the capitalist world from social change—even if the change be peaceful, orderly, and *democratic*. Iran in 1953, Guatemala in 1954, the Dominican Republic in 1962, Brazil in 1964, and Chile and Uruguay in 1973 are cases in point. In all these countries popularly elected governments began instituting progressive changes for the benefit of the destitute classes and began to nationalize or threatened to nationalize U.S. corporate holdings. And in each instance, the United States was instrumental in overthrowing these governments and instituting right-wing regimes that accommodated U.S. investors and ruthlessly repressed the peasants and workers. Similarly, in Greece, the Philippines, Indonesia, East Timor, and at least ten Latin American nations, popular governments were overthrown by military oligarchs—largely trained and financed by the Pentagon and the CIA—who prove themselves friendly to capitalism.[31]

For all their talk about "human rights," U.S. government leaders have propped up regimes throughout the world that have used assassination squads, torture, and terror to support the allies of the corporate world order. In many U.S.-supported states, strikes have been outlawed, unions destroyed, wages cut, and dissidents murdered.[32]

This policy of containing social change in order to make the world safe for capitalism has had its serious setbacks. In the post World-War-II era, successful national liberation movements in China, Cuba, Vietnam, Cambodia, Laos, Mozambique, Nicaragua, and elsewhere have vanquished corporate social orders and have instituted popular socialist governments. If the U.S. government lost the war in Indochina, it was not for want of trying. Both Democratic and Republican administrations spent $150 bil-

---

30. Cypher, "The Basic Economics of 'Rearming America.'"

31. See Stephen Schlesinger and Stephen Kinzer, *Bitter Fruit, The Untold Story of the American Coup in Guatemala* (Garden City, N.Y.: Doubleday, 1982); and James Petras and Morris Morley, *The United States and Chile: Imperialism and the Overthrow of the Allende Government* (New York: Monthly Review Press, 1975). In the 1980s, some of the military rulers stepped aside to allow for civilian rule, as happened in Argentina, Brazil, and the Philippines, but with little change in the class structure, the pattern of foreign investment, and the distribution of wealth and poverty.

32. See Noam Chomsky and Edward Herman, *The Washington Connection and Third World Fascism* (Boston: South End Press, 1979); Penny Lernoux, *Cry of the People* (Garden City, N.Y.: Doubleday, 1980).

lion and more than ten years prosecuting that war, dropping almost 8 million tons of bombs, 18 million gallons of chemical defoliants, and nearly 400,000 tons of napalm. Over 40 percent of Vietnam's plantations and orchards were totally destroyed by chemical herbicides, as were over 40 percent of its forest lands and much of its fish and sea resources. Several million Vietnamese, Laotians, and Cambodians were killed, millions more were maimed or wounded or left contaminated by Agent Orange and other toxic chemicals, and almost 10 million were left homeless.[33] Some 57,000 Americans lost their lives and hundreds of thousands more were wounded or permanently disabled. But the war did bring enormous benefits to a tiny segment of the American population: corporate defense contractors like DuPont, ITT, and Dow Chemical.[34]

By the 1980s, the interventionist pattern was repeating itself, as the United States supported a bloody intervention against Nicaragua and a counterinsurgency in El Salvador that included the massive bombing of the Salvadoran countryside by a Salvadoran air force trained, financed, and equipped by the United States.[35]

If we define "imperialism" as that relationship in which one country dominates, through use of economic and military power, the land, labor, resources, finances, and politics of another country, then the United States is the greatest imperialist power in history. The American empire is of a magnitude never before equaled. More than a half-million American military personnel are stationed in hundreds of military bases around the globe, costing over $5 billion a year. The military has some 8,500 strategic nuclear weapons and 22,000 tactical ones deployed throughout the world. The U.S. Navy deploys a fleet larger in total tonnage than all the other navies of the world combined, consisting of missile cruisers, nuclear submarines, nuclear aircraft carriers, destroyers, and spy ships, which sail every ocean and make port on every continent. The United States has trained and equipped over 2 million troops and police in foreign lands; the purpose of this militarization has been not to defend these countries from outside invasion but to protect capital investments and the ruling oligarchs from the dangers of domestic insurgency.

---

33. *New York Times*, October 2, 1972; *Guardian*, September 24, 1975.

34. William Hoffman, "Vietnam: The Bloody Get-Rich-Quick Business of War," *Gallery*, November 1978, p. 42. Hoffman notes that the top ten defense firms grossed $11.6 billion in contracts during the Vietnam War.

35. Millions of dollars in U.S. aid given to the contras (the right-wing exiles who oppose the revolutionary government in Nicaragua) were funneled into offshore banks and private companies or in other ways were not accounted for, according to a General Accounting Office investigation: *New York Times*, June 12, 1986. On U.S. counterinsurgency in Latin America, see Edward Herman, *The Real Terror Network* (Boston: South End Press, 1982).

With only 5 percent of the earth's population, the United States expends one-third of the world's military funds. Two-thirds of the discretionary portion of the federal budget (that is, the portion not obligated by Social Security) is spent on war preparation. Despite a nuclear "overkill" capacity that can destroy the entire world more than twenty-five times over, the U.S. nuclear arsenal continues to grow at the rate of three H-bombs each day. Since World War II, more than $120 billion in U.S. *military* aid has been given to some eighty nations.[36]

This American global expansionism is designed to prevent competing social orders from emerging, especially those having a noncapitalist way of using wealth and labor. The *profits* of empire flow into corporate hands, while the growing military and investment *costs* are largely borne by the American taxpayer. This is not to say that U.S. expansionism has been impelled by the profit motive alone, but that various other considerations—such as national security and patriotism—are defined in a way that serves the material interests of a particular class. Indeed, much of what passes for "the national interest" in capitalist America, not surprisingly, has been defined from the perspective of a capitalist social order. "A serious and explicit purpose of our foreign policy," President Eisenhower observed in 1953, "[is] the encouragement of a hospitable climate for investment in foreign nations."[37] Since American "security" is supposedly dependent on American power, and such power depends in part on American wealth (i.e., a "sound economy," "secure markets," "essential raw materials," etc.), then policies that are fashioned to expand U.S. corporate wealth abroad are presumed to be in the national interest. Thus, we avoid any question as to whose interests are benefited by military-industrial global expansionism, at whose cost, and in pursuance of whose particular definition of "security" and "national interest."

TAXES: HELPING THE RICH IN THEIR TIME OF GREED

The corporate-dominated state uses taxation as well as public spending to redistribute wealth in an upward direction. Taking into account all local, state, and federal sales, excise and income taxes, as well as Social Security, we find that lower-income people pay a higher percentage of their earnings than do upper-income people, while generally getting less for what they

36. About two-thirds of every year's foreign aid package consists of military aid.
37. *New York Times*, February 3, 1953, quoted in Harry Magdoff, *The Age of Imperialism* (New York: Monthly Review Press, 1969) p. 126.

pay. Even a capitalist organ like the *Wall Street Journal* admitted: "One of the ironies of the federal tax system is its bias against the poor." And in 1985, after several years of the Reagan tax cuts, the *Washington Post* reported: "Taxes on the working poor have sky-rocketed while taxes on the well-to-do and on profitable corporations have declined dramatically."[38]

On the Upper East Side of Manhattan, within a few blocks on and around Fifth Avenue, there live members of many of America's richest families: Rockefellers, Mellons, Fricks, Pulitzers, Woolworths, Guggenheims, Belmonts, and Vanderbilts, those who were once known as the super-rich "Four Hundred." This area produces one of the highest per capita number of Ivy League graduates, U.S. ambassadors, and other top political and corporate leaders, and also "the smallest proportionate return of personal income tax to the national treasury."[39] The wealthier the person, the greater the opportunities to enjoy lightly taxed or tax-free income from various kinds of investments and from business and professional deductions. According to a 1985 congressional report, the wealthiest 30,000 Americans paid little or no taxes, and 3,170 millionaires paid no tax.[40]

It has been argued that if the wealthy were more heavily taxed this would make no appreciable difference in federal revenue since they are relatively few in number. In fact, if rich individuals and top corporations paid a progressive income tax of 50 percent, with no loopholes, shelters, or major deductions, there would be no federal deficit and enough to pay for all federal expenditures for aid to dependent children, education, child care, occupational safety, housing, environmental protection, and medical care.[41]

---

38. *Wall Street Journal*, December 30, 1985; *Washington Post*, April 14, 1985. In 1980, a family of four living at the poverty level paid less than 2 percent of its income in federal taxes. By 1986, that same family handed over 10.4 percent of its earnings: Anthony Lewis, "The Fairness Issue," *New York Times*, December 19, 1985; also Lewis's column, *New York Times*, February 6, 1986.

39. Bernard Livingston, *Closet Red* (New York: Waverly Publishers, 1985), p. 36.

40. Unpublished report by Representative J. J. Pickle (D-Tex.), Chairman, Subcommittee on Oversight, Committee on Ways and Means, House of Representatives (Washington, D.C.), released August 1, 1985; also Ronald Pasquariello, *Tax Justice* (Lanham, Md.: University Press of America, 1985). Upper-income people often pay less than meets the eye. Thus, Ronald Reagan might pay almost 10 percent, or $35,000, on his $375,000 "adjusted gross income" (income after deductions). But his actual income before deductions is upward of $1 million or more, so the effective tax is really closer to 3 percent, less than the rate paid by over 95 percent of the working population.

41. Hundreds of billions of dollars would be saved. During the Reagan era, inheritance taxes on the wealthiest estates were sharply reduced; this alone allowed an estimated tax break in 1982–1985 of $15.6 billion for the beneficiaries of very large fortunes. Incidentally, a top tax rate of 50 percent means half of everything over $200,000 or so, not 50 percent of the entire income. It is a graduated rate.

While the share of federal revenues coming from working taxpayers has been rising, the portion paid by corporations has dropped from 50 percent in 1945 to 14 percent in 1979 to 6.2 percent in 1983. While making billions in profits each year, the largest banks and industrial firms pay little or no taxes. Some, in fact, enjoy a negative tax rate, meaning their paper losses and credits so exceed their stated income that they actually receive cash rebates from the government. In 1981 commercial banks enjoyed an average tax rate of *minus* 12.6 percent; and Northrup, the aerospace manufacturer, had a tax rate of *minus* 103 percent.[42] Every year, over 100 of the largest private utilities collect taxes on their monthly billings to customers, but by taking advantage of write-offs, they are able to pocket most of what they collect, amounting to billions of dollars. In addition, an estimated 350,000 companies are illegally withholding Social Security and income taxes from their employees' paychecks and then pocketing the money. Few of these delinquent firms have been prosecuted.[43]

Generous tax breaks are supposed to spur new investments, but studies show that industries do not reinvest these windfall proceeds nor use them to create new jobs. In fact, firms paying little or no taxes have cut back on jobs; their tax savings are more often turned into higher dividend payments to stockholders and higher executive salaries.[44] It is argued that heavier taxes on the rich would leave them less money to invest and would therefore depress the economy and hurt us all. As just mentioned, the rate of investment today, now that the rich pay less taxes than ever, is no better, and if anything somewhat more sluggish, than in earlier years. The super-rich are no cause for prosperity. Numerous Third World nations have their super-wealthy class without a corresponding benefit to their peoples. At the same time, countries like Sweden tax their rich companies and individuals heavily yet enjoy a higher and more equitable standard of living than do we.[45]

For many decades, the federal income tax law was ostensibly progressive. A *progressive* income tax is one that takes a higher percentage of income from the rich than from the poor, the assumption being that the

42. Citizens for Tax Justice, *Corporate Income Taxes in the Reagan Years* (Washington, D.C., 1984) *Economic Notes*, November 1984, pp. 6–7; *Boston Herald*, August 29, 1985; *Denver Post*, October 6, 1984; *Parade*, April 8, 1984. In 1983, a working single mother, with three children and a salary of $10,500, paid more federal taxes than Boeing, General Electric, DuPont, Texaco, Mobil, and AT&T combined—even though these corporations had profits totaling $13.7 billion: *Washington Post*, May 13, 1985.

43. Study by Environmental Action Foundation, reported in the *Daily World*, July 26, 1985. *Moneysworth*, October 13, 1975.

44. Citizens for Tax Justice report in the *Washington Post*, January 28, 1985; and John Bryan, Jr.'s column in the *Washington Post*, May 14, 1985.

45. Herbert Inhaber, "How Rich Should the Rich Be?" *New Leader*, April 16, 1984, p. 12.

rich can better afford it. However, as just noted, the progressive features of the federal income tax were undermined by the many tax benefits afforded the wealthy.

A *proportionate* income tax, or "flat rate" tax, imposes the same rate on everyone, so that both rich and poor persons pay, say, 20 percent of their income. A person who earns $10,000 then pays $2,000 in taxes, and one who earns $1 million pays $200,000. Those who advocate a progressive income tax consider a flat tax to be unjust, for while both are paying the same rate, and the richer person is paying more dollars, the poorer person will have a harder time of it, since a greater percentage of his or her salary is needed for basic necessities. Since he has so fewer of them, each dollar has a greater impact on the well-being and survival needs of the lower-income person.

A *regressive* tax takes the most money from those who have the least. When both a modestly paid worker and a high-income executive pay $2,972 on their Social Security, one is paying 7 or 8 percent of his income and the other only 1 or 2 percent. Sales and excise taxes are regressive, because low- and middle-income people use a higher portion of their earnings for the goods and services so taxed. And when rich and poor persons pay the same thirty-five cents tax on a gallon of gas, they are sacrificing markedly different portions of their income.

The 1986 "Tax Reform" law contains some progressive features: it removes from the tax rolls some 6 million of the very poorest families (leaving on the rolls many millions more who are below or near the poverty level). It increases the standard deduction—a small assistance to low- and middle-income families with children. Capital gains will be taxed the same as other income rather than at less than half the regular rate, as was previously the case. Limits will be put on the paper losses used in tax shelters by the rich. And most of the worst corporate deductions will supposedly be eliminated. I say "supposedly" because special exceptions were granted to rich individuals and corporations, and subsequent ambiguities, loopholes, imaginative accounting practices, and special-favor amendments will likely allow yet more corporate money to escape taxation.[46]

The 1986 tax law also eliminates the progressive income tax, a historic gain for the rich. When Reagan came into office, the top tax bracket was 70 percent. It was reduced to 50 percent in 1981 and to 28 percent in the 1986 law and applies to everyone making over $29,750. Persons making below that sum will pay 15 percent. By reducing rates to these two brackets, the 1986 law comes close to being a flat tax: both the autoworker

46. *New York Times*, June 6, 1986; *Washington Post*, September 29, 1986.

who makes $29,900 and the auto executive who makes $2,000,000 will pay the same rate. But the new law is worse than a flat rate, for it also retains many of the regressive deductions that disproportionately benefit high-income people. It also reduces corporate income tax from 46 to 34 percent. Business meals and entertainment expenses are still 80 percent deductible, while unemployment compensation and some scholarships are no longer tax-exempt. *The 1986 tax law channels at least 16 percent of the total tax relief to half of 1 percent of the upper-income bracket, those making $200,000 or more.*

The only federal tax that has been cut during the Reagan years is the income tax, the only one with progressive features. More regressive levies, such as payroll taxes, user fees, and sales and excise taxes have all been increased.[47] Each successive tax law has shifted an increasingly heavier tax burden onto those of middle and low income.

DEFICIT SPENDING AND THE NATIONAL DEBT

As government plays a continually more active role in maintaining capital accumulation, it must spend greater and greater sums; in fact, it must expend more than it collects in revenues, a process known as "deficit spending." To meet its deficits the government borrows from financial institutions, wealthy individuals, and other creditors in the United States and abroad, in effect borrowing on the future earnings of the people to shore up the present earnings of the wealthy. Today the United States is the greatest debtor nation in the world, owing more than all Third World countries combined.

Conservative leaders who sing hymns to a balanced budget on Sunday have been among the wildest deficit spenders during the rest of the week. The Nixon and Ford administrations produced record peacetime deficits, and President Reagan's budget deficits threaten to run off the charts, being several times larger than previous peacetime and *wartime* budgets.[48] In 1940 the national debt was $43 billion; the costs of World War II brought it to $259 billion. By 1981, it climbed to $794 billion. In six years under Reagan, the debt ballooned to over $2 *trillion*, and should reach $2.7 trillion by the time he leaves office, or triple what it was when he entered the White House.[49]

---

47. George Mitchell, "Tax Relief for the Middle Class, Too," *Washington Post*, June 9, 1986; Victor Perlo, "Reagan Tax Bill," *People's Daily World*, August 30, 1986.

48. "Deficit Spending—A Hard Habit to Break," *U.S. News and World Report*, January 19, 1981; Richard DuBoff, "What Do the Reagan Deficits Really Mean?" *In These Times*, February 20–26, 1985.

49. *Washington Post*, February 14, 1986; *New York Times*, June 28, 1986.

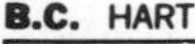

Nor can this runaway debt be blamed on the liberal Democrats in Congress who supposedly vote profligate sums for welfare and human services. During the first five Reagan years, social spending was cut $114.8 billion. And Congress appropriated *less* in discretionary spending than Reagan requested: $2.237 trillion as opposed to $2.249 trillion. The growth in deficit spending has been due to (a) the hundreds of billions in tax cuts given to rich individuals and corporations, and (b) gargantuan military budgets.[50]

As with the debts incurred by Third World nations, the U.S. national debt grows at an increasingly faster rate. The government not only borrows more, but must do so at higher rates and on shorter terms, so that the interest paid on the national debt has been growing twice as fast as the budget itself. In 1978, the interest payment was $49 billion; in 1981, $96 billion; in 1986, $144 billion. Every year a higher portion of the debt payment is on the interest alone and less and less for retirement of the principle. By 1989, about 80 percent of all government borrowing will go to pay for interest on money previously borrowed.[51]

The interest paid out on the federal debt is the second largest item in the discretionary budget (after military spending) and *represents a sum almost three times the amount spent on federal welfare payments to the poor*. Under Reagan, the increase in interest payments more than equals all the money saved by cuts in social services. The deficit is being financed at a cost to the living standards of the populace. Drawn as taxes from the working public, interest payments (consisting of 32 percent of every tax

50. *Washington Post*, September 26, 1960 and July 24, 1985. Conservatives blame the deficit on major benefit programs such as Social Security; see remarks by Senator Pete Domenici (R-N.M.), *Washington Post*, August 2, 1985. Actually, Social Security does not add to the deficit. It is self-supporting and, in fact, brings in more money than it pays out, so that it actually reduces the deficit somewhat. See correspondence, *Public Citizen*, April 1986, p. 10.

51. Joe Kahn, "The National Debt," *Economic Notes*, May–June 1985. On the financial devastation wrought by the "Reagan Revolution" see Center for Popular Economics, *Economic Report of the People* (Boston: South End Press, 1986).

dollar) go to banks, investment firms, and rich individuals, and constitute an upward redistribution of wealth. By buying up government bonds and securities, wealthy creditors can put their surplus capital into the federal deficit and watch it grow risk-free at public expense. We and our children will be paying increasingly larger sums to service an astronomical debt. As Karl Marx wrote in *Capital* (volume 1): "The only part of the so-called national wealth that actually enters into collective possessions of modern peoples—is their national debt."

In 1985, Congress enacted the Gramm-Rudman-Hollings Balanced Budget Act (stampeded through the Senate without benefit of a single committee hearing), which mandates an increasingly lower deficit for each year's budget until the budget is balanced in the 1990s. Should that deficit be exceeded, the act authorizes across-the-board automatic cuts. However, Gramm-Rudman leaves untouched all tax benefits for the rich and 38 percent of the military budget—the two items that contribute most to the deficit. (In fiscal 1987, more than 60 percent of the military budget was exempted.) Also exempt was the $144 billion in interest payments on the debt and various entitlements such as Social Security. Gramm-Rudman will cut mercilessly into human services and various other programs.[52]

As we have seen, the outputs of the political system benefit mostly those who own the wealth of the nation and do so at the expense of the working populace. In almost every enterprise, government has provided business with opportunities for private gain at public expense. Government nurtures private capital accumulation through a process of deficit spending, offers an endless market in the defense and space industries, and provides financial aid and military protection to support the global expansion of multinational corporations. From ranchers to resort owners, from corporate executives to bankers, from automakers to missile makers, there prevails a welfarism for the rich of such stupendous magnitude as to make us marvel at the big businessman's audacity in preaching the virtues of self-reliance whenever lesser forms of public assistance threaten to reach hands other than his own.

How to limit and reverse the class bias and economic oppression of federal policies? Some urgent early steps would be: (1) cut out the obvious instances of waste and duplication in our military budget; (2) negotiate arms reductions and détente with the Soviets which would then allow us to substantially reduce the bloated, titanic military establishment that is sinking the nation into a debt abyss; (3) eliminate the billions sent to often

52. Ronald Pollack, "No Way To Balance the Budget," *New York Times*, October 23, 1985; also *New York Times*, January 16, 1986.

corrupt foreign militarists and the billions in hidden subsidies to corporations abroad; (4) eliminate the subsidies and welfare handouts to rich corporations and rich agribusiness at home; (5) expand socially useful services such as environmental protection, conservation, housing, transportation, medical care, education, urban rehabilitation, and the like (discussed in the next chapter); (6) pass a tax law with a progressive rate, and that eliminates loopholes and special favors to the wealthy class; (7) initiate a wealth tax or capital accumulation tax. On this last point: only the rich can make substantial money on their money, needing proportionately less of it for consumption, even when living well. Even a 1 percent tax on assets, most of which would be paid for by the 840,000 super-rich families, would generate $100 billion annually and cut the budget deficit in half.[53]

As we shall see in the chapters ahead, there are reasons why measures like these are not pursued by those who rule in our name.

53. Arthur Carter, "How About a Capital Accumulation Tax?" *New York Times*, September 23, 1986.

7

Health, Environment, and Welfare: The Sacrificial Lambs

The plutocracy rules but not always quite in the way it would like. From time to time, those of wealth and power must make concessions to popular resistance, giving a little in order to keep a lot, taking care that the worst abuses of capitalism do not cause people to question and then agitate against the system itself. The concessions thus extracted by the democratic forces of society become the base from which to launch further struggles. For instance, the class struggles that brought important gains during the Great Depression of the 1930s did not end there. In the half-century that followed, labor unions, minorities, the poor, environmental groups, peace groups, women's-rights groups, public-interest organizations, and other progressive-minded people continued to press their fight against economic and social injustice. In response to this popular pressure, the federal government initiated a series of human services programs that bettered the lot of many, although failing to reach millions, including many of the people most in need. In recent years even these inadequate gains have come under attack.

THE POOR GET LESS (AND LESS)

In the 1960s, large sums were allocated for a "war on poverty" that brought no noticeable betterment to millions living in destitution. Some $7 billion was invested by federal, state, and local governments in the impoverished Appalachia region, yet the bulk of the poor remained "largely untouched" by a poverty program that was "chiefly a boon for the rich and for the entrenched political interests," specifically merchants, bankers, the coal industry, and road contractors.[1]

Other government assistance programs either (1) do not reach the neediest, or (2) have proven to be insufficient in scope, or (3) have been substantial and even somewhat effective but subjected to heartless cutbacks. For example, federal aid to education has been skewed more toward middle-class communities than toward the very poorest. And aid to higher education tends to favor the elite universities rather than community colleges and commuter schools.[2] Generally the federal government spends more money in rich counties than in poor ones. Federal transfer payments such as Social Security, workers' compensation, and unemployment and disability benefits distribute billions of dollars more to people earning moderate to middle incomes than to those in the lower brackets.[3]

Social Security is inadequate for the needs of many old persons, yet three-fifths of the elderly depend on it for their support, and Social Security reduced the poverty rate among the elderly from about 35 percent in 1959 to 14.1 percent by 1983. While other industrial countries are lowering the retirement age, and in socialist countries men can retire at age sixty and women at fifty-five, in the United States a 1983 law reduced Social Security benefits and raised the retirement age from sixty-five to sixty-seven (beginning in about two decades).[4]

All federal food programs combined, including school lunches, reach only a minority of the indigent. In-kind (noncash) benefits, such as Medicaid (medical payments for the poor), food stamps, and subsidized housing, fail to reach about 40 percent of the nation's poor. Nearly half the poor people in America are children. Most of the families of these children receive little or no government assistance.

The budget cuts initiated by the Reagan administration exacerbated the situation, penalizing "millions of poor, minority and handicapped youths."[5] School breakfast programs, reaching mostly children from low-

---

1. *New York Times*, November 29, 1970, quoting officials in the Office of Economic Opportunity.

2. Family income is a more decisive determinant of who goes to college than high-school performance. Every year hundreds of thousands of academically qualified high-school graduates do not continue their education because of insufficient funds. The Reagan cuts in scholarship funds have made it even more difficult for them; see correspondence, *New York Times*, October 18, 1986.

3. Gordon Tullock, *Economics of Income Distribution* (Hingham, Mass.: Kluwer, 1983).

4. Paul Light, *Artful Work, the Politics of Social Security Reform* (New York: Random House, 1985); *New York Times*, March 14, 1985. For a general study of domestic policy outputs see Benjamin Page, *Who Gets What from Government* (Berkeley: University of California Press, 1983).

5. According to the Children's Defense Fund, a children's advocate group: *Washington Post*, January 29, 1985; also *Washington Post*, July 7, 1982; and *American Children in Poverty*, a report by the Children's Defense Fund (Washington, D.C., January 1984). The

income families, have been severely cut. In all, between 1982 and 1986 over $114 billion in federal funds were cut from food stamp programs, Social Security, college scholarships, legal services for the poor, remedial education, nutrition programs for poor children, and federal welfare for the aged, blind and disabled.[6] The Comprehensive Employment and Training Administration (CETA), employing hundreds of thousands of people (70 percent of them women) to staff day-care centers, libraries, and centers for the disabled and aged, was entirely abolished, as was the Summer Feeding Program which provided meals for one million poor children.[7]

Generally, those people with the fewest economic resources and the least political clout were made to bear the greatest austerity under "Reaganomics." Translated from abstract figures into human experience, the cuts have meant more hunger and malnutrition, especially for infants, children, the disabled, and the elderly; more isolation and unattended illnesses; more homeless, jobless, and desperate people; more pathology, unhappiness, and suffering among those least able to defend themselves.[8]

The Reagan cuts were defended as a way of getting "welfare chiselers" off the dole. But of the more than eleven million recipients of Aid to Families with Dependent Children (AFDC, or "welfare"), almost all are children from low-income households and single mothers with no means of support. Less than one percent are able-bodied men. While there may be occasional instances of fraud, the AFDC program is one of the most strictly supervised programs in the federal government.[9] Contrary to conservative myths, (1) most welfare recipients are White; (2) most stay on welfare for an average of not more than two years; (3) welfare mothers do not have lots of children in order to collect lots of welfare (most AFDC families are small, consisting of only a mother and one or two children); (4) recipients do not live in luxury (they receive combined food, rent, and clothing allotments that are drastically below the poverty level); (5) the swelling welfare rolls have not been due to mass epidemics of laziness but

---

Supplemental Security Income (SSI), supposedly the "safety net" for low-income aged, blind, or disabled persons, was cut by Reagan. After paying heating bills, SSI recipients had sixty dollars or less each week to pay for all necessities. At least 33 percent of those eligible for aid are not reached: *New York Times*, March 14, 1985.

6. *Washington Post*, September 26, 1986, and October 3, 1984.

7. *Washington Post*, July 20, 1986 and February 20, 1985. Anthony Champagne and Edward Harpham, *The Attack on the Welfare State* (Prospect Heights, Ill.: Waveland Press, 1984).

8. See Champagne and Harpham, *The Attack on the Welfare State; Washington Post*, May 16, 1986 and June 10, 1982; *Newsweek*, April 5, 1982; *New York Times*, June 25, 1982.

9. Contrary to conservative claims, virtually none of the cuts in assistance programs were directed at fraud; nearly all dealt blows to the poorest families, according to the Project on Food Assistance and Poverty, a Washington-based public interest group: Geoffry Becker, "More Food Reductions for the Hungry?" *Guardian*, December 30, 1981.

to chronically high unemployment rates and to the cutbacks in day-care arrangements for children of single mothers.[10]

Finally, welfare payments are *not* the cause of our huge deficits. Welfare spending is not more than 5 or 6 percent of the federal budget. As already mentioned, interest payments, big tax cuts, and military spending have been the culprits. As for human services, "the big spending has been on retirement income and medical care for the middle class while programs for the poor . . . have lagged far behind inflation."[11]

Even before the Reagan cuts, one welfare expert estimated that for every two people receiving support, two or three did not get the assistance to which they were entitled, and this did not include persons who received payments smaller than they legally deserved. Millions fall through the tattered "safety net," being too young for Social Security, too old for AFDC assistance, not disabled enough for disability benefits, not covered by unemployment benefits (or their benefits have run out), and unable to collect welfare even though in need of it. Welfare is hardly an adequate solution to the problems of the poor, but "eliminating welfare payments in the absence of other economic and social opportunities is . . . a worse solution."[12]

"URBAN REMOVAL" AND "MESS TRANSIT"

Federal housing programs offer another example of the difficulties of providing equitable services in a capitalist society. While new housing is beyond the means of at least 75 percent of the nation's families, federal programs have provided lavish assistance to better-income homeowners in the form of low-cost credit and tax deductions. Almost all of the $60 billion or so deducted by homeowners each year (many times the amount spent on welfare) goes to people at the upper-income levels. Some 53 percent of the subsidized mortgage loans made by the government have gone to more affluent families that could have bought homes without help.[13]

---

10. Cesar Perales, "Myths About Poverty," *New York Times*, October 26, 1983. Studies indicate that one out of every five or so unemployed women is jobless because she is unable to make satisfactory child-care arrangements: *Child Care and Equal Oportunity for Women*, booklet of the U.S. Commission on Civil Rights (Washington, D.C., 1981).

11. Editorial, *Washington Post*, December 16, 1983.

12. Frances Fox Piven and Richard Cloward, *The New Class War* (New York: Pantheon, 1982), p. 4.

13. Chester Hartman (ed.), *America's Housing Crisis* (Boston: Routledge and Kegan Paul, 1983). Federal aid to low-income public housing was phased out by 1986 in favor of "moderate-income" housing, including federal cash and tax subsidies to complexes renting apartments at $3000 a month: *Washington Post*, July 20, 1986.

Most of the billions spent by the Department of Housing and Urban Development (HUD) have been channeled into the private sector of the economy in response to the profit interests of developers, banks, and speculators, producing few homes for people who cannot afford market prices.[14] Private housing developments built with federal assistance are often rented to low-income people for a year or two in order to qualify for federal funds, then renovated or sold to other private owners who, not held to the original contract, evict the tenants and turn the units into high-priced rentals or condominiums. Many already sound houses are rehabilitated with federal funds so that landlords can then drive out the poorer residents and make a greater return on their investments.

Urban renewal is better described as "urban removal." By the power of eminent domain the government does for investors what they cannot do for themselves—namely, forcibly buy large tracts of residential areas from reluctant small owners and small businesspeople, or from speculators who, armed with inside information, buy up land in the "condemned" area for quick resale to the city at substantial profit. Then the city sells this land, often at less than the market value, to developers, underwriting all investment risks on their behalf. The losses suffered by the municipality are usually made up by federal funds and constitute another multibillion-dollar public subsidy to private capital.[15]

The public housing that actually did reach the poor in any serviceable manner came under strong attack from the Reagan administration. Rents on low-income public housing were raised, and virtually all low-income construction has been eliminated. Between 1981 and 1986, the administration slashed $17 billion from public housing programs, and reduced the existing stock of subsidized housing through the displacement of indigent occupants, sales to high-income private investors, planned deterioration, and demolitions.[16] The goal was to eliminate some 100,000 public housing units by 1988, while continuing to subsidize the private housing industry through tax write-offs and easy-term loans.[17]

---

14. G. C. Thelen, Jr., "Homes for the Poor: The Well-Insured Swindle," *Nation*, June 26, 1972, pp. 814–16; *Guardian*, June 16, 1976.

15. Paul Baran and Paul Sweezy, *Monopoly Capital* (New York: Monthly Review Press, 1968); Hartman, *America's Housing Crisis*.

16. Gale Cincotta, correspondence, *New York Times*, May 3, 1986; Hartman, *America's Housing Crisis*, pp. 1–3.

17. Ward Sinclair, "U.S. Accused of Taking Homes from Poor and Selling to Rich," *Washington Post*, October 29, 1983. Sinclair notes that more than half of the federally subsidized low-income homes in the Virginia area "have gone to high-income investors and rents charged to tenants have doubled and tripled over their previous mortgage payments." See also the *Washington Post*, January 1, 1985.

Meanwhile, the private housing industry did not "take up the slack" on behalf of the homeless and the poor—as was supposed to happen. If anything, there has been a diminishing supply of low- and moderate-rent domiciles on the private market, as 2.5 million people lose their homes each year from evictions, foreclosure, higher rents, and neighborhood "gentrification." Finally, to put itself still more firmly on the side of investors, bankers, and landlords, the Reagan administration started to withhold federal aid from cities that enacted effective rent controls.[18]

The transportation system provides another example of how private profit takes precedence over public need. Earlier in this century the transporting of passengers and goods was done mostly by electric car and railroad. One mass-transit railway car can do the work of fifty automobiles, and railroads consume one-sixth the energy of trucks to transport goods. But these very efficiencies are what make railroads so *un*desirable to the oil and auto industries. For over a half-century the corporate response has been to undermine the nation's rail and electric-bus systems.

Consider the fate of Los Angeles. In 1935 a once beautiful Los Angeles was served by one of the largest interurban railway systems in the world, covering a 75-mile radius with 3,000 quiet, pollution-free electric trains that carried 80 million people a year. But General Motors and Standard Oil of California, using dummy corporations as fronts, purchased the system, scrapped its electric transit cars, tore down its power transmission lines, and placed GM diesel buses fueled by Standard Oil on Los Angeles's streets. By 1955, 88 percent of the nation's electric-streetcar network had been eliminated by collaborators like GM, Standard Oil, Greyhound, and Firestone. In short time, they cut back city and suburban bus services, forcing people to rely increasingly on private cars. In 1949, General Motors was found guilty of conspiracy in these activities and fined the devastating sum of $5,000.[19]

Given the absence of alternative modes of transportation, people become dependent on the automobile as a way of life so that their need for cars is often as real as their need for jobs—and mass transit devolves into "mess transit." The social costs of the automobile are staggering. About 45,000 people are killed on the highways each year and hundreds of thousands are injured and maimed. More than 60 percent of the land of most U.S. cities is taken up by the movement, storage, and servicing of vehicles. Whole neighborhoods are razed to make way for highways. The

---

18. James Ridgeway, "The Administration's Attack on the Homeless," *Village Voice*, February 14, 1984; Hartman, *America's Housing Crisis*.

19. Bradford Snell, *American Ground Transport* (Washington, D.C.: Government Printing Office, 1973); Jonathan Kwitny, "The Great Transportation Conspiracy," in Cargan and Ballantine (eds.), *Sociological Footprints*, 2nd ed. (Belmont, Calif.: Wadsworth, 1982).

automobile is the single greatest cause of air pollution in urban areas. In most suburban communities at least 40 percent of police work is directly related to automobiles, as is a good portion of ambulance and hospital service.[20]

The automobile requires communities to spread out, causing (a) premature obsolescence of streetcar neighborhoods whose compactness cannot accommodate cars; (b) higher food transportation costs as farms on the metropolitan fringe are displaced by suburban sprawl; (c) higher costs for sewage construction, road maintenance, and other thinly spread services. But as the number of cars grows so do the profits of the oil, auto, trucking, tire, cement, construction, and motel businesses. At the same time mass transit—the most efficient, cleanest, and safest form of transporting goods and people—falls into further decay.[21]

The government's role has been to subsidize the auto industry with multibillion-dollar highway programs while slashing rail services. Between 1946 and 1980, federal aid to highways amounted to $103 billion compared with $31 billion for air transportation and $6 billion for rail.[22] Much of the money pumped into the railroads ended up as dividends to stockholders and credit payments to banks.[23]

One of the more blatant giveaways to private corporate interests has been the "privatization" of Conrail. The government created Conrail on the ruins of Penn Central and six other northeastern lines which themselves had been brought to bankruptcy by profit milking. Fortified by $3 billion from the U.S. treasury and an intelligent management, Conrail was built into an efficient and profitable giant railroad system with $800 million in cash reserves by 1985. But with the complicity of supporters in Congress, President Reagan sold Conrail to private stockholders at less than half its value, supposedly to bring in new revenues.[24]

Most municipal transit systems are funded by deficit spending with tax-free bond issues sold to wealthy individuals and banks. In any one year these bondholders receive millions of dollars in interest payments, causing transit systems to cut services and raise fares as they go deeper into debt. The cities themselves are going deeper into the red. And as debt accumu-

---

20. Snell, *American Ground Transport*; also James Bush, "Would America Have Been Automobilized in a Free Market?" *New York Times*, February 10, 1985.

21. Bush, "Would America Have Been Automobilized . . . ."

22. Philip Weinberg, "Amtrak is Rolling," *Amicus*, Winter 1980, pp. 7–11.

23. In 1976, flushed with billions in subsidies from the federal government, railroads stripped themselves of their own cash assets and distributed millions of dollars to their stockholders in what was one of the highest dividend payments in history: *Workers World*, March 12, 1976.

24. Charles Curtis, "'Privatization': Govt. Gift to Corps.," *The Socialist*, April 1986, p. 3; *New York Times* editorial, May 20, 1986; *In These Times*, February 20–26, 1985, p. 2.

lates, a city must pay an increasingly large portion of its budget just to service that debt.[25] In order to pay out millions of dollars to their rich creditors, cities like New York have had to close down day-care centers, drug rehabilitation programs, health clinics, senior-citizen services, and park services for children, and lay off tens of thousands of hospital and sanitation workers, firefighters, and teachers.[26]

HEALTH AND SAFETY FOR NOBODY

Consumer protection is another area in which government does an insufficient job of protecting the public and actually advances the interests of private producers at the citizen's expense. The result is a market infested with overpriced, adulterated, and unsafe products; false advertising and planned obsolescence. The Food and Drug Administration (FDA) tests but 1 percent of the millions of yearly shipments of marketed drugs and foods, and approves drugs for public use on the basis of unreliable data supplied by the drug industry itself.[27] Drug companies spend $1 billion a year to promote sales—three times more than they spend on research and development.[28]

In 1985, the Census Bureau reported that 35 million Americans lacked any kind of health insurance. Millions live in areas where treatment is unavailable except at high fees, and where public hospitals are closing down for lack of funds. Medical bills in private hospitals are 23 percent higher for each patient than in hospitals that are not investor-owned. Nearly 16 million American families, or about one family in five, incur catastrophic out-of-pocket medical costs each year; about a third of these

---

25. William Tabb and Larry Sawers (eds.), *Marxism and the Metropolis* (New York: Oxford University Press, 1984).

26. Jack Newfield, "Who Killed New York City?" *New Politics*, Winter 1976, pp. 34–38; Ronald Berkman and Todd Swanstrom, "A Tale of Two Cities," *Nation*, March 24, 1979, pp. 297–99.

27. Alan Anderson, "Neurotoxic Follies," *Psychology Today*, July 1982, pp. 30–42; Sidney Wolfe, M.D., Christopher Coley, and the Health Research Group, *Pills That Don't Work* (New York: Farrar, Straus, 1981). Hundreds of hair dyes, food additives, cosmetics, and drugs marketed for years without FDA testing have been linked to cancer and birth defects: *New York Times*, July 22, 1973 and March 18, 1975; Colman McCarthy, "Dangerous Drugs," *Washington Post*, November 6, 1982.

28. But the companies spend nothing on rare and often fatal diseases because the market is not big and profitable enough. N. R. Kleinfield, "'Orphan' Drugs Caught in Limbo," *New York Times*, July 20, 1986; *Washington Post* editorial, January 3, 1983; "Orphan Diseases," *Scientific American*, January 1983. The Reagan administration opposed attempts by Congress to subsidize the production of medications for rare diseases.

have incomes below the poverty level.[29] In sum, medical costs have soared, yet people are receiving not better care, only more expensive care, if any at all.

Too often, the first thing patients receive in a hospital emergency room is an examination of their wallets. An estimated one million are refused emergency care each year because they cannot show proof of ability to pay, others are ejected from hospitals in the midst of an illness because they are out of funds, others are bankrupted by medical bills despite supposedly "comprehensive" private insurance, and still others suffer iatrogenic illness and death in hospitals that are below minimal standards of cleanliness, safety, and staffing.[30]

While many people have no medical coverage of any kind, over 20 million, mostly low-income and elderly, do respectively benefit from Medicaid and Medicare. But the greatest beneficiaries have been the doctors and hospitals that overcharge, give unnecessary treatment, and fraudulently bill the government for over $3.4 billion annually.[31] The padded bills became so astronomical that federal and state governments turned to paying fixed, limited sums per illness, regardless of the amount of care extended. So instead of loading on tests and treatments, the medical industry is now tempted to provide as little service as possible in order to pocket as much of the fixed insurance payments as possible.[32]

Defenders of medicine-for-profit argue that no one is denied medical care; they point to the glut of doctors and beds that exist in many private hospitals. But these hospitals are interested exclusively in the highly profitable market of insured, *paying* customers, and turn away those who cannot pay. Many Americans have discovered that an oversupply of doctors and beds does not add up to increased access to medical care.[33]

Federal medical assistance leaves much to be desired. Medicare is more burdensome to low-income elderly who pay 25 percent of their annual income for health care, compared to less than 3 percent paid by high-income elderly.[34] The entire health system is unfair to the millions of

---

29. Howard Waitzkin, *The Second Sickness: Contradictions of Capitalist Health Care* (New York: Free Press, 1983); *New York Times*, August 11, 1983; Spencer Rich, "Catastrophic Health Bills Found in 1 in 5 Families," *Washington Post*, June 7, 1986.

30. *Washington Post*, March 21, 1984; James Bryan, "For-Profit Medicine Is a Major Threat to Good Care," *Washington Post*, July 24, 1985; Stanley Wohl, M.D., *The Medical-Industrial Complex* (New York: Harmony Books, 1984).

31. Harvey Rosenfield, "Fraudulent Billing Costs," *Public Citizen*, February 1986, pp. 19–20.

32. David Himmelstein and Steffie Woolhandler, "Medicine as Industry," *Monthly Review*, April 1984, pp. 13–25.

33. *Washington Post*, June 30, 1985.

34. *New York Times*, March 13, 1986.

Americans who pay the federal taxes that heavily subsidize medical-school education for doctors but who cannot afford visits to those same doctors.[35] Assistance to the poor under Medicaid has been slashed—with growing numbers of fatalities for those denied hospitalization. With the Reagan cutbacks, child-health care also has declined and the number of infants who die because of a lack of postnatal care has increased.[36]

Medical care, much like agriculture, housing, and transportation, is organized as a publicly subsidized private enterprise whose purpose is to make a profit for those who control it. Dr. Bernard Winters points out:

> Just as our defense budget has little to do with actually defending the United States, so our health budget has little to do with maintaining the health of the American people. It is a costly, wasteful mechanism for funneling money to a sprawling medical industry that encompasses not only physicians and hospitals but equipment manufacturers, pharmaceutical corporations, banks and insurance companies. The impulse that drives this industry is the same that drives every industry—the maximization of profit.[37]

One cannot talk about the health of America without mentioning the awesome problem of occupational safety. Every year more than 14,000 workers are killed on the job; another 100,000 die prematurely, and 400,000 become seriously ill from work-related diseases, such as black lung and cancer. Five million on-the-job injuries occur each year. About 20 million Americans work with chemicals that can damage the nervous system, even in small doses. All told, one out of every four workers suffers from occupationally connected diseases.[38]

Industrial work may always carry some risk, but the present carnage is due mostly to inadequate safety standards and lax enforcement of codes. Thus, almost all coal-mine accidents could be avoided if proper safeguards were employed. Work conditions in U.S. mines are among the worst in the world.[39] Company money spent on safety for workers (and consumers) rather than on production for profits is money spent in the worker's interest rather than the owner's. So, Johns-Manville continued to subject

---

35. *Washington Post*, May 23, 1983.

36. *New York Times*, December 17, 1984 and February 13, 1983; *Los Angeles Times*, November 15, 1984.

37. Bernard Winter, M.D., "Health Care: The Problem Is Profits," *Progressive*, October 1977, p. 16.

38. Daniel Berman, *Death on the Job* (New York: Monthly Review Press, 1978); Anderson, "Neurotoxic Follies"; Wendy Chavkin (ed.), *Double Exposure: Women's Health Hazards on the Job and at Home* (New York: Monthly Review Press, 1984); *Washington Post*, January 24, 1985.

39. In socialist countries there is much more emphasis on worker safety in mining and other industries: *New York Times*, October 26, 1974; also the report of a West Virginia miner who visited the Soviet Union, *United Mine Workers Journal*, November 1, 1974.

its workers to asbestos for decades after learning they would suffer lung damage and cancer—rather than face new production and safety costs and lawsuits from injured workers.[40] As one farm worker testifies:

> I began to see how everything was so wrong. When growers can have an intricate watering system to irrigate their crops but they can't have running water inside the houses of workers. Veterinarians tend to the needs of domestic animals but they can't have medical care for the workers. They can have land subsidies for the growers but they can't have adequate unemployment compensation for the workers. They treat him like a farm implement. In fact, they treat their implements better and their domestic animals better. . . . Now because of the pesticides, we have many respiratory diseases. The University of California at Davis has government experiments with pesticides and chemicals, to get a bigger crop each year. They haven't any regard as to what safety precautions are needed.[41]

For years organized labor has fought for laws to protect workers. In 1970, Congress finally created the Occupational Safety and Health Administration (OSHA). In the chemical industry alone, OSHA regulations brought a 23-percent drop in accidents and sickness, averting some 90,000 illnesses and injuries at a yearly cost to industry of $140 per worker. Yet the agency's resources are vastly insufficient. The OSHA has only enough inspectors to visit each workplace once every eighty years. After President Reagan took office, the number of OSHA inspectors was cut by 16 percent. As of 1986, OSHA had an "acceptable" death and injury level: the national average. Only plants that exceeded that average were inspected. And the average kept rising as OSHA began exempting firms from inspection and weakening safety standards.[42]

Existing workers' compensation laws usually place the burden of proof on the injured worker, provide no penalties when industry withholds or destroys evidence, and allow long delays in procedure that work against the disabled and the penurious. The law also imposes a statute of limitation, which makes it difficult to collect on diseases that have a long latency period. Only about 10 percent of the millions of injured workers actually get any benefits. And those who receive workers' compensation forfeit

---

40. Richard Abel "Torts," in David Kairys (ed.), *The Politics of Law: A Progressive Critique* (New York: Pantheon, 1982); Paul Brodeur, *Outrageous Misconduct* (New York: Pantheon, 1985).

41. Quoted in Studs Terkel, *Working* (New York: Pantheon, 1972), p. 12.

42. Ruth Ruttenberg and Randell Hudgins, *Occupational Safety and Health in the Chemical Industry* (New York: Council on Economic Priorities, 1981); Bill Dennison, "Murder at the Workplace," *Daily World*, May 21, 1986; Joan Claybrook, *Retreat from Safety: Reagan's Attack on America's Health* (New York: Pantheon, 1984).

their right to sue a negligent employer. Thus, the program actually shields industry from liability.[43]

ON BEHALF OF POLLUTION AND RADIATION

Like sin, pollution is regularly denounced but vigorously practiced. Strip mining and deforestation by coal and timber companies continue to bring ruination to our forest lands. Six million acres of topsoil are eroded each year by chemicalized farming. Great quantities of industrial effusion have been dumped into our rivers and lakes. Meanwhile acid rain, a deadly combination of pollutants from factories and automobiles, is doing its share to destroy crops, forests, lakes, wildlife, and human life.

Industry introduces some one thousand new chemicals into the marketplace annually, often with insufficient or fraudulent information about their effects on health and environment. Food additives, household cleansers, and herbicides used for lawns have been linked to cancer. Billions of pounds of buried toxic wastes, leaking from thousands of sites, contaminate wide areas of groundwater, and cause birth defects, liver and kidney diseases, and cancer. Dioxin, one of the deadliest of all chemicals, used as a defoliant in Vietnam, is applied as an herbicide on American pasturelands and forests, and even as a weed killer in residential areas, causing birth abnormalities and cancer. In all, *over one billion pounds of chemicals are released into the environment each day*. This situation, say some ecologists, makes the air we breathe, the water we drink, and the food we eat the leading causes of death in the United States.[44]

According to estimates by the Environmental Protection Agency (EPA), about 91 percent of all Americans, over 200 million people, have detectable levels of PCBs (a toxic chemical compound) in their fatty tissues, and virtually everyone is exposed to pesticides, many of which are known to be carcinogenic. Pesticides are appearing in underground water supplies despite earlier assurances that they would not pass through the soil. Areas with noticeably high pesticide runoff, such as parts of the

43. Mark Reutter, "Workmen's Compensation Doesn't Work or Compensate," *Business and Society*, Fall 1980, pp. 39–44.

44. Michael Brown, *Laying Waste: The Poisoning of America by Toxic Chemicals* (New York: Pantheon, 1980); *New York Times*, March 16, 1983, and November 18, March 10, and May 22, 1985; Jonathan King, "The Poisoning of America's Drinking Water," *Public Citizen*, October 1985, pp. 14–20; Linda Martin, "Herbicide for Lawns Is Linked to Cancer," *New York Times*, October 30, 1986; William Ashworth, *The Late Great Lakes* (New York: Knopf, 1986); *Washington Post*, September 12, 1980, contains a summary of the U.S. Surgeon General's report on toxic chemicals.

agricultural Midwest, have high instances of leukemia and other cancers.[45] Drawing on an incomplete listing, an EPA study found that since early 1980 at least five accidents a day have released toxic chemicals from factory facilities and have killed 136 people and injured nearly 1,500. Had the entire country been surveyed, the number of accidents would have been about three times higher.[46]

Everyone is victimized by environmental contamination, but some more than others. One study found that poor people are more likely to get cancer and die from it than rich people, partly because the poor have less access to health care and are more likely to delay seeking treatment. But the poor also *develop* cancer at significantly higher rates because they generally live in areas that are more highly contaminated by industrial toxins and automobile pollution. They are also more likely to work at dirtier, nonunion jobs where there is even less protection from occupational hazards than at unionized worksites.[47]

Pollution continues unabated because production costs are cheaper and profits are higher when industrial wastes can be dumped into the environment. The cost of monitoring production, the cost of disposing of industrial effluents (which compose 40 to 60 percent of the loads treated by municipal sewage plants), the cost of developing new water sources (while industry and agribusiness consume 80 percent of the nation's daily water supply), and the costs of tending to the sickness and disease caused by pollution do not enter the accounts of industrial firms but are passed on to the public.

In response to a growing public outcry, Congress did create the EPA and passed the Clean Air Act of 1970, which saved an estimated 14,000 lives a year and billions of dollars in health, property, and vegetation damage. Two years later Congress passed the Clean Water Act, which brought improvements to a number of our rivers and lakes. Nevertheless, given the urgency of our environmental needs, the government's record is dismal. Federal controls on pesticides vary from dangerously lax to nonex-

---

45. *New York Times*, March 6 and September 6, 1986. Increased use of pesticides create generations of insects more resistant to chemical controls. In the last thirty-five years, pesticide use has increased twelvefold and crop losses to insects and other pests have almost doubled: Robert Van Den Bosch, *The Pesticide Conspiracy* (Garden City, N.Y.: Doubleday, 1978); *Washington Post*, September 26, 1984. For an excellent bimonthly that offers organic, economical, and nonchemicalized ways of farming, see *The New Farm* (Emmaus, Pa.), a monthly publication on alternative agriculture.

46. *New York Times*, October 3, 1985. Hazardous toxic waste sites exist at thousands of U.S. military facilities. The Pentagon hopes to begin cleaning these up "no later than 1993" at a cost of $5 billion to $10 billion: *New York Times*, February 28, 1985.

47. Study by the American Cancer Society reported in *People's Daily World*, October 11, 1986.

istent. The EPA does not effectively screen new chemicals and has regulated but a few of the tens of thousands of toxic emissions that contaminate our environment. Along with the Food and Drug Administration and other agencies, the EPA has preferred to collaborate with big-business polluters.[48]

48. Karl Grossman, *The Poison Conspiracy* (Sag Harbor, N.Y.: Permanent Press, 1983); Ruth Norris (ed.), *Pills, Pesticides, and Profits* (Croton-on-Hudson, N.Y.: North River Press, 1982); *Washington Post*, June 12, 1985; *New York Times*, July 10, 1984 and March 13, 1986. One example: when Gulf Resources and Chemical Co., which made $25 million in profits one year, refused to spend $880,000 to clean up a smelting plant and threatened to close the plant, EPA and OSHA granted five-year delays on worker safety and emission standards: *Guardian*, October 7, 1981.

In 1971 a presidential commission estimated that it would cost $105 billion to clean up the nation's air, water, and ground pollution, *less than what the military spends in five months*. The best that Congress could do in 1986, over Reagan's opposition, was to pass a toxic cleanup superfund that allocated $9 billion to be spent over five years.[49] During its tenure, the Reagan administration sought to weaken or abolish almost all environmental protections (inadequate as they already were) because they were supposedly too costly to industry. But one study revealed that government and industry regularly exaggerated the costs of complying with environmental rules by upwards of 200 percent.[50]

The heavily chemicalized methods pushed by the Department of Agriculture is harmful to farmers' wallets as well as to the environment, costing farmers $40 billion a year in pesticides, chemical fertilizers, fuel, and machinery, and driving many of them into bankruptcy. Yet the Reagan administration, concerned for the welfare of the chemical industry, gave no support to less costly, environmentally protective organic farming and instead fired the only full-time specialist dealing with regenerative farming in the Department of Agriculture.[51]

Another major menace to health and safety is nuclear power. Serious mishaps that came close to being major catastrophes have occurred at Three Mill Island in Pennsylvania and at reactors in Middletown, Penn.; Detroit; Hanford, Wash.; Brown's Ferry, Ala.; Oak Harbor, Ohio; Gore, Okla.; and Salem, N.J. Repeated malfunctions have plagued almost each one of the eighty nuclear plants in the United States.[52] According to the Nuclear Regulatory Commission (NRC), there are about 4,000 mishaps each year. Radioactive buildups are regularly vented into the environment. At the Callaway reactor in Missouri, for example, radioactive gases were released on the average of once a week. Reactors employed by the

49. *New York Times*, October 21, 1986.

50. *Guardian*, July 2, 1980; Jonathan Lash, *A Season of Spoils, The Story of the Reagan Administration's Attack on the Environment* (New York: Pantheon, 1984).

51. *Washington Post*, March 31, 1984. Pesticides banned in the United States make their way back to our dinner tables anyway. The pesticide producers just ship them abroad to be used on foreign-grown produce, much of which is then imported into the United States: *Daily World*, October 8, 1985. For a broad critique, see Michael Fox, *Agricide* (New York: Schocken Books, 1986).

52. "U.S. Nuclear Plant 'Mishaps' Are Still Repeated," *Baltimore Sun*, November 24, 1984; *New York Times*, April 29, 1986; also John Fuller, *We Almost Lost Detroit* (New York: Crowell, 1976); Ralph Nader and John Abbotts, *The Menace of Atomic Energy*, rev. ed. (New York: Norton, 1979); "We Almost Lost Salem," *Progressive*, May 1983, pp. 12–13. Ian Gilbert and Elliot Negin, "America's Chernobyls," *Public Citizen*, August 1986, pp. 12–14. Nuclear plants are so hazardous that insurance companies refuse to handle them. Accidents have also occurred in Canada, France, and India. The most serious so far was at Chernobyl in the USSR in 1986, causing scores of deaths; widespread contamination of food and livestock in the Ukraine, Scandinavia and parts of Western Europe; and billions of dollars in damage.

miltary are said to be even more dangerous than commercial ones and account for half of all radioactive waste.[53]

The radioactive emissions resulting from the mining, milling, storage, and shipment of nuclear materials are far in excess of "permissible" levels established by the NRC. No one has ever demonstrated there is such a thing as a "permissible" level of exposure. The best scientific evidence indicates that *any* amount of emission can damage health and genetic structure. Extraordinarily high rates of cancer, birth deformities, and deaths have been found among populations residing within fifteen miles of nuclear plants. Nuclear wastes, some of which remain radioactive for 250,000 years, are building up in the soil and the silt of rivers. The nuclear industry has no long-term technology for safe waste disposal nor for the entombment or decontamination of old nuclear plant sites—some of which are approaching the end of their 40-year life expectancy.[54]

The promise of nuclear power was that it would be safe, clean, and cheap. It is none of these. The construction of nuclear plants now involve cost overruns of 400 to 1000 percent. Electric rate increases of 25 to 50 percent or more are looming for millions of customers in various states because of the costs of nuclear reactors. A plant built in Midland, Michigan was estimated at $350 million but ended costing $4.43 billion. The New York Shoreham plant, originally priced at $261 million, ended up costing $4.1 billion. In addition, for years to come, taxpayers and customers will be paying off the many billions of dollars spent on 100 reactors that have been canceled by the end of 1983 because of economic and safety reasons—without receiving any electricity for their pains.[55]

In regard to nuclear power, the federal government's role has been true to form, that of a faithful servant of industry. For years, the government spent billions to subsidize the development and use of nuclear energy. It also promoted false notions that nuclear energy was safe and cheap, and

---

53. Kay Drey, "Pathway to the Environment," *In These Times*, May 21–27, 1986, p. 15. "Military Nuclear Wastes: The Hidden Burden of the Nuclear Arms Race," *Defense Monitor* (Washington, D.C., 1981).

54. Nader and Abbotts, *The Menace of Atomic Energy*, pp. 72–81. A White House Task Force estimated as early as 1979 that over one million Americans have already become victims of "low-level" radiation: *Potomac Alliance Newsletter* (Washington, D.C., October 1979); Marvin Resnikoff, *The Next Nuclear Gamble: Transportation and Storage of Nuclear Waste* (New York: Council on Economic Priorities, 1983); John Gofman, M.D., *Radiation and Human Health* (San Francisco: Sierra Club Books, 1982); *New York Times*, April 10, 1979; Virginia Witt, "What To Do with Old Nuke Power Plants?" *Guardian*, February 24, 1982. Hundreds of thousands of truck shipments of contaminated waste pass over U.S. highways close to populated areas and other vehicles, vulnerable to leakage and accident: *Washington Post*, February 4, 1982.

55. See the excellent series by Matthew Wald in the *New York Times*, February 26–28, 1984; also *New York Times*, May 27 and September 11, 1986; *Wall Street Journal*, October 14, 1983.

repeatedly suppressed findings by its own scientists that demonstrated to the contrary. The government also has allowed private industry and the military to deposit radioactive nuclear wastes into fifty ocean dumps that stretch along the east and west coasts of the United States, including prime fishing areas. Radioactive fallout from underground tests by the military is regularly vented into the atmosphere. The NRC still does a dangerously inadequate job of addressing the safety issue and enforcing safety standards. And the government spends almost nothing on alternative fuel sources such as solar, geothermal, and tidal energies. By 1986, even though there were hundreds of thousands of people around the world already relying on solar heating devices, President Reagan had succeeded in abolishing all expenditures for solar energy development.[56]

In the energy field as elsewhere, we discover the contradiction between our human needs and our economic system, a system whose primary goal is to produce whatever brings the highest corporate profit regardless of the waste, cost, ecological damage, and health hazards. And we see that government is an insufficient bulwark against this social malpractice and often a willing handmaiden.

Do Government Programs Work?

Of the billions of dollars in public funds spent ostensibly for housing, medical care, transportation, and energy, a good portion ends up as subsidies to business. Thus, we keep priming a leaky pump, attempting to rectify the social ills of capitalism through a capitalist system that itself is organized primarily to serve the private investor. Yet we should not overlook the fact that social spending programs sometimes do "work"—in limited but important ways. This may explain why conservatives want to eliminate them—not because they don't work but because they do. For when they serve popular interests, they create problems and risks for the owning class.

For instance, environmental protections—if tough enough and properly enforced—do improve the quality of the water we drink and air we breathe; and occupational safety does prevent injuries and save lives.[57] But such measures cut into profits by adding to production costs. And they

56. Anna Gyorgy, et al., *No Nukes* (Boston: South End Press, 1979), pp. 92–94, 225–295; "The Fading Dream of NRC Reform," *Nucleus* (Report to the Union of Concerned Scientists Sponsors, Cambridge, Mass.), Spring 1983; Douglas Foster, "You Are What They Eat," *Mother Jones*, July 1981, pp. 18–25; *New York Times*, May 23, 1983.

57. John Schwarz, *America's Hidden Success* (New York: W. W. Norton, 1983), pp. 59–69; *Washington Post*, January 1, 1985.

place limits on industry's ability to use human labor and the environment solely as it sees fit.

Another example discussed earlier: Conrail demonstrated that a government-owned rail system could give better service at less cost than the investor-owned lines it replaced. But this very success is intolerable to conservatives who correctly see nonprofit public ownership as a threat to the private-profit system. So, Conrail was "privatized" at a bargain price.

Public housing programs did dramatically reduce overcrowding and substandard housing between 1940 and 1980,[58] but they also created a housing supply that competes with the private housing industry, and this does not sit well with investors. Other liberal programs have worked to some degree. Joseph Califano, Jr., a former member of President Carter's cabinet, credits public medical assistance with increasing life expectancy in the United States by five years, from seventy to seventy-five. Food stamps, SSI, and the Women, Infants and Children program (WIC) have helped the very poorest and the disabled to survive, offering them a potentially more productive existence. And without Social Security almost nine million more elders would be living in abject poverty. In general, without federal assistance programs, the number of people living in poverty would easily double.[59] But while these programs are funded mostly by the working populace, they also take some money from the wealthy and from employers; they redistribute income in a downward, instead of upward, direction and therefore are opposed by those in the higher social reaches.

The attack on human services and entitlements, which is the essence of "Reaganomics" (and every other economically conservative agenda), makes sense from a particular class and ideological perspective. Fewer regulations and protections mean more profits. Less public assistance, more cuts in disability and unemployment insurance and in Social Security, a higher retirement age, and a freezing of minimum wages deprive millions of people of alternative sources of income, forcing many back into the job market, thereby intensifying the competition for employment.[60] This, in turn, deflates the price of labor and helps keep wages from cutting into profits—which partly explains why profits remain so high during

58. Schwarz, *America's Hidden Success*, pp. 48–50.

59. *Washington Post*, September 27, 1982, and April 20 and May 24, 1985; *New York Times*, March 14, 1985 and February 3, 1986; also "How Bad Was Liberalism?" *The Progressive Review*, Washington, D.C., May–June 1985.

60. President Reagan revealingly complained that federal aid has allowed the unemployed poor to be the only group that did not need to move elsewhere in search of jobs: *New York Times*, June 20, 1982. Bereft of public assistance, low-income people presumably would be forced to range more widely to compete with others for jobs, adding to the labor surplus and deflating wages.

times of stagnation. Even though the pie is not growing, those at the top manage to get a larger slice through the upward redistribution of income.

In addition, eliminating human services supposedly will make people stop "running to the government for a handout" and teach them to "rely on themselves"—thereby leaving government with more funds to help defense contractors, bankers, and all the other businesspeople who run to the government for a handout whenever it suits them.

8

Law, Repression, and Democratic Struggle

Some government programs are designed to take the edge off popular discontent and avoid serious challenges to the politico-economic system. But government does not rely solely upon spending programs to keep the people quiescent. There are sterner measures. Besides the carrot, there is the stick. Behind the welfare bureaucracy, there stand the police, courts, prisons, and the various agencies of "national security" like the FBI and the CIA.

A DOUBLE-STANDARD LAW

Since we have been taught to think of the law as a neutral instrument serving the entire community, it is discomforting to discover that laws are often written and enforced in the most tawdry racist, sexist, and class-biased ways. In most conflicts between management and workers, for instance, the law intervenes on the side of management. The protection of corporate property is deemed tantamount to the protection of society itself and of benefit to all, even to those who possess no corporate assets. The very definition of what is and is not lawful contains a class bias. Hence, the theft of merchandise from a neighborhood store is unlawful, while the theft of the store itself and the entire surrounding neighborhood in an urban "renewal" program instigated by investment speculators, bankers, and public officials is hailed as an act of civic development.

The law's proximity to capital and its distance from labor can be seen in the curriculum of the average law school: one learns corporate, tax, insurance, and realty law; torts and damages; and even labor law chiefly

from the perspective of those who own the property. Owners, trustees, and landlords have "rights," but workers, students, consumers, and tenants have troublesome "demands." Under the law, management may call in the police to lock out workers, but workers cannot call in the police to drive out management. University trustees may bring in the police to suppress striking students, but students cannot call on the police to control unaccountable trustees.

The biases written into the law, which reflect the often unjust property relations of the society, are compounded by the way the law is enforced. Even when the letter of the law is on their side, working people have little else going for them. They are least able to seek redress of grievances through the courts, seldom having the time or money. And when they find themselves embroiled in court cases, it is almost always at the initiative of bill collectors, merchants, or landlords, who regularly use the courts as a means of asserting their property interests.

The law does little to protect us from white-collar crimes like embezzlement, fraud, business-related arson, overpricing, and violations of environmental and occupational safety. Such crimes cost the public over $40 billion a year, a figure that excludes antitrust violations like price-fixing, which may amount to as much as another $160 billion. In the period from 1983 to 1985 alone, General Electric admitted it defrauded the Pentagon; the Bank of Boston admitted it failed to report $1.22 billion in cash transactions, including what was later discovered to be laundered drug money; U.S. Steel pleaded no contest to charges of illegally dumping toxic wastes; Sperry Corporation confessed to falsifying bills for work on the MX missile; Rockwell agreed to reimburse the government for excessive billing on the space shuttle; and Exxon had to refund $1.49 billion for violating

1. *Newsday*, November 4, 1985; *New York Times*, May 3 and March 29, 1985; Joan Claybrook, "White Collar Crime Boom," *Public Citizen*, July/August 1985, p. 5; Mark Green and John Berry, "White Collar Crime as Big Business," *Nation*, June 8, 1985, p. 704–707.

price controls.[1] According to the pro-business *U.S. News and World Report*, 115 of the top 500 corporations "have been convicted in the past decade of at least one major crime or have paid civil penalties for serious misbehavior." Among the very biggest firms "the rate of documented misbehavior has been even higher."[2] Many companies are repeat offenders.

People fear street crime more than the white-collar variety because of the immediacy of its violence and because of its vivid and constant portrayal in movies and television shows. But the loss of dollars and lives from "unsafe products, pollution, and price-fixing greatly exceeds that from all [street crime] in America."[3] Yet the corporate criminals seldom go to jail. Honeywell ignored defects in gas heaters resulting in twenty-two deaths and seventy-seven crippling injuries, for which it was fined $800,000. Tycoon C. Arnholt Smith pleaded no contest to charges of looting one of his companies of $100 million through the use of phony stock deals and bank loans, for which he received a $30,000 fine and a two-year suspended sentence. E. F. Hutton copped a plea to 2,000 felony counts of wire and mail fraud involving hundreds of banks and was fined $2 million. Johns-Manville Corporation suppressed information about the asbestos poisoning of its workers; when ordered to pay damages in civil court Manville declared bankruptcy to avoid payment. Wedtech, a defense contractor, admitted to forging $6 million in invoices submitted to the Defense Department, but was not barred from bidding on future government contracts and no criminal charges were filed. An executive of Eli Lilly pleaded no contest to charges that he failed to inform the government about the effects of Oraflex, a drug the company knew had been tied to twenty-six deaths in the United States and to deaths abroad. He was fined $15,000.[4]

Guilty companies are often provided with special stipulations and negotiated settlements or are let off with light fines. The average fine against companies with serious workplace safety violations, according to Representative George Miller (D-Cal.), is $239, a figure not likely to terrorize Wall Street. And offenders often ignore the penalties imposed on them. According to a Senate investigation, $185.6 million in fines was owed by white-collar criminals who could pay but who simply did not.[5]

"Crime in the suites" may be due less to the venality of executives and more to the nature of the profit system. Many businesspeople have argued

---

2. *U.S. News* is quoted in Green and Berry, "White Collar Crime . . ." p. 704; see also Marshall Clinard and Peter Yeager, *Corporate Crime* (New York: Free Press, 1986).

3. Green and Berry, "White Collar Crime . . ." p. 704; Robert Elias, *The Politics of Victimization* (New York: Oxford University Press, 1985).

4. *New York Times*, September 12, 1985 and November 9, 1986; *Newsday*, November 4, 1985. For earlier findings see Edwin Sutherland, *White Collar Crime* (New York: Holt, Rinehart and Winston, 1949).

5. *Washington Post*, September 30, 1983.

that their illegal actions were not designed to line their pockets with someone else's money but were done "under pressure to get their profits up, or because the competition forced them to it."[6]

While tender toward business, the law has been harsh toward labor. Courts will impose injunctions and multimillion-dollar fines to break strikes and cripple unions. Leaders of public-employment unions have been jailed up to one year for strikes deemed illegal.[7] When companies refuse to sign new contracts with unions, improve safety standards, or make other expenditures on the grounds that it would be too costly, what can the workers do? Philip Green describes some of the legal difficulties they face:

> Suppose the workers . . . demand to see the books. They cannot; *the law* protects corporations from having to accede to that demand. If they then go on strike, they will probably lose a prolonged strike, because *the law*—that is, *the state*—forbids mass picketing, secondary boycotts and all the other tactics that would give the workers a chance to overcome their lack of accumulated capital. Suppose further, having lost their strike, they then sit in, seize the plant: *the state* will send in armed forces to remove them.[8]

CRIMINAL ENFORCEMENT

The criminal-law enforcement process is all too frequently tainted by racial, gender, ideological, and class biases. Who you are may be as important as what offense you commit. A public defense attorney who specializes in juvenile cases notes the difference between the way the enforcement system works against low-income and middle-income minors: "It's strange how the schoolyard fights and shoplifting cases in middle-class neighborhoods rarely result in the youngsters' being charged. The police call the kids' parents to pick them up, and they send them home with a warning to stay out of trouble. But when the same incidents happen in the less affluent neighborhoods, children are arrested and charged and brought to court."[9] Arrest situations often have enough ambiguity to allow authorities some discretion in determining charges. Whether a situation is

---

6. Joe Sims, "The Prosecution of Price-Fixing," in Mark Green and Robert Massie, Jr. (eds.), *The Big Business Reader* (New York: Pilgrim Press, 1980), pp. 50–51. At the same time, the people at the top *do* line their pockets: the systemic pressures for corporate crime rarely work against personal greed.

7. *Guardian*, June 14, 1978.

8. Philip Green, "Two Cheers for the State," *Nation*, April 14, 1979, p. 400.

9. Diane Shust, "They Call It 'Juvenile Justice,'" *Washington Post*, November 30, 1986; also Robert Lefcourt (ed.), *Law Against the People* (New York: Random House, 1971).

treated as "disorderly conduct" or "assault" depends somewhat on the judgment of the law enforcers and their feelings about the suspect's social status.

At arraignment the judge has the option of doing anything from releasing defendants on their own recognizance to imposing a bail high enough to keep them in jail until the trial date—which might come a couple of years later—as was the fate of numerous Black Panthers arrested and held on bonds of as high as $200,000, even though eventually found innocent.[10] This "preventive detention" allows the state to incarcerate and punish individuals without having to convict anyone of a crime.[11]

One study found 73 percent of all indigent people arrested were denied pretrial release as opposed to 21 percent of "respectable," middle-class persons.[12] Most of the people held in county and municipal jails have been convicted of no crime but are awaiting either a trial or hearing. Poor people are more likely to be denied bail and persuaded to plead guilty to reduced charges (plea bargaining).[13] Ninety percent of all defendants plead guilty without a trial; of the other 10 percent, more than half are convicted of something.

Like medical service, legal service in our society best serves those who can pay for it. The corporate executive with top legal assistance experiences a different treatment from the law than the poor person with a court-appointed lawyer who sometimes sees the defendant for the first time on the day of the trial. Public defenders can provide able legal service, but because of insufficient funds, disproportionate numbers of arrests in low-income areas, and other problems, they are often overworked and understaffed. Many indigents, especially in the lower courts, are deprived of a lawyer, being encouraged by judges to waive their right to counsel.[14]

In many states, prospective jurors are chosen from voter registration

---

10. The Black Panthers were a Black Political group during the late 1960s and early 1970s that advocated socialist revolution.

11. Jerome Skolnik, "Judicial Response in Crisis," in Theodore Becker and Vernon Murray (eds.), *Government Lawlessness in America* (New York: Oxford University Press, 1971), p. 162; Herman Schwartz, "Bad Times in the Bail Jail," *Nation*, June 30, 1979, pp. 782–84.

12. Stuart Nagel, "Disparities in Criminal Procedure," *UCLA Law Review*, 14, August 1967, pp. 1272–1305.

13. Contrary to the belief that plea bargaining gives the criminal an easy way out, most ordinary defendants end up with sentences as severe as any they would have received had they stood trial, according to one study of street-crime convictions: *Morning Union* (Springfield, Mass.), August 21, 1978.

14. Jeffrey Reiman, *The Rich Get Richer and the Poor Get Prison* (New York: Wiley, 1979); Jerold Auerbach, *Unequal Justice* (New York: Oxford University Press, 1976) The Reagan administration cut 25 percent from the budget of the Legal Services Corporation, the federal agency which funds law firms that deal with poverty and public interest issues: *Los Angeles Times*, April 7, 1987.

rolls, county tax lists, or street lists which underrepresent racial minorities, women, young people, and the poor. Prospective jurors have been subjected to secret background checks by prosecutors seeking to exclude political nonconformists and dissenters.[15]

The judges who preside over trials—if we are to believe Hollywood portrayals—are distinguished-looking persons who calm courtroom passions with wise and measured admonitions, while showing fear and favor toward none. In reality, according to one investigator, many judges are marked "by cruelty, stupidity, bias against the poor, short tempers or total insensitivity to civil liberties."[16] Investigations in New York found widespread sale of judgeships to moneyed persons. Once on the bench, these individuals commonly sold "not guilty" verdicts to businesspeople, crime-syndicate bosses, and corrupt politicians brought before them. Similar practices could be found in other states.[17]

Judges not only tend to favor the prosecution, they usually *are* former prosecutors, sometimes "presiding over cases in which members of their former offices are sitting at the prosecution table," according to the well-known trial lawyer, William Kunstler.[18]

Judges seem more inclined to identify with the defendant if they are drawn from the same social class as are judges. Studies of state courts find that judges were more inclined to send poorly educated, low-income persons to prison and less likely to give them suspended sentences or probation than better educated, higher-income persons convicted of the same crimes.[19]

Leniency is for the affluent, severity for the indigent. Only 18 percent of white-collar embezzlers go to prison for an average of fifteen months and many have their sentences dropped. But 89 percent of working and poor people convicted of larceny spend an average of ten-and-a-half years behind bars. Some examples might serve: a judge imposed a small fine on a stockbroker who had made $20 million through illegal stock manipulations and, on the same day, sentenced an unemployed Black man to one year in jail for stealing a $100 television set from a truck shipment.[20] Exxon

---

15. *New York Times*, April 19, 1976.

16. Jack Newfield, "The Next 10 Worst Judges," *Village Voice*, September 26, 1974, p. 5; also Charles Ashman, *The Finest Judges Money Can Buy* (Los Angeles: Nash, 1973). A majority of federal judges in the South and in major cities outside the South belong to all-White segregated clubs: *Washington Post*, September 20, 1979.

17. Newfield, "The Next 10 Worst Judges."

18. William Kunstler, correspondence in the *New York Times*, October 23, 1986.

19. Reiman, *The Rich Get Richer* . . . Ray Bloomberg, "Court Justice Tied to Middle-Class Values," *Quaker Service Bulletin*, 54, Spring 1973, p. 8; also Nagel, "Disparities in Criminal Procedure."

20. Leonard Downie, Jr., *Justice Denied* (New York: Praeger, 1971); *Workers World*, June 12, 1981.

Corporation was accused of taking millions of tons of fresh water from the Hudson River, which it sold to overseas refineries, while dumping millions of gallons of contaminated water into the river. The penalty: a civil settlement in which Exxon agreed to pay the state of New York $1.5 million (a fraction of the profits made on the fresh water sales). And while that case was being settled, a twenty-year-old youth in Houston was sentenced to fifty years for robbing two people of one dollar as they left a restaurant.[21]

The trick is to steal big. Two wealthy contractors, who received $1.2 million in government contracts for work they never did, were ordered to pay $5,000 in fines and do 200 hours of "community service."[22] In contrast, relatively minor defendants who are less well-connected can receive punishments that have an eighteenth-century severity about them. In Norfolk, Virginia, a man got ten years for stealing eighty-seven cents; a youth in Louisiana received fifty years for selling a few ounces of marijuana, and another in Virginia got forty years for doing the same. When a five-time petty offender stole $73, a Dallas court gave him 1,000 years in prison. A New Orleans judge gave a four-time petty offender life imprisonment for possession of a stolen television set. Another man spent fifteen years in prison for filching $2.43 in stamps from a post office in Illinois.[23]

Consider how the law was applied in this case: an unemployed farm worker, Thomas Boronson, and his family were eating one meager meal a day from money earned by selling their blood. Boronson and a friend, Lonnie Davis, took over a welfare office in a desperate attempt to get the several hundred dollars owed by the state to the Boronsons. One of Boronson's children was a sick infant who had been denied medical care because the family could not pay. Boronson and Davis were arrested and convicted of kidnapping, assault, and robbery, even though the welfare workers refused to press charges. They were sentenced to nine and seven years respectively.[24]

Some conservatives argue that, instead of "coddling criminals," we can reduce crime by using more police and imposing harsher sentences. In fact, the United States locks up more people per capita, for longer times, than any other advanced industrial nation except South Africa. By 1985, there were more than twice as many Americans in prison than in 1970 and the number of police more than doubled between 1957 and 1977, yet

21. *Daily World*, June 9, 1984.

22. *Washington Post*, May 30, 1979. On why the law has been ineffective against organized crime see Jonathan Kwitny, *Vicious Circles: The Mafia in the Marketplace* (New York: W. W. Norton, 1979).

23. *New York Times*, August 5, 1984; Gary Cartwright, "The Tin-Star State," *Esquire*, February 1971, p. 100; Reiman, *The Rich Get Richer* . . ..

24. *Guardian*, May 26, 1976.

during this same period crime rates rose over 400 percent. Nor are the more punitive states, like Texas, safer than the others.[25]

There are many causes for crime: individual ones such as greed, venality, and pathological passions, but also social ones such as racism and bad economic conditions. The vast majority of America's 450,000 inmates are poor; they are disproportionately Afro-American and Latino, and before incarceration were chronically unemployed or underemployed. Blacks tend to get substantially longer prison terms than Whites convicted of the same crimes, even when the Black person is a first-time offender and the White person a second- or third-time offender.[26]

The U.S. government spends more money imprisoning one person for a year than the cost of a year's education at Harvard. Yet most American prisons remain overcrowded, unhealthy places, breeding violence, rape, and disease. Prisoners who protest the bad conditions are likely to be subjected to official retribution.[27] As people feel increasingly threatened by the crime and violence of American society and the anticrime media hype, most states have reinstituted the severest of all punishments—the death penalty.

Proponents of capital punishment contend that it acts as an effective deterrent, and is a more just punishment for capital crimes than incarceration. Opponents note that there is no data supporting the notion that the death penalty deters capital crimes and much evidence showing that it is applied in racist and class-biased ways, almost exclusively against racial minorities and poor Whites. "I don't know of a wealthy person ever executed in the United States," observes a former long-time warden of San Quentin prison.[28] Capital punishment is also arbitrarily applied. Some child-killers and cold-blooded mob murderers are paroled after ten to fifteen years while a low-income White like John Spenkelink is executed for killing a man who had robbed, beaten, and raped him.[29]

---

25. *Washington Post*, February 20, 1984; Elliot Currie, *Confronting Crime* (New York: Pantheon, 1985).

26. Haywood Burns, "Can a Black Man Get a Fair Trial in This Country?" *New York Times Magazine*, July 12, 1970, pp. 5, 38–46; Frank L. Morris, "Black Political Consciousness in Northern State Prisons," paper presented at the National Conference of Black Political Scientists, New Orleans, May 1973; *Denver Post*, May 1, 1977. The U.S. prison population is about 50 percent White, 47 percent Black, and 3 percent other.

27. *Washington Post*, December 3, 1986; Jessica Mitford, *Kind and Usual Punishment: The Prison Business* (New York: Vintage, 1974); *Ithaca* (N.Y.) *New Times*, February 1, 1976.

28. *The Progessive Review* (Washington, D.C.), May–June 1985, p. 4. Representative John Conyors, correspondence, *New York Times*, May 30, 1984; also *New York Times*, October 16 and March 13, 1986; Hugo Adam Bedau and Chester Pierce (eds.), *Capital Punishment in the United States*, (New York: AMS Press, n.d.). The San Quentin warden is quoted in Peter Ross Range, "Will He Be the First?" *New York Times Magazine*, March 11, 1979.

29. *Washington Post*, January 16, 1985. As of 1985, 1,513 people were under sentence of death;, about half were Afro-American, Latino, Asian, or Native American, and the other half were poor Whites: *Workers World*, December 12, 1985.

The most compelling argument against capital punishment is that it leaves no room for redress should an innocent person be condemned; in effect, it assumes the infallibility of a very fallible enforcement process, one frequently tainted by perjury on the part of law officers and witnesses, the suppression of troublesome evidence by prosecutors, incompetent work by defense lawyers, and the prejudices of judges and juries.[30] At least 25 demonstrably innocent persons have been executed in the United States since 1900 and more than 343 have been wrongly convicted of capital crimes. In one part of New Jersey alone, a clergyman recently managed to get authorities to free three men wrongly convicted of capital

30. Wendell Rawls, Jr., "On Death Row, Two Muse on Luck," *New York Times*, August 7, 1982. Ten percent of the people on death row are without counsel; some are mentally ill: Robert Sherrill, "Electrocution Binge," *Nation*, November 24, 1984, p. 555.

crimes who had served many years behind bars. If they and hundreds of innocents like them had been executed instead of given prison terms, there would have been no opportunity to reopen their cases and amend the injustice.[31]

All this is not to suggest that we should be "soft" on crime. It is no crime to be against crime. Strong, effective, and even-handed law enforcement is needed to protect the public from organized mobs and corporate crime, as well as street criminals, child molesters, and dangerous psychopaths. What often is lacking is just the kind of even-handed laws and effective enforcement that would make our communities safer places.[32]

To sum up: poor and working-class persons, the uneducated, and the racial minorities are more likely to be arrested, less likely to be released on bail, more likely to be induced to plead guilty, more likely to go without a pretrial hearing even though entitled to one, less likely to have a jury trial if tried, more likely to be convicted and receive a harsh sentence, and less likely to receive probation or a suspended sentence than are mobsters, businesspeople, and upper- and middle-class Whites in general. "The rich have little reason to fear the system and the poor have little reason to respect it."[33]

Women of upper-class social background are more likely to receive favored treatment at the hands of the law than are low-income people of either sex. But class aside, women suffer legal injustices of their own.[34] Incarcerated women are subjected to sexual assault and exploitation by male guards.[35] One study found pervasive courtroom bias against women. Female lawyers were routinely demeaned and patronized by male judges and attorneys; female witnesses were considered less credible than male witnesses by judges who viewed women as emotional and untrustworthy. Frequently failing to recognize a wife's contribution to a marriage, judges distributed property inequitably in divorce settlements and tended to treat lightly a woman's efforts to obtain child-support payments.[36]

Every year thousands of women are seriously injured because of repeated beatings from their mates, yet the law is seldom enforced in such

31. *New York Times*, November 9, 1986. More than 100 inmates have asked the clergyman, James McCloskey, for help: *Washington Post*, November 17, 1986; see also Philip Shenon, "How Errors Convicted Wrong Man," *New York Times*, March 15, 1984. On the execution of twenty-five innocent people see the study prepared by Hugo Adam Bedau and Michael Radelet, released by the American Civil Liberties Union, November 1985.

32. Consider the lackadaisical police work that has allowed various thrill-killers and serial murderers to operate for years on end without being detected. See, for example, Tim Cahill, *Buried Dreams*, (New York: Bantam, 1984).

33. Senator Philip Hart, "Swindling and Knavery, Inc.," *Playboy*, August 1972, p. 162.

34. Karen De Crow, *Sexual Justice* (New York: Random House, 1974).

35. Ann Jones, "Sex Exploitation Behind Bars," *Nation*, April 17, 1982, pp. 456–59.

36. *New York Times*, April 20, 1986.

cases.[37] Nor has the law proved to be as effective as one would hope in protecting women from sexual harassment on the job or breaking down discriminatory employment and wage practices. Some of the largest corporations admit to a policy of paying women less for doing the same work as men. Along with immigrant workers and child workers, women historically have served as a reserve army of labor, paid less so as to keep wage rates down for all workers.[38] Women who have agitated for equal pay, prison reform, day care, lesbian rights, and legalized abortion have been the object of FBI and CIA surveillance.[39]

After years of struggle, working women have made important gains, organizing themselves into unions as nurses, clerical workers, and factory employees. In noticeable numbers women are moving into professions and occupations previously thought "unsuitable" for them. Women have won maternity leave from several hundred corporations. And as women challenge traditional roles, more men are learning to share in child-rearing and family chores. These changes, however, have invited attacks from conservatives who resist any form of gender, class, and wage equalization.[40]

Homosexuals are another group who have been the target of popular bias and legal oppression. In 1978, the Supreme Court ruled that a teacher could be fired for no other reason than being a homosexual. In 1976 and again in 1986, the Court ruled that the Constitution does not protect homosexual relations between consenting adults even in the privacy of their own homes.[41] Men and women have been discharged from the armed services because they were gay. Mothers have been denied custody of their children on the grounds that their lesbian preferences made them unfit parents. Gay-rights organizers have been beaten and arrested by law officers in various cities and gay bars have been raided by police.[42]

Public concern over AIDs, a sexually transmitted lethal disease that afflicts men and women equally in some countries but predominantly homosexual males in this country, has further fueled antigay sentiments.

---

37. Del Martin, *Battered Wives* (New York: Pocket Books, 1983); Faith McNulty, *The Burning Bed* (New York: Bantam, 1981).

38. Kate Abell, "Economic Oppression of Women," *Political Affairs*, April 1984, pp. 15–18.

39. Letty Cottin Pogrebin, "The FBI Was Watching You," *Ms.*, June 1977, pp. 37–44.

40. For an example of government opposition to women's struggles, see Kim Lacy Rogers and Thomas Zoumaras, "Meese versus Affirmative Action," *In These Times*, October 2–8, 1985.

41. *Gish v. Board of Education of Paramus, N.J.* (1976); *Doe v. Commonwealth's Attorney* (1976) and *Bowers v. Hardwick* (1986). In nineteen of the twenty-four states with sodomy statutes, the law applies to heterosexual persons as well, those who might dare engage in oral sex.

42. Doug Ireland, "Open Season on Gays," *Nation*, September 15, 1979, pp. 207–10; Clifford Guy Gibson and Mary Jo Risher, *By Her Own Admission* (Garden City, N.Y.: Doubleday, 1977).

Nevertheless the organized struggles launched by gays in recent years have succeeded in changing homophobic attitudes among many heterosexual people, and progress has been made against anti-gay housing and employment practices.

Law enforcement represents the largest budget item of many local governments, yet not much progress has been made against organized crime and corporate crime. Police work concentrates mostly on small-time drug dealing, gambling, and larceny.[43] Racial minorities and low-income Whites have many more personal encounters with police brutality than middle-class White "respectables."[44] Investigations of police departments in Philadelphia, Los Angeles, New York, Houston, and various other places reveal that brutality is widespread and often tolerated by department commanders. The victims are almost always Afro-American, Latino, or low-income Whites. Few of the officers involved in police brutality have ever been indicted, convicted, or given substantial sentences.[45]

The history of the labor movement in the United States reveals a pattern of police harassment and violence. From the earliest days of industrial conflict to today, agents of the law have defended corporate property against the interests of workers. Police have either looked the other way or actively cooperated when company goons and vigilantes attack union organizers and picketers. In recent years, in various parts of the country, police have attacked striking construction workers, farm workers, truckers, miners, meatpackers, and factory-workers, arresting and badly injuring hundreds. Many workers have been imprisoned for resisting court injunctions against strikes and pickets. In Harlan County, Kentucky, a striking coal miner was shot to death by a scab, as was a farm worker in Texas. In Elwood, Indiana, within a period of a few months, seven strikers were shot by company goons. In Wilmington, California, a striker at an oil refinery was killed and several others severely injured when a company truck crashed through a picket line. In all these instances police

---

43. Elias, *The Politics of Victimization*. A decline in street crime in recent years has been due to demographics: most violent crimes are committed by young males between eighteen and twenty-six. Today, there are fewer in this cohort because of the birthrate decline in the early 1960s: *Washington Post*, April 23, 1984.

44. David Bayley and Harold Mendelsohn, *Minorities and the Police* (New York: Random House, 1968), pp. 29–30.

45. See "Homocide Squad," *Inquiry*, July 7–21, 1980, p. 4; Joan Walsh, "Police Brutality Divides Milwaukee," *In These Times*, September 9–15, 1981, p. 6; Murray Kempton, "The Harlem Policeman," in Becker and Murray (eds.), *Government Lawlessness in America*, pp. 47–49; *Newsweek*, July 4, 1977; Sara Blackburn (ed.), *White Justice* (New York: Harper and Row, 1972); *Guardian*, March 18 and November 11, 1981; *Daily World*, December 16, 1981 and July 1, 1982; *New York Times*, April 30 and 31, 1985; and the documentary film by Richard Cohen on the Los Angeles Police Department, *Deadly Force* (San Francisco: Hound Dog Films, 1982).

apprehended no one despite eyewitness evidence of the identity of the killers.[46]

The law and its enforcement agents do many worthwhile things. Many laws enhance public safety and individual security. The police sometimes protect life and limb, direct traffic, administer first aid, assist in times of community emergency, and perform other services with commendable dedication and courage.[47] But aside from this desirable *social-service* function, the police serve a *class-control* function—that is, they must protect those who rule from those who are ruled. And they protect the interests of capital from those who would challenge the inequities of the system. The profiteering corporate managers, plundering slumlords, swindling merchants, racist school boards, self-enriching doctors, special-interest legislators, and others who contribute so much to the scarcity, misery, and anger that lead to individual crimes or mass riots leave the dirty work of subduing these outbursts to the police. When the police charge picket lines—beating, gassing, and occasionally shooting workers—they usually are operating with a court injunction that allows them to exert force in order to protect the interests of the corporate owners.

The police confront dangers and social miseries of a kind most of us can only imagine. They deal with the waste products of an affluent, competitive corporate society: corpses in the street, back-alley muggers, pimps, child molesters, winos, heroin pushers, psychopaths, the ill-fed, the ill-housed, the desperate, and the defeated. The slums are not the problem, they are the *solution*; they are the way capitalism deals with the surplus people of a market economy. And for all they cost the taxpayer in crime, police, and welfare, the slums remain a source of profit for certain speculators, arsonists, realtors, big merchants, and others. But they do present problems of violence and social pathology that need to be contained. And that is the job of the police: to sweep protest and poverty under the rug—even if it takes a club or gun. Repressive acts by police are not the aberrant behavior of a few psychotics in uniform but the outgrowth of the kind of class-control function that law officers perform and rulers insist upon—which explains why the police are able to get away with murder.

---

46. For some recent instances see *Daily World*, July 29, 1982, and January 24, 1984. On labor's struggle see Richard Boyer and Herbert Morais, *Labor's Untold Story*, 3rd ed. (New York: United Electrical, Radio and Machine Workers, 1972), passim. For an analysis of the class function of the police see *The Iron Fist and the Velvet Glove: An Analysis of the U.S. Police*, 2nd ed., written and published by the Center for Research on Criminal Justice (Berkeley, Calif., 1977).

47. See Jill Freedman, *Street Cop* (New York: Harper and Row, 1981) for a compassionate photographic essay on the struggles of police at the street level to keep the victims of society from victimizing each other. Another sympathetic treatment of police is Mark Baker, *Cops; Their Lives in Their Own Words* (New York: Simon and Schuster, 1985).

Some police are aware of the class function they serve. Former Boston Police Commissioner Robert DiGrazia summed it up:

> We are not letting the public in on our era's dirty little secret: that those who commit the crime which worries citizens most—violent street crime—are, for the most part, the products of poverty, unemployment, broken homes, rotten education, drug addiction and alcoholism, and other social and economic ills about which the police can do little, if anything.
>
> Rather than speaking up, most of us stand silent and let politicians get away with law and order rhetoric that reinforces the mistaken notion that police—in ever greater numbers and with more gadgetry—can alone control crime. The politicians, of course, end up perpetuating a system by which the rich get richer, the poor get poorer, and crime continues.[48]

THE REPRESSION OF POLITICAL DISSIDENCE

Among those whom the law treats repressively are persons and organizations who oppose capitalism and advocate alternative economic orders. According to the established ideology, capitalism is an essential component of Americanism and democracy. It follows that anticapitalists are antidemocratic, un-American, and a "subversive threat" to the national security, thus fair game for repression. The repression is directed against communists and other anticapitalists and eventually against anyone else who shows an active interest in progressive causes. Under the guise of defending democracy, security agencies often impose severe limitations on democratic rights.

When directed toward social reforms that might benefit the working populace, the law usually proves too weak for effective change. But when mobilized against political dissenters, the resources of the law appear boundless, and enforcement is pursued with a punitive vigor that itself becomes lawless. Dissident groups have had their telephones tapped and their offices raided by law officers. Members of these groups have been threatened, maligned, beaten, murdered, or arrested on trumped-up charges, held on exorbitant bail, and subjected to costly, time-consuming trials that, whether won or lost, paralyze their leadership, exhaust their funds, and consume their energies. With these kinds of attacks, the government's message comes across loud and clear: people are not as free as they think. They may challenge class relations and government policies,

---

48. Quoted in *Parade*, August 22, 1976. Perhaps even in the best of circumstances there is a "criminal element" who will resort to violent and unlawful means to get what they want. Not all crime is a direct reaction to social deprivation and class inequity, but a great deal of it is.

but their public utterances and private behavior will be watched by one or more of the many security agencies. If they persist, they may encounter the repressive legal mechanism of the state.[49]

Thus, almost all of the one hundred or so murders of civil-rights activists during the 1960s were committed by police and White vigilantes. Yet the state was able to catch but a few of the perpetrators and none were convicted of murder.[50] From 1968 to 1971, police attacked the headquarters of the Black Panthers (a Black Marxist organization) in more than ten cities, smashing typewriters, stealing thousands of dollars in funds, and arresting, beating, and shooting the occupants in well-planned, unprovoked attacks. More than forty Panthers were killed by police in that period, and over three hundred were arrested, with many imprisoned for long periods without bail or trial.[51]

In Orangeburg, South Carolina, police fired into a peaceful campus demonstration, killing three Black students and wounding twenty-seven others; many were shot in the back while fleeing. In 1970, police killed several unarmed Black students at Jackson State, Mississippi, who were engaging in a demonstration, and National Guardsmen killed four White students and maimed two others who were participating in an antiwar protest at Kent State University in Ohio. In the latter two instances, the evidence gathered by government agencies clearly indicated that the lives of law officers and Guardsmen were never in danger. In both cases, grand juries refused to indict the murderers but did indict demonstrators, including several who had been wounded.[52]

The list of killings could go on, but the pattern remains the same: law-enforcement agents used lethal weapons against strikers, protestors, and political radicals, none of whom were armed, a few of whom were reported to be hurling rocks or shouting hostile remarks. In almost every instance, an "impartial investigation" by the very authorities responsible for the killings exonerated the uniformed murderers and their administrative chiefs.

Protestors against the Vietnam War were attacked by police on dozens of campuses throughout the country and in major demonstrations in Chicago, New York, and Los Angeles. During the 1970s and 1980s, Black

---

49. Becker and Murray, *Government Lawlessness in America*; Morton Halpern, et al., *The Lawless State* (New York: Penguin 1976); Jessica Mitford, *The Trial of Doctor Spock* (New York: Knopf, 1969); Jason Epstein, *The Great Conspiracy Trial* (New York: Vintage, 1971).

50. Blackburn, *White Justice*.

51. For the FBI's role in instigating and assisting in these police attacks see *Chicago Tribune*, April 20 and June 12, 1976.

52. Jack Nelson and Jack Bass, *The Orangeburg Massacre* (New York: World, 1969); I. F. Stone, "Fabricated Evidence in the Kent State Killings," *New York Review of Books*, December 3, 1970, p. 28; *New York Times*, May 4, 1976 and May 7, 1978.

socialist leaders like Martin Sostre in Buffalo, New York; Frank Shuford in Santa Ana, California; Ben Chavis in Wilmington, North Carolina; and Eddie Carthan, former mayor of Tchula, Mississippi, involved in progressive community causes against landlords, owners, and drug pushers, were hit with trumped-up charges of drug dealing, arson, assault, and (in Carthan's case) even murder, and convicted on the testimony of witnesses who subsequently recanted.[53] These leaders and numerous associates received sentences of over thirty years each. Sostre served nine years, Chavis five years, and Carthan two years, before they managed to regain their freedom—assisted by the efforts of progressive and humanitarian groups.[54]

The state also has more subtle instruments of oppression than the club and the gun. One of these is the grand jury. Supposedly intended to weigh the state's evidence and protect the innocent from unjustifiable prosecution, the grand jury has usually been turned into its opposite—doing what the prosecution wants. A common device is to suspend the Fifth Amendment right against self-incrimination by granting witnesses immunity from prosecution. If they then refuse to testify, they can be imprisoned for contempt. The upshot is to turn people into involuntary informers regarding any conversation or activity to which they have been privy. The grand jury is often used to carry out "fishing expeditions" to intimidate persons engaged in dissident political activities. People have been required to appear without benefit of counsel and without being told the nature of the investigation. They can be forced to answer any question about political ideas and associations with friends, neighbors, or relatives or face imprisonment for refusing to do so.[55]

For years "loyalty and security" tests were used to deny public employment to people of leftist persuasion, in violation of First Amendment guarantees of free speech. Anticapitalist dissenters encounter oppression within the private sector of society as well. Employees who agitate for better working conditions or enunciate unpopular opinions risk loss of job.[56]

---

53. *New York Times*, December 25, 1975; *Guardian*, September 24, 1975 and May 11, 1983; *Outfront* (Amherst, Mass.), August 1976, p. 9; *Daily World*, August 31, 1983; Shuford Defense Committee *Newsletter*, January 1978.

54. Shuford has been in prison for over 10 years, serving a 30-year sentence.

55. For example, in 1983 five supporters of a Puerto Rican liberation movement were sentenced to three years in jail by a grand jury for refusing to answer questions: *Guardian*, June 29, 1983 and December 26, 1984; also Marvin Frankel and Gary Naftalis, *The Grand Jury* (New York: Hill and Wang, 1977); "Crime Victims," *Nation*, June 12, 1982, p. 706.

56. For instances of employees fired because their bosses disapproved of their political views see Max Gordon, "Can Business Fire at Will?" *Nation* July 14–21, 1979, pp. 42–44; *Daily World*, August 25, 1984. For attempts by Congress to deny employment to dissidents see *Nation*, January 3–10, 1981, p. 6.

The Internal Revenue Service (IRS) is another government agency used as an instrument of political control to discourage the free circulation of ideas critical of plutocracy. The IRS has repeatedly gone after left-leaning organizations and publications (and the individuals and small foundations supporting them), harassing them with audits, seizing their records, and denying them tax-exempt status.[57]

The government also decides which ideas we may be exposed to from abroad. The Immigration and Nationality Act of 1952, also known as the McCarran-Walter Act, permits the State Department and the Immigration and Naturalization Service to exclude anyone who might be affiliated with Communist, anarchist, or terrorist groups, or who might in any way engage in activities "prejudicial to the public interest" or harmful to "national security." Every year under these sweeping provisos, dozens of Marxist and other socialist scholars, authors, artists, performers, journalists, scientists, doctors, and trade-union leaders, who may have been critical of U.S. policies, have been denied visas and prevented from entering the United States to participate in cultural events and conferences to which they had been invited by private groups.[58]

Former officials of repressive right-wing regimes, along with Eastern European ex-Nazis, Salvadorean death-squad leaders like Roberto D'Aubuisson, and almost any emigré from a Communist country gain ready entry into the United States as visitors or permanent residents. In contrast, refugees fleeing political repression in El Salvador, Chile, and other right-wing regimes have been denied entry or have even been seized and deported back to their countries, often to face jail and death.[59] By now it should be no mystery why persons of the violent right are allowed in while their victims on the left are not. The left generally opposes the capitalist class order, while the right supports it.

While we are taught that the United States has no political prisoners, in truth, there has been a long history of American political repression against those who resist the powers and policies of the moneyed class.

---

57. *New York Times*, February 26, 1974.

58. For some recent cases see *Washington Post*, June 29, 1984, April 25, 1985, and September 27, 1986; *New York Times*, December 13, 1985 and September 3, October 16 and 18, and November 19, 1986. While American trade unionists are frequently invited to the Soviet Union, their Soviet counterparts are prevented by our government from visiting the United States; or on the rare occasions they have been allowed in, they have been prohibited from meeting with American labor union people: *Daily World*, December 30, 1982; June 3, 1983; April 27, 1984; and April 29, 1986.

59. Gil Loescher and John Scanlan, *Calculated Kindness, Refugees and America's Half-Open Door* (New York: Free Press, 1985); *New York Times*, March 14, 1986; *Guardian*, March 23, 1983. The government also has banned documentary films from abroad which are critical of American policies, and has tried to prevent the foreign distribution of American-made documentaries critical of the official viewpoint: *New York Times*, October 30, 1986.

Eugene Debs and some 6,000 other socialists, pacifists, and radical IWW organizers were imprisoned during the First World War or deported during the Palmer raids immediately afterward. The anarchists Sacco and Vanzetti were executed for a crime most investigators say they never committed. Numerous war resisters were arrested during World War II and the Korean War. The Smith Act of 1940 prohibited the mere advocacy of revolutionary ideas and was used to jail scores of American Communists and other leftists, including Gus Hall, General Secretary of the Communist Party, USA, who spent nine years in prison for his political beliefs.[60]

Others spent time in jail for refusing to cooperate with congressional witch-hunts during the McCarthy era. The Taft-Hartley Act of 1947 was used to purge Communists from trade unions. The FBI set up a national security file containing the names of persons to be rounded up and put into detention camps without due process. Julius and Ethel Rosenberg were convicted of espionage and executed, on what many critics feel was flimsy or nonexistent evidence. During the Vietnam War, several thousand youths were jailed for refusing to serve in what they felt was an unjust war; many thousands more chose exile. During the 1960s, almost every antiwar activist who occupied a position of national or even local leadership, and many who did not, were arrested at one time or another. Many stood trial or were jailed or went underground.[61]

During the 1970s and 1980s, several hundred political persons were incarcerated, some of whom are now serving life sentences because of armed encounters with the police. Others were held in "preventive detention" for resisting grand jury investigations, or on weapons charges, illegal interstate travel, or "sedition" and "seditious conspiracy"—though no evidence was presented linking them to any violent act. In prison, as of 1987, were members of the American Indian Movement, the Black Liberation Army, Puerto Rican nationalists, Irish nationalists, Chicano and North American revolutionary activists—and unaffiliated persons who were supportive of these various movements.[62] Among America's political prisoners must be numbered the fifty-seven members of Plowshares, a peace group that jackhammered the concrete around a Minuteman missile silo in Kansas in 1984. For this protest action against nuclear weapons,

---

60. See Stanley Kutler, *The American Inquisition* (New York: Hill and Wang, 1983); Gil Green, *Cold War Fugitive* (New York: International Publisher, 1985); William Schneiderman, *Dissent on Trial* (Minneapolis: Marxist Educational Press, 1983).

61. See the American Civil Liberties Report edited by Norman Dorsen, *Our Endangered Rights* (New York: Pantheon, 1984); also Thomas Emerson, *The System of Freedom of Expression* (New York: Vintage, 1971); Walter and Miriam Schneir, *Invitation to an Inquest* (New York: Penguin, 1973).

62. For lists of political prisoners as of 1986 see *The Insurgent* (Newsletter of the Committee to Fight Repression), 2, Summer 1986.

eleven of the Plowshares protestors were each sentenced to eighteen years in prison.[63] Contrary to what we have been taught, political prisoners are as American as apple pie.

AGENTS OF NATIONAL INSECURITY

At least twenty well-financed federal agencies (of which the FBI and CIA are the best publicized) and hundreds of state and local police units engage in surveillance and suppression of dissenting groups. The federal government has poured billions of dollars into research and law-enforcement hardware for state and local police. The unrestricted adoption of surveillance technology by police moved a Rand Corporation engineer to speculate that "we could easily end up with the most effective, oppressive police state ever created."[64] According to one police official, there are more law officers throughout the country "on political intelligence assignments than are engaged in fighting organized crime."[65] In the 1980s, authorities in various states reactivated police Red squads to spy on, infiltrate, and harass lawful groups, targeting peace advocates and organizations opposed to U.S. policies in Central America.[66]

A Senate subcommittee revealed in 1975 that federal agencies alone maintain 858 data banks containing 1.25 *billion* files, mostly on individuals supected of harboring unorthodox political views.[67] Data on political dissenters are sometimes fed to the press, employers, and landlords in attempts to cause difficulties for the people under surveillance.

Of the one million police in the United States, only half are sworn to uphold the law; the rest are employed by private corporations to spy on and harass striking workers, union organizers, and various "cause" groups

---

63. Colman McCarthy's column, *Washington Post*, November 23, 1986; Helen Woodson, "Random Thoughts from the First Year in Prison," *The Witness*, March 1986, pp. 14–15. Included among those receiving eighten years were a mother of eleven children and a priest. The Minuteman had been falsely presented as a purely defensive weapon in a hardened encasement designed to withstand and then retaliate against an enemy attack. Plowshare people demonstrated that the silo's concrete could not even withstand a jackhammer let alone an enemy missile, and that the Minuteman was really a first-strike weapon.

64. Quoted in Robert Barkan, "New Police Technology," *Guardian*, February 2, 1972; Frank Donner, *The Age of Surveillance* (New York: Knopf, 1980); Les Gapay, "Pork Barrel for Police," *Progressive*, March 1972, pp. 33–36.

65. Quoted in Frank Donner, "The Theory and Practice of American Political Intelligence," *New York Review of Books*, April 22, 1971, p. 28; *Washington Post*, December 6, 1984.

66. Susan Jaffe, "The Spies in the Peace Movement," *Mother Jones*, August 1983; Frank Donner, "The Return of the Red Squads," *Nation*, October 12, 1985, pp. 329, 339–42.

67. *New York Times*, October 3, 1975. For instances of illegal federal harassment see David Garrow, *The FBI and Martin Luther King, Jr.* (New York: Penguin, 1983).

that might prove troublesome to business. These private firms keep over 100 million secret files on Americans and enjoy the collaboration of federal agents and local police.[68] Perhaps one reason authorities cannot win the "war on crime" and the "war on drugs" is they are too busy fighting the war on political protest and social justice.

In pursuance of that goal, the FBI launched—with White House authorization—a Counterintelligence Program (COINTELPRO) designed, in the words of the FBI's late director J. Edgar Hoover: "to expose, disrupt, misdirect, discredit, or otherwise neutralize" members and supporters of antiwar, Black nationalist, and socialist groups.[69] The Bureau has conducted hundreds of illegal break-ins against political organizations and individuals. Undercover agents have attempted to sabotage the legal operations of dissident groups and foment conflict within and among them.[70] As the *New York Times* finally noted in 1974: "Radical groups in the United States have complained for years that they were being harassed by the Federal Bureau of Investigation and it now turns out that they were right."[71]

The FBI has spied on political opponents of the White House, including journalists, congressional representatives, and members of congressional staffs. The Bureau has infiltrated various labor unions in attempts to brand them as "communist controlled" and has cooperated with management in secret surveillances of union strike activities. The FBI keeps a "security index" of some 15,000 persons, mostly members of anticapitalist groups, who are slated for arrest and detention in case of a "national emergency"—although the law authorizing this practice was declared unconstitutional.[72] In 1982, as part of the FBI war against leftist ideas, FBI director William Webster attacked the National Lawyers Guild and other progressive groups because they "produce propaganda, disinformation and legal assistance [that] may be even more dangerous than those who actually throw the bomb."[73]

---

68. George O'Toole, *The Private Sector: Rent-a-Cops, Private Spies and the Police-Industrial Complex* (New York: Norton, 1978); Jim Hougan, *Spooks: The Haunting of America* (New York: Morrow, 1978); James Rule, *Private Lives and Public Surveillance* (New York: Schocken, 1974).

69. Quoted in the *Village Voice*, September 9–15, 1981, p. 25.

70. *New York Times*, November 22, 1977. Continuing into the 1980s, peace activists have complained of intimidating visits by FBI agents, tampering and disappearance of mailings, telephone taps, and office break-ins: *Guardian*, June 8, 1983, December 19, 1984, and March 5, 1986; also Newsletter of Organizing Committee for Peace, Washington, D.C., February 21, 1984.

71. *New York Times*, November 24, 1974.

72. On the surveillance of journalists and members of Congress see *New York Times*, December 4, 1975. On the use of FBI agents against organized labor see *Guardian*, July 5, 1978. On national emergency detention see *New York Times*, August 3 and October 25, 1975.

73. Quoted in *Daily World*, July 3, 1982; also *Atlantic Journal*, January 9, 1981.

In contrast to the way they treat the left, the FBI and the police have provided support to right-wing extremist groups in their attacks against progressives. In San Diego, the FBI financed a cryptofascist outfit called the Secret Army Organization, whose activities ranged from burglary and bombings to kidnapping and attempted murder.[74] The Senate Intelligence Committee revealed in 1976 that the FBI organized forty-one Ku Klux Klan chapters in North Carolina, and that Klan members in the pay of the FBI worked less as informants and more as instigators. FBI informants were present when Klan members and Nazis committed murder and other acts of violence against civil-rights activists and anti-Klan demonstrators; the informants did nothing to stop the perpetrators, and in some instances assisted the murderers by procuring weapons for them and directing them to the location of their victims.[75]

Political violence as such has never bothered the FBI nor the police; it depends on who is using it against whom. When asked by Congresswoman Pat Schroeder (D-Colo.) what they intended to do about the fifteen or so right-wing paramilitary terrorist training camps within the United States, including five in Florida run by Cuban exiles who participated in the Bay of Pigs invasion, a Reagan-appointed Justice Department official said the camps did not appear to be in violation of any federal criminal statute.[76] In 1974, when two Chicano socialists were killed by bombs planted in their cars, the FBI made no arrests. A powerful bomb wrecked the offices of several progressive and civil-liberties groups in New York, injuring three people; the police made only a perfunctory investigation. A right-wing Cuban exile terrorist group claimed credit for some twenty-one bombings between 1975 and 1980 and for the murder of a Cuban diplomat in New York; the group escaped arrest in all but two of the bombing attacks.[77] After a series of threats, an antinuclear organizer was shot dead in Houston and an assistant was seriously wounded; police came up with not a clue.[78]

---

74. *San Francisco Examiner*, January 11, 1976.

75. Alex Chams, "Grand Jury Investigates Klan Killings," *In These Times*, September 22–28, 1982, p. 10; *New York Times*, May 12, 1985; Patsy Sims, *The Klan* (New York: Stein and Day, 1978); Earl Caldwell's report in *Rights* (National Emergency Civil Liberties Committee) March–April 1983, pp. 3–4; and Caldwell's column, *New York Daily News*, January 19, 1983; *Guardian*, February 23, 1983; *Daily World* April 9, 1983; Michael Parenti and Carolyn Kazdin, "The Untold Story of the Greensboro Masacre," *Monthly Review*, November 1981, pp. 42–50. Hundreds of Nazi war criminals have lived in the United States, some of them employed by U.S. security agencies that knew of their past political crimes: Howard Blum, *Wanted: The Search for Nazis in America* (New York: Quadrangle, 1977); Erhard Dabringhaus, *Klaus Barbie* (Washington, D.C.: Acropolis Books, 1984)

76. James Ridgeway, "Looney Tune Terrorists," *Village Voice*, July 23, 1985, p. 23.

77. Jeff Stein, "Inside Omega 7," *Village Voice*, March 10, 1980, p. 1, 11–14; *Cuba Update* (Center for Cuban Studies, New York), October 1980, p. 3.

78. *Guardian*, February 4, 1981; *New Age*, July 1979, p. 10.

In Chicago, after repeated death threats, Chicano union organizer and Communist, Rudy Lozano, who effectively worked to unite Latinos, Afro-Americans, and Whites around progressive causes, was shot dead in his home in midday by an intruder who stole nothing. According to family members, paramedics who arrived at the scene thought they could save Lozano's life, but police blocked them from attempting to revive him, claiming they did not want him touched because "evidence might be destroyed."[79] On her way to a meeting with a *New York Times* reporter, Karen Silkwood was killed in a mysterious car crash. Evidence showed that her automobile had been knocked off the road by a heavier vehicle. The papers she had in the car exposing Kerr-McGee corporation for radiation safety negligence, were never recovered. Police said her death was just another auto accident.[80]

In 1984, an antinuclear activist parked his vehicle near the Washington Monument and proclaimed he would blow it up in protest of U.S. nuclear arms escalations. Though it was hard to see how he could accomplish his threat and—as it turned out, he possessed no explosives—he was deemed a "terrorist" and shot dead by security forces when he attempted to drive away. That same year, antiabortion activists who called themselves "Warriors of God" and who *did* use explosives in more than twenty bombings and burnings of family planning clinics, were deemed by FBI director William Webster not to be terrorists because it had not been demonstrated to his satisfaction that the perpetrators were "a definable group."[81] Likewise in 1986, more than twenty-five break-ins occurred at homes and offices of opponents of Reagan's Central American policies in different parts of the country. In each case no property was stolen. Yet FBI director William Webster said that these were just individual cases and he could discern no links between them.[82]

The FBI's budget for undercover work has escalated from $1 million in 1977 to $12.5 million in 1984. And the number of its covert operations has increased five times over.[83] Making the world safe for capitalism is a massive enterprise. Taken together, government security agencies expend over $12 billion a year on intelligence and covert action at home and

79. *Daily World*, June 10, 1983.

80. Howard Kohn, *Who Killed Karen Silkwood?* (New York: Summit, 1981); Richard Rashke, *The Killing of Karen Silkwood* (New York: Penguin, 1981).

81. *New York Times* editorial, December 7, 1984.

82. *Washington Post*, December 5, 1986. On occasion when Klan-Nazi groups have attacked the police themselves or robbed banks, the FBI and other law-enforcement agencies have moved against them: *Washington Post*, July 18, 1985; *Guardian*, May 1, 1985.

83. Nat Hentoff, "Someone to Watch Over Us," *Washington Post*, June 10, 1984.

abroad. This is at best a rough estimate, since Congress has no exact idea how much money security agencies are spending or for what purposes.[84]

A word must be said about the Central Intelligence Agency. With a legal mandate only to gather intelligence overseas and prohibited from domestic spying, the CIA nevertheless has been heavily involved in wire-tapping and break-ins against Americans engaged in protest activities here in the United State. In addition:

1. For twenty years the CIA opened the mail of private citizens. (When the FBI found out about this illegal practice, it became an active participant.)

---

84. See the House Select Committee report on the CIA excerpted in *Village Voice*, February 16, 1976. CIA officials questioned by the committee refused to state the size of their budget.

2. The CIA admitted to maintaining surveillance on members of Congress and infiltrating congressional campaign organizations.
3. The CIA has given money to private corporations but has refused to disclose the purpose of such payments. The agency owns a complex of companies whose profits are used as it sees fit, and it keeps millions of dollars in secret accounts in banks in Switzerland and the Cayman Islands.
4. The CIA has worked with right-wing Cuban exiles and notorious foreign intelligence agencies of such countries as Chile, South Korea, and Iran (under the Shah), allowing them to terrorize exiles from these countries residing in the United States.
5. The CIA keeps hundreds of college professors on its payroll; it has secretly financed the writings of academics like Professor Samuel Huntington of Harvard, and subsidizes publishing houses and periodicals. Its agents participate in academic conferences and it conducts its own intern- and resident-scholar conferences.
6. The CIA has infiltrated and financed student, labor, scientific, and peace groups. It has financed research programs on mind-control drugs at universities and elsewhere, sometimes on unsuspecting persons, and was responsible for the death of at least one government employee.
7. The CIA has equipped, trained, and supported local police forces even though the National Security Act of 1947 states that the CIA "shall have no police, subpoena, law enforcement powers or internal security functions."[85]

It has been revealed that the White House and the Treasury and Commerce departments were infiltrated by CIA agents, that the CIA was involved in the Southeast Asia heroin trade, that it used notorious mobsters to assist in CIA assassination plots, that it routinely provides covert aid to foreign politicians and political parties even though U.S. law prohibits the practice, and that it retained a stockpile of poisonous gas despite a presidential order to destroy it.[86]

---

85. For documentation of the preceding points, see Ralph McGehee, *Deadly Deceits: My 25 Years with the CIA* (New York: Sheridan Square Publications, 1983); Darrel Garwood, *Undercover: 35 Years of CIA Deception* (New York: Grove, 1985); David Wise, *The American Police State* (New York: Random House, 1976); Victor Marchetti and John Marks, *The CIA and the Cult of Intelligence* (New York: Knopf, 1974); Halperin, et al., *The Lawless State; New York Times*, June 4 and July 1, 1977, May 9, 1978, November 5, 1985, and February 14, 1986; Vitaly Petrusenko, *A Dangerous Game, CIA and the Mass Media* (Prague: Interpress, n.d.); Jack Anderson, "CIA Returns to Campus Spying," *Washington Post*, October 12, 1984; Jack Anderson and Joseph Spear, "How CIA Moved Some Arms Deal Money," *Washington Post*, December 9, 1986; John Marks, *The Search for the Manchurian Candidate* (New York: Times Books, 1979); David Remnick, "A Mind is a Terrible Thing to Waste," *Washington Post National Weekly Edition*, August 12, 1985, pp. 9–10.

86. *New York Times*, June 11 and 20, 1975; July 9 and 10, 1975; April 13, 28, and 29, 1976; August 2, 1977; June 11, 1982; *Newsweek*, June 7, 1982; Alfred McCoy, *The Politics of Heroin in Southeast Asia* (New York: Harper and Row, 1973).

The CIA's crimes against the peoples of other nations are too numerous to record here in any detail. In various Latin American countries, the agency has used military force, terror, and sabotage to bring down democratically elected governments and install reactionary dictatorships friendly to American corporate interests. It has infiltrated and fractured the trade-union movements of other nations. It has funded and trained secret armies, torture squads, death squads, and "destabilization" campaigns. It has been involved in the assassination of labor, peasant, and student leaders in various nations.[87]

Public exposure of CIA illegal actions in the United States led to several investigations of the agency but no indictments of any CIA officials. A 1978 executive order by President Carter designed to discourage unlawful CIA acts was countermanded in December 1981 by President Reagan's executive order that permits the CIA and FBI to carry out domestic covert operations, including the infiltration and disruption of organizations and individuals "believed" to have sympathies with foreign groups or powers. The new order allows the CIA to equip, train, and support local police, and authorizes intelligence agencies to enter secret contracts with corporations, academic institutions, other organizations, and individuals for the provision of services and goods.[88]

It has been argued that a strong intelligence community is needed to gather information essential for government policymakers. But the CIA has been involved in *covert actions* including economic, political, and military sabotage; disinformation campaigns directed against the American public itself; mercenary wars; acts of terror and destabilization against other nations—activities that go beyond intelligence gathering and beyond the CIA's lawful mandate. As one former CIA officer confessed:

> My view, backed by 25 years of experience is, quite simply, that the CIA is the covert action arm of the presidency. Most of its money, manpower and energy go into covert operations that . . . include backing dictators and overthowing democratically elected governments. . . . The CIA uses disinformation, much of it aimed at the U.S. public, to mold opinion. . . .
>
> But if the Agency actually reported the truth about the third world, what would it say? It would say that the United States installs foreign leaders, arms their armies and empowers their police to help those leaders repress an angry,

87. Garwood, *Undercover: 35 Years of CIA Deception*; Wise, *The American Police State*; Philip Agee, *Inside the Company* (London: Allen Lane, 1975); Philip Agee, Louis Wolf, et al., *Dirty Work: The CIA in Western Europe* (Secaucus, N.J.: Lyle Stuart, 1979); also past and present editions of *Covert Action Information Bulletin* (Washington, D.C.). Jesse Leaf, an ex-CIA agent active in Iran, reported that CIA operatives instructed the Shah's secret police on interrogation "based on German torture techniques from World War II" and that the torture project was "all paid for by the U.S.A." *New York Times*, January 7, 1979.

88. *New York Times*, December 5, 1981.

> defiant people; that the CIA-empowered leaders represent only a small fraction who kill, torture and impoverish their own people to maintain their position of privilege.
>
> This is true intelligence, but who wants it? So instead, the Agency . . . labels the oppressed as lackeys of Soviet or Cuban or Vietnamese communism fighting not for their lives but for their communist masters. It is difficult to sell this story when the facts are otherwise, so the Agency plants weapons shipments, forges documents, broadcasts false propaganda, and transforms reality. Thus it creates a new reality that it then believes.[89]

In 1982, at the urging of the Reagan administration, Congress passed a law that made it a crime to publish any information that might lead to the disclosure of the identities of present or former intelligence agents and informers, even if the information came from already published sources. Under the law, some news reports and articles about CIA and FBI unlawful covert activities become illegal.

Watergate and the Iran-Contra Connection

In June 1972, a group of ex-CIA agents were caught breaking into the Democratic party headquarters in the Watergate building in Washington. Subsequent investigations revealed that the burglary was part of an extensive campaign involving political espionage, electoral sabotage, wiretapping, theft of private records, and illegal use of campaign funds—planned and directed by members of Nixon's campaign staff and White House staff. Persons close to the president testified that Nixon failed to respond to warnings of cover-up efforts by White House staff members, and that he himself was involved in the Watergate skulduggery, and in cover-up activities. Then it was discovered that tapes of all Oval Office conversations had been maintained, and these revealed that the charges were true and Nixon had been lying to the public. In August 1974, facing impeachment proceedings, Nixon resigned from office. Vice-President Gerald Ford succeeded to the presidency and promptly pardoned Nixon for all crimes relating to Watergate, including any that might come to light at some future time.[90] Nixon retired on a fat presidential pension.

Congress and the press treated Watergate as a deviant instance of government lawlessness. In fact, for many decades these same practices had been employed against the political left. What shocked the establish-

---

89. Ralph McGehee, *Deadly Deceits*, pp. xi and 194.

90. Members of the Nixon administration found guilty in the Watergate affair were given relatively light sentences.

ment politicians was that this time the crimes were committed against a segment of the establishment itself—specifically the Democratic Party and mainstream newspeople.[91]

In 1986, another scandal rocked the White House and shocked the nation. It was discovered that after six years of relentless condemnations of terrorism, the Reagan administration had been sending millions of dollars worth of secret arms shipments to Iran, a country linked closely to terrorists. Then, as part of a covert operation to bypass Congress, the law, and the Constitution, the funds had been funneled to the Nicaraguan mercenaries known as the "contras." Funds also may have been diverted to pay for the television campaign expenses of conservative Republican candidates in the 1986 election. President Reagan admitted full knowledge of the arms sales to Iran, although in his public statements he vastly understated the amount sent. But he claimed he had no idea as to the disposition of the money earned from those sales. He asked the American public to believe that the various unlawful policies were created and carried out by subordinates, including his own National Security Advisor, without being cleared with the president.

Reagan pledged his full cooperation, yet after the initial revelations about the scandal he did little to clear up the mystery. He offered no complete public testimony and volunteered none of the information his administration possessed regarding the development of the Iran-contra scandal. He left it to Congress to do the digging. When a number of his estwhile subordinates took the Fifth Amendment and refused to answer questions before congressional investigating committees, Reagan had only kind words for them. Each new day of investigation unearthed new contradictions and gaps in the statements made by the president and other members of his administration.[92]

MIND CONTROLS FOR LAW AND ORDER

In their never-ending campaign to contain the class struggle and control behavior unacceptable to the existing order, authorities have moved beyond clubs, bullets, and eavesdropping devices and are resorting to such things as electroshock, mind-destroying drugs, and psychosurgery. Since the established powers presume that the present social system is virtuous, then those who are prone to violent or disruptive behavior, or who show

---

91. Nixon claimed he had the "inherent executive power" under the Constitution to commit even criminal acts when impelled by what he considered to be national security considerations. As he said in a television interview, May 19, 1977: "When the president does it, that means it is not illegal." Scratch a president and you find a divine rights monarch.

92. At the time of writing, February 1987, the affair is still unfolding. See the *Washington Post* and *New York Times* from the end of November 1986 onward.

themselves to be manifestly disturbed about the conditions under which they live, must be suffering from *inner* malfunctions that can best be treated by various mind controls. Not only are political and social deviants defined as insane, but sanity itself has a political definition. The sane person is the obedient one who lives in peace and goes to war on cue from his leaders, is not too much troubled by the inhumanities committed against people, is capable of fitting into one of the mindless job slots of a profit-oriented hierarchical organization, and does not challenge the established rules and conventional wisdom. Since authorities accept the present politico-economic system as a good one, then anything that increases its ability to control dissident persons is also seen as good.

Among the mind-control methods employed, probably the most inhumane is psychosurgery, better known as lobotomy, an operation that modifies behavior by destroying brain cells. Hundreds of such operations are reported in the nation each year, with an unknown number going unreported. Advertised as a cure for anger, anxiety, depression, espousal of unpopular political opinions, and refusal to take orders, psychosurgery has been used on rebellious prison inmates, psychiatric patients, incarcerated political dissenters, "hyperactive" children, and distressed women. In most cases, drastic personality changes result: individuals become compliant, emotionally dulled, and show a striking deterioration in memory and intelligence.[93]

Prison inmates who propagate revolutionary or Black nationalist ideas or who engage in prison protests have been singled out for mind-control programs. Prisoners like the socialist Stephen Kessler, charged with disrupting a federal penitentiary by "promoting racial unity, collectivizing the inmate population, attempting to secure legislative inquiries . . . into prison conditions and being involved with outside radical groups," are placed in "behavior modification" units to be subjected to mind-altering drugs, beatings, forced rectal searches, prolonged shackling, isolation, and other tortures.[94] In the words of one Oklahoma prisoner: "As long as

---

93. Lani Silver, et al., "Surgery to the Rescue," *Progressive*, December 1977, p. 23; David Schutts, *Lobotomy: Resort to the Knife* (New York: Van Nostrand Reinhold, 1982). For the horrifying story of how a spirited, politically dissident actress was railroaded in the 1940s into an asylum, tormented, raped, drugged, and finally lobotomized into submission, see William Arnold, *Frances Farmer: Shadowland* (New York: McGraw-Hill, 1978). For general critiques of the hidden oppressions and ideological biases of the mental health industry see Bruce Ennis, *Prisoners of Psychiatry* (New York: Avon, 1972); Philip Brown (ed.), *Radical Psychology* (New York: Harper and Row, 1973); Ronald Leifer, *In the Name of Mental Health* (New York: Science House, 1969); Seymour Halleck, *The Politics of Therapy* (New York: Science House, 1971); Elliot Valenstein, *Great and Desperate Cures* (New York: Basic Books, 1986).

94. *New York Times*, February 20, 1974; *Guardian*, January 21, 1976. At least 5,000 psychiatric patients were killed each year by mind-control drug treatments during the 1960s and early 1970s: Morton Silverman and Phillip Lee, *Pills, Profits and Politics* (Berkeley, Calif.: University of California Press, 1974).

prisoners confine themselves to gambling, shooting dope, running loan rackets and killing each other, everything is fine. Let them pick up a book on Marx's theory of dialectical materialism and they are immediately branded a communist agitator and locked in solitary confinement."[95]

In a class-action suit against the special "control unit" in Marion Federal Penitentiary, Warden Ralph Aaron testified that the program was used "to control prisoners with revolutionary attitudes and tactics." Federal Judge James Foreman agreed, noting in *Bono* v. *Saxbe* that the control unit had been used "to silence prison critics . . . religious leaders . . . [and] economic and philosophical dissidents. Often no showing was made as to how these persons disrupted the . . . running of the institution."[96]

Behavior-modification programs use several approaches. One technique is to put the prisoner in solitary confinement under excruciating conditions of filth, cold, insufficient food, and sensory deprivation and make piecemeal improvements in each of these conditions as a reward if he develops the kind of attitude and behavior patterns desired by the authorities. The conversion must be a "sincere" one. "Reformed" prisoners are then forced to inform upon their fellow inmates and engage in marathon sessions to help break them. Those "reformed" prisoners who refuse to cooperate are once more subjected to behavior-modification torture themselves.[97]

Not even minors are exempt from institutional oppression. More than a million children are kept in orphanages, reformatories, and adult prisons. Most have been arrested for minor transgressions or have committed no crime at all and are jailed without due process. Ninety percent of the children brought into juvenile court are impoverished and of those incarcerated, a majority are Black or a member of some other minority. Many are subjected to beatings, sexual assault, prolonged solitary confinement, mind-control drugs, and, in some cases, psychosurgery.[98]

Medical aggression perpetrated against poor people, especially racial minorities, includes the sterilization of women without their knowledge or consent. One of every four Native American women of childbearing age is sterilized. One of every three women in Puerto Rico has been sterilized, most of them involuntarily. In Los Angeles and parts of the Southwest,

---

95. Letter from Chuck Stots, inmate in Oklahoma State Prison, *Liberation*, February 1975, p. 5.

96. For the statements by Warden Aaron and Judge Foreman see respectively, Phyllis Roa, correspondence in *New York Review of Books*, March 9, 1978; and Chuck Nowlen, "A Prison on Trial," *Progressive*, April 1980, p. 28.

97. *Guardian*, May 29, 1974.

98. Thomas Cottle, *Children in Jail* (Boston: Beacon Press, 1977); Kenneth Wooden, *Weeping in the Playtime of Others* (New York: McGraw-Hill, 1976).

Chicano women have been forcibly sterilized. And in parts of the South, Black girls whose mothers are on welfare are routinely sterilized when they turn fifteen. While the federal government limits funding for Medicaid abortions, thus depriving low-income women of access to medically safe abortions, the government continues to fund sterilization operations for low-income people.[99]

Some people are mentally dysfunctional or gravely retarded and need institutional help. But because of meager funding, understaffing, and inadequate facilities, public mental hospitals are designed to fail them. During the 1970s, the public outcry against the treatment accorded mentally ill persons provided fiscally pressed states with an excuse to close down facilities so that the 535,000 mentally ill or mentally retarded or senile patients in state facilities in 1960 were reduced to 281,000 by 1981. Once again, when a public service failed to deal with a problem correctly or sufficiently, the conservative response was to diminish the public service. What occurred, however, was not a "deinstitutionalization" but a "privatization" and a "reinstitutionalization," as large numbers of former inmates were dumped into private-profit nursing homes, boarding houses, and flophouse hotels— places gravely deficient in medical care, recreational facilities, and health and safety standards. "If the old institutions were 'warehouses,' the new institutions are deathtraps."[100] The condition for most nonaffluent mental patients has gone from bad to worse. Many now live on the street.

THE DEMOCRATIC STRUGGLE

Police, judges, FBI and CIA agents, behavior-modification experts, and psychosurgeons all have one thing in common: while they do a dismal job of fighting crime, drugs, and social pathology, they work effectively to make the world safe for those on top by exercising repressive control over those below. They help the capitalist class protect itself from its own people, all in the name of peace and security, normality and health, law and order.

---

99. Claudia Dreifus, "Sterilizing the Poor," *Progressive*, December 1975, pp. 13–18. Evidence of massive involuntary sterilization of American Indians was unearthed by a GAO study: *East West Journal*, March 1977, p. 10. Federal regulations designed to protect low-income Medicaid patients from involuntary sterilizations are regularly ignored by the states: *Washington Post*, July 17, 1981.

100. Mary Ellen Schoonmaker, "Home, on the Curb," *In These Times*, April 28–May 4, 1982, p. 16; *Washington Post*, May 21, 1981. City and county jails are becoming dumping grounds "for millions of poor, homeless and mentally disturbed Americans who have no other place to go": *Washington Post*, June 17, 1983.

The law is an instrument—one among many—whereby the ruling interests control the populace and at the same time legitimate the existing order. When the law is written so as to deprive democratic forces of the very means of changing it—as when it restricts freedom of speech and assembly, the right to organize, bargain collectively, and strike, then the law often will be violated by popular struggle. In time, either the repressive law becomes too costly and is rescinded or not enforced, or the repression intensifies until the popular movement is discouraged and broken.

As social contradictions deepen and people mobilize, the law appears less as an unshakable rock upon which society rests and more as a resource of ruling class power. Yet, important democratic victories have been won by popular forces, most notably by the labor movement, and by minorities, peace movements and civil-liberties groups. Freedom of speech and assembly, freedom not only to talk back but to fight back, was not "given to us by our Founding Fathers"; these freedoms are the product of people actively struggling to better their lot and shape their own destiny.[101] In fact, the framers of the Constitution did not believe that freedom of speech included the right to criticize the government without risk.[102] Nor did subsequent generations of elites believe that the Constitution allowed people to oppose slavery, build labor unions, support the enfranchisement of women, limit the workday, abolish child labor, oppose U.S. military ventures, and advocate socialism. In each of these struggles, advocates were imprisoned or in other ways targeted by authorities. In each instance, the right to oppose officialdom was finally legitimated to some extent by bold, militant mass expressions of dissent, by struggles in the political process, in the streets, at the worksite, and even in the courts themselves. Popular struggle in the legal arena has brought victories, for ultimately the law is not what the judges say it is, but what the people say it is—on those occasions they can manage to make themselves heard strongly enough.[103]

Upon becoming a professor of law at Harvard in 1829, Joseph Story announced that the lawyer's most "glorified and not infrequently perilous" duty was to guard the "sacred rights of property" from the "rapacity" of the majority. The lawyer and the law were the "solitary citadel" that stood between property and property redistribution.[104] Today, lawyers, like

101. David Kairys, "Freedom of Speech," in David Kairys (ed.), *The Politics of Law* (New York: Pantheon, 1982), pp. 140–171.

102. Leonard Levy, *Emergence of a Free Press* (New York: Oxford University Press, 1985).

103. For an account of how progressive groups have litigated for civil rights, civil liberties, and human needs, see Ann Giner (ed.), *Human Rights Docket* (Berkeley, Calif.: Meikeljohn Civil Liberties Institute, 1979).

104. Quoted in Elizabeth Mensch, "The History of Mainstream Legal Thought," in Kairys, *The Politics of Law*, p. 20.

politicians, have learned to be more circumspect in their expressions of devotion to the owning class and more inclined to talk about "justice for all." To be most effective as an instrument of class control, the law must win the acceptance of those it seeks to control. To do this, it must give the appearance of neutrality and evenhandedness. But to maintain that appearance, it must at times make actual concessions and abide by its professed restraints and standards. Even if intended only as legitimating deceptions, the concessions become soft spots of vulnerability, through which democratic forces can sometimes press for greater gains. The law is an instrument of class control but an imperfect one, for successful struggles have been fought to defeat retrogressive laws and pass progressive ones.

To preserve its legitimacy and popular acceptance, the ruling class must maintain democratic appearances and to do that it must not only lie, distort, and try to hide its exploitations and unjust privileges, but must occasionally give in to popular demands. In time, the legitimating ideology becomes a two-edged sword. Ruling-class pronouncements about "democracy" and "fair play" place some limitations on ruling-class power, once the public takes democracy and fair play seriously and fights for them.[105]

The victories won, however, are never totally secure. In the 1980s, the Reagan administration's Attorney General, Edwin Meese, launched an active campaign to gut the Freedom of Information Act, imposed lifetime censorship agreements on government workers, and called for sweeping restrictions on constitutionally protected speech and a weakening of the writ of habeas corpus and of protections from unlawful searches and seizures. A stagnant capitalism does not easily coexist with a vibrant democracy. By diluting our democratic rights, and thus weakening the populace's ability to advance its interests, rulers are better able to secure the existing class structure.

Our democratic freedoms today would be a lot safer and more of a reality if we understood that they were won by political struggle and will have to be defended and expanded by more struggle. Democracy is fulfilled only by winning greater equality in legal and material conditions, and by gaining greater popular control and accountability over the productive forces as well as the political institutions and wealth of society.

105. For a fuller exposition see my "Monopoly Capitalism and Culture," *Political Affairs*, March 1985, pp. 3–12.

9

The Mass Media: Free and Independent?

One of the most important purveyors of plutocratic culture is the mass media (newspapers, magazines, radio, and, above all, television). The media help propagate the dominant myths and images. They select most of the information and misinformation we use to define sociopolitical reality. How we view issues and events, even what we define as an issue or event, are largely determined by those who control the communications world. By enlarging our vision through technology, we have actually surrendered control over much of our own sensory intake.[1] Even those of us who are often critical of news distortions are inclined to accept what we see, hear, or read in the media. Are our media free and independent? If not, how free can *we* be?

HE WHO PAYS THE PIPER

For all the talk about a free press, it comes as a shock to some people to discover that the major media are an increasingly concentrated component of corporate America, being themselves giant companies or subsidiaries of conglomerates controlled by a small number of top banks and corporations, and a handful of rich conservative tycoons like Rupert Murdoch and Walter Annenberg. Murdoch, for instance, owns major newspapers in England, Australia, New York, and Chicago, a European cable network, and is co-owner of 20th Century Fox and a chain of television stations in

1. Robert Cirino, *Don't Blame the People* (New York: Vintage, 1972), pp. 30–31; Herbert Schiller, *The Mind Managers* (Boston: Beacon Press, 1973).

the United States. Another example: the Tribune Company owns, besides the *Chicago Tribune* and the Chicago Cubs, television stations in Los Angeles, Atlanta, New Orleans, and Denver, five radio stations, fifteen cable television systems, and the *New York Daily News*.[2] As Charles Perlik, president of the Newspaper Guild, observed: "The news industry has always been a business, run by businessmen—and an occasional businesswoman. Today it is in danger of being run—and overrun—by financiers."[3]

Of the "independent" television stations, 80 percent are affiliates of one of the three major networks, NBC, CBS, and ABC. Except for the local news, practically all the shows they run are network programs. Most of the remaining "independents" are affiliated with NET, the "educational" network, which receives most of its money from the Ford Foundation (controlled largely by the Morgan and Rockefeller banks) and a few allied foundations. The Ford Foundation picks NET's board of directors and reserves the right to inspect every program produced with Ford money.

Newspapers show a similar pattern of ownership. Two-thirds of the 1700-odd dailies, controlling 80 percent of circulation, are owned by chains like Gannett and Knight-Ridder. The trend in ownership concentration continues unabated, as the large chains buy not only independent papers but other chains. The "free and independent American press" is largely a monopoly press. Less than 4 percent of American cities have competing newspapers under separate ownership; and in cities where there is a "choice," the newspapers offer little variety in ideological perspective and editorial policy. In general, newspapers vary mostly from moderately conservative to ultraconservative, with a smaller number that are centrist or tepidly liberal.

Most of the "independent" dailies rely on the wire services and big-circulation papers for stories, syndicated columnists, and special features. Like television stations, they are independent more in name than content. Coverage of national and local affairs is usually scant, superficial—consisting of a few brief "headline" stories and a number of conservative or simply banal commentaries and editorials.[4]

Along with the accelerated concentration of ownership is the growing trend toward cross-media conglomerates, as corporations and banks en-

---

2. Herbert Schiller, "Behind the Media Merger Movement," *Nation*, June 8, 1985, pp. 696–98.

3. Charles Perlik, address before the Newspaper Guild, reprinted in the *Daily World*, November 7, 1985. As of the 1980s, the majority of all American newspapers, magazines, radio and television stations, publishing houses, and movie studios were controlled by fifty giant corporations, which themselves interlocked financially with massive industries and major banks: Ben Bagdikian, *The Media Monopoly* (Boston: Beacon Press, 1983).

4. *New York Times*, February 15, 1977; James Aronson, *Packaging the News* (New York: International Publishers, 1971); Herbert Schiller, *Communication and Cultural Domination* (New York: Pantheon, 1978).

gage in mammoth multibillion-dollar takeovers of newspapers, television and radio stations, magazines, publishing houses, and movie studios. What fuels these record-breaking mergers? As one conservative publication explains: "The profits are almost unbelievable."[5] Like other businesses, the media corporations are diversified and multinational, controlling print, broadcast, and film outlets throughout Latin America, Asia, and the Middle East—as well as in Europe and North America.[6]

Government coercion and official censorship are not the only threats to freedom of the press. As a report by one group of scholars noted, protection against the state is not enough: "The owners and managers of the press determine which person, which facts, which version of the facts, and which ideas shall reach the public."[7] The pro-business, conservative, and centrist biases of the mainstream media are readily evident. Given the media's pattern of ownership and dependency on big-business advertising, labor unions have few opportunities to present programs on the needs and struggles of working people. Peace activists seldom get a chance to challenge the military-industrial complex. Information favorable to existing socialist countries is systematically suppressed. Little positive exposure is given to anti-imperialist alternatives emerging throughout the world, or to the socialist critique of capitalism at home, or to domestic left protest on a number of major issues.

Of the many interesting documentaries made by independent film producers, dealing critically with racism, women's oppression, labor oppression, corporate environmental abuse, the FBI, and U.S. imperialism in Central America and elsewhere, few if any have ever gained access to commercial movie houses or major television networks. In 1986, for instance, the documentary, *Faces of War*, revealing the destructive U.S.-supported counterinsurgency waged against the people of El Salvador, was denied broadcast rights in twenty-two major television markets.[8]

Journalists express concern about having their stories killed, about getting reassigned, passed over for promotion, and fired.[9] *New York Times* columnist Tom Wicker testifies:

> When I was *Times* bureau chief in Washington, I was a member of the League of Gentlemen [i.e., the established elite]; otherwise I never would have been

---

5. *U.S. News and World Report*, May 13, 1985.

6. Herbert Schiller, *Mass Communication and American Empire* (New York: Augustus Kelley, 1969).

7. Report by the Commission on Freedom of the Press, quoted in Cirino, *Don't Blame the People*, p. 47.

8. Joan Walsh, "Direct Response: The Answer Is No," *In These Times*, January 22–28, 1986. For a study of the political and class biases of the mainstream media see Michael Parenti, *Inventing Reality: The Politics of the Mass Media* (New York: St. Martin's Press, 1986).

9. *Inventing Reality*, chapter 3.

> bureau chief. Time after time, good reporters . . . complained about not being able to get stories in the paper. And time after time I said to them, "You're just not going to get *that* in the *New York Times* . . . it's too reliant on your judgment rather than on official judgment, it's too complex, it contradicts the official record more flagrantly than the conventions of daily journalism allow."[10]

News reports on business rely mostly on business sources and allow little space for the views of antibusiness critics, or the communities and individuals afflicted by business. Reports about State Department or Pentagon policies rely heavily on State Department and Pentagon releases. Media coverage of the space program uncritically accepts the government's claims about the program's desirability and seldom gives exposure to the arguments made against it.[11]

AN OFFICIAL PRESS

Far from being vigilant critics, most news organizations share the counter-revolutionary, anticommunist assumptions and vocabulary of the media magnates who own them. For years the press has supported cold-war policies, indulging in an unremitting Soviet-bashing and a hatred and fear of existing socialist societies that is so formidable in its ideological monopoly as to permeate even much of the American left. The Vietnam War was portrayed in the media as a noble but ill-conceived venture, with little attention given to the underlying class interests and to the horrendous devastation wreaked by U.S. forces upon the Vietnamese people and their society and environment.[12]

The U.S. media ignored the slaughter by the right-wing Indonesian military of some 500,000 Indonesians, just as it ignored the genocidal campaign waged by this same military in East Timor and the massive repression, torture, and murder of progressives in Uruguay, Guatemala, Argentina, Paraguay, Brazil, Zaire, the Philippines, and other U.S.-supported pro-corporate regimes.[13] For twenty-five years, the Shah of Iran, a

---

10. Quoted in Kevin Kelly, "'League of Gentlemen' Rates Media," *Guardian*, February 13, 1985.

11. Parenti, *Inventing Reality*; also David Paletz and Robert Entman, *Media Power Politics* (New York: Free Press, 1981).

12. Noam Chomsky and Edward Herman, *After the Cataclysm: Postwar Indochina and the Reconstruction of Imperial Ideology* (Boston: South End Press, 1979).

13. After ignoring the Indonesian genocide for twelve years, the *New York Times* reported that the Indonesian chief of security had announced that "500,000 Communists" were slaughtered after the right-wing takeover in 1965: *New York Times*, December 21, 1977; also Chomsky and Herman, *The Washington Connection*, pp. 41–204; Paletz and Entman, *Media Power Politics*, pp. 213–35.

friend of the U.S. oil companies and a product of the CIA, maimed and murdered tens of thousands of dissident workers, students, peasants and intellectuals. For the most part, the American press ignored these terrible happenings and portrayed Iran as a citadel of stability and the Shah as an enlightened modernizer. However, when the Polish government cracked down on the Solidarity union in Poland in December 1981, resulting in the death of several miners and the incarceration of several thousand other people, every network, newspaper, and newsmagazine gave these events top-story play for weeks on end. During this very same period, a fascist government in Turkey executed thousands of workers and dissenters and jailed tens of thousands, yet this brutal repression went largely unmentioned.

The business-owned media treats the atrocities of U.S.-sponsored rightist regimes with benign neglect while casting a stern, self-righteous eye on popular revolutions, as in Nicaragua. Generally the press defames leftist movements and governments and supports those right-wing pro-capitalist dictatorships that are clients of the multinational corporations.[14]

When seven political parties participated in elections in Nicaragua in 1984, with each accorded funds and free television time by the government during a campaign judged to be fair and open by teams of observers from neutral countries, the U.S. media—following the White House line—treated the election as a rigged affair conducted under "unfair conditions." The news media never provided evidence to support that conclusion, but simply repeated the charges in successive news stories and editorials. That same year, however, the U.S.-sponsored election held in El Salvador between two right-wing candidates, under highly coercive and restricted conditions—including the lack of secret ballots—was hailed in the U.S. press as a great blossoming of democracy (in a country where most of the labor-union leadership had been assassinated along with thousands of other opponents of the regime).[15]

When President Reagan denounced the Soviet Union as the perpetrator of international terrorism, the U.S. press, for the most part, dutifully parroted this line despite the absence of any supporting evidence and a good deal of evidence to the contrary. When the President announced that his Strategic Defense Initiative (SDI) or "Star Wars" project was a "defensive shield" against enemy missiles, the news media implicitly accepted that characterization and gave short shrift to the opposing viewpoint that SDI was part of an offensive, first-strike arsenal. When Reagan suddenly

---

14. Parenti, *Inventing Reality*, passim.
15. Ibid., pp. 198–202; also Edward Herman, *The Real Terror Network* (Boston: South End Press, 1982).

declared he was for arms control and nuclear disarmament, after twenty years of denouncing the idea of trying to negotiate arms agreements with the Soviets, the press took him at his word and pretty much reported things his way, even though he then refused to join the Soviets in a moratorium on nuclear testing, refused to join them in a nuclear freeze and in a no first-use nuclear pledge, violated SALT II arms limitations, made ready to violate the antiballistic missile (ABM) treaty, and dismissed every Soviet arms offer as a publicity stunt.[16]

The workings of the capitalist political economy remain another area uncharted by the news media. The need to invest surplus capital; the tendency toward a falling rate of profit; the drive toward profit maximization; the instability, recession, inflation, and underemployment—these and other such problems are treated superficially, if at all, by newspersons and commentators who have neither the knowledge nor the permission to make critical analyses of multinational corporatism. Instead, economic adversity is ascribed to innocent and unavoidable causes, such as "hard times." One television commentator put it this way: "Inflation is the culprit and in inflation everyone is guilty."[17] When economic news *is* reported, it is almost always from management's viewpoint.

Each evening the network news programs faithfully report the Dow Jones stock-exchange averages, but stories deemed important to organized labor are scarcely ever touched upon, according to a study made by union members.[18] Reporters fail to enlist labor's views on national questions. Unions are usually noticed only when they go on strike, but the issues behind the strike, such as job security, occupational and public safety, and resistance to loss of benefits are seldom acknowledged. The misleading impression is that labor simply turns down "good contracts" because it wants too much for itself.

There are few militantly progressive and no avowedly socialist commentators and editorialists in the mass media. Of the liberal columnists and commentators, most take care to present themselves as judiciously moderate—that is, they avoid class issues and direct confrontations with class power, knowing full well who their employers are and under what limits they are working.[19] Some liberal commentators have been refused radio spots even on the relatively infrequent occasions they have had

16. Parenti, *Inventing Reality*, pp. 130–35, 148–51; William Dorman, "The Media: Playing the Government's Game," *Bulletin of the Atomic Scientists*, 41, 1985, pp. 118–124, and William Dorman, "Soviets Seen Through Red-tinted Glasses," *Bulletin of the Atomic Scientists*, 41, 1985, pp. 18–22.

17. Channel Nine News, Ithaca, N.Y., February 11, 1976.

18. International Association of Machinists and Aerospace Workers, *Network News and Documentary Report* (Washington, D.C.), July 30, 1980.

19. Herbert Gans, *Deciding What's News* (New York: Vintage, 1979).

sponsors who would pay. When independent liberal groups manage to muster enough money to buy broadcasting time or newspaper space, they still may be denied access to the media—as has happened to those wanting to run ads against the Vietnam War, the nuclear arms buildup, and U.S. intervention in Central America.[20]

Denied access to the major media, the political left has attempted to get its message across through little magazines and radical newspapers, publications that suffer chronic financial difficulties and sometimes harassment from police, FBI, rightist vigilantes, the IRS, and the U.S. Postal Service.[21] Dissenters also attempt to make themselves heard by mobilizing great numbers of people in public protest. But popular demonstrations against official policies are often trivialized, undercounted, and accorded minimal coverage by the business-owned media. The September 1981 march on Washington, in which a half million working people protested Reagan's policies, was the largest ever to take place in that city. In June 1982, upwards of a million people marched in New York to protest nuclear armaments in the largest demonstration in U.S. history. However, neither historic event received direct coverage (unlike the marriage of England's Prince Charles or the funeral of Monaco's Princess Grace). The networks preferred to concentrate on sporting events on those days, giving but a few minutes of evening news to these massive expressions of popular sentiment.[22]

This is not to say that the press is entirely immune to mass pressures. If, despite the media's misrepresentation and neglect, a well-organized and persistent public opinion builds around an issue or set of issues, the press eventually feels compelled to acknowledge its existence. If the popular opinion is strong and widespread and *if it does not attack the capitalist system as a system*, it can occasionally break through the media-controlled sound barrier, albeit with selected images. On occasion, acts of skulduggery and cover-up are committed in high places involving no class-wide interest as such but leaving prominent personages—presidential cabinet members or even the president—vulnerable before the law. When elite power is thus weakened for a time and held accountable to law in a democratic way, then it is hard to keep the press from digging into the story, especially an important one like the Watergate scandal or the Iran-

20. Cirino, *Don't Blame the People*, pp. 90, 302; Parenti, *Inventing Reality*, pp. 71–72; *Washington Post*, November 21, 1982.

21. Geoffrey Rips, *The Campaign Against the Underground Press* (San Francisco: City Lights Books, 1981); William Preston, Jr., "'Balancing' the News: How the Post Office Controls the Circulation of Information," *World Magazine*, April 3, 1986, p. 14.

22. Todd Gitlin, *The Whole World Is Watching* (Berkeley: University of California Press, 1980), passim.

contra connection. In such instances, conservatives are convinced the press is a liberal conspiracy dedicated to wrecking the system.[23]

While the press cannot regularly violate the fundamental class interests of media moguls and corporate advertisers, it must also market a product called "the news," which is credible to the general public. Therefore, there are sometimes limits to how the media can suppress and distort things, especially when popular feelings are high and the public is demanding explanations about unemployment, plant closings, pollution, poverty, inflation, crime, overseas interventions, the arms race, bloated military budgets, or whatever. The media's need to deal with such subjects, usually haphazardly and superficially but sometimes in ways that are revealing and troublesome to the powers that be, also leads conservatives to the conclusion that the media are infected with "liberal" biases.[24]

To combat what they see as the ideological "softness" of the centrist media, hardcore ultraconservatives have launched repeated attacks on specific newspersons and have induced corporations to withdraw their advertising support from certain programs. They have organized corporate proxy fights against those news organizations deemed not sufficiently sympathetic to the right's message, and have poured millions of dollars into building new media outlets to compete with the centrist media; these include the religious right's radio network, consisting of 1,300 local stations, and two national networks PTL and CBN; each has almost as many affiliates as ABC. Spreading the gospel is only one concern of the Christian rightists; most of the programming is, economically conservative, militaristic, phobically anticommunist, antiunion, and hostile toward the needs of minorities.[25]

It is said that a free and independent press is a necessary condition for democracy, and it is frequently assumed that the United States is endowed with such a press. While the news in "totalitarian" nations is controlled, we Americans supposedly have access to a wide range of competing sources. In reality, the controls exerted in the United States, while more subtle than in some other countries, leave us with a press that is far from "free" by any definition of the word. When it comes to getting the other side of the story, Americans are a rather deprived people. U.S. programs

---

23. For a discussion of the media's failure to get at the whole Watergate story see Andrew Kopkind, "The Unwritten Watergate Story," *More*, November 1974; Robert Holsworth and J. Harry Wray, *American Politics and Everyday Life* (New York: Wiley and Sons, 1982), pp. 89–91.

24. For a more extensive discussion see my *Inventing Reality*, passim.

25. Mike Zagarell, "'Lighting Freedom's Way,'" *World Magazine*, November 8, 1984, pp. 8–9; and Zagarell's "The Ultra-right Media Web," *World Magazine*, October 25, 1984, pp. 15–16; Marie Shear, "Laxalt, the *Bee*—and Play It Safe Press," *Columbia Journalism Review*, January/February 1985, p. 16.

can be heard throughout Eastern Europe via Voice of America. American films are regularly shown in socialist countries. Twenty percent of the television shows in Poland come from the United States. American novels and other books are translated and widely read in the Soviet Union and Eastern European countries. Cubans can watch Miami television and listen to a half dozen U.S. radio stations and to Spanish-language Voice of America programs. But how many Americans are exposed to the media and literature of socialist countries? More importantly, how many Americans get information about their *own* country, from *within* their own country, that is contrary to the capitalist orthodoxy? Perhaps we Americans should think more of ourselves and worry less about others. We should want the same good things for ourselves that we so fervently desire for Soviets and Cubans, namely the opportunity to hear and express iconoclastic, antiestablishment views in our national media without fear of censorship and reprisal.

THE POLITICS OF ENTERTAINMENT

While the entertainment sector of the media, as opposed to the news sector, supposedly has nothing to do with politics, entertainment programs in fact undergo a rigorous political censorship. Shows that treat controversial, antiestablishment subjects often have trouble getting sponsors and network time. The censorship code used by Proctor and Gamble, the largest television advertiser in the United States, for programs it sponsors states in part: "Members of the armed forces must not be cast as villains. If there is any attack on American custom, it must be rebutted completely on the same show."[26] Truly radical themes are eschewed by both the networks and Hollywood. On the rare occasions a leftist film is produced, such as *1900*, or *Reds*, or *Burn* it is likely to be accorded a limited distribution.

But entertainment shows contain plenty of politics of their own. Be it adventure film, prime-time drama, or soap opera, adversities are caused by ill-willed individuals rather than by the economic and social system in which they live, and problems are solved by individual effort within the system rather than collective effort against it. Evening soap operas like "Dallas" and "Dynasty" depict a corporate world of ruthless tycoons engaged in an amoral pursuit of wealth, power, and sex—but the audience is invited to identify with, rather than reject, it all.

Revolutionaries and foreign agents are seen as menacing our land, and the military and police as protecting it. Movies like *Rambo* glorify the

---

26. Eric Barnouw, *The Television Writer* (New York: Hill and Wang, 1962), p. 27.

killing of Communists and depict Russians as subhumans who delight in torture and atrocity. Other films like *Red Dawn* and *Invasion USA*, and television specials like ABC's "Amerika," offer fantasy depictions of the conquest of the United States by Soviet troops—assisted by Cubans and Nicaraguans. The message is clear: the Soviets are our inexorable enemy and we had better not expect to live in peace and friendship with them.

In the world of Hollywood and television, physical assault and other kinds of aggressive behavior are a regular indulgence. Conflicts are defined and resolved by generous applications of violence. Nefarious violence is met with righteous violence, although it is often difficult to distinguish the two. The brutal and sometimes criminal behavior of law officers is portrayed sympathetically as one of those gutsy realities of life. One study of "cop and crime" shows found that police actions habitually violate the constitutional rights of individuals. The profound importance of the concept of due process is lost as television police carry out illegal searches and break-ins, coerce suspects into confessing, and regularly use homicidal violence against suspected criminals in shoot-'em-up endings. Studies indicate that these kind of programs help condition the public into accepting authoritarian law-and-order solutions (including the death penalty) and helping to create a climate of opinion that allows for repressive police actions.[27]

In the media, women appear less often than men and primarily in subsidiary roles as housewives, secretaries, and girlfriends, who are usually incapable of initiating responsible actions of their own. In media advertisements it is even worse: women seem predominantly concerned with being cheery, mindless handmaidens who shampoo a fluffy glow into their hair, wax floors shiny bright, make yummy coffee for hubby, and get Junior's grimy clothes sparkling clean. One-fifth of all television time is taken up with commercials that often characterize people as loudmouthed imbeciles whose problems are solved when they encounter the right medication, cosmetic, or cleanser. In this way, industry confines the social imagination and cultural experience of millions, teaching people to define their needs and life-styles (and those of hubby, wifey, and baby) according to the dictates of the commodity market.[28]

For years, characters who were Afro-American, Latino, or some other

---

27. Stephen Arons and Ethan Katsh, "How TV Cops Flout the Law," *Saturday Review*, March 19, 1977, pp. 11–18. Studies show that adults become more belligerent after large doses of television violence and more fearful of racial minorities, cities, and criminal attack: Richard Saltus, "The Research Shows Cop Shows Make Us Violent," *Leisure*, February 21, 1976, p. 22; George Gerbner's report in *Psychology Today*, April 1976, finds that heavy television viewers are more convinced that more police repression is needed to control crime.

28. For a study of how advertising has been used to create the kind of consumerism needed by capitalism, see Stuart Ewen, *Captains of Consciousness* (New York: McGraw-Hill, 1976).

ethnic minority were given little exposure except in unflattering stereotyped roles. When minorities have made appearances in cop shows, it has been most often as crooks, pimps, informers, or persons in need of assistance from White professionals. Working people in general, be they White, Black, Latino, or whatever, have little representation in the entertainment media except as uncouth, simple persons, hoodlums, sidekicks, and other stock characters. The tribulations of working-class people in this society—their struggle to make ends meet; the specter of unemployment; the lack of decent recreational facilities; the victimization by unscrupulous landlords and realty developers; the loss of pensions and seniority; the bitter strikes and the historical and ever-present battle for unionization, better wages, and work conditions; the dirty, noisy, mindless, dangerous quality of industrial work; the lives wrecked by work-connected injury and disease—these and other realities are given little if any dramatic treatment in the business-owned media.[29]

In recent years, however, partly in response to the public pressure of a more politically advanced audience, there have been changes for the better. Various television series like "Hill Street Blues," "St. Elsewhere," "Cagney and Lacey," "Who's the Boss," and "Hail to the Chief" have offered plots with some social content and have projected women and minorities as intelligent and capable persons, sometimes as doctors, lawyers, district attorneys, police lieutenants, or as occupying other positions of authority and empowerment. Situation comedies continue to be loaded with a contrived and frenetically aggressive or downright silly humor. But in some of the better ones, like "The Cosby Show," minorities are portrayed as intelligent, likable, and decent people. And in a few rare films, such as *Norma Rae*, the struggles of working people have been given respectful attention.

Not all air time is given to commercial gain. The Federal Communications Commission requires that broadcasters devote some time to public-service announcements. Like the free space donated by newspapers and magazines, this time is monopolized by the Advertising Council, a group composed of representatives from the networks and big business. No public-interest groups are represented. While supposedly "nonpolitical," the Council's "public service" commercials laud the blessings of free enterprise and falsely claim that business is "doing its job" in hiring veterans, minorities, and the poor. Workers are exhorted to take pride in their work and produce more for their employers—but nothing is said about employers paying more to their workers. The ads blame pollution on everyone (but

29. Generally, unions are presented as selfish, violent organizations that are likely to do their members no good: Ralph Johnson, "World Without Workers: Prime Time's Presentation of Labor," *Labor Studies Journal*, 5, Winter 1981, p. 203.

not on industry) and treat littering as the major environmental problem. In general, social and political problems are reduced to individual failings or evaded altogether. Air time that could be used by conservationists and labor, consumer, and other public-interest groups has been preempted by an Advertising Council that passes off its one-sided ads as noncontroversial and nonpartisan.[30]

REPRESSING THE PRESS

On those rare occasions when the news media expose the murky side of official doings, they are likely to encounter serious discouragements from public authorities. Government officeholders treat news that places them in an unfavorable light as "slanted" and criticize reporters for not presenting the "accurate" and "objective" (that is, uncritical and supportive) viewpoint. These kinds of attacks allow the media to appear as defenders of free speech against government pressure, instead of supporters of the established order as they more commonly have been.

The federal government has used the FBI to harass and arrest newspersons who persist in writing troublesome news reports. The Justice Department won a Supreme Court decision requiring reporters to disclose their information sources to grand-jury investigators, in effect reducing the press to an investigative arm of the courts and the prosecution—the very officialdom over whom it is supposed to act as a watchdog. Dozens of reporters have since been jailed or threatened with prison terms on the basis of that decision.[31] On repeated occasions the government has subpoenaed documents, tapes, and other materials used by news media. Such interference imposes a "chilling effect" on the press, a propensity—already evident in news reports—to slide over the more troublesome aspects of a story and censor oneself in order to avoid censorship by those in power.

To offer one of numerous recent examples: in May 1986, William Casey, then CIA director, threatened to prosecute NBC, the *Washington Post*, and other media, for printing stories that supposedly violated "national security." One of these stories concerned an American who was charged with selling the Soviets information about how U.S. submarines were spying in Soviet harbors. But if the Soviets already knew about this, then suppressing the story would only keep it from the American people. While the U.S. government attempts to prevent unauthorized leaks to the

---

30. Keenen Peck, "Ad Nauseum," *Progressive*, May 1983, pp. 44–45.

31. William Porter, *Assault on the Media* (Ann Arbor: University of Michigan Press, 1977); *United States* v. *Caldwell* (1972); also *New York Times*, September 4, 1976, and November 19, 1978.

press, it itself continually leaks information when it serves official purposes. As *New York Times* columnist James Reston noted, the administration "leaks the baloney it thinks people will swallow, and threatens to sue anybody who publishes information it wants to suppress."[32]

In 1986 the Reagan administration admitted that it had generated misinformation against Libyan leader Colonel Qaddafi as part of a campaign to overthrow him. This revelation evoked shocked comments from newspaper editors and executive producers of news shows—as if it were the first time the government had ever tried to manipulate the press.[33] In fact, most American presidents and other top officials have attempted to manipulate the news flow. Usually they win the cooperation of the press in killing "sensitive" stories and planting favorable ones. Members of the press knew our government was flying U-2 spy planes over Soviet territory; they knew our government was planning an invasion of Cuba at the Bay of Pigs; they knew there were facts about the Tonkin Bay incident in Vietnam that differed from the official version; they knew the United States was engaged in a massive, prolonged saturation bombing of Cambodia. But in each instance, they chose to act "responsibly" by not informing the American public. "Journalistic responsibility" should mean the unearthing of true and significant information. But the "responsibility" demanded by government officials and often agreed to by the press means the opposite—the burying of some piece of information precisely because it is troublesomely true and significant.

In 1983, the White House refused to let reporters cover the U.S. invasion of Grenada, thus making certain that the public would get only the official version. This was the first time in U.S. history the press had been banned from covering a war. "The exclusion of reporters during the first days of the Grenada invasion gave new meaning to the concept that no country can limit the freedom of others without also limiting it for itself."[34] While these curbs were supposed to be temporary, the government came up with a set of guidelines in October 1984 that were to be imposed on all future surprise military operations; these included limiting the number of reporters to a select pool, imposing press blackouts, and restricting coverage.[35]

---

32. *New York Times*, May 21, 1986.

33. For examples of their responses see *New York Times*, October 3, 1986.

34. Mike Zagarell, "News Reporting—the Military Vies for Command," *World Magazine*, November 1, 1984, p. 8.

35. See the critical correspondence by Max Kozlof, *New York Times*, October 21, 1984. As it was, reportage of Grenada was dismal. Most of the press uncritically went along with unsubstantiated White House claims that the invasion was intended to rescue Americans attending medical school there, that the island (population 110,000) was a Cuban military bastion and a strategic Soviet threat to U.S. security, and that the Grenadian revolutionary

The relationship between the CIA and the press offers another example of how the media have been anything but free and independent. More than four hundred American journalists, including nationally syndicated columnists, have carried out secret assignments for the CIA over the last three decades, either gathering intelligence and doing espionage abroad or writing the kind of stories that create a climate of opinion supportive of the CIA's policy objectives. Included among these have been personnel from the *Washington Post*, CBS, NBC, ABC, *Time*, *Newsweek*, *Wall Street Journal*, *U.S. News and World Report*, and the Associated Press. The CIA has also conducted surveillance of news reporters to determine their information sources and has infiltrated various news services. The Agency has owned outright more than 240 media operations around the world, including newspapers, magazines, publishing houses, radio and television stations, and wire services, and has partially controlled many more.[36]

Government manipulation of the press is a constant enterprise. Every day the White House, the Pentagon, and other agencies release thousands of self-serving statements and reports to the media, many of which are then uncritically transmitted to the public as information from independent news sources. White House staffers meet regularly with network bosses and publishers to discuss and complain about specific stories and reporters. They withhold information or feed misleading data to troublesome journalists. And in the 1980s the administration increased its control over what becomes news by severely reducing reporters' expectations about having full access. As the *New York Times*'s Washington editor, Bill Kovach, stated: "[The administration's] whole attitude is that government information belongs to the government." Helen Thomas of UPI, dean of the White House press corp, complained: "They [the administration] pick the story every day. They pick the one that will almost invariably wind up on the nightly news, and that's the one they answer questions on or give access to information about. [On] a lot of events, we're absolutely blacked out, and if you don't like it, too bad. The whole attitude is: We will tell you what we think you should know."[37]

From what has been said so far it should be clear that one cannot talk about a "free press" apart from the economic and political realities that

---

government intended aggressive actions against neighboring islands. The press concentrated on the success of the invasion and implicitly accepted its legitimacy, saying little about the social and economic accomplishments of the revolutionary government that was deposed by American military force.

36. Carl Bernstein, "The CIA and the Media," *Rolling Stone*, October 20, 1977; Stuart Loory, "The CIA's Use of the Press: A Mighty Wurlitzer," *Columbia Journalism Review*, September/October, 1974, pp. 9–18; Vitaly Petrusenko, *A Dangerous Game, CIA and the Mass Media* (Prague: Interpress, n.d.).

37. Both Kovach and Thomas are quoted in *Washington Post*, June 10, 1985.

determine who owns and controls the media. As Schiller asks: "How may at least a part of the nation's information and cultural apparatus be rescued from near-total corporate control and made accountable and accessible to the viewing, listening and reading public?"[38]

There is no such thing as unbiased news. All reports and analyses are selective and inferential to some inescapable degree—all the more reason to provide a wider ideological spectrum of opinions and not let one bias predominate. If in fact we do consider censorship to be a loathsome danger to our freedom, then we should not overlook the fact that the media are *already* heavily censored by those who own and control them. The very process of selection allows the cultural and political biases and class interests of the selector to operate as a censor. Some measure of ideological heterodoxy could be achieved if public law required all newspapers and broadcasting stations to allot substantial portions of space and time to a diverse array of political opinion, including the most progressive and revolutionary. But given the interests the law serves, this is not a likely development.

An existing statute, known as the Fairness Doctrine, requires that unpaid time be given to an opposing viewpoint—only if a particular editorial opinion is voiced, which discourages some stations from engaging in discussions of political questions. The law makes no requirement as to the diversity of the opposing viewpoints, so usually the range is between two slightly different establishment stances. In the 1980s, the Reagan administration all but ceased enforcing the Fairness Doctrine, with the consequence that advocacy advertising by corporations and well-financed conservative private organizations rose dramatically. In 1985, these interests spent an estimated $1.8 billion to communicate their views on a variety of public issues. Advocacy ads tend to be emotionally charged appeals paid by corporate sponsors who often hide behind public-service sounding names.[39]

Ultimately the only protection against monopoly control of the media is ownership by the people themselves, with legally enforceable provisions allowing for the maximum participation of conflicting views. As A. J. Liebling once said, freedom of the press is guaranteed only to those who own the presses. In Europe some suggestive developments have taken place: the staffs of various newspapers and magazines like *Der Stern* in Germany and *Le Figaro* in France have used strikes to achieve greater editorial control of the publications they help produce. And *Le Monde*'s

38. Schiller, "Beyond the Media Merge Movement."

39. S. Prakash Sethi, "Beyond the Fairness Doctrine," *New York Times*, August 10, 1986; also *Washington Post*, October 3, 1981 and February 8, 1985. Congress's attempt to extend the life of the Fairness Law was vetoed by President Reagan: *New York Times*, June 25, 1987.

management agreed to give its staff a 40 percent share in the profits and a large share in managerial decisions, including the right to block any future sale of the paper.[40]

While they point to alternative forms of property control, these developments are themselves not likely to transform the property relations of a capitalist society and its mass media. With few exceptions, those who own the newspapers and networks will not relinquish their hold over private investments and public information. Ordinary citizens will have no real access to the media until they come to exercise control over the material resources that could give them such access, an achievement that would take a different kind of economic and social system than the one we have. In the meantime, Americans should have no illusions about the "free press" they are said to enjoy.

40. Aronson, *Packaging the News*, p. 99.

10

The Greatest Show On Earth: Elections, Parties, and Voters

As noted earlier, most institutions in America are ruled by self-appointed business elites who are answerable to no one. Presumably the same cannot be said of government, since a necessary condition of our political system is the popular election of those who govern, the purpose being to hold officeholders accountable to the people who elect them. But does it work that way? Not usually.

The American two-party electoral system, with its ballyhoo and hoopla, its impresarios and stunt artists, is the greatest show on earth. Campaign time is show time, a veritable circus running for over 12-month periods, brought into our living rooms via television as a form of entertainment. The important thing is that the show must go on—because it is more than just a show. The two-party electoral system performs the essential function of helping to legitimate the existing social order. It channels and limits political expression, and blunts class grievances. It often leaves little time for the real issues because it gives so much attention to the contest per se: who will run? who is ahead? who will win the primaries? who will win the nomination? who will win the election? It provides the form of republican government with little of the substance. It covers the plutocratic system with a democratic facade, giving an appearance of popular participation while being run by and for a select handful of affluent contestants.

But people are tiring of the show. They complain of the quality of the candidates, the lack of real choice, the absence of real issues, the endless primaries, and the vast expenditures of campaign funds. As they watch the parade of clowns and acrobats, elephants and donkeys, they feel something urgent is being trivialized.[1] This public disenchantment is a worrisome development for faithful allies of the existing politico-economic system, who are concerned about "a party system in decline."[2] They understand it is a serious matter when one of the crucial legitimating institutions of the established order, the two-party electoral system, finds its own legitimacy waning.

THE SOUND AND THE FURY

For generations, the electoral circus was run by professional party politicians who were sufficiently occupied by the pursuit of office and patronage to remain untroubled by questions of social justice. Alan Altshuler describes the machine politicos:

> Though they distributed favors widely, they concentrated power tightly. Though their little favors went to little men, the big favors went to land speculators, public utility franchise holders, government contractors, illicit businessmen, and of course the leading members of the machines themselves. . . . The bosses . . . never questioned the basic distribution of resources in society. Their methods of raising revenue tended toward regressivity. On the whole, the lower classes paid for their own favors. What they got was a *style* of government with which they could feel at home. What the more affluent classes got, though relatively few of them appreciated it, was a form of government which kept the newly enfranchised masses content without threatening the socio-economic status quo.[3]

Old-fashioned political machines can still be found in a number of cities, but they seldom exercise influence beyond the local level.

State, local, and national party organizations have declined over the last two decades, for several reasons:

1. Now that so many states have adopted the direct primary, candidates no longer seek out the party organization for a place on the ticket

---

1. In 1980, a Gallup poll found that voters most disliked the length of campaigns, the amount of mudslinging, the lack of issue discussion, and the high campaign costs, in that order. See *Washington Post*, November 23, 1980. The mudslinging "negative ads" of the 1986 congressional campaigns reportedly were distasteful enough to some voters as to cause them to stay home.

2. For example: Everett Ladd, Jr., *Where Have All the Voters Gone?* (New York: W. W. Norton, 1978), an expanded version of articles by a political scientist written on assignment for *Fortune* magazine.

3. Alan Altshuler, *Community Control* (New York: Pegasus, 1970), pp. 74–75.

but instead can independently pursue the nomination through the ballot box.[4]

2. Campaign finance laws, which allocate federal election funds to candidates rather than to parties, have weakened party resources.

3. Now that television can reach everyone at home, the precinct captain is less needed to canvas the neighborhood.

The outcome is a decline in party organization, an increase in primary contests open to anyone who has the rich backers or personal wealth to pay for individualized staffs and costly media campaigns. Rather than relying on the party for exposure, personnel, expertise, and contacts with the electorate, today's candidate is more likely to bring in a campaign management firm complete with private pollsters and media experts.[5]

Besides making things vastly more costly, this transition to elections-by-television has done little to elevate the quality of political discourse and much to reduce it still further to a kind of spot-advertisement campaign heavily dependent upon candidate image manipulation, a kind of politics that offers little accountability to the electorate and little attention to questions of economic and social justice.

Another problem is the limited choice offered by the two major parties. It is not quite accurate to characterize the Republicans and Democrats as Tweedledee and Tweedledum. Were they exactly alike in image and posture, they would have even more difficulty than they do in maintaining the appearances of choice. Therefore, it is preferable that the parties be fraternal rather than identical twins. From the perspective of those who advocate a basic change in national priorities and a restructuring of class power, the question is not, "Are there differences between the parties?" but, "Do the differences make a difference?" On most fundamental economic class issues, the similarities between the parties loom so large as frequently to obscure the differences. Both the Democratic and Republican parties are committed to the preservation of the private corporate economy; huge military budgets; the use of subsidies, deficit spending, and tax allowances to bolster business profits; the funneling of public resources through private conduits, including whole new industries developed at public expense; the use of repression against opponents of the existing class structure; the defense of the multinational corporate empire;

4. Seventeen states held primaries in 1968; thirty-six in 1980: Jack Walker, "Reforming the Reforms," *Wilson Quarterly*, 5, Autumn 1981, p. 88.

5. Frank Sorauf, *Party Politics in America*, 3rd ed. (Boston: Little, Brown, 1976), pp. 416–17. Herman Talmadge, former senator from Georgia, complained: "Today it's advertising agencies. They take some fellow, dress him up in their fashion, teach him to read from some idiot board for 20 seconds": *New York Times*, October 6, 1986.

and intervention against social-revolutionary elements abroad. In short, Republicans and Democrats are dedicated to strikingly similar definitions of the public interest, at great cost to the life chances of underprivileged people at home and abroad.

The lack of real class differences between the major parties is evident to the corporate business elites:

> Top executives may still be Republican, but they are no longer *partisan*. . . . Most of them have come to think it does not usually make all that much difference which party wins, and indeed that business and the country often fare better under the Democrats. Observes Rawleigh Warner, Jr., the chairman of Mobil: "I would have to say that in the last ten to fifteen years, business has fared equally well, if not better, under Democratic administrations as under Republican administrations." Other top executives echo Warner's sentiments.[6]

So, in a different tone, do progressive labor leaders like William Winpisinger, president of the International Association of Machinists: "We don't have a 2-party system in this country. We have the Demopublicans. It's one party of the corporate class, with two wings—the Democrats and Republicans."[7]

Rather than sharpening the partisan differences between the major parties, the accession of Ronald Reagan, an unequivocal right-wing conservative, seemed to blur them still further, as many Democrats retreated from a liberal agenda. None of Reagan's programs, neither the cutbacks in domestic services, nor the massive tax cuts favoring the upper-income brackets, nor the sharp escalation in the cold war and in miltary spending could have been enacted without help from a substantial number of Democrats.[8]

From a progressive point of view, the problem with the Democrats is not that they are worse than or as bad as the Republicans, but that they are *perceived* as being far less conservative than they really are. They are seen as the party of labor, the poor, and the minorities, when they have been the party of the business subsidies, tax breaks, and big military budgets almost as much as the GOP. The upshot is that popular constituencies decide that the Democrats have their hearts in the right place and are doing the best they can under the circumstances.[9] They forget that the Democrats are a major force in creating those circumstances.

---

6. Ladd, *Where Have All the Voters Gone?* p. 17.
7. *Guardian*, Special Report, Fall 1981.
8. See the discussion in Thomas Ferguson and Joel Rogers, *Right Turn, The Decline of the Democrats and the Future of American Politics* (New York: Hill and Wang, 1986).
9. Skipper Canis, "Better a Wolf in Wolf's Clothing," *Progressive*, October 1980, p. 32; also Michael Kinsley, "The Shame of the Democrats," *Washington Post*, July 23, 1981.

The similarities between the parties do not prevent them from competing vigorously for the prizes of office, expending huge sums in the doing. The very absence of significant disagreement on fundamentals makes it all the more necessary to stress the personalized features that differentiate oneself from one's opponent. As with industrial producers, the merchants of the political system have preferred to limit their competition to techniques of packaging and brand image. With campaign buttons and bumper stickers, television commercials and radio spots, with every gimmick devoid of meaningful content, the candidate sells his image as he would a soap product to a public conditioned to such bombardments.[10] His family and his looks; his experience in office and devotion to public service; his sincerity, sagacity, and fighting spirit; his military record, patriotism, and his determination to limit taxes, stop inflation, improve wages, and create new jobs by attracting industry into the area; his desire to help the worker, farmer, and businessperson, the young and old, the rich and poor, and especially those in between; his eagerness to end government waste and corruption and making the streets and the world itself safe by strengthening our laws, our courts, and our defenses abroad, bringing us lasting peace and prosperity with honor, and so forth—such are the inevitable appeals that like so many autumn leaves, or barn droppings, cover the land each November.[11] As someone once said: You can't fool all the people all of the time, but if you can fool them once it's good for four years.

This is not to deny there are significant differences between—and within—the major parties. Generally, progressives and liberals are more likely to find a home in the Democratic party and conservatives in the GOP. During the New Deal era, Democratic support came predominantly from racial and ethnic minorities, urban workers, Southerners, Catholics, and lower-income groups, while Republican strength rested mostly with White Protestants, middle-class professionals, Midwesterners, New Englanders, rural people, businesspeople, and upper-income strata. For several decades, however, the traditional constituency alignments have been shifting. Republicans are now regularly elected in the South and Democrats in Maine and Vermont, as patterns of one-party regional dominance break down and the parties become more national in scope.

Superimposed upon the old cleavages of class, religion, and region is the new ideological alignment which has led to a trading of supporters

---

10. Sidney Blumenthal, *The Permanent Campaign* (Boston: Beacon Press, 1980); Joe McGinnis, *The Selling of the President 1968* (New York: Simon and Schuster, 1970).

11. On the issueless, emotionalized political advertising in the 1984 campaign: Philip Dougherty, "Advertising: Reagan's Emotional Campaign," *New York Times*, November 8, 1984.

between the two parties. Democrats have gained new support among urban and suburban professionals outside the South who cannot abide the social conservatism and nuclear-minded foreign policy of hardline Republicans. Meanwhile, the Republicans have made inroads among well-to-do White Southerners and socially conservative Northern Whites, including Catholic ethnics. These conservative Democrats are attracted not to moderate Republicans but to right-wing Republicans. "Strom Thurmond, Jesse Helms, S. I. Hayakawa, John Connally, and Ronald Reagan all used to be Democrats, and all of them, as conservatives, found themselves out of place in their party. They 'realigned' and took many of their supporters with them."[12]

Recent studies also show that the Democratic Party has become, in terms of its supporters' income, increasingly bottom-heavy, and the GOP increasingly top-heavy.[13] Aware of conservative Republican hostility toward labor unions, organized workers have remained mostly in the Democratic column. Enduring the brunt of the antiegalitarian "Reagan Revolution," Blacks vote even more solidly Democratic than before. To a lesser extent, women also favor the Democratic party, since they are concerned about unequal opportunities in pay, employment, and promotion—and they see the Republicans as hostile to ERA and affirmative action.[14] Ironically, then, even as the major party organizations go into decline, and even as campaign advertising becomes increasingly mindless and manipulative, party labels are developing more ideological significance among the voters. And among the candidates too, "conservative" is increasingly associated with Republicans and "liberal" with Democrats.

THE TWO-PARTY MONOPOLY

Whatever their differences, the two major parties cooperate in various stratagems to maintain their monopoly over electoral politics and discourage the growth of progressive third parties. All fifty states have laws, written and enforced by Republican and Democratic officials, regulating and frequently discouraging third-party access to the ballot. Minor parties are required to gather large numbers of signatures on nominating petitions. In Pennsylvania, third-party candidates for statewide office must obtain the signatures of 36,000 registered voters within a three-week

---

12. William Schneider, "Realignment: the Eternal Question," *PS*, 15, Summer 1982, p. 452.

13. Survey data from the Center for Political Analysis, Ann Arbor, Mich., cited in *Washington Post*, February 5, 1984.

14. *Washington Post*, November 3, 1982 and November 5, 1986.

period. The requirements are becoming ever more rigorous: between 1980 and 1984, the states of Indiana and North Dakota, for instance, quadrupled the number of signatures needed, and Alabama went from none to 11,000.

In addition, a minor party faces limitations on where and when petitions may be circulated, who may circulate them, and who may sign. In Texas, every signer must not only be a registered voter but one who did not cast a ballot in the preceding presidential primary and who could recall his or her eight-digit voter identification number. In West Virginia, persons who sign a petition on behalf of a third party forfeit all rights to vote in that year's major-party primaries. A minor party must pay Florida ten cents for every signature it submits in that state. In Louisiana, an independent candidate must pay a $5,000 filing fee. In some states a nonrefundable filing fee must be paid just for the privilege of *trying* to get on the ballot. A third party would need over $750,000 in filing fees and other expenses to get on all state ballots in one national election. Petitions are often thrown out by hostile officials on trivial and sometimes false and unlawful technicalities, compelling minor parties to pursue court battles that further strain their limited financial resources.[15]

In the early 1980s, in at least seven states, some of the prohibitive restrictions against third parties were struck down after court battles.[16] Another positive development was the bill introduced by Representative John Conyers (D-Mich.) and eleven cosponsors to eliminate existing barriers to ballot access and institute a uniform federal election law.

It has been argued that restrictive ballot requirements are needed to screen out frivolous candidates. But who decides who is "frivolous"? And what is so deleterious about allegedly frivolous candidates that the electorate must be protected from them by all-knowing Democratic and Republican officials? In any case, the few states that allow an easy access to the ballot—such as Iowa and New Hampshire where only 1,000 signatures are needed and plenty of time is allowed to collect them—have suffered no invasion of frivolous or kooky candidates.

---

15. On the barriers against third-party electoral participation see Jimmie Rex McClellan, *Two-Party Monopoly* (Ph.D. dissertation, Institute for Policy Studies, Washington, D.C., 1984); Simon Gerson, *Does the U.S. Have Free Elections?* (New York: International Publishers, forthcoming); Richard Walton, "The Two-Party Monopoly," *Nation*, August 30–September 6, 1980, pp. 176–78; Joelle Fishman, "Connecticut Third CD—Ballot Status Retained" *Political Affairs*, January 1981, pp. 16–20.

16. See for instance *West Virginia Libertarian Party* v. *Manchin* (1982); *Socialist Workers Party* v. *Secretary of State* (1982). More recently however, a conservative Supreme Court in a 7 to 2 decision upheld a Washington state law that requires minor-party candidates to win at least 1 percent of the total primary election vote in order to be placed on the general election ballot: *Munro* v. *Socialist Workers Party* (1986), in effect depriving minor parties of ballot access.

The Federal Election Campaign Act of 1974 generously appropriates public funds to the two major parties (granting them over $110 million in 1986, divided equally between them, and including matching funds for primary campaigns and millions of dollars for their respective national conventions. But third-party candidates can receive public financing only *after* an election, and only if they glean 5 percent of the vote (about four million votes), something nearly impossible to achieve without generous funds and regular media access. "It's a classic Catch-22 situation: you don't get the money unless you get the 5 percent of the vote; you don't get the 5 percent unless you get the money."[17] Although exempted from federal monetary benefits under the 1974 act, third parties must observe all the act's record-keeping and reporting requirements and are subjected to its limitations on contribution and expenditure. A Federal Election Commission set up by the act, with a designated composition of three Republican and three Democratic commissioners, spends most of its time looking into the accounts of smaller parties and filing suits against them and other independent candidates. Thus, two private parties have been endowed with public authority to regulate the activities of other parties whose existence is otherwise ignored by federal law.[18]

According to a 1977 survey, half the nation's 13-year-olds believe it is against the law to start a third party.[19] In a sense they are correct: the electoral law is so written and applied by and for the major parties as to accord them something of an official status. We Americans would balk at seeing any particular religious denomination designated *the* state religion, to be favored by the law over all other religions; indeed, the Constitution forbids it. Yet we have accepted laws that, in effect, make the Democrats and Republicans *the* official state parties. At a time when they are less popular and less accepted than in a century, "this status serves to sustain them."[20]

The system of representation itself limits the opportunities of third parties. The single-member-district elections used throughout most of the United States tend to magnify the strength of the major parties and the weakness of the smaller ones, since the party that polls a plurality of the vote, be it 40, 50, or 60 percent, wins 100 percent of a district's representation with the election of its candidate, while smaller parties, regardless of their vote, receive zero representation. This is in contrast to a system of

---

17. Walton, "The Two-Party Monopoly," p. 177.

18. McClellan, *Two Party Monopoly*, Even the Postal Service does its bit to protect the two-party monopoly by granting lower rates to Republicans and Democrats while denying the same privilege to other parties: Walton, "The Two-Party Monopoly"; Gerson, *Does the U.S. Have Free Elections?*

19. *Progressive*, March 1977, p. 14.

20. Walton, "The Two-Party Monopoly."

proportional representation, existing in many western countries, which provides a party with legislative seats roughly in accordance with the percentage of votes it wins, assuring minor parties of some parliamentary presence. Duverger notes that under the winner-take-all system "the party placed third or fourth is underrepresented compared with the others: its percentage of seats is lower than its percentage of votes, and the disparity remains constantly greater than for its rivals. By its very definition proportional representation eliminates this disparity for all parties."[21] Thus, in the 1983 election in the United Kingdom, a third-party coalition of Social Democrats and Liberals known as the Alliance won almost 26 percent of the popular vote but less than 4 percent of the seats in the House of Commons.[22]

The winner-take-all single-member-district system deprives the minority parties not only of representation but eventually of voters too, since not many citizens wish to "waste" their ballots on a party that seems incapable of achieving a legislative presence. Some political scientists argue that proportional representation is undesirable because it encourages the proliferation of "splinter parties" and leads to legislative stalemate and instabilty. In contrast, the two-party system allows for a consensus politics devoid of fragmentation and polarization. American democracy is based on the measured competition of the two-party system, we are told.

In fact, through most of this century, in many parts of the country, one party has dominated over the other (as is still true in many rural and urban locales), so that the two-party system has been, in large part, a patchwork of one-party dominances.[23] Nor is it clear why present forms of "stability" and "consensus" are to be treated as sacrosanct. Stability is often just another word for "keeping things as they are." And consensus usually means collusion between the major-party leaders on the fundamentals of policy and class interests. Furthermore, we might wonder whether stalemate and fragmentation—supposedly the products of multiparty systems—do not characterize the *present* political system with its lack of coherent agendas and popularly accountable actions.

The monopoly electoral system is rigged in other ways so as to thwart

---

21. Maurice Duverger, *Political Parties* (New York: Wiley and Sons, 1955), p. 248, and the discussion on pp. 245–55; E. E. Schattschneider, *Party Government* (New York: Holt, Rinehart and Winston, 1960), pp. 74–84. In 1947, Benjamin Davis and Peter Cacchione, Communists elected to the city council in New York, lost their seats when the city shifted from proportional representation to single-member districts. The change was intended to freeze out the Communists and other dissident parties. Proposals were introduced to abolish proportional representation in local elections in Cambridge, Massachusetts, in 1972 after victories by a few radically oriented candidates.

22. *New York Times*, June 12, 1983.

23. Theodore Lowi, "Toward a More Responsible Three-Party System," *PS*, 16, Fall 1983, p. 699.

challenges from *within* as well as without the two-party system. A common device is *redistricting*, changing the boundaries of a constituency to guarantee a preferred political outcome. Consider this report on Jackson, Mississippi:

> While Blacks make up 47 percent of the population of this Mississippi capital city, no Black has been elected to city office here since 1912. . . . Since 1960, White suburbs have been annexed three times, each time substantially diluting Black voting strength just as it appeared Blacks were about to become a majority. And each election, like this one, has been characterized by racial bloc voting and increasingly apathetic Black voters.
>
> "Many Blacks in Jackson have just given up," [state legislator Henry] Kirksey said.[24]

One form of redistricting is the *gerrymander*. District lines are drawn in elaborately contorted ways so as to maximize the strength of the party that does the drawing.[25] Sometimes the purpose is to weaken the electoral base of progressive members in Congress, or in state legislatures, or in city councils, or to dilute the electoral strength of new or potentially dissident constituencies. In 1981, in Philadelphia, a Latino community of 63,000 anticipated control of at least one, and possibly two, seats in the Pennsylvania Assembly. Instead, their cohesive community was divided into a number of districts, none of which had more than a 15 percent Latino population. Chicago's Puerto Rican and Mexican-American community suffered a similar plight that same year. And the New York City Council split 50,000 working-class Black voters in Queens into three predominantly White districts, making them a numerical minority in all three. Although composing nearly 50 percent of New York's population, Blacks and Latinos have been able to elect only eight representatives of a forty-three member council, in part because of gerrymandering.[26]

If, despite rigged rules and official harassments, dissident groups continue to prove viable, then authorities are likely to resort to more violently

---

24. *Washington Post*, June 19, 1981. Blacks are nearly 12 percent of the population but compose only slightly more than 1 percent of the elected and appointed officials in the country: Jesse Jackson's commentary in *Washington Post*, June 16, 1986.

25. Named after an early practitioner of the method, Governor Elbridge Gerry of Massachusetts, who employed it in 1812, and "salamander," from the odd shape of the district. Congressional districts and state legislative districts are drawn by the state legislatures, subject to veto by the governors. City council districts are drawn by the municipal legislatures, usually subject to the approval of the mayor.

26. Juan Cartagena, "The Reapportionment Game," *Guild Notes*, March–April 1983, p. 4; *Daily World*, June 12 and July 30, 1981. Regarding redistricting struggles between Democrats and Republicans in California and Indiana, see *Wall Street Journal*, October 2, 1985 and excerpts from Declaration in *Badham* v. *Eu* by Bernard Grofman, Gordon Baker, Bruce Cain, and others, *PS*, 18, Summer 1985, pp. 538–581.

coercive measures. Almost every radical group that has ever managed to gain some grass-roots organizational strength has become the object of official violence. The case of the American Socialist party is instructive. By 1918, the Socialist party held 1,200 offices in 340 cities including seventy-nine mayors in twenty-four different states, thirty-two legislators, and a member of Congress. In 1919, after having increased its vote dramatically in various locales, the Socialists suffered the combined attacks of state, local, and federal authorities.[27] Their headquarters in numerous cities were sacked by police, their funds confiscated, their leaders jailed, their immigrant members deported, their newspapers denied mailing privileges, and their elected candidates denied their seats in various state legislatures and in Congress. Within a few years the party was finished as a viable political force. While confining themselves to legal and peaceful forms of political competition, the Socialists discovered that their opponents were burdened by no similar compunctions. The guiding principle of ruling elites was—and still is: *When change threatens to rule, then the rules are changed.*

The biggest handicap faced by third-party candidates—and progressive candidates within the major parties—is procuring the ever-increasing amounts of campaign funds needed to win and retain office. Money is the lifeblood of electoral politics, helping to determine the availability of personnel, organization, mobility, and that most important of all ingredients, media visibility. Without money the politician's days are numbered. Commenting on the plight of reformers in Congress, Representative Charles Vanik observed: "As things are now, the public-interest members here have no reward except personal satisfaction. In the long run most of them face defeat by the big-money people. Many of the best men who come here lose after one or two terms."[28]

Besides coping with money problems, progressive candidates must try to develop a plausible image among a citizenry conditioned for more than a century to hate socialists, communists, and other leftists. They find themselves dependent for exposure on mass media that are owned by the conservative interests they are attacking. They see that, along with the misrepresentations disseminated by a hostile press, the sheer paucity of information and haphazard reportage can make meaningful campaign dialogue nearly impossible. The dissenters compete not only against well-financed opponents but also against the media's many frivolous and stupefying distractions. Hoping to "educate the public to the issues," they

---

27. James Weinstein, *The Decline of American Socialism* (New York: Monthly Review Press, 1967).

28. Quoted in Richard Harris, "Annals of Politics," *New Yorker*, August 7, 1971. For a more detailed discussion of money in campaigns, see chapter 12.

discover that the media allow little opportunity for the expositions needed to make their position understandable to voters who might be willing to listen.

Candidates who hope to reach a mass electorate are largely dependent on mass media. For most voters the campaign has little reality apart from its media version. Since the media do not cover a third party's campaign, most people remain unaware of its existence. During presidential campaigns the television networks give the Democratic and Republican candidates ten to fifteen minutes of prime-time coverage every evening, while minor-party presidential candidates receive but a few minutes' exposure, if that, in their *entire* campaign. By withholding coverage from minor-party candidates while bestowing it lavishly on major-party ones, the media help perpetuate the two-party monopoly—at the very time more Americans are withdrawing their allegiance from the major parties.[29]

On those infrequent occasions when progressive dissenters win office as mayors, governors, or federal or state legislators, they often find themselves burdened by administrative duties or relegated to obscure legislative tasks. If they attempt changes, they run into the opposition of other elected and bureaucratic officials and of economic interests larger and more powerful than they. They frequently decide that "for now" they must make their peace with the powers that be, holding their fire until some future day when they can attack from higher ground. To get along they decide to go along. Thus begins the insidious process that lets a person believe he is still opposing the ongoing arrangements when in fact he has become a functional part of them. There are less subtle instances of cooptation, as when reformers are bought off with favors by those who hold the key to their survival. Once having won election, they may reverse their stands on fundamental issues and make common cause with established powers, to the dismay of their supporters.

Or they may not. Despite all discouragements and temptations, dedicated progressives—like Harold Washington, mayor of Chicago; Gus Newport, former mayor of Berkeley, California; and Bernard Sanders, mayor of Burlington, Vermont—are able to build, within the narrow limits of their office, honest, democratic, progressive administrations beneficial to ordinary voters.

In sum, of the various functions a political party might serve—(1) selecting candidates and waging election campaigns, (2) articulating and debating major issues, (3) formulating coherent and distinct programs, and (4) implementing a national program when in office—our parties fulfill none of these functions with any distinction. The parties are loose

29. McClellan, *Two-Party Monopoly*, Chapter 6.

conglomerations organized around one common purpose: the pursuit of office. For this reason, American parties have been characterized as "nonideological." And indeed they are—in the sense that their profound ideological commitment to capitalism at home and abroad and to the ongoing class structure is seldom made an explicit issue. The major parties have a conservative effect on the consciousness of the electorate and on the performance of representative government. They operate from a commonly shared ideological perspective that is best served by the avoidance of iconoclastic politico-economic views and by the suppression or cooptation of dissenters. In their common effort to blur and pass over fundamental issues, the major parties prevent class divisions from sharpening and serve the valuable function of maintaining a noisy, apolitical politics, distracting us from the real problems and narrowing the scope of participation while giving a busy appearance of popular government.[30]

According to democratic theory, electoral competition keeps political leaders accountable to their constituents. Politicians who wish to remain in office must respond to voter preferences in order to avoid being replaced by their rivals in the next election. But do the conditions of electoral competition actually exist? As noted earlier, legal, political, and moneyed forces so limit the range of alternatives as to raise serious questions about democratic accountability.

About one out of every ten Representatives are elected to Congress with no opposition in either the primary or the general election. During the 1970s and 1980s, from 90 to 96 percent of incumbents who sought congressional office were reelected.[31] Death and voluntary retirement seem to be the important factors behind the turnover in representative assemblies. In this respect, legislative bodies bear a closer resemblance to the nonelective judiciary than we would imagine.

THE RIGHT TO VOTE

Supposedly one of the great gifts of our democracy is the right to vote for the candidate of one's choice. But, as we have noted, the "choice" is often narrow and prestructured by a variety of undemocratic features. Further-

30. Following the 1968 Democratic Convention, reforms were instituted providing more equitable representation at Democratic party conventions for women, Blacks, and young people. These reforms were attacked by conservative Democrats, including academics, who argued that party professionals would be denied sufficient representation. Recent research indicated that such fears are unfounded: reform has not forced party regulars out of decision-making roles: Dennis Sullivan, Jeffrey Pressman, and Christopher Arterton, *Explorations in Convention Decision Making* (San Francisco: W. H. Freeman, 1976).

31. *Washington Post*, September 8, 1982 and November 6, 1986.

more, although two centuries of struggle have brought real gains in extending the franchise, the opportunity to vote is still not available to everyone.

From the early days of the Republic, rich propertied interests sought to limit popular participation. Large numbers of propertyless White males, and all indentured servants, women, Blacks (including freed slaves), and native American Indians had no access to the ballot. In the wake of working-class turbulence during the 1820s and 1830s, formal property qualifications were abolished for White males. And after a century of agitation, women won the right to vote with the adaption of the Nineteenth Amendment in 1920. In 1961, the Twenty-third Amendment allowed District of Columbia residents to vote in presidential elections (but they are still denied full voting representation in Congress). In 1971, the Twenty-sixth Amendment lowered the minimum voting age to eighteen for all elections.

The Fifteenth Amendment, ratified in 1870, written as it were in the blood of civil war, prohibited voter discrimination because of race. But it took another century of struggle to make this right something more than a formality. In 1944, the Supreme Court ruled that all-white party primaries were unconstitutional.[32] Decades of agitation and political pressure (augmented by the growing voting power of Blacks in Northern cities), led to the Civil Rights Acts of 1957 and 1960, the Voting Rights Acts of 1965, 1970, 1975, and 1985, and several crucial Supreme Court decisions.[33] Taken together, these measures (a) gave the federal government and courts power to act against state officials who were discriminating against non-Whites at the polls, and (b) eliminated state restrictions—such as long-term residency requirements, literacy tests, and poll taxes—that had sharply reduced the electoral participation of the poor and less educated. The result was that in certain parts of the South, Blacks began voting in visible numbers for the first time since Reconstruction.

Yet low-income people, be they Black, Latino, or White, still vote at about half the rate of the more affluent,[34] according to a 1984 report. One reason is that while legal restrictions have been removed, administrative barriers remain largely in place. "There is still only one registration office in most counties; it is still usually open only during working hours; and it is likely to be administered by political appointees hostile to minority groups and the poor."[35] In a county in Texas, officials closed down all but one of

---

32. *Smith* v. *Allwright* (1944).

33. The Supreme Court decisions are: *Harper* v. *Virginia State Board of Elections* (1966) on poll taxes, and *Dunn* v. *Blumstein* (1972) on residency requirements.

34. *New York Times*, August 18, 1984.

35. Richard Cloward and Frances Fox Piven, "Trying to Break Down the Barriers," *Nation*, November 2, 1985, p. 436.

thirteen polling places, and that one was a considerable distance from the major Black and Latino population centers. As a result, minority voter turnout plummeted from 2,300 to 300.[36] "In Mississippi," notes one voter registration organizer, "a person has to sign up both at a town courthouse and then at the county courthouse. This can mean driving ninety miles in some cases."[37]

Administrative barriers exist nationwide, not just in the South, and are directed at the working class as a whole. More than half of the major registration suits filed during the 1984 campaign were taken against election officials in Northern states.[38] According to the standard view, working-class people and the poor have a low turnout because they are wanting in information, education, and civic involvement. But if they are so naturally inclined to apathy, one wonders why entrenched interests find it necessary to erect such elaborate barriers against their participation.

With conservatives controlling the White House and the Justice Department through most of the 1980s, the discouragements—particularly against those likely to vote against the Republican ticket—intensified. Reagan administration officials threatened to cut off federal aid in attempts to get state and local agencies to deny space in their buildings for registration booths. They urged states to prohibit registration drives at food lines, and some did so. Voting-rights activists who tried to register people in welfare offices were arrested. In 1984, the Republican-appointed Postmaster General issued an unprecedented order prohibiting postal employees from taking part in voter registration efforts even on lunch breaks and in nonwork areas—because the union had endorsed the Democratic presidential candidate and was therefore judged to be engaging in politically partisan activity. Likewise the government issued an advisory opinion that federal employees whose union had endorsed a candidate may not engage in voter registration.[39]

In 1986 carloads of FBI agents streamed into five Southern counties that had Black majorities and interrogated over 2,000 Black voters about whether their absentee ballots were fraudulently cast. While they found no evidence of fraud, they did intimidate some voters into thinking twice about ever voting again and they indicted eight voting-rights activists on 215 criminal charges. Five of the activists were acquitted; two plea-bargained to misdemeanors and one was convicted of violations less serious than those that White registrars had long been committing with impunity.

---

36. John Conyers, Jr. and Neil Kotler, "The Blacks," *Progressive*, October 1982, p. 40.
37. Joe Madison of the NAACP, quoted in the *Guardian*, February 22, 1984, p. 3.
38. Cloward and Piven, loc. cit.
39. Jack Anderson, "U.S. Squelches Some Voter Drives," *Washington Post*, October 27, 1985.

The Alabama state legislature passed a "reidentification" law requiring counties with a concentration of low-income, anti-Reagan voters to re-register at inconvenient hours in obscure locations, with hostile officials presiding over the process. Since many poor Blacks were without transportation and many were still economically dependent on Whites, the result was a marked decrease in Afro-American registration.[40]

Another ploy is to institute at-large elections, a rarity in Southern towns before 1965, now all but universal, and not unknown in Northern locales where Blacks and Latinos are gathering numerical strength. Instead of election by district, the at-large election gives a winner-take-all victory to one or another citywide slates, allowing complete White domination and freezing out minority representation.[41] Given all these discouragements it is no wonder that many poor people are nonvoters.

To worsen matters, nonvoting has a feedback effect. For as fewer among the poor and the racial minorities vote, the politicians pay even less attention to them, further convincing the nonparticipants that the realm of politics is inaccessible to them and that there is no reason to go to the polls—thereby intensifying the cycle of powerlessness.[42] Thus, the unresponsiveness of the system discourages the participation and diminishes the influence of the very people who are most in need of democratic representation.

NONVOTERS AND MEANINGFUL PARTICIPATION

The false campaign claims propagated by politicians are a further discouragement to voting. With good reason people complain: "Politicians tell us one thing to get our votes and then do another thing once they are elected." If many politicians are dissemblers and half-truth artists, it is not necessarily because they are morally flawed in their personalities (although some of them are indeed so). Rather, they are caught in the contradiction

40. See *Vote Fraud Trials Threaten Democracy* (Alabama Blackbelt Defense Committee, Gainesville, Ala., February 1986). Two years earlier the Justice Department indicted two Afro-American women; they were convicted and sentenced to four and five years, the stiffest sentences ever in an Alabama voting-fraud case. Their crime? Of the thirty-nine elderly Blacks whose absentee ballots they gathered, one infirm lady said they signed her name to the ballot; all the others said they signed their own names.

41. Chuck Foger, "The March Back," *City Paper* (Washington, D.C.), January 11, 1985, p. 8.

42. A key factor in the drop in voter participation is "the decline in beliefs about government responsiveness": Paul Abramson and John Aldrich, "The Decline of Electoral Participation in America," *American Political Science Review*, 76, September 1982, p. 519. Voter turnout in the 1980 and 1984 presidential elections and primaries and in the 1986 congressional elections were the lowest in more than twenty years: *Washington Post*, September 27, 1986; and Simon Gerson's column in the *People's Daily World*, November 28, 1986.

of having to be both a "candidate of the people" and—if they want to survive and advance—a servant of the particular needs of rich and powerful contributors and of the systemic needs of multinational capitalism.

Many people fail to vote, because (1) they do not find anyone who appeals to them, and (2) they have trouble believing that voting makes a difference. Interviews in various districts in Pittsburgh found many people complaining that there was no one to vote for in the 1984 Democratic primary. They did not like the incumbent president (Ronald Reagan) nor believed that any of the Democratic candidates were much better. And they doubted that anything would change. Some finally went to the polls but with little enthusiasm.[43] Of those Americans who had voted for Carter in 1976, 28 percent were so turned off by his subsequent doings and so unmoved by his challenger, Reagan, that they stayed home in 1980.[44] A nationwide survey in 1982 found that "for the great majority of citizens interviewed" nonvoting was a result of the anger and frustration they harbored toward the choices available. Some felt there was a dearth of qualified candidates; others complained that candidates did not care about voters. As one 44-year-old female factory worker in New Jersey said: "I wasn't interested in any of the candidates. They weren't helping poor people, they were helping the rich."[45]

It has been argued that since nonvoters tend to be among the less educated and more apathetic, then it is just as well they do not exercise their franchise. Since they are likely to be swayed by prejudice and demagogy, their activation would constitute a potential threat to our democratic system.[46] Behind this reasoning lurks the dubious presumption that better-educated, upper-income people who vote are more rational and less compelled by narrow self-interests and racial and class prejudices, an impression that itself is one of those comforting prejudices upper- and middle-class people have of themselves.

Some writers argue that low voter turnout is symptomatic of a "politics of happiness": people are apathetic about voting because they are fairly

---

43. Survey reported on the CBS evening news, April 11, 1984. In Reagan's "overwhelming" victories in 1980 and 1984, less than 30 percent of the eligible voters in the nation voted for him; almost 50 percent stayed home. In midterm congressional elections over the last twenty years, nonparticipation has ranged from 55 to 65 percent.

44. Elizabeth Drew, "A Political Journal," *New Yorker*, February 20, 1984.

45. *Washington Post*, September 23, 1982.

46. For a typical example of this view see Seymour Lipset, *Political Man* (Garden City, N.Y.: Doubleday, 1960), pp. 215–19. Occasionally, there is an admission by the well-to-do that voting should be limited not to protect democracy but to protect the well-to-do. A letter to the *New York Times* (December 6, 1971) offered these revealing words: "If everybody voted, I'm afraid we'd be in for a gigantic upheaval of American society—and we comfortable readers of the *Times* would certainly stand to lose much at the hands of the poor, faceless, previously quiet throngs. Wouldn't it be best to let sleeping dogs lie?"

content with the way things are going.[47] Certainly some people are blithely indifferent to political issues—even issues that seem to affect their lives in important ways. But generally speaking, the many millions of Americans outside the voting universe are not among the more contented but among the less affluent and more alienated, displaying an unusual concentration of socially deprived characteristics. The "politics of happiness" is usually nothing more than a cover for the politics of discouragement. What is seen as apathy may really be antipathy. In any case, apathy is often a psychological defense against powerlessness and frustration. Nonparticipation is not the result of contentment or lack of civic virtue but an understandably negative response to the political realities people experience.[48]

Many regular *voters* share the disillusionment of alienated nonvoters, manifesting low interest in the election's outcome and a low trust in public officials. About the same number of voters as nonvoters are convinced that government is run "for a few big interests" rather than for the benefit of all the people. This would suggest that many people vote less because of substantive issues than out of a ritualized sense of civic duty. For them the vote is an exercise more of civic virtue than civic power.[49] This raises the question of who really are the deadwood of democracy: the "apathetic" or the "civic minded," those who see no reason to vote or those who vote with no reason?

Of course, there are other inducements to voting besides a sense of civic obligation. Voters who ascribe undesirable traits to one party are sometimes then inclined to find virtue in the other. Thus, the suspicion that Democrats might favor Blacks and labor unions leads some Whites to assume that the Republican party is devoted to their interests, a conclusion that may have no basis in the actual performance of Republican officeholders. Similarly, the identification of Republicans as the party of big business suggests to some working-class voters that, in contrast, the Democrats are *not* for business but for the "little man," a conclusion that may be equally unfounded in most instances.

---

47. Heinz Eulau, "The Politics of Happiness," *Antioch Review*, 16, 1956, pp. 259–64; Lipset, *Political Man*, pp. 179–219.

48. Penn Kimball, *The Disconnected* (New York: Columbia University Press, 1972); David Hull and Norman Luttbeg, *Trends in American Electoral Behavior*, 2nd ed. (Itasca, Ill.: F. E. Peacock, 1983), pp. 85–94. One national survey found that nonvoters are not among the more content; they just do not believe their votes would bring any changes for the better: *New York Times*, September 25, 1983.

49. On the attitudes of alienated voters see *New York Times*/CBS News poll: *New York Times*, November 16, 1976 and November 16, 1980; Angus Campbell, et al., *The American Voter* (New York: Wiley and Sons, 1960), pp. 103–6. A *Washington Post*/ABC News poll finds: "To some extent, many people continue to go to the polls because they feel they have to—that their vote is important—and not because they like the choices offered them": *Washington Post*, September 23, 1982.

"I'M HAVING SECOND THOUGHTS ABOUT THE ELECTION... I'M NOT SURE I VOTED AGAINST THE RIGHT PERSON."

When magnified by partisan rhetoric, the differences between the parties appear worrisome enough to induce millions of citizens to vote—if not *for* then *against* someone. Voters who have no great hope that the incumbent will do much for them, might persistently fear that the challenger will make things even worse. Or conversely, they may dislike the challenger but reluctantly vote for him only because the incumbent has become unbearable. This lesser-of-two-evils appeal is the single most effective inducement to voter participation and is a marvelous ruling-class device. The people are offered a candidate who violates their interests and who is dedicated to the preservation of capitalism at home and abroad, then they are presented with another candidate who promises to be even worse. Thus, they are not so much *offered* a choice as *forced* into one.[50]

---

50. *New York Times*/CBS News poll found that voters participating in 1980 presidential primary contests most frequently cited "the lesser of evils" as the determinant of candidate choice: *New York Times*, June 4, 1980. A 1984 survey found that voters seemed most clear on who they wanted to vote *against*: 43 percent were determined to oppose Reagan and 48 percent were set against Mondale: "Voters Know What They Don't Like," *Business Week*, June 11, 1984.

On those infrequent occasions when a dedicated candidate emerges who has a chance of winning and who demonstrates his or her commitment to the people, constituents are more inclined to participate, for they begin to perceive that voting can influence public policy and that there is a real—and realistic—choice. In Burlington, Vermont, for instance, six years of rule by the Progressive Coalition (1981–87), led by socialist mayor Bernard Sanders, brought marked improvements in the city government. The condition of Burlington's streets, sidewalks, and sewers noticeably improved. Youth employment programs and cultural activities were implemented. Against the opposition of landlords and business, the Sanders administration attempted to institute a more equitable distribution of the tax burden and reforms in utility rates, while imposing no new property taxes on homeowners. Significantly enough, voter turnout in Burlington—especially in the low-income districts—increased dramatically. City council races no longer went uncontested and thousands of people regularly turned out for public hearings on various issues.[51]

Studies show that when presented with distinct issue-linked choices, voters do respond, in the large, according to their policy preferences. Black turnout increases significantly when an election offers a Black candidate who is perceived as concerned with the needs of the Afro-American community—even when the prospects for victory are modest. The 1986 Senatorial elections brought victory mostly to candidates who stressed bread-and-butter issues like jobs, Social Security, Medicare, and the plight of farm families.[52]

The argument is sometimes made that if deprived groups have been unable to win their demands from the political system, it is because they are numerically weak compared to White, middle-class America. In a system that responds to the democratic power of numbers, a minority poor cannot hope to have its way. The deficiency is in the limited numbers of persons advocating change and not in the representative system, which operates according to majoritarian principles. What is curious about this argument is that it is never applied to more select minority interests—for instance, oilmen. Now oilmen are far less numerous than the poor, yet the deficiency of their numbers, or of the numbers of other tiny minorities like bankers, industrialists, and millionaire investors, does not result in any lack of government responsiveness to their wants. On most important matters government policy is determined less by the majoritarian principle

---

51. Steven Soiter, "Socialist Sanders Wins Big in Burlington," *Guardian*, March 20, 1985, p. 7.

52. V. O. Key, Jr., with Milton Cummings, Jr., *The Responsible Electorate* (Cambridge, Mass.: Harvard University Press, 1966); Benjamin Page and Richard Brody, "Policy Voting and the Electoral Process," *American Political Science Review*, 59, March 1965, p. 27; Conyers and Kotler, "The Blacks"; *Washington Post*, November 29, 1986.

and more by the economic strength of private interests. The fact that government does little for the minority poor does not mean that it operates according to majoritarian principles, for it does very little for the working majority in general and quite a bit for privileged economic minorities.

THE DEMOCRATIC INPUT

There are two sweeping propositions that might mistakenly be drawn from what has been said thus far: (1) It does not matter who is elected. (2) Elected officials are indifferent to voter desires and other popular pressures. Both these notions are far from being the whole picture.

Many people reject voting not only because they feel there is no choice but because they see politics itself as something that cannot deliver anything significant even if a dedicated candidate is elected. And given the plutocratic dominance of the two-party monopoly, they are not too far wrong. Yet it should be noted that even within the confines of capitalist public policy, people's lives can be affected for better or worse by what happens within the electoral realm. Having correctly observed that two-party elections are designed to blur real issues, some people incorrectly conclude that what Democrats and Republicans do once elected to office is also inconsequential and farcical. In truth, major-party policies can have an important effect on our well-being—as the previous chapters on what government does in the realm of health, education, the environment, taxation, and foreign and military policy testify.

In Western Europe, benefiting from the more democratic system of proportional representation, left-wing parties have established a viable presence in parliaments, even ruling from time to time. While this has never proven sufficient to bring the structural changes needed for socialism, the left-wing parties have helped create labor conditions superior to those found in the United States. Be it disposable income, paid vacations, family allowances, safety conditions, protection from speed-ups, the right to collective bargaining, or job security, American employees have less protection and fewer benefits than their French, German, Scandinavian, and Benelux counterparts. Among industrialized capitalist nations, the United States possesses one of the highest unemployment rates and one of the lowest levels of social services. Lacking any form of organized mass challenge to the existing distribution of wealth and income, and possessing a two-party monopoly that effectively freezes out a socialist critique, U.S. capitalism is even more successful than European capitalism in shifting onto the working populace the cost of public programs and business subsidies, and the austerities caused by capital flight abroad, foreign competition, and cutbacks in human services.[53]

> Countries like Finland and Sweden, where parties are perceived to have clear class practices, have higher rates of electoral involvement, higher voter turnout, and more extensive welfare states than those that don't have these practices. Indeed, societies in which the political and economic instruments of labor are perceived as class instruments have lower income inequality between the top and bottom layers, a higher percentage of GNP allocated to social expenditures, a higher level of overall progressive taxation, and lower unemployment. It is in those countries in which class practices within the working class do not exist and in which labor operates as one more interest group (highly divided into different subgroups, each one looking out for its own), that we find a depoliticization of the population, with low voter turnout and a fragmentation of politics. This is precisely what is happening in today's U.S.[54]

Aside from the differences between nations, within the U.S. context itself it can be said that while many electoral contests are meaningless, some reflect real differences between reactionary and progressive forces. Who is elected, then, *can* make a difference within a limited but important range of policy options.

In addition, there is ample evidence indicating that elected representatives are not totally indifferent to voter demands, since—along with money—votes are still the means to office and empowerment.[55] To be sure, officeholders often respond with deceitful assurances. For instance, dozens of members of Congress who pledged to vote *against* draft registration in 1978 voted *for* it in 1980. The heaviest applause line in Jimmy Carter's 1977 Inaugural Address was his vow to "move this year a step towards our ultimate goal—the elimination of all nuclear weapons from this Earth." But his administration then went on to build two or three more bombs a day. In an elaborate publicity campaign President Reagan pledged a war against narcotics—and then went on to cut federal funds for drug rehabilitation programs in 1987.

Politicians frequently make false assurances and empty promises, but the pressures of democratic opinion and the need to maintain electoral

53. "Labor at Home and Abroad," *Economic Notes*, January 1985, pp. 1–15; James Petras and Robert Rhodes, "The Reconstruction of U.S. Hegemony," *New Left Review*, May–June 1976, pp. 37–53.

54. Vicente Navarro, "The 1980 and 1984 U.S. Elections and the New Deal," *Social Policy*, Spring 1985, pp. 3–10.

55. See Benjamin Page and Robert Shapiro, "Effects of Public Opinion on Policy," *American Political Science Review*, 77, 1983, pp. 175–190.

support sometimes force them to place limits on how single-mindedly they may serve the moneyed powers and how unresponsive they may remain to the needs of ordinary people. Popular sentiments and actions directed at a number of issues such as Social Security, a negotiated arms settlement with the Soviet Union, the removal of U.S. troops from Lebanon, and sanctions against South Africa, moved officeholders, including conservative ones, to take stances that were not normally part of their elitist inclinations. Another example: in 1986, determined to veto toxic-waste legislation passed by Congress, President Reagan ended up reluctantly signing the bill into law "because the president listened to the plaintive cries of Republicans up for re-election."[56]

To summarize some points in this chapter: Important structural and material factors so predetermine the range of electoral choices as to raise a serious question about the representative quality of the political system. Being enormously expensive affairs, elections are best utilized by those interests endowed with the resources necessary to take best advantage of them. Politics has always been principally "a rich man's game." Ironically, the one institutional arrangement ostensibly designed to register the will of the many serves to legitimize the rule of the privileged few and often excludes those most in need.

The way people respond to political reality depends on the way that reality is presented to them. If large numbers have become apathetic and cynical, including many who vote, it is at least partly because the electoral system and the two-party monopoly resist the kind of creative involvement that democracy is supposed to nurture. It is one thing to say that people tend to be uninvolved and poorly informed about political life. It is quite another to maintain a system that propagates these tendencies with every known distraction and discouragement. Elections might better be considered a symbol of democratic governance than a guarantee of it, and voting often seems to be less an exercise than a surrender of sovereignty.

Still, in the face of all discouragements, third-party challenges continue to arise among people who seek a democratic alternative—bringing to mind the observation made years ago by the great American socialist Eugene Debs: "I would rather vote for what I want and not get it than vote for what I don't want and get it." These are not always the only two choices. A third-party vote is not necessarily a wasted vote. Third parties often have an impact on the major parties, forcing them to incorporate issues and adopt stances originating outside the two-party ideological monopoly.

---

56. *New York Times*, October 21, 1986, quoting a conservationist spokesperson.

Finally, even within the two-party context, elections remain one of the potential soft spots in the capitalist political order, vulnerable to the impact of popular sentiments. When an issue wins broad, well-organized support and receives some attention in the media, then officeholders cannot remain supremely indifferent to it. The grass-roots pressures of demonstrations, civil disobedience, strikes, boycotts, riots, and other forms of popular agitation, along with the mobilization of voters and involvement in electoral campaigns can have a direct effect on who is elected and how they behave once in office.

11

Who Governs? Leaders, Lobbyists, or Labor?

Those who control the wealth of this society have an influence over its political life far in excess of their number. They have the inside track on how government must deal with the (capitalist) economy. The owning class has the power to influence policy decisions through the control of jobs and the withholding of investments. In addition, since no system automatically maintains and reproduces itself, the capitalists use some portion of their vast wealth to finance or exercise trusteeship over social and educational institutions, foundations, think tanks, publications, and mass media, thereby greatly influencing society's ideological output, its values and information flow. This power does not result in total ideational domination but it usually gives the plutocracy a preponderate influence in setting the outer limits of respectable discourse and shaping the nation's political agenda.

Along with these broad systemic powers, the owning class tends to political affairs in a more direct way. The capitalists occupy public office or see that persons loyal to them do. In that way they can (1) best pursue their own particular interests, and (2) safeguard the capitalist social order in its entirety.

THE RULING CLASS

Alexis de Tocqueville once said that the wealthy have little desire to govern the working people, they simply want to use them.[1] Yet, members of the

1. Alexis de Tocqueville, *Democracy in America*, vol. 2 (New York: Vintage, 1945), p. 171.

owning class seldom have been slow in assuming the burdens of public office. Not every important political leader is rich but many are, and those who are not are usually beholden to moneyed interests. Not all wealthy persons are engaged in ruling; some prefer to concentrate on other pursuits. The ruling class, or plutocracy, consists largely of the politically active members of the owning class.

From the beginning of the Republic to modern times, the top leadership positions—including the presidency, vice-presidency, the cabinet, and Supreme Court—have rested predominantly in the hands of White males from wealthy families, with most of the remainder being of upper-middle class origins (moderately successful businesspeople, commercial farmers, and professionals). In recent times, political leaders have been drawn from the directorships of big corporations, the prominent law firms and banks of Wall Street, and, less frequently, from the military, elite universities, foundations, and the scientific establishment. Of those who went to college more than a third went to elite Ivy League schools.[2] The men who ran the nation's defense establishment in the decades after World War II, "were so like one another in occupation, religion, style and social status that, apart from a few Washington lawyers, Texans and mavericks, it was possible to locate the offices of all of them within fifteen city blocks in New York, Boston and Detroit."[3]

The wealthy carry into public life many of the class interests and values that shape their business careers. Be they of "old families" or newly arrived, liberal or conservative, they do not advocate democratic alternatives to the economic system under which they prosper. The few rich persons who adopt markedly left leanings are not invited into positions of power. Conversely, persons from relatively modest class background such as Richard Nixon, attract the financial backing that enables them to rise to the top by showing themselves to be faithful guardians of the privileged circles. Some politicians, academic advisors, and journalists are coopted into the ruling ranks, but for the most part, the plutocracy recruits its top members from its own social class. In any case, the crucial factor is not the

---

2. Sidney Aronson, *Status and Kinship in the Higher Civil Service* (Cambridge, Mass.: Harvard University Press, 1964); Philip Burch Jr., *Elites in American History*, vols. 1–3 (New York: Holmes and Meier, 1980, 1981); G. William Domhoff, *The Powers That Be* (New York: Vintage, 1979); Beth Mintz, "The President's Cabinet," *Insurgent Sociologist* 5, Spring 1975, pp. 131–148; John Schmidhauser, *The Supreme Court* (New York: Holt, Rinehart and Winston, 1960). Legend has it that most U.S. presidents rose from humble origins. In fact, almost all came from families of a higher socioeconomic status than almost ninety percent of the American population: Edward Pessen, *The Social Background of the Presidents* (New Haven, Conn.: Yale University Press, 1984). Throughout most of our history, working-class children rarely have been able to secure the higher education and advanced professional training necessary to put them on the road to prominent political office.

3. Richard Barnet, *Roots of War* (New York: Atheneum, 1972), pp. 48–49.

"The Duke and Duchess of A.T. & T., the Count and Countess of Citicorp, the Earl of Exxon, and the Marchioness of Avco. The Duke of Warnaco . . ."

class origin of leaders but the class interest they serve. The question is not only who governs, but whose interests and whose agenda are served by who governs, who benefits and who does not—which is why so much attention is given in this book to policy outputs.

Government and business elites are linked by institutional, financial, and social ties and move easily between public and private leadership posts. Policy-advisory organizations, with their interlocking network of corporate and political notables, play an unofficial but influential role in shaping U.S. policies and recruiting elites for leadership posts during both Democratic and Republican administrations. One of the more prominent of these policy organizations is the Council on Foreign Relations (CFR), which had a major influence in creating the International Monetary Fund and the World Bank. In the 1960s, the CFR advocated U.S. military intervention in South Vietnam and diplomatic relations with China. In 1980, the CFR strongly recommended a sharp escalation in military spending and a harder line toward the Soviets. All of these positions were, in turn, eventually adopted by whomever was in the White House. The private companies with the most members on the CFR have been Morgan Guaranty Trust, Chase Manhattan Bank, Citibank, and IBM.[4]

Much of the CFR membership overlapped with the Trilateral Commission, an assemblage of business and political elites from the major capitalist countries, initiated by David Rockefeller for the purpose of coordinating and protecting international capitalism in a changing world. Other prominent elite organizations include the Committee for Economic Development (CED), which consists of about two hundred business leaders. Working through study groups aided by academic specialists, the CED produces policy statements on a range of domestic and international issues. "Several of the statements bear a striking similarity to government policies that were enacted at a later time."[5]

Then there is the Business Council, composed of the nation's top financiers, bankers, and industrialists, drawn from such companies as Chase Manhattan Bank, Morgan Guaranty Trust, General Electric, and General Motors. Ostensibly an independent organization, Business Council members hold regular three-day private meetings with top government officials in a posh hotel just outside Washington, where they conduct panels and hold informal talks.[6]

Organizations like the Council on Foreign Relations, the CED, the Trilateral Commission, and the Business Council avoid promoting the interests of particular enterprises and seek to develop policies for the overall system. Rather than being special-interest lobbyists, they are ideological or class-interest lobbyists. Their influence is drawn from their systemic position, from the persuasiveness that inheres in the enormous economic power they wield. Their influence also is realized in their capac-

---

4. G. William Domhoff, *Who Rules America Now?* (New York: Simon and Schuster, 1983). Regarding their social ties: many elites go to the same schools, work in the same firms, intermarry, and vacation together. For almost a century, the top decision makers in business and government have gathered every summer at Bohemian Grove, a male-only retreat in California: G. William Domhoff, "Politics Among the Redwoods," *Progressive*, January 1981, pp. 32–36.

5. Domhoff, *Who Rules America Now?*, p. 89.

6. The 154 Business Council members listed in *Who's Who in America* together held 730 directorships in 435 banks and corporations, as well as 49 foundation trusteeships, and 125 trusteeships with 84 universities: Domhoff, *Who Rules America Now?*, p. 134. For a detailed listing of the membership and business affiliations of the Business Council (and of the CED and CFR), see Philip Burch Jr., "The American Establishment: Its Historical Development and Major Economic Components," *Research in Political Economy*, vol. 6 (Greenwich, Conn.: JAI Press, 1983), pp. 83–156.

ity—unique among social groups—to fill top government posts with persons from their ranks or at least persons friendly to their interests.

Members of these upper-class organizations have served as U.S. presidents, vice-presidents, secretaries of state and defense, and other cabinet positions, and have at times virtually monopolized the membership of the National Security Council, the nation's highest official policy-making body.[7] President Ford appointed fourteen CFR members to positions in his administration. Seventeen top members of President Carter's administration were Trilateralists, including Carter himself and Vice-President Mondale.

As an ultraconservative, Ronald Reagan ostensibly stood closer to the new wealth of the Sunbelt than his more establishment predecessors, closer to right-wing advisory groups like the Center for Strategic and International Studies, and the Heritage Foundation, and business groups like the conservative National Association of Manufacturers (NAM). Yet his top administrators included chief executives of Wall Street investment houses and directors of New York banks. At least a dozen of them and thirty-one advisors were members of the Council on Foreign Relations. In its composition the Reagan crew was really not too different from earlier millionaire-dominated administrations.[8]

LOBBYISTS AND THEIR INTERESTS

Corporate elites are also heavily involved in lobbying and the selection of candidates for elective office, activities that involve less reliance on social position as such and more active use of large sums of money. The importance of money in campaigns will be treated in the next chapter. Here we will concentrate on lobbying.

Lobbyists are persons hired by interest groups to influence legislative and administrative policies. Some political scientists see lobbying as a

---

7. Holly Sklar (ed.), *Trilateralism* (Boston: South End Press, 1980). Domhoff, *Who Rules American Now?*; Burch, "The American Establishment . . ."; Laurence Shoup, *The Carter Presidency and Beyond* (Berkeley, Calif.: Ramparts Press, 1980).

8. Ron Brownstein and Nina Easton, *Reagan's Ruling Class* (Washington, D.C.: Center for the Study of Responsive Law, 1982); Domhoff, *Who Rules America Now?*, pp. 139–40. Supposedly a cleavage exists between "Eastern Establishment" capitalists and Sunbelt capitalists. In fact, major wealth does not divide along those regional lines. The Rockefellers have as much invested in oil, defense, and high technology in the Southwest as any "cowboy capitalist," who, in turn, usually has holdings in the East. The major division is ideological, between "moderate" conservatives and ultraconservatives. But on many issues the two tendencies manage to find common ground. A partial list of big contributors to Ronald Reagan's presidential campaigns include not only Texan oil and silver billionaires but also Eastern Establishment capitalists like David Rockefeller, chairman of Chase Manhattan.

"communication process": the officeholder's perception of an issue is influenced primarily by the information provided him or her—and the lobbyist's job is to be the provider. But this process does not occur in a social vacuum. Often the arguments made on behalf of an issue are less important than who is making them and what interests he or she represents. As one congressional committee counsel explains it: "There's the 23-year-old consumer lobbyist and the businessman who gives you $5,000. Whom are you going to listen to?"[9]

Supposedly the techniques of the "modern" lobbyist consist of disseminating data and giving informative testimony before legislative committees rather than the obsolete tactics of secret deals and bribes.[10] In fact, the development of new lobbying techniques have not brought an end to the older, cruder ones. Along with the slick brochures, expert testimony, and technical reports, corporate lobbyists still have the succulent campaign contributions, the secret slush funds, the "volunteer" campaign workers, the fat lecture fees, the stock awards and insider stock market tips, the easy term loans, the high-paying corporate directorship upon retirement from office, the lavish parties and prostitutes, the prepaid vacation jaunts, the luxury hotels and private jets, the free housing and meals, and the many other hustling enticements of money. "Many a financial undertaking on Capitol Hill," writes Washington columnist Jack Anderson, "has been consumated in cold cash—that is, with envelopes or briefcases stuffed with greenbacks, a curious medium for honorable transactions."[11]

Summing up the power of lobbyists, former Speaker of the House Tip O'Neill said: "The grab of special interests is staggering. It will destroy the legislative process."[12] It has certainly destroyed much legislative integrity. The case of Claude Wild, Jr., is instructive. As a vice-president of Gulf Oil and a lobbyist over a twelve-year period, Wild had the full-time job of passing out about $4.1 million of Gulf's money to more than 100 U.S. senators and representatives, eighteen governors, and scores of judges and local politicians. His gift list included Presidents Lyndon Johnson, Richard

---

9. Peter Kinzler quoted in "Business Battles Back," *Environmental Action*, December 2, 1978, p. 14.

10. Lester Milbrath, *The Washington Lobbyists* (Chicago: Rand McNally, 1963), p. 185 and passim; also Douglass Cater's comparison of the "new" with the "old" NAM in his *Power in Washington* (New York: Random House, 1964), p. 208.

11. *Washington Post*, August 7, 1980. For other examples, see Jack Anderson's column, *Washington Post*, May 21, 1985; Shiela Kaplan, "Join Congress, See the World," *Common Cause Magazine*, September/October 1986, pp. 17–23. A remarkable eyewitness account of the seamy side of lobbying is Robert Winter-Berger, *The Washington Pay-Off* (New York: Dell, 1972); also Lawrence Gilson, *Money and Secrecy* (New York: Praeger, 1972).

12. Jack Anderson, "Lobbyists: The Unelected Lawmakers in Washington," *Parade*, March 16, 1980, p. 4.

Nixon, Gerald Ford, and Jimmy Carter (when he was governor of Georgia). Over a ten-year period, four oil companies paid out $8 million in illegal payments to forty-five members of Congress.[13]

"Everyone has a price," Howard Hughes once told an associate who later recalled that the billionaire handed out about $400,000 yearly to "councilmen and county supervisors, tax assessors, sheriffs, state senators and assemblymen, district attorneys, governors, congressmen and senators, judges—yes, and vice-presidents and presidents, too."[14]

Many large corporations have a special division dedicated to performing favors for officeholders. A 1979 report stated that the American Petroleum Institute, an organization of oil, gas, and petrochemical companies, spends $75 million a year in lobbying efforts in Washington and has a dozen full-time lobbyists. The oil industry employs over 600 people to pressure Congress and government agencies.[15] The Chamber of Commerce, with its 89,500 corporate members, $20 million annual budget, and 1,200 local "Congressional watch committees," can bring down a snowstorm of mail and a mountain of pressure on the lawmakers and is regarded as "very effective" on Capitol Hill.[16] Of special note is the Business Roundtable, the "trillion-dollar voice" of big business, considered by many to be the most powerful lobby in Washington. The Roundtable is composed of 190 chief executives of the nation's blue-chip corporations, one or another of whom are always in contact with key figures in the White House, the cabinet, and Congress. Credited with thwarting or watering down antitrust, environmental, pro-labor, pro-consumer, and tax-reform measures, the Roundtable exercises an influence over government eclipsing even that of the National Association of Manufacturers and the United States Chamber of Commerce.[17]

The big-time Washington lobbyists are usually attorneys or businesspeople who have proven themselves articulate representatives of their firms, or ex-legislators, or ex-congressional aides, or former bureaucrats

---

13. According to SEC investigators: *Washington Post*, March 22, 1976. On Claude Wild and the Gulf payments, see *Wall Street Journal*, November 17, 1975; *Philadelphia Bulletin*, November 12, 1975; *Washington Post*, June 24, 1979.

14. Howard Kohn, "The Hughes-Nixon-Lansky Connection," *Rolling Stone*, May 20, 1976, p. 44.

15. Jack Newfield, "Oil: The Imperial Lobby," *Village Voice*, November 5, 1979, p. 1. On other oil lobbying efforts, see *New York Times*, December 10, 1985.

16. Anderson, "Lobbyists: The Unelected Lawmakers . . ."

17. Many Roundtable members also belong to the Business Council. Roundtable officers "have immediate access to many legislators just because they are the heads of their corporations": "Business Battles Back," p. 13; Mark Green and Andrew Buchsbaum, *The Corporate Lobbies* (Washington, D.C.: Public Citizen, 1980); Philip Burch Jr., "The Business Roundtable," *Research in Political Economy*, vol. 4 (Greenwich, Conn.: JAI Press, 1981), pp. 101–127.

with good connections.[18] Whatever their varied backgrounds, the one common resource lobbyists should have at their command in order to be effective is money. Money buys what one House aide called that "basic ingredient of all lobbying"—*accessibility* to the officeholder and, with that, the opportunity to shape his or her judgments with arguments of the lobbyist's own choosing. But this takes more than just accessibility. As Woodrow Wilson once pointed out:

> Suppose you go to Washington and try to get at your Government. You will always find that while you are politely listened to, the men really consulted are the men who have the big stake—the big bankers, the big manufacturers, and the big masters of commerce. . . . The masters of the Government of the United States are the combined capitalists and manufacturers of the United States.[19]

It is, then, something more than "information flow" that determines influence, the decisive factor being not just the message but the messenger. The ability to disseminate information to decision makers and propagate one's cause itself presumes access to organization, expertise, time, and labor—things money can buy. In addition, the mere possession of great wealth and the control of industry and jobs give corporate interests an advantage unknown to ordinary working citizens, for business's claims are paraded as the "needs of the economy" and, as it were, of the nation itself. Having the advantage of pursuing their interests within the framework of a capitalist system, capitalists can pretty much limit the range of solutions.[20]

Surveying the organized pressure groups in America, E. E. Schattschneider notes: "*The system is very small.* The range of organized, identifiable, known groups is amazingly narrow; there is nothing remotely universal about it."[21] The pressure system, he concludes, is largely dominated by business groups, the majority of citizens belonging to no organization that is effectively engaged in pressure politics.

The pressure system is "small" and "narrow" only in that it represents a

---

18. Or even former vice-presidents, see Alexander Cockburn and James Ridgeway, "A Specter Haunting Mondale," *Village Voice*, February 22, 1983. Pressure group influence at the state and local levels is even more blatant than in Washington. A prominent banking official in Albany, N.Y., summed it up: "I don't buy legislators dinners, I buy legislators": *Times-Union* (Albany), January 19, 1974. On lobbying in Maryland see Margaret Shapiro, "Lobbyist For Hire," *Washington Post*, March 14, 1983.

19. Quoted in D. Gilbarg, "United States Imperialism" in Bill Slate (ed.), *Power to the People* (New York: Tower, 1970), p. 67.

20. On how power is used not only to pursue interests but to define them, see Michael Parenti, *Power and the Powerless* (New York: St. Martin's Press, 1978).

21. E. E. Schattschneider, *The Semi-Sovereign People* (New York: Holt, Rinehart and Winston, 1960), p. 31. Italics in the original.

highly select portion of the public. In relation to government itself, the system is a substantial operation. Some 15,000 lobbyists prowl the Capitol's corridors and lobbies (whence their name). Others seek favorable rulings from agencies within the vast bureaucracy. Still others are engaged in public relations. Lobbyists make themselves so helpful that members of Congress sometimes rely on them to perform tasks normally done by congressional staffs. Lobbyists will draft legislation, write speeches, and plant stories in the press on behalf of cooperative lawmakers. Lobbyists "put in millions of hours each year" to make the world a better place for their clients, "and they succeed on a scale that is undreamed of by most ordinary citizens."[22] A favorable adjustment in rates for interstate carriers, a special tax benefit for a family oil trust, a high-interest bond issue for big investors, a special charter for a bank, a tariff protection for auto producers, the leasing of public lands to a company, emergency funding for a faltering aeronautics plant, a postal subsidy for advertising firms, the easing of safety standards for a food processor, the easing of pollution controls for a chemical company, a special acreage allotment for peanut growers and tobacco growers, an investment guarantee to a housing developer, a lease guarantee to a construction contractor—all these hundreds of bills and their thousands of special amendments and the tens of thousands of administrative rulings, which mean so much to particular interests and arouse the sympathetic efforts of legislators and bureaucrats, will go largely unnoticed by a public that pays the monetary and human costs and seldom has the means to make its case—or even to discover it has a case.

Attempting to speak for the great unorganized populace, public-interest groups make many proposals for reform but have few of the resources that push officeholders in a reformist direction—especially when their proposals are directed against powerful, entrenched interests in the economy. The relative sparsity of power resources (the most crucial being money) limits the efforts of citizen groups and makes problematic their very survival. Substantial sums are needed just to maintain an office and a tiny staff. Without affluent patrons, the public-interest group faces an uncertain future and is likely to perish. Many are forced to devote an inordinate amount of their time foraging for funds rather than acting as representatives of the public interest.[23]

Some political scientists have theorized that the diversity of cultural,

22. Richard Harris, "Annals of Politics: A Fundamental Hoax," *New Yorker*, August 7, 1971, p. 56; Anderson, "Lobbyists: The Unelected Lawmakers . . ."; Walter Shapiro, "courting the Class of '82," *Washington Post Magazine*, November 7, 1982; Jack Anderson's column, *Washington Post*, June 16, 1984.

23. Jack Walker, "The Origins and Maintenance of Interest Groups in America," *American Political Science Review* 77, 1983, pp. 403–4.

economic, regional, religious, and ethnic groups in our society creates cross-pressured allegiances that mitigate the partisanship of any one organized interest. While this may be true of certain broad constituencies, it does not seem to apply to the more powerful and politically active segments of the business community whose interlocking memberships seem to compound rather than dilute their class commitments and power.[24]

Certainly the multiplicity of interests within the business community creates problems of cohesion, but these diverse groups are capable of (a) collusion around common class interests, and (b) giving mutual support to each other's special projects. For instance, when defending their depletion allowance, the oil companies mobilized merchant fleet owners, truckers, county highway commissioners, asphalt companies, gas station owners, the National Rifle Association, representatives of military-industrial interests, bankers, and some gamblers.[25] It is not too much to suppose that at least some of these groups, in turn, received support from the oil lobby when pressuring for their interests.

"Grass-Roots Lobbying"

Pressure-group efforts are directed not only at officeholders but also at the public. Corporations and trade associations spend nearly one billion dollars a year on "grass-roots lobbying," whereas environmental, consumer, and other public-interest groups spend three-tenths of one percent of that amount.[26] Grant McConnell offers one description of a grass-roots campaign:

> The electric companies, organized in the National Electric Light Association, had not only directly influenced Congressmen and Senators on a large scale, but had also conducted a massive campaign to control the substance of teaching in the nation's schools. Teachers in high schools and grammar schools were inundated with materials. . . . Each pamphlet included carefully planted disparagement of public ownership of utilities. The Association took very active, if inconspicuous, measures to insure that textbooks that were doctrinally impure on this issue were withdrawn from use and that more favorable substitutes were produced and used. College professors . . . were given supplemental incomes by the Association and, in return, not infrequently taught about the utility industry with greater sympathy than before. . . . Public

24. Burch, "The Business Roundtable," p. 117.
25. Robert Engler, *The Politics of Oil*, 2nd ed. (Chicago: University of Chicago Press, 1976), pp. 390–391.
26. "Business Battles Back," p. 12.

libraries, ministers, and civic leaders of all kinds were subjected to the propagandistic efforts of the electric companies.[27]

Consider also business's campaign against the formation of a federal consumer-protection agency. Trade associations got thousands of their local business members throughout the country to send letters to their representatives and senators. The Business Roundtable hired a public-relations firm to produce editorials and editorial cartoons opposing the consumer agency and sent them free of charge to small daily and weekly newspapers—over 800 of which reproduced them without mention that they were political announcements from the Roundtable. "The use of such 'canned' editorial material from special interest groups is a routine practice among small newspapers."[28]

Pressure groups hide behind front organizations that have up-lifting, public-service sounding names. Take, for example, the Committee for Energy Awareness, which launched a slick $30-million television advertising and lobbying campaign to convince everyone that nuclear energy is safe. This "concerned citizens" group never got around to mentioning that it gets millions of dollars from the nuclear industry. Likewise, the American Council on Science and Health reports that saccharin does not cause cancer, chemical pesticides are safe, formaldehyde is not carcinogenic, and there is no link between heart disease and a high-fat, high-cholesterol diet. This self-labeled "public-interest group" receives substantial funds from food, petroleum, and chemical companies.[29]

Some grass-roots lobbying is intended to build a climate of opinion favorable to the corporate giants rather than to push a particular piece of legislation. The steel, oil, and electronics companies do not urge the public to support the latest tax-loophole bill or business handout—if anything, they would prefer that citizens not trouble themselves with such matters—but they do "educate" the public, telling of the many jobs they create, the progress and services they provide, the loving care they supposedly give to the environment, and so on. This kind of "institutional advertising" attempts to place the desires of the giant firms above politics and above controversy—a goal that is itself highly political. Rather than selling their particular products, the corporations sell the business system itself.[30]

---

27. Grant McConnell, *Private Power and American Democracy* (New York: Knopf, 1966), p. 19.

28. "Business Battles Back," p. 13.

29. Howard Kurtz, "Hiding Behind a Name," *Washington Post*, January 27, 1985. Liberal and left-wing groups also have high-sounding names like Common Cause and Center for Science in the Public Interest, but, as Kurtz notes, these groups do not front for specific financial interests like many of their counterparts on the right and they tend to be more candid about their funding sources.

30. See Michael Parenti, *Inventing Reality: The Politics of the Mass Media* (New York: St. Martin's Press, 1986), chapter 4, "The Big Sell."

On various occasions progressive groups in various states were able to place referenda on the ballot regarding nuclear power, public ownership of utilities, rent control, and other things. Opinion polls showed that often these referenda were backed by large majorities in the early stages of the campaign, only to be voted down after business interests launched multi-million-dollar media assaults. Increasingly, the referendum is being employed by conservative organizations which utilize computerized direct-mail appeals to raise funds and gather signatures.[31] Besides working outside the democratic system, business does well within it, using the power of money to successfully propagandize its viewpoint and harness the power of numbers.

DOES LABOR HAVE TOO MUCH POWER?

According to one survey, more than two out of three Americans approve of labor unions and want them to thrive, yet many are concerned that unions have become too powerful an influence in public life.[32] In reality, unions cannot match business in material resources and political influence. Federal and state governments have proven far more responsive to business than to labor, passing "right-to-work" laws and imposing legal restrictions on strikes, boycotts, and labor organizing activities. The result is that union organizing has become increasingly difficult and unions have declined from 30 percent of the work force in 1950 to 18 percent in 1986.

The right to organize was supposedly guaranteed over a half-century ago under the National Labor Relations Act of 1935. But the law has become more a hindrance than a help to workers who want to organize. The National Labor Relations Board (NLRB), an independent federal agency dealing with labor-management disputes, was stacked with pro-business Reagan appointees during the 1980s, thus enabling it to apply the law in ways far more beneficial to management than labor. The NLRB (1) often refused to enforce employees' statutory rights against arbitrary firings, including illegal discharges for union activities, (2) ruled that middle management could vote in union certification elections, (3) delayed actions on cases, causing backlogs of three years or more—during which time many unionizing drives were stalled and defeated, (4) imposed only token fines on management for serious violations of the law.[33]

---

31. *New York Times*, November 4, 1984; *In These Times*, January 14–20, 1981.

32. *Washington Post*, February 7, 1982.

33. *Labor News* (Racine, Wisc.), February 10, 1984; David Moberg, "Obstacles to Union Organizing," *In These Times*, July 11–24, 1984, p. 5; Dennis Schaal, "How Bad Can the NLRB Get?" *Guardian*, January 16, 1985, p. 7. It is "virtually impossible, under today's laws and the way these laws are administered to organize a construction site," according to one high AFL-CIO official: *New York Times*, February 24, 1985.

In addition, management has increased its own efforts at union busting—which is now a major industry with more than a thousand consulting firms doing a $500 million-yearly business teaching companies how to prevent workers from organizing and how to get rid of existing unions. Various industries also use the threat of plant closings to extract benefit and wage concessions from unions "amounting to billions of dollars." [34]

To juxtapose Big Labor with Big Business, as do some American government textbooks, is to overlook the fact that businesspeople have a near monopoly on the top decision-making positions in government. While labor can sometimes play an effective role on behalf of social legislation, it does not come close to matching the spending and lobbying powers of big business in Washington and in the state capitals. Nor can it match business ownership of the major media and the hundreds of millions of dollars business spends in propagandizing issues through the media. Total corporate profits are about 500 times greater than the total income of labor unions. In recent electoral campaigns, business has outspent labor by about 4 to 1. If we add the huge sums given to lawmakers and lobbyists between elections or spent on referenda campaigns and the funds from individual fat cats and wealthy candidates, the ratio is more like 10 to 1.[35] This is not to discount organized labor as a political force but to refute the notion that it has become so powerful as to ride roughshod over business and government. Far from having too much power, unions have been fighting for their lives against hostile laws, court rulings, NLRB decisions, negative images in the business-owned media, and government witch-hunting that purged the labor movement of Communists—who were among its most effective leadership and most militant rank and file.[36]

Some people complain that unions are corrupt and undemocratic. In a few cases, to be sure, union leaders become union dealers, powerful and undemocratic in relation to their own membership, pilfering union funds, colluding with gangland thugs to intimidate the rank and file into submission, while acting as tame junior partners of management, cooperating in speed-ups, and doing little to assist the membership. In return, they win

34. *New York Times*, June 13, 1982; Peter Ajemian, "Union Busters," *Public Citizen*, April 1986, pp. 14–19. In 1957 about 100 workers were dismissed for union activities; by 1983 the number had climbed to 10,000: *Washington Post*, July 20, 1986.

35. Thomas Ferguson and Joel Rogers, *Right Turn* (New York: Hill and Wang, 1986); *Washington Post*, February 21, 1982; *Guardian*, February 18, 1981. For a more detailed discussion of campaign spending, see chapter 12.

36. Richard Boyer and Herbert Morais, *Labor's Untold Story* (New York: United Electrical, Radio and Machine Workers, 1972), pp. 340–80. In recent years some besieged unions have been forced to accept two-tier contracts, allowing the company to provide less wages or benefits for workers hired after a certain date. This brings more profits to the owners and divides and weakens the work force. The "lower" tier resents the "privileged" workers and the inferior contract, while the "privileged" tier is targeted for layoffs by management because it is better paid.

management's ready acceptance as a union.[37] Yet this kind of corruption tends to be concentrated in less than 1 percent of all locals. (In contrast, 11 percent of the biggest corporations have been involved in fraud, bribes, tax evasion, or other unlawful acts over the last decade.) As for union democracy, the rank and file participate in union elections at far higher rates than in national elections, with as many as 16 percent being nominated or elected to union office over a three-year period. In most unions the entire membership gets to vote on a contract. Local union leaders are defeated in democratic elections at higher rates than incumbent members of Congress.[38]

It has been said that unions discriminate against nonunion workers and allow their members to get away with poor performance and low productivity. In fact, union members do make more money than nonunion workers, but the latter also benefit from the struggles of organized labor when their bosses make concessions in order to keep unions out. A unionized work force usually is more productive than a nonunion one paid the same compensation because it has a lower rate of turnover and more stable labor relations. Furthermore, criticisms and challenges from unions induce better management performance.[39]

Unions have also been attacked for causing both inflation and recession. As noted in chapter two, wage increases do not drive up prices but usually lag behind price-profit growth. Labor's share of the national income has remained the same or actually has receded during the last two decades of inflation. As for recession, it is argued that unions drive up labor costs forcing companies to mechanize and cut back on jobs, move to cheaper labor markets, or go bankrupt. To be sure, under capitalism the demands of labor are not automatically accommodated and do create problems for the capital accumulation process. But given the boom-and-bust cycles endemic to capitalism, it is a bit much to give the capitalists credit for the boom and blame the workers for the bust. If the charge were true we might expect that as unions decline, the economy would flourish. But the very opposite has happened. When unions lost membership during the 1970s and 1980s there was no great economic resurgence, but there were several record recessions. Also in states where unions have been traditionally weak (e.g., Alabama, South Carolina, and Mississippi), the standard of living has been lower than in states where unions have a stronger presence. So with Third World countries that have weak or nonexistent unions as compared to the better unionized and more pros-

37. For one example, see Dan Moldea, *The Hoffa Wars* (New York: Paddington Press, 1978).
38. Richard Freeman and James Medoff, *What Do Unions Do?* (New York: Basic Books, 1984).
39. Ibid.

perous nations of Western Europe and Scandinavia. Unions correlate with prosperity rather than with poverty.

Far from being the autocratic, all-powerful bullies they are made out to be, labor unions are a vital part of whatever democracy we have. They have been an important voice for their members and for the general public. The AFL-CIO played a vital role in the passage of the 1963 and 1964 civil-rights bills and has supported national health insurance, low-income housing, mass transportation, consumer protection, equitable tax reform, and the Equal Rights Amendment and has opposed repressive measures such as emergency detention. Many unions have backed pollution and environmental controls and antinuclear measures in coalitions with other organizations. Some of the more progressive unions broke with the militaristic cold-war mentality of the AFL-CIO leadership and supported nonintervention in El Salvador.[40]

MONEY CORRUPTS

If, as they say, power corrupts, it usually gets a helping hand from money. The influence system is a money system in search of special favors from officeholders who are burdened by huge campaign bills and often expensive tastes. In recent years there have been reports of corruption involving federal, state, and local officials throughout the nation. In Congress, "corruption is so endemic that it's scandalous," the corruptors usually being "the major economic interest groups and the wealthy individuals who together largely dominate campaign financing."[41] In just one six-year period, the number of public officials convicted in courts of law included three cabinet officers, three governors, thirty-four state legislators, twenty judges, five state attorneys general, twenty-eight mayors, eleven district attorneys, 170 police officers and a U.S. vice-president who pleaded no contest—and this included only those unlucky or clumsy enough to get caught.[42] The Nixon administration was implicated in scandals involving

40. See *The People's Lobby*, AFL-CIO Report on the 98th Congress, 1983–84 (Washington D.C., March 1985); also Andrew Levison, *The Working-Class Majority* (New York: Penguin Books, 1974).

41. George Agee, director of the National Committee for an Effective Congress, quoted in Harris, "Annals of Politics . . ." p. 62.

42. *Washington Post*, January 1 and December 10, 1981. The Knapp Commission report found that the largest drug dealer in New York City was the police department itself: Robert Elias, *The Politics of Victimization* (New York: Oxford University Press, 1985). For instances of major corruption in Texas, Nebraska, Pennsylvania, Virginia, Chicago, New York, and San Diego, Calif., see *New York Times*, December 27, 1982; June 3, 1983; August 26 and December 27, 1984; October 13, 1985; March 15 to March 27, 1986; *Washington Post*, February 21, 1984; *Nation*, October 13, 1984. For instances of corruption in the FBI, see *New York Times*, January 15 and December 6, 1978; and Sanford Ungar, *FBI: An Uncensored Look Behind the Walls* (Boston: Little, Brown, 1976).

the sale of wheat, an out-of-court settlement with ITT, price supports for dairy producers, corruption in the Federal Housing Administration, stock-market manipulations, and political espionage (the Watergate affair).

The career of Nelson Rockefeller provides an impressive example of money doing its thing. When he was being considered for appointment to the U.S. vice-presidency to replace Spiro Agnew (who had just resigned in exchange for the dropping of charges of bribery, extortion, and income-tax evasion), Rockefeller admitted to having given nearly $1.8 million in gifts and loans to eighteen public officials, including $50,000 to Henry Kissinger, an erstwhile Rockefeller employee, three days before Kissinger became national security advisor to President Nixon. Rockefeller also gave $650,000 to the chairman of the Port Authority of New York. (The Rockefellers' Chase Manhattan Bank has large bond holdings in the Port Authority.) At a Senate hearing, Rockefeller insisted these payments were simply manifestations of his esteem for the recipients. "Sharing has always been part of my upbringing," he told the senators, none of whom doubled over with laughter. None of them reminded him that New York law prohibits public employees from accepting any gift greater than $25. Nor did any of them wonder aloud whether a "gift" to public officials who make decisions affecting one's private fortune might not better be called a "bribe." Instead Congress confirmed Nelson Rockefeller as vice-president of the United States.[43]

Every administration has had its scandals but the number of high-level members of the Reagan administration accused of unethical or illegal conduct is without precedent—110 by early 1986, with the number climbing well beyond that as the Iran-contra affair unfolded later that year. These included at least three cabinet members, a CIA director, several White House staff members, several advisors and aides from the National Security Council, and numerous administrative agency heads. The charges include fraud; illegal or improper stock dealings; tax-code violations; failure to make proper financial disclosures; perjury; obstructing congressional investigations; accepting illegal or improper loans, gifts, and favors; and using public resources to aid personal interests. Only a few went to jail, many resigned, and many stayed on after the Justice Department concluded there was insufficient reason to prosecute, including Attorney General Edwin Meese.[44]

---

43. *Newsweek*, October 21, 1974; *New York Times*, October 7, 1974.

44. See the compilation in the *Washington Post*, April 27, 1986. Meese answered: "I don't recall" or some such amnesic response at least 79 times when questioned by the Senate Judiciary Committee, about the financial bounties he had accepted from persons whom he then recommended for appointment to cushy government jobs. Reagan himself has been in long association with persons attached to underworld figures: see Dan Moldea, *Dark Victory: Ronald Reagan, MCA, and the Mob* (New York: Viking Press, 1986).

Some observers see corruption as a more or less acceptable fact of life. Passing a little money under the table is just another way of oiling the wheels of government and getting things done. But corruption has gone beyond the petty bribe to reach momentous proportions. Rather than being a violation of the rules of the game, corruption is the name of the game. It is not so much a matter of finding a few bad apples as noting that the barrel itself is rotten. Corruption in government promotes policies that lead to permanent public indebtedness, inefficiency, and waste; it drains the public treasure to feed the private purse; it vitiates laws and regulations that might otherwise safeguard occupational, health, environmental, and consumer interests; it undermines equal protection of the law, producing favoritism for the few who can pay and injury and neglect for the many who cannot.

Besides denouncing corruption we should understand the politico-economic system that makes it ubiquitous. The temptation for corporate interests to use large sums of money to win decisions that bring in vastly larger sums is strong, especially since those who would be the guardians of the law themselves have their palms out or are in other ways beholden to the corrupting powers. If the powers and resources of the social order itself are used for the maximization of private greed and gain, and if the operational ethic is "looking out for number one," then corruption will be chronic rather than occasional, a systemic product rather than merely an outgrowth of the politician's flawed character.

12

Congress: The Pocketing of Power

In order to guard against democratic "excesses," the framers of the Constitution separated state functions into executive, legislative, and judicial branches and installed a system of checks and balances. These measures were designed to forestall popular action and prevent fundamental changes in the class order. The framers understood what some theorists today seem to have forgotten: in a society in which private wealth is in the hands of a few, the *diffusion* of power among the various segments of government does not necessarily mean the *democratization* of power but more likely the opposite. Confrontations between concentrated private wealth and fractured public power do not usually yield democratic results. Fragmented power is more readily pocketed by well-organized, moneyed private interests and is thereby less responsive to the mass public.

Looking specifically at the United States Congress, one is struck by how the diffusion of power has led to undemocratic results and how the power of money has preempted the power of the electorate.

A CONGRESS FOR THE MONEY

The fragmentation of power begins with the election system itself. Rather than slates of candidates backed by a cohesive party organization united around a common program, elections are individualized district-by-district contests, fueled more by personalized candidate appeals and "image issues" than by substantive issues. As already noted, the major weapon in all these campaigns is money. More and more of it is needed to pay for staff, direct-mail operations, continuous polling, phone banks, computerized services, publicity experts, and media time.

"Congress is the best money can buy," said the humorist Will Rogers a half-century ago. The quip is truer than ever. Elections in 1980 and 1984, from local ballot issues to the White House, cost from $1.2 billion to $1.8 billion, more than twice the cost of the 1976 elections. In both 1980 and 1984, special-interest political action committees (PACs) outspent political parties. The 1986 midterm congressional elections by themselves probably went over $1 billion. Nor can these astronomical sums be blamed on inflation. Between 1972 and 1982, inflation climbed 100 percent, but spending for House races increased 450 percent and for Senate races, 500 percent.[1]

Coming from corporations, trade associations, and rich individuals, most of the money not surprisingly finds its way into the coffers of the more conservative of the two capitalist parties. Thus in the 1970s and 1980s, Republicans outspent Democrats by 5 to 1 margins.[2] However, money knows no firm party lines, only class lines. Both of the capitalist parties (but none of the anticapitalist ones) receive millions of dollars from PACs. To hedge their bets, some big donors sometimes give money to both candidates running against each other in the same race.[3] Democratic incumbents with strategic committee seats are often better funded by business PACs than their Republican challengers.

Members of Congress go where the money is, scrambling for the congressional committee assignments that deal with the issues of greatest interest to big donors.[4] In a two-year period, nine members of the Senate Finance Committee received $547,000 in campaign funds from oil and gas interests. During the first seven months of 1983, the forty-two members of the House Energy and Commerce Committee received $1.8 million, an average of $40,000 per member (with senior members getting the lion's

1. On the role of money see: Herbert Alexander, "Political Parties and the Dollar," *Society*, January/February 1985, pp. 55–57; Herbert Alexander, *Financing Politics* (Washington, D.C.: Congressional Quarterly, 1984). Elizabeth Drew, *Politics and Money* (New York: Macmillan, 1983); David Nichols, *Financing Elections: The Politics of an American Ruling Class* (New York: Franklin Watts, 1974); Statement by John Warren McGary, Federal Election Commission, before Subcommittee of the Senate Appropriations Committee, April 9, 1986, p. 2; also *Washington Post*, May 3 and 8, 1983; February 3, 1984; *New York Times*, October 21, 1984; Mark Green, "When Money Talks, Is it Democracy?" *Nation*, September 15, 1984, pp. 200–204.

2. *Washington Post*, January 17, 1982, May 7, 1985, and August 29, 1986; *New York Times*, August 22 and October 29, 1986. But Democrats are not totally bereft of "moderate conservative" fat cats: see *Washington Post*, November 28 and October 25, 1984; and G. William Domhoff, *Fat Cats and Democrats* (Englewood Cliffs, N.J.: Prentice Hall, 1972).

3. For examples see Carole and Paul Bass's report in *In These Times*, October 3–9, 1984, p. 6; and Ivan Boesky's campaign contributions reported in *Washington Post*, August 29, 1986.

4. See Op-Ed page, *New York Times*, May 4, 1986.

share), mostly from corporate PACs representing a variety of industries that the committee dealt with. Other especially well-oiled committees are those dealing with taxes, appropriations, and—most lucrative of all—defense contracts.[5]

Some politicians insist that campaign contributions do not influence them. Senator Durenberger (R-Minn.) maintained that the $62,775 he received from the chemical industry "hasn't had any effect on me. These people contributed in the hope that I'd be a senator, and not on the

5. David Marinass, "PAC Heaven," *Washington Post*, August 21, 1983; Jack Newfield, "Oil: The Imperial Lobby," *Village Voice*, November 5, 1979, pp. 1, 15–17; *New York Times*, June 16, 1986; Jack Anderson, "Ways and Means: A Seat Can Be as Good as Gold," *Washington Post*, October 26, 1982; Gordon Adams, *The Iron Triangle: The Politics of Defense Contracting* (New York: Council on Economic Priorities, 1981).

condition that I'd vote for their legislation."[6] But why was the chemical industry so keen on having Durenberger as senator? Possibly because they were utterly taken by his personal qualities, more likely because he voted the way they liked on most issues. *Politicians may claim that money does not influence their votes, but their votes have an influence on the money flow*. The thirty senators still in office who voted *against* the oil depletion allowance received an average of $3,275 in oil-industry contributions. The twenty-eight senators who voted *pro-oil* received an average of $41,659 from oil interests—more than twelve times as much.[7] Big contributors might be fooled or strung along now and then, but they do not give away money for nothing and do not reward lawmakers who habitually vote against their interests.

There is ample testimony provided by legislators themselves on how they feel obliged to vote as their PAC contributors want.[8] One candidate who ran for a House seat, only to be outspent (and defeated) by his conservative opponent, noted: "Campaign money becomes an overriding factor. Constant trips to raise money eat you up and get in the way of talking about issues and meeting voters. It poses a problem for many candidates. They are tempted to compromise their positions in return for PAC money."[9] Announcing to the Senate Democratic Caucus that he was leaving office to become a religious lay worker, Senator Harold Hughes said his conscience would no longer allow him to continue in politics because of the way he had been forced to raise money in order to run. At the same gathering, Senator Hubert Humphrey also discussed his pangs of conscience (as recorded by James Abourezk who was then a senator):

> In all his years in politics [Humphrey] said, nothing was as demeaning and degrading as the way he had to raise money. He was in a highly emotional state as he told of how ashamed he was of the things he had to do to extract campaign money from contributors. He spoke of how politicians are treated by those who contribute, of how candidates literally had to sell their souls. Both Hughes and Humphrey clearly touched a nerve in those present at the caucus.[10]

---

6. Quoted in *Washington Post*, November 17, 1980. A veteran congressional aide observed that some lawmakers "come to really believe that the guy who gives the big dough is the best guy and that helping him is in the public interest"—quoted in Richard Harris, "Annals of Politics: A Fundamental Hoax," *New Yorker*, August 7, 1971, p. 54.

7. Newfield, "Oil: The Imperial Lobby," p. 15. Note how the American Medical Association hands out large sums to lawmakers who vote its way and little or nothing to those who have supported progressive health measures: see the study "Take $2000 and Call Me in the Morning," *Common Cause*, Washington, D.C., 1983.

8. For specific testimony see Green, "When Money Talks . . .," p. 202.

9. Thomas Cronin quoted in Dom Bonafede, "Textbook Candidate," *PS*, Winter 1983, p. 55.

10. James Abourezk, "Clear Out PACs, Clean Up Congressional Campaigns," IPS feature release, Institute For Policy Studies, Washington, D.C., March 18, 1986.

More money is spent on campaigns because—among other reasons—more money is available. The 1974 Federal Election Campaign Act, backed by subsequent court decisions and Federal Election Commission rulings, allows corporations to form PACs that can solicit contributions from stockholders and all employees. Now able to spend as much of corporate funds as they please on candidates of their choice, these PACs have exploded in number: 776 in 1978, 954 in 1980, 1,327 in 1982, 4009 in 1984. As of 1987, individuals could give a maximum of $1000 to candidates, $5000 to a PAC, and $20,000 to a political party. But a wealthy person could get around that limit by giving in the name of other persons. A PAC could contribute a maximum of $5000 to a candidate, but with no limit on what it could spend independently on any candidate. Political parties can donate a range of sums to congressional contests, up to $1 million for Senate races in larger states.

Various methods have been used to evade spending limits, with the Republicans being the most inventive since they have more to spend: PACs are used as conduits to allow individuals to exceed limits; funds in excess of legal limits are channeled through the backdoor via unregulated state parties. Presidential candidates set up tax-exempt foundations to receive unlimited amounts of unreported but tax-deductible contributions. Excess funds ("soft" funds) are used for voter registration drives among constituencies that favor a particular party.[11]

It is claimed that since PACs are so numerous and diverse, they cancel each other out. To be sure, sometimes they do conflict, and organized labor's PACs certainly represent a countervailing (albeit weaker) force against the corporate tide. But more often, rather than canceling each other out, corporate PACs move in the same direction with cumulative impact. Meanwhile the homeless, the hungry, the unemployed, the unattended sick, the migrant workers, the small farmers—and on most issues, the ordinary citizens and consumers—have no PAC connections, certainly none with the muscle of the corporate PACs.

It has been argued that money is not a major influence on elections, since well-financed candidates have sometimes lost. Other variables such as incumbency and the state of the economy are said to be more crucial. Of course there are other variables, and of course the biggest spender does not *always* win, but electoral figures confirm the maxim that the better financed candidate *usually* wins: thus over the last decade or more, the

---

11. Congress's efforts to restrict campaign spending have been undermined by the Supreme Court, which tortuously reasoned that limits on spending were an infringement on the right to free speech: see chapter 15. Individuals and PACs have no limits on what they may spend on their own for candidates (as opposed to what they may contribute to specific PACs and candidate committees): *Washington Post*, March 19, 1985.

bigger spenders won in over 80 percent of the House and Senate races and in most of the gubernatorial contests.

In any case, who wins is not the only way to measure the influence of money. Republican losses would probably be much greater if they did not enjoy such a financial superiority in key races. In the 1982 New York gubernatorial contest, Lewis Lehrman, a political unknown and rabid ultraconservative, came from way behind in the opinion polls to within three points of defeating the popular Democrat Mario Cuomo. Would he have done as well without the $14 million of his personal fortune which he expended in the race? Would he have even been nominated to head the GOP ticket? Would Cuomo have won without the $6 million *he* spent in the campaign? Even if the candidate who wins spends less, he usually spends quite a lot. He may not need to have the most funds but he must have enough. Without money there is no campaign to speak of—as third-party candidates have long known.[12]

COMMITTEE GOVERNMENT AND SPECIAL INTERESTS

Once elected, how do the legislators go about their work? For years, power in Congress rested with the twenty or so standing (i.e., permanent) committees in each house that determined the destiny of bills: rewriting some, approving a few, and burying most. The committees were dominated by chairpersons who rose to their positions by seniority—that is, by being repeatedly reelected, a feat best accomplished in a safe district or predominantly one-party state. This explains why Southern Democrats monopolized the chairmanships for years. Seniority increased a legislator's influence within Congress and thereby attracted an increasing amount of moneyed support, and moneyed support helped reassure reelection and seniority. With two-party competition growing in the South and elsewhere, committee chairpersons have started coming from non-Southern states and less conservative urban and suburban districts. Seniority also determined the assigning of members to committees and the selection of subcommittee chairpersons.

Although seniority remains the rule in both houses, the House Democratic Caucus instituted a number of changes to weaken the hold of

12. Richard Joslyn, Marc Howard Ross, Michael Weinstein, "Election Night News Coverage," *PS*, Summer 1984, pp. 568–570; *Washington Post*, November 4, 7, and 17, 1982; Green, "When Money Talks . . ." p. 204. Money not only often determines who wins but who runs. Candidates sometimes are backed by party leaders explicitly because they have personal wealth and are therefore more likely to wage an effective campaign: Frank Lynn, "With Eye to November, Dyson Stresses Wealth," *New York Times*, August 26, 1986.

committee chairpersons, removing several from their positions and expanding the powers of subcommittees.[13] No longer can chairpersons arbitrarily select subcommittee chairpersons, nor stack a subcommittee with members of their own choice, or cut its budget. Totaling over 300 in the House and Senate combined, the subcommittees have staffs of their own and fixed legislative jurisdictions. Advancement within the subcommittees, as within the full committees, is still mostly by seniority. Departures from seniority occur more frequently than in earlier decades and probably a little more frequently in the House than in the Senate. On occasion, the House Democratic Caucus will pass over the most senior person when selecting a committee chairperson or remove one who has not worked well. Chairmanships are sometimes contested in Caucus elections by several candidates.

House Democrats have restored some powers to the Speaker of the House, giving him more input in the selection of committee members and in the formulation of policy. The Speaker's ability to coordinate policy, however, is insufficient to overcome so much divided authority. Furthermore, as legislators rely less on party leaders for campaign funds and a place on the ballot, the leadership exercises less leverage over them. The atomized campaign system makes for a more atomized legislature. House rules limit the powers of committee chairpersons but not subcommittee chairpersons, some of whom do not always act in a democratic way.

The fragmented committee system in Congress, then, has been replaced by a still more fragmented "subcommittee system," lacking a central leadership to garner support for popular constituencies deprived of lobbyists and PACs. "More than mere specialization, the subcommittee permits development of tight little cadres of special interest legislators and gives them great leverage."[14] In agriculture, for instance, cotton, corn, wheat, peanut, tobacco, and rice producers compete for federal support programs; each interest is represented on a particular subcommittee of the Senate and House Agricultural Committees by senators and representatives ready to do battle on their behalf.[15] The fragmentation of power within the subcommittees simplifies the lobbyist's task of controlling legislation. It offers the special-interest group its own special-interest subcommittee. To decentralize power in this way is *not* to democratize it. The

13. Both parties in both houses have a caucus (or "conference"), which consists of the entire membership of the party in that particular house. In each house, the party with a majority controls the committee and subcommittee chairmanships. Democrats in the Senate weakened seniority somewhat by deciding in 1970 that a senator could chair only one committee and sit on not more than one of the major standing committees; this allowed freshmen senators somewhat better access to important committee assignments.

14. Douglass Cater, *Power in Washington* (New York: Random House, 1964).

15. *Washington Post*, August 12, 1985.

separate structures of power tend to monopolize decisions in specific areas for the benefit of specific groups. Into the interstices of these substructures fall the interests of large segments of the unorganized public.

Whether Congress is organized under a committee system, a subcommittee system, or a strong centralized leadership—and it has enjoyed all three in its history—it seems unchanging in its dedication to business interests. A few examples:

> A Senate reclamation law revision exempts the big irrigators in the West from acreage limitations, continuing hefty tax subsidies. A House committee relieves asbestos producers of sharing the cost of removing their cancer-causing insulation from schoolhouses. A 2-year-old strip mine control law is dealt a stunning blow in the Senate under pressure from coal companies.
>
> Hospital cost-containment legislation is bottled up by a powerful hospital-doctor lobby that contributed more than $1.6 million to campaigners in 1977–1978. Sugar producers are voted a 15.8 cents-a-pound price increase and milk producers' price supports are extended by a House committee. Sand and gravel and limestone pit operators win an exemption from safety training requirements. The House waters down a windfall profits tax proposed on the affluent oil industry, whose PACs spent better than $1 million in the last two congressional elections.[16]

Congress produces an array of protections, grants, subsidies, leases, franchises, in-kind supports, direct services, noncompetitive contracts, loan guarantees, loss compensations, and other forms of public largesse to private business. Every few years, Congress engages in a bipartisan stampede to sustain the same (or an increasingly inequitable) system of taxation. Every year, Congress votes hundreds of billions for bloated military budgets and hundreds of millions for right-wing dictatorships throughout the Third World.

But Congress also knows how to save money. In recent years, it has refused to provide $9 million for a disease-control center dealing with tuberculosis, even though some 15 million Americans have TB. It cut 5 million doses out of the federal immunization program for children, for a grand saving of $10 million, and reduced venereal-disease programs by 25 percent despite increases in that disease. To teach people rugged self-reliance, Congress cut food programs for infants and senior citizens, assistance programs for the disabled, home-care and therapy programs for

16. *Washington Post*, September 23, 1979. For additional examples, see *Washington Post*, October 1, 1982. Defense contractors offer one of the biggest pork barrels. Almost 90 percent of the billions spent on Star Wars goes to contractors in states with senators who sit on the two key Senate committees that vote funds for the program: "Star Wars: The Economic Fallout," Council on Economic Priorities (Washington, D.C., 1986).

the infirm and handicapped, and medical care, job, and housing programs for the poor and elderly.[17]

What has failed to appear on Congress's agenda is any notion of major structural changes in class and power, of moving the economy toward nonprofit forms of production for social use rather than production for corporate gain. As an integral product of the existing politico-economic system, Congress is not likely to initiate a transformation of that system. Congress cannot try a new recipe because it is too committed to slicing up the existing pie.

On occasions when public opinion is aroused, Congress is likely to respond by producing legislation that appears to deal with the problem while lacking real muscle. Thus we are treated to a lobbyist-registration act that does little to control lobbyists and an occupational-safety act that has grossly insufficient enforcement provisions. Or Congress is capable of ignoring strong public sentiments. After years of large peace demonstrations and with opinion polls showing a majority against the Vietnam intervention, the legislators were still voting huge appropriations for the war by lopsided majorities.[18] In the face of a nationwide consumer meat boycott and a deluge of letters and calls protesting inflation, Congress chose to listen to "cattlemen, banking and business interests and food merchants" and voted down all proposals for price freezes.[19] In 1982 a massive grass-roots movement for a bilateral, verifiable freeze on nuclear weapons swept the country like few things in our history, yet Congress continued to vote for major escalations in nuclear weapons systems. And in 1986 opinion polls showed that by large majorities the public opposed aid to the Nicaraguan mercenaries who were waging war against Nicaragua from U.S.-furnished bases in Honduras, yet Congress voted $100 million in aid.

At other times lawmakers will heed an aroused public—especially as election time approaches. Before the 1982 and 1986 congressional elections, even under the threat of President Reagan's vetoes, the Congress pushed through a number of important human services and environmental programs. But normally the populace exercises an influence over our lawmakers that is more episodic than durable. Given the demands made on his or her time by job and family, and the superficial and often misleading coverage of events by the media, the average wage earner has little opportunity to give sustained, informed attention to more than a few broad issues, if that.

---

17. *Washington Post*, July 9, 1982; *Daily World*, August 20, 1982.

18. "Save This House," bulletin by the National Committee for an Effective Congress, Washington D.C., 1982; *Washington Post*, November 7, 1982.

19. *Washington Post*, January 17, 1982.

Worse still, Congress is inclined to remove itself from scrutiny whenever the people get too interested in its affairs. Congressional committees, especially those dealing with military spending, appropriations, and taxes, hold many of their sessions behind closed doors. While public-interest advocates are often kept in the dark, business groups enjoy a ready access to committee reports. "The thing that really makes me mad is the dual standard," complained a Senate committee staff member. "It's perfectly acceptable to turn over information about what's going on in committee to the auto industry or the utilities but not to the public."[20]

Secrecy can envelop the entire lawmaking process: a bill cutting corporate taxes by $7.3 billion was (1) drawn up by the House Ways and Means Committee in three days of secret sessions, (2) passed by the House under a closed rule after only one hour of debate with (3) about thirty members present for the (4) non-roll-call vote. Sometimes the lawmakers themselves do not know what is going on. Thus during conference committee negotiations on what became the Deficit Reduction Act of 1984, Dan Rostenkowski (D-Ill.), chairman of the House Ways and Means Committee, Robert Dole (R-Kan.), Senate majority leader, and Donald Regan, Secretary of the Treasury and former Wall Street executive for Merrill Lynch, slipped a special tax-straddle provision into the final package allowing some commodity traders (including Merrill Lynch) to roll their tax liability forward year after year. Neither the Senate nor the House ever debated or even knew about this $1.2 billion tax dodge.[21]

Just as important as the special legislation for special friends is the influence exerted by Capitol Hill on the executive branch to get government contracts, government jobs, and favorable administrative rulings for business clients. In this capacity, the lawmaker again often acts as little more than an extension of the lobbyist. Speaking from direct observations on the Hill, one observer concludes that the lobbyist's main job is to circumvent existing laws and get preferential treatment "for clients who have no legal rights to them." To achieve this the lobbyist pays cash to "one or more members of Congress—the more influential they are, the fewer he needs." They, in turn, make the contact with the executive agency handling the matter.[22]

The impact of money is sometimes limited by such factors as cultural norms, the need to maintain representative democratic appearances, and the pressure of popular agitation. While moneyed interests may not

---

20. Mark Green et al., *Who Runs Congress?*, 2nd ed. (New York: Bantam Books/Grossman, 1972), p. 56.

21. Both Rostenkowski and Dole accepted thousands of dollars in campaign contributions from these same Wall Street firms: *Washington Post*, June 3, 1985.

22. Robert Winter-Berger, *The Washington Pay-Off* (New York: Dell, 1972). Winter-Berger offers astonishing eyewitness testimony in his book.

always get their way, they *usually* do. If money were not effective, why would corporations and others spend so much of it on politics? Certainly corporate heads do not feel contributions are wasted. William May, chairman of the American Can Corporation, comments on his company's PAC contributions: "I've got to admit the money does have an impact. There is no doubt about it."[23]

LOOKING OUT FOR THEMSELVES

Members of Congress will sometimes act as pressure politicians without prodding from any pressure group, either because they are so well attuned to the group's interests or have lucrative holdings of their own in the same industry. Legislators with large farm holdings sit on committees that shape agricultural subsidy programs which directly benefit them. Fully a third of the lawmakers hold outside jobs as lawyers or officers of corporations, banks, and other financial institutions that closely link them "with the very industries they were elected to oversee."[24] More than a third of the senators make money every time the military budget increases, for they have investments in firms that rank among the top defense contractors. Almost half the Senate and over a hundred House members have interests in banking, including many who sit on committees that deal with banking legislation. What is called "conflict of interest" in the judiciary and executive branches is defined as "expertise" in the Congress by lawmakers who use their public mandate to legislate on behalf of their private fortunes.

Plutocracy—rule for the rich by the rich—prevails in Congress. Members of both houses are becoming richer. With unusual candor, Senator Daniel Patrick Moynihan (D-N.Y.) remarked: "At least half of the members of the Senate today are millionaires. That has changed the nature of the body. We've become a plutocracy. The dependence on party and leadership just isn't there. The Senate was meant to represent the interests of the states; instead, it represents the interests of a class."[25] The lower chamber too is going upper class, in what one critic called an "evolution from a House of Representatives to a House of Lords."[26] Because of a Supreme Court ruling that allows wealthy candidates to expend as much as they want of their own money on their own campaigns, rich individuals

---

23. Mark Green and Jack Newfield, "Who Owns Congress?" *Washington Post Magazine*, June 8, 1980, p. 12.

24. *Washington Post*, September 5, 1979 and February 7, 1985.

25. Quoted in *New York Times*, November 25, 1984.

26. Mark Green quoted in Steven Roberts, "The Rich Get Richer and Elected," *New York Times*, September 24, 1985.

have an additional advantage in gaining party nominations. Furthermore, because most PAC contributions go to incumbents, it is more necessary than ever for challengers to have a private source of wealth. Thus the new House members of the 99th Congress had 400 percent more in personal assets than had the new members of the previous Congress.[27]

The people who represent us in Congress are certainly not *financially* representative of us. Almost all have personal incomes that put them in the top 1-percent bracket. As Philip Green notes, our rulers experience a vastly different life from those over whom they rule. Transportation policy is made by people who fly in heavily subsidized private planes and who never have to search for a parking space or endure the suffocation of a rush-hour bus. Agricultural policy is shaped by legislators who never tried keeping a family farm going. Safety legislation is devised by lawmakers who never worked in a factory or mine. Medical policies are made by persons who never have to wait in a crowded clinic.[28] The same legislators who impose austerity programs on working people vote themselves fat pay raises and a tax-free income.[29]

Some members of Congress pilfer from the public treasure. They travel for fun at government expense under the guise of conducting committee investigations; they place relatives on the payroll and pocket their salaries or take salary kickbacks from staff members; they charge both the government and a private client for the same expense; they use committee staff workers for personal campaign purposes; they use unspent travel allocations and unspent campaign contributions for personal indulgences; they keep persons on the staff payroll whose major function is to perform sexual favors.[30]

Venality takes more serious forms. Mark Twain once said, "There is no distinctly American criminal class except Congress." Since World War II, more than sixty-five lawmakers or their aides have been indicted or convicted of bribery, influence peddling, extortion, and other crimes. And those were only the ones unlucky enough to get caught. Numerous other

---

27. Roberts, "The Rich Get Richer . . ." The legislators financial disclosure do not cover their net worth and are often "incomplete, misleading or useless": *Congressional Quarterly*, September 2, 1978. More thorough disclosures would likely reveal more millionaires: *Washington Post*, May 21, 1982. Millionaire representatives are a phenomenon found at the state level as well. In a poor state like West Virginia, an estimated half of the state legislators are millionaires, many of them coal-mine owners; almost none are environmentalists: Jean Callahan, "Cancer Valley," *Mother Jones*, August 1978, p. 40.

28. Philip Green, *Retrieving Democracy* (Totowa, N.J.: Rowman and Allanheld, 1985), pp. 177–78.

29. In 1981 members of Congress voted enough new tax breaks for themselves so as to avoid paying any income taxes: *Washington Post*, January 14, 1982.

30. *Washington Post*, August 13, 1982; *New York Times*, April 5, 1983 and September 29, 1985; Shiela Kaplan, "Join Congress, See the World," *Mother Jones*, September/October 1986, pp. 18–24.

members have retired from office to avoid criminal charges. All in all, Capitol Hill seems to have a higher per-capita crime rate than inner-city Detroit.

Under the Ethics in Government Act, the House and Senate ethics committees are charged with overseeing and enforcing ethics codes—a task they have neither the inclination nor staff to perform. In 1976, at least nineteen senators were implicated in a multimillion-dollar slush fund run by oil companies. Because of the publicity given the case, the Senate Ethics Committee, which had not investigated a senator's ethics in ten years, finally initiated an inquiry—which it dropped a short time later without calling any corporate witnesses (including oil lobbyists who were willing to name names).[31] The House Ethics Committee has suffered from a similar sluggishness. When a member of the Korean CIA, testifying before the committee, named thirty legislators to whom he had given almost $1 million in bribes in exchange for votes in support of his government, the Ethics Committee responded by indicting only two ex-members of Congress.[32]

THE LEGISLATIVE LABYRINTH

As intended by the framers of the Constitution, the very structure of Congress has a conservative effect on what the legislators do. The staggered terms of the Senate—with only one-third elected every two years—are designed to blunt any mass sentiment for a sweeping turnover. The division of the Congress into two separate houses makes legislative action all the more difficult, giving an advantage to those who desire to prevent reforms. With bicameralism, lobbyists have more opportunities to exert pressure and more places to set up roadblocks; legislation that gets through one house can often be buried or multilated in the other house.

A typical bill before Congress might go the following route: after being introduced into, say, the House of Representatives, it is committed to a committee, where it can be pigeonholed or gutted by the chairperson, or parceled out to various subcommittees for extensive hearings, where it might then meet its demise. Or it might be reported out of subcommittee

31. *Boston Globe*, September 22, 1976. The chairperson of the Senate Ethics Committee in the 98th Congress, Senator Malcolm Wallop (R-Wyo.) believed that senators should not have to disclose their financial holdings and could decide their own conflicts of interest. He even criticized the whole idea of a code of ethics. No wonder his colleagues picked him for the job: *Washington Post*, December 31, 1982.

32. An earlier probe had disclosed that 115 members of Congress had taken bribes from South Korean agents. Executive officials were also implicated: *New York Times*, July 11, 1977; *Workers World*, June 2, 1978.

to full committee either intact or greatly diluted or completely rewritten. In the event it is reported out of the full committee, the bill is sent to the Rules Committee, which might pigeonhole it, thus killing it. Or the Rules Committee could negotiate with the standing committee for a rewriting of certain provisions. Or the House might vote—by at least two-thirds—to bypass or take the bill away from the Rules Committee and bring it directly to the House floor for debate and a vote. Usually the Rules Committee provides a rule for the bill, regulating the amount of time for debate and what provisions may or may not be open for amendment. Then the bill goes to the House, which can reject or amend the rule. The House resolves itself into the Committee of the Whole House (allowing suspension of House rules including quorum requirements) to debate, amend, pass, or reject the bill, or recommit it to the originating committee for further study. If passed by the Committee of the Whole, the House reconstitutes itself and then decides the bill's fate.

If the bill is passed by the House, it is sent to the Senate which either places it directly on its calendar for debate and vote or refers it to a standing committee to repeat the same process of subcommittee and committee hearings and amendments. It can die in committee or be sent to the Senate floor. The Senate might defeat the bill or pass the House version either unchanged or, more likely, amended. If the House refuses to accept the Senate amendments, a conference committee is put together consisting of several senior members from each house. Should the conference committee be able to reach a compromise, the bill is returned to both houses for a final vote.[33] If passed by both houses, the bill goes to the president who either signs it into law or vetoes it. (A bill that does not make it through both houses before the next congressional election must be reintroduced and the entire process begun anew.) The president's veto can be overridden only by two-thirds of the members of each house who are present and voting. If the president fails to sign the legislation within ten days after passage, it automatically becomes law unless Congress adjourns in that time, in which case it has been "pocket vetoed" and so dies.

The bill that survives this legislative labyrinth to become law may be only an *authorization* act—that is, it simply brings some program into existence. Congress then must repeat the entire legislative process for an *appropriations* bill to finance the authorized policy—something the lawmakers occasionally fail to do. Congress's task is made no easier by the duplication of bills and overlapping committee jurisdictions. For instance,

33. More than one conference committee has rewritten a bill on its own. Thus in 1985 a House-Senate conference committee approved a $302.5 billion military budget that restored money for all of the twenty-two weapon systems that either the House or Senate had voted to kill: *New York Times*, July 26, 1985.

there are twenty-two House committees and subcommittees dealing—none of them too successfully—with the problems of the aged.

Also worth mentioning are the various parliamentary devices, from time-consuming quorum calls to Senate filibusters, which make it easier to thwart action. The rule in the Senate allows a small but determined number of senators to engage in limitless debate and thereby filibuster a bill to death or dilute it by exercising the threat of filibuster. For decades the filibuster was a weapon of last resort used by Southern senators to block civil rights legislation. In more recent times, as conservatives in Congress sought to roll back past democratic gains and introduce New Right legislation, the filibuster was used most frequently—with mixed success—as a defensive measure by liberals.

No doubt the legislative labyrinth serves a worthwhile filtering purpose at times. About 80 percent of the bills that run the obstacle course fail to become law, and many of these are better left buried. But the lawmakers' wisdom is not the only determinant of what gets through; class power is also at work. Corporate and financial interests usually get what they want and are able to stymie what they oppose. A $100 million bill to fund summer jobs for unemployed youth is debated in Congress from December 1983 to July 1984, with dozens of attempts at crippling amendments. But when Continental Illinois Bank is about to go bankrupt, billions of dollars are handed out practically overnight without any kind of deliberation by the appropriate congressional committees. Multibillion-dollar tax breaks for the rich and multibillion-dollar defense contracts are passed in a matter of days with little debate, while a minor pilot project supplying school breakfasts for a small number of the millions of malnourished children in America is debated at great length.[34] In 1981 Congress cut domestic programs by $87 billion in a few months, undoing legislative programs that had taken many years of struggle to achieve. The big financial interests may not always win, but they seem to have the fast track in Congress.

One Democratic senator reminded his party colleagues that they were too responsive to moneyed interests and were neglecting to keep up appearances as "the party of the people." In a speech on the Senate floor urging that the scientific patents of the $25 billion space program not be given away to private corporations but applied for public benefit, Russell Long (D-La.) candidly remarked: "Many of these [corporate] people have much influence. I, like others have importuned some of them for campaign contributions for my party and myself. Nevertheless, we owe it to the people, now and then, to save one or two votes for them. This is one

34. *New York Times*, May 18, 1984; Sam Marcy, "State Capitalism and the Collapse of Continental Illinois," *Workers World*, August 9, 1984, p. 9.

such instance. . . . We Democrats can trade on the dubious assumption that we are protector of the public interest only so long if we permit things like these patent giveaways."[35] Here Senator Long provided a perfect example of how the need to maintain democratic appearances can sometimes lead to taking an actual democratic stance.

Congress is less bicameral than "multicameral." For all their activity, 100 senators and 435 representatives, in a subcommittee system of fragmented power and beholden to an array of pressure groups, are unable to produce a coherent, national program. The lawmakers confine their legislative efforts to several specialized subcommittees, trying to build up some expertise in limited areas, giving little attention to the interrelatedness and systemic nature of these problems. On matters outside their domain, they defer to their other specialized (and special-interest) colleagues.

Congress "is at best a collection of well-intentioned people who have fallen back on a service role while making a great deal of noise about larger issues."[36] Members of Congress spend a good deal of time on casework for constituents, making calls to public agencies on behalf of private interests, and answering the huge quantity of mail they receive. Legislators perform constituent service for the many while making policy for the few. They do small favors for small people and big favors for big people, winning votes from the former and campaign money from the latter.

Special-interest legislators often achieve working majorities in Congress by "logrolling," a process of mutual trade-offs that is not the same as compromise. Rather than checking one another as in compromise situations, and thus blunting the selfish demands of each, interest groups end up supporting one another's claims at the expense of those who are without power in the pressure system. For example, legislators hoping to maintain a price support program for sugar interests will swap votes with legislators seeking to protect steel subsidies.[37]

For some members of Congress getting reelected is their major concern; for others it is their only concern. In any case, the great majority of them are quite successful at it. In the nineteenth century, half or more of every new House was made up of freshmen representatives. Even as late as the 1940s, freshmen composed upwards of 30 percent. Today the turnover has dropped to between 11 and 13 percent and this includes those members who voluntarily retire from office. Between 1956 and 1984, incumbents who sought reelection were returned to their seats 92 percent of the time.

---

35. *Washington Monthly*, April 1972, p. 18.
36. Sanford Ungar, "Bleak House: Frustration on Capitol Hill," *Atlantic*, July 1977, p. 38. Ungar was referring to the House, but his description applies to the Senate as well.
37. *New York Times*, October 2, 1985.

In 1986, of the 393 House members who ran for reelection, 385 won, for a record 98 percent.[38] There are a number of reasons why incumbents prevail:

1. Campaign funding. Incumbents have already demonstrated an ability to muster enough money and organization to win. And once in office they have numerous opportunities to build up still more moneyed support. About 80 percent of PAC money goes to incumbents, 10 percent to challengers, and 10 percent to open seats.[39]

2. Better press coverage. Incumbents have had years of public exposure and voter recognition, while challengers usually have not. Incumbents who have built strong support in their districts are likely to win both more coverage and more favorable press treatment than are their opponents.[40] Challengers find that one of the few lines of attack open to them is to focus on issues, but the media tend to downplay or ignore issues.

3. Resources of office. Members of Congress have the resources of the office itself, including staff, franking privileges, travel allowances, and the opportunity to perform favors for voters. Such resources give the incumbent a built-in advantage estimated at millions of dollars.

4. One-party predominance. A good many districts heavily favor one party over the other. Despite increasing two-party competition around the nation, the number of incumbents winning by majorities of 60 percent or more has also gone up; and in 1986 nearly 25 percent of the Democrats and 17 percent of the Republicans had no opponent at all. This apparent contradiction suggests that, in many instances, it is not the one-party predominance that creates an incumbency advantage but the incumbent's overbearing advantage in money, press, and resources that has created the one-party predominance, discouraging challengers from attracting enough financial support or from even entering the race.[41]

Despite the advantages of incumbency, there is a higher retirement rate. In recent years many members of Congress have been finding their jobs more demanding and less rewarding. The work load has greatly increased. Campaign costs have escalated, and fund raising takes up more and more time, especially for the less affluent and more progressive lawmakers who do not easily win the favors of wealthy contributors. Special-interest groups are more numerous and more demanding. The erosion of

---

38. Charles Jones, *The United States Congress* (Homewood, Ill.: Dorsey Press, 1982), p. 79; *Washington Post*, January 6, 1985 and November 23, 1986.

39. *Washington Post*, November 23, 1986.

40. Peter Clarke and Susan Evans, *Covering Campaigns: Journalism in Congressional Elections* (Palo Alto, Calif.: Stanford University Press, 1983); John Orman, "Media Coverage of the Congressional Underdog," *PS*, Fall 1985, pp. 754–59.

41. Norman Ornstein et al., *Vital Statistics on Congress*, 1984–1985 edition (Washington, D.C.: American Enterprise Institute, 1984), p. 38.

the seniority system has diminished the rewards of political longevity. The inability "to get things done" and "make a difference" frustrates the more idealistic legislators, and the attractions of highly lucrative jobs in private industry lure the less idealistic ones. Hence, record numbers of lawmakers are voluntarily retiring, at almost a 10-percent annual rate in recent years. Congress is less often a place where one settles in for life.[42]

It is not quite accurate to call Congress "unrepresentative." It is representative of the power distributions of the wider society in that "power goes to those . . . legislators who service powerful interests, while isolation goes to those who merely represent powerless people."[43] Behind Congress there stands the entire corporate social order, with its hold over the economic life of the nation and the material resources of society; its control of information and mass propaganda; its dominant influence over most cultural and social institutions; its well-placed policymakers, organized pressure groups, high-paid lobbyists, influence-peddling lawyers, and big-money contributions.

A Touch of Democracy

Given all this, it is surprising that any democratic victories are won in Congress. Yet progressive elements do manage to get things through from time to time. The lawmakers are not entirely untouched by popular pressures. Votes still count and therefore so do voters. Thus legislators frequently "vote their district" (or their state, in the case of senators). Some appropriations are "pork barrel"—that is, money for projects that are not the most essential or economical but are highly visible representations of the legislators' ability to get federal funds for their home district. But many appropriations are worthwhile, bringing needed jobs and services to the ordinary folks back home: a post office, a cancer clinic, a program for the handicapped, an adult training project, and the like.

The legislators also perform useful detailed watchdog functions over administrative agencies, checking to see why a Labor Department field office is not functioning, why a Social Security office is being closed, why vacancies in an agency investigating racketeering have not been filled, why a report on wage rates at rural hospitals has not been released, and other such matters. This watchdog function is itself an important democratic pressure on behalf of popular interests, prodding and checking a recalcitrant and often conservative executive leadership. The most useful watchdog of government, the General Accounting Office (GAO), was created by Congress to investigate everything from military waste to en-

42. *New York Times*, March 27 and November 13, 1978.
43. Ralph Nader, "Making Congress Work," *New Republic*, August 21–28, 1971, p. 19.

vironmental abuse. The GAO operates at the request of specific legislators and reports only to Congress (and the public), making revelations that provide important ammunition for democratic struggles.

Congress, then, is not just an arena of special interests. It is also a place where larger critical issues are raised concerning U.S. policies at home and abroad. To the extent that democratic forces have any impact on the policy process, it is likely to be through Congress. There are liberal and avowedly progressive groupings in the national legislature that often represent something more than corporate-military power. Such legislators will often respond to the needs of the many rather than the greed of the few, impelled both by their own political commitment and by popular pressure. But what victories they win are almost always hard-fought and hard-won, for the legislative high ground is usually occupied by the conservative coalition, composed mostly of Republicans and Southern Democrats (more recently named "boll weevil" Democrats who sided with the Reagan program). They frequently manage to block the liberal agenda somewhere along the legislative labyrinth or in open votes in Congress. And when the White House is controlled by the Right as during the Reagan era, then the ultraconservatives are able to score decisive victories against the hard-won gains of labor and the Left.

The liberal-labor coalition in Congress has to win some portion of the moderate conservatives to their side in order to achieve major legislative victories against the ultraconservatives. This is more likely to happen during times of strong social agitation as in the 1930s and 1960s, when moderates are convinced that concessions are in order.[44] Major splits within the business community provide an opening wedge for reform forces. But when business is unifiedly against something, there is little chance of popular gain. "Recent evidence supports the view that major business lobbies appear to be able to exercise a de facto veto over measures they oppose. If business lobbies don't object, reform measures can become law; if they do, they can't."[45]

On rare occasions a unified business community may be defeated, as in 1935 when Congress passed the National Labor Relations Act, which gave the force of law to collective bargaining between employers and unions—despite the vehement oppostion of virtually the entire business class. But as Domhoff points out, that was the first major defeat the corporate class had suffered on a labor issue in U.S. history—and given the subsequent rollback of the Taft-Hartley Act (1947) and other such laws—the only major defeat thus far.[46]

---

44. G. William Domhoff, *Who Rules America Now?* (New York: Simon and Schuster, 1983), p. 145.
45. Mark Green and Michael Calabrese, *Who Runs Congress?*, 3rd ed. (New York: Bantam Books, 1979), p. 28.
46. Domhoff, *Who Rules America?* p. 145–46.

In sum, there is a genuine measure of struggle and indeterminancy in the policy-making process. Congress is still a place where democratic inputs can be registered. Progressive forces within the legislative body can apply democratic pressure in their watchdog capacity and can on occasion mount attacks against a conservative status quo or maintain some (partially successful) defense against ultraconservative rollback. However, the overall evidence suggests that the moneyed powers are the predominant influence in Congress, and that, for all the reasons discussed above, the legislators do more to sustain than change the existing system of class power and privilege.

13

The President: Guardian of the System

In this chapter our task is to take a nonworshipful look at what presidents do and why they do it. The president, we are told, plays many roles: chief executive, "chief legislator," commander-in-chief, head of state, and party leader. Seldom mentioned is the role of guardian and representative of capitalism. The president is the embodiment of the executive-centered political system that defends American corporate interests at home and abroad.

SALESMAN OF THE SYSTEM

As authoritative figures whose opinions are widely publicized, presidents do their share to indoctrinate the American people into the ruling-class ideology. Every modern president has had occasion to praise the "free enterprise system" and denounce collectivist alternatives. President Carter proclaimed himself "an engineer, a planner and a businessman" who understood the value of "minimal intrusion of government in our free economic system."[1] One description of President Ford could easily apply to any number of other presidents: "[He] follows the judgment of the major international oil companies on oil problems in the same way that he amiably heeds the advice of other big businesses on the problems that

1. *Seattle Post-Intelligencer*, July 16, 1976. When I refer to the president as *he*, I only am recognizing that every president so far has been a man. I do not mean to rule out the possibility that a woman may eventually occupy the office.

interest them. . . . He is . . . a solid believer in the business ideology of rugged individualism, free markets and price competition—virtues that exist more clearly in his mind than they do in the practices of the international oil industry."[2]

The president is the top salesman of the system, conjuring up reassuring images about the state of the union. He would have us believe that our social problems and economic difficulties can be solved with enough "vigor" and "resolve," as John Kennedy used to say; or with "hard work" and "toughing it out," as Richard Nixon put it; or with a return to "self-reliance" and a "spiritual revival," as Ronald Reagan urged. A massive oil spill wreaks ecological destruction on the Santa Barbara coast—and President Nixon conducts an "inspection tour" along one of the beaches especially cleaned up for the event, falsely announcing that the damage has been repaired. The nuclear plant at Three Mile Island comes close to a disastrous meltdown, venting large amounts of radioactive gases into the atmosphere—and President Carter appears at the site with his wife Rosalyn to reassure the American public that everything's under control. The space shuttle *Challenger*, plagued by serious safety problems, blows up on takeoff, killing its entire crew—and within hours President Reagan appears on television to laud their sacrifice as yet another glorious step in humanity's progress.

"America is number one," proclaimed President Nixon, although millions of Americans at the bottom of the heap were feeling less than that. "America is standing tall. America is back. America is the greatest," exulted President Reagan, to a nation with millions underemployed, 35 million living below the poverty level, a record trade deficit, and a runaway national debt. Prosperity, our presidents tell us, is here or not far off—but so is the Red Menace and the wild-eyed terrorists, against whom we must guard with huge military budgets and a strong internal security system. Presidents usually downplay crises except the ones needed to bolster defense spending and interventionism abroad.

Whether Democrat or Republican, liberal or conservative, the president tends to treat capitalist interests as synonymous with the nation's well-being. Presidents will greet the expansion of big business and big profits as manifestations of "a healthy *national* economy" and as good for the "*national* interest." They will describe the overseas investments of giant corporations as "*United States* investments abroad," part of "*America's* interests in the world," to be defended at all costs—or certainly at great cost to the populace.

At the Constitutional Convention, the wealthy planter Charles Pinckney proposed that no one qualify for the presidency who was not worth at

2. William Shannon, *New York Times*, July 22, 1975.

least $100,000—a rich person's sum in 1787. While the proposal was never written into the Constitution, it seemingly has been followed in practice. The individuals who have occupied the highest office, with a few notable exceptions, have come from the highest income brackets. Since World War II, almost all presidential candidates on the Democratic and Republican tickets have been millionaires either at the time they first campaigned for the office or by the time they departed from it. In addition, presidents have drawn their top advisers and administrators primarily from industry and banking and have relied heavily on the judgments of corporate leaders.[3]

Like other politicians, the individuals who run for president procure vast sums from the rich to defray their campaign costs. Big contributors

3. See the discussion in chapter eleven on the plutocracy. The president lives like a multimillionaire in a rent-free, 132-room mansion, the White House, set on an 18-acre estate, with a $2 million maintenance budget and a domestic staff of eighty-three, including six butlers, a well-stocked wine cellar, a private movie room, a gymnasium, tennis courts, a bowling alley, and a heated outdoor swimming pool. In addition, the president has the free services of a private physician, a dozen chauffeured limousines, numerous helicopters, and jets, including Air Force One—which costs $5,221 an hour to fly. (Every trip Reagan took to California at the taxpayers' expense cost about the equivalent of 100,000 meals in food stamps.) The president has access to country retreats, free vacations, a $70,000 yearly expense allowance—and for the few things the president must pay for, a $200,000 annual salary. Journalists and political scientists have described the presidency as a "man-killing job." Yet presidents live better and longer than the average American man. And after leaving office they can count on a comfortable pension.

may disclaim any intention of trying to buy influence, insisting that they give freely because they "believe" in the candidate and think the candidate will pursue policies beneficial to the national interest. That they view the national interest as something often indistinguishable from their own interests does not make their support hypocritical but all the more sincere. Their image of a better America is a product of their own class experiences and values.

If it should happen, however, that after the election the big contributors find themselves or their firms burdened by a problem that only the White House can handle, they see no reason why they shouldn't be allowed to exercise their rights like any other citizens and ask their elected representative, who in this case happens to be their friend, the president of the United States, for a little help.

While appearing to be an opponent of the special interests and protector of the national interest, the president is as capable of trading favors for money as any other influence-peddling politician—only on a grander scale. The Nixon administration helped settle a multibillion-dollar suit against ITT and received a $400,000 donation from that corporation.[4] Reagan pushed through the deregulation of oil and gasoline prices and received more than $200 million from the oil companies for his campaigns. He opposed federal gun controls—to the satisfaction of the National Rifle Association, one of his special-interest supporters. And he was able to get massive tax cuts for corporations and rich individuals and fat contracts for the defense industry, all of whom were among his biggest contributors.[5]

It is said that the greatness of the office lends greatness to its occupants; even persons of mediocre endowment supposedly grow in response to the presidency's responsibilities and powers. Closer examination shows that White House occupants have been just as readily corrupted as ennobled by the power of the office, inclined toward self-righteous assertion, compelled to demonstrate their toughness and decisiveness, intolerant of, and irritated by, public criticism, and not above using their power in unlawful ways. Thus, at least six presidents employed illegal FBI wiretaps to gather incriminating information on rival political figures.[6] The White House tapes, which recorded the private Oval Office conversations of President Nixon, revealed him to be a petty, vindictive, bigoted man who manifested a shallowness of spirit and mind that the majestic office could cloak but

4. *New York Times*, January 11 and June 15, 1973; also Anthony Sampson, *The Sovereign State of I. T. T.* (New York: Stein and Day, 1973).

5. Juan Williams, "Reagan Is the Real King of the Special Interest Groups," *Washington Post*, April 1, 1984; Noel Rerof, *Daily World*, May 8, 1981.

6. Joanne Omang, "Secret Hoover Files Show Misuse of FBI," *Washington Post*, December 12, 1983.

not transform.[7] President Reagan was observed to have repeatedly fabricated stories and anecdotes about nonexistent events. The Iran-contra affair revealed him to be a deceptive manipulator who pretended to support one policy while pursuing another, and who felt himself to be unaccountable to Congress and to the law itself.[8]

THE TWO FACES OF THE PRESIDENT

Presidents make a show of concern for public causes, using images intended to enhance their popular appeal; thus Roosevelt had his "New Deal," Truman his "Fair Deal," Kennedy his "New Frontier," Johnson his "Great Society," and Reagan his "American Renaissance." Behind the fine-sounding labels one discovers much the same record of service to the powerful and neglect of the needy.

Consider John Kennedy, a liberal president widely celebrated for his devotion to the underdog. In foreign affairs, Kennedy spoke of international peace and self-determination, yet he invaded Cuba after Castro nationalized the holdings of United States corporations. He drastically increased military expenditures, instituted new counterinsurgency programs throughout the Third World, and sent troops to Vietnam. In domestic matters, Kennedy presented himself as a champion of civil rights yet he refrained from taking legal action to support antidiscrimination cases or to prevent repeated attacks against civil-rights organizers in the South. Kennedy talked as if he were a friend of working people, yet he imposed wage restraints on unions at a time workers' buying power was stagnant or declining, and he opposed introduction of the 35-hour work week. He also instituted tax programs and deficit-spending policies that carried business profits to all-time highs without reducing unemployment.[9]

Conservative presidents, such as Richard Nixon and Gerald Ford, manifested the same tendency to talk for the people and work for the corporate elites. Both of them voiced their support for environmental protection while opening new forest lands for commercial exploitation and

---

7. Official audits revealed that President Nixon spent $2 million of the taxpayers' money on improvements for his private estates and underpaid his taxes by more than $400,000. On occasion, he requested the Internal Revenue Service to stop auditing the incomes of close friends: *New York Times*, June 21, 22, and 25, 1973, and April 4, 1974.

8. On Reagan's fabrications see Mark Green and Gail MacColl, *Ronald Reagan's Reign of Error* (New York: Pantheon, 1983); also Robert Lindsey, "Reagan Disputed on Work Program," *New York Tmes*, April 13, 1986. On Reagan's misrepresentations regarding Iran-contra, see the *Washington Post* and *New York Times* from November 26, 1986, onward.

9. Ian McMahan, "The Kennedy Myth," *New Politics*, Winter 1968, pp. 40–48; Richard Walton, *Cold War and Counter-Revolution: The Foreign Policy of John F. Kennedy* (Baltimore: Penguin Books, 1972); Bruce Miroff, *Pragmatic Illusions* (New York: McKay, 1976).

opposing the regulation of strip mining. Both gave lip service to the problems of the Vietnam veteran, the plight of the elderly, and the needs of the poor, yet opposed extending benefits and services to these groups and even supported cutbacks.[10]

President Carter supplied the same admixture of liberal rhetoric and conservative policy. He promised to cut the military budget and instead increased it. He promised to "reduce the commerce in arms sales," but arms sales under his administration rose to new levels. While he talked of helping the needy, Carter proposed cutbacks in summer youth jobs, child nutrition programs, and other benefits. After campaigning as a friend of labor, he went on to oppose most of the AFL-CIO legislative program. Like his predecessors, he continued to dole out multibillion-dollar credits and subsidies to big business.[11]

The gap between rhetoric and policy became a vast chasm during the Reagan years. In 1986, Reagan called for a "war on drugs" but cut funding for drug treatment and prevention by almost one-third. He repeatedly hailed our veterans for their great sacrifices but offered a budget that cut veterans' health-care benefits in 1985. He participated in media events celebrating the indomitable courage of the disabled, but repeatedly tried to cut funds for the disabled. After Reagan opposed any extension of Social Security benefits, the Republican National Committee spent $1 million in television ads giving him credit for winning the 7-percent increase Congress had passed. Before an audience of Black Republicans in Washington, D.C., Reagan described himself as a champion of racial equality when in fact he had opposed an extension of the Voting Rights Act, had advocated tax breaks for segregated private schools, had drastically reduced enforcement of civil-rights laws, and had cut inner-city assistance programs. He claimed his administration had appointed more Latinos, Blacks, and women to top policy and judiciary posts than any previous administration, when actually, as compared to the Carter administration, he reduced such appointments by anywhere from 60 to 80 percent.

In 1980 candidate Reagan said he opposed Selective Service registration, but once in office he reactivated it. That same year candidate Reagan supported the federal air traffic controllers' union in their claims that air traffic was dangerously overcrowded and that they were plagued by stressful work conditions and obsolete equipment; but once in office President Reagan refused to negotiate these issues and broke the union, firing all 11,400 of its striking members. Running for reelection in 1984, Reagan

---

10. For instance, *New York Times*, September 11 and October 8, 1975.

11. Christopher Lydon, "Jimmy Carter Revealed: He's a Rockefeller Republican," *Atlantic*, July 1977, pp. 50–59; Frank Browning, "Jimmy Carter's Astounding Lies," *Inquiry*, May 5, 1980, pp. 13–17.

announced that his tax cuts had benefited the poor and not the rich—even though the figures said otherwise; he claimed his administration was waging a vigorous defense of the environment while he did little to enforce environmental laws and opposed congressional efforts in that direction.[12]

In foreign affairs, Reagan repeatedly accused Cuba, Nicaragua, and other noncapitalist countries of an unwillingness to negotiate, but he himself repeatedly rebuffed Nicaraguan and Cuban overtures for friendly relations and refused to seriously negotiate arms limitations with the Soviets. Through the use of blockades, embargoes, military forays, nuclear escalations, and menacing pronouncements he launched a campaign of confrontation and destabilization aimed at socialist nations—while he assured the American public that the United States government sought only friendly and peaceful relations with other countries.[13]

The President's Systemic Bind

If presidents tend to speak one way and act another, it is less likely due to some inborn flaw shared by the varied personalities who occupy the office than to something in the nature of the office itself. Like any officeholder, the president plays a dual role in that he must satisfy the major interests of corporate America and at the same time make a show of serving the people. He differs from other politicians in that the demands and expectations of his office are greater and therefore the contradictions deeper. More than any other officeholder, he deals with the overall crises of capitalism, for he is the national executive, but also the only nationally elected leader (along with the vice-president, of course), and hence the focus of mass attention and mass demand. So the president, even more than other politicians, is caught between the demands of democracy and plutocracy.

Although some presidents may try, they discover they cannot belong to both the corporations and the people. Occasionally a president may be instrumental in getting Congress to allocate monies and services for the

12. James Nathan Miller, "Ronald Reagan and the Techniques of Deception," *Atlantic Monthly*, February 1984, pp. 62–68; *Washington Post*, August 29, 1982, June 17 and 19 and July 13, 1984, September 27, 1986; *New York Times*, July 30 and 31, 1982; December 27, 1985. How to explain Reagan's electoral victories? The poor performance of the economy in 1980 proved to be Carter's undoing and led to the Reagan landslide. During the recession of 1981, Reagan's approval rating dropped 60 percent. It was the improved performance of the economy in 1984—with inflation, unemployment, and interest rates down, and a gain in real income for much of the middle class—that gave Reagan his reelection landslide: Seymour Martin Lipset, "The Elections, the Economy and Public Opinion, 1984," *PS*, Winter 1985, pp. 28–38.

13. For a critique of U.S. foreign policy see my *The Sword and The Dollar: Imperialism, Revolution, and the Cold War* (St. Martin's, forthcoming); also the discussion and sources cited in chapter six.

American public, but whatever his intentions, he comes no closer to solving the deep structural problems of the political economy, for he cannot both serve capitalism as capitalism needs to be served and at the same time drastically transform it. He cannot come up with a solution because he is part of the problem, or part of the system that creates the problem.

While members of Congress are the captives of the special interests, the president, elected by the entire country, tends to be less vulnerable to pressure groups and more responsive to the needs of the unorganized public—at least this is what political scientists taught after years of observing presidents like Roosevelt, Truman, and Kennedy tussling with conservatives in Congress. As we have seen, our various presidents resemble the average pressure politician to a greater extent than we were taught. Nevertheless, the president is more likely to see the ramifications that issues have for the overall system than the average member of Congress, who is concerned primarily with the problems of his or her district or state and the desires of his or her campaign contributors. (Even when the chief executive does represent special interests, he is less likely to be recognized as doing so, for he can define his policies on behalf of oil companies, banks, and military contractors as necessary for the security and well-being of the nation itself.)

The growth of capitalism from a diverse array of small, local producers to national and multinational conglomerates has necessitated an increasingly active role by the federal government. The government has helped secure markets for the bigger corporations by subsidizing them at the expense of smaller interests and by imposing regulations that limit the small firm's opportunity to compete successfully. Presidents have been instrumental in thus "rationalizing" the economy. In representing the more powerful, advanced financial and industrial interests, the president has played a systemic role, updating the economy and getting businesspeople to accept a modern, state-regulated, state-supported capitalism.

The president must do for capitalism what individual capitalists cannot do for the system or for themselves. First, he must reconcile conflicts between major producers. Thus, he might go against the interests of some importing companies to protect an industry that is being hurt by foreign imports. Or he might wipe out a shellfish industry to build a shoreline plant for the nuclear industry. Generally, he decides these interest-group conflicts in favor of heavy industry and big finance as against light industry and small business—again because the bigger interests play a bigger role in the entire corporate system.

Second, on behalf of the capitalist system as a system the president sometimes must oppose the interests of individual companies, keeping them in line with the overall needs of the corporate economy: hence he might oppose tariff protections for particular firms in order to avoid having foreign countries retaliate by closing their markets to American trade. Or he might do battle with an industry like steel to hold prices down in order to ease the inflationary effects on other producer interests. When engaged in such conflicts the president takes on an appearance of opposing the special interests on behalf of the common interest. *In fact, he might be better described as protecting the common interests of the special interests.*

Third, as the only elected officeholder accountable to a national constituency, and as the focus of popular expectation and constant attention from the media, the president does feel the pressure more than anyone else to solve the nation's problems. It is his task, if anyone's, to ameliorate the hardships of the populace and discourage the tendency toward disruption, protest, and troublesome rebellion. There are limits to how inequitable and oppressive the politico-economic system can be. Those who work too single-mindedly for the privileged classes run the risk of undermining the system. So, billions are spent on social programs to blunt the discontent that the underprivileged feel, wedding them to the system—by means of the dole. Here, too, presidents, especially liberal ones, have been the key force in the process of reform. It is usually the president's task to convince the business class that new concessions are needed to defend the old order. By accepting labor unions, minimum-wage laws, social programs, and the like, the president may incur the wrath of the more conservative elements of the business community who see such things as the beginning of the end. Again, the president's role is an innovative one, but it is intended to reform rather than transform the existing system.

The success any group enjoys in winning the intervention of the president has less to do with the justice of its cause than with the place it occupies in the class structure. If a large group of migrant workers and a small group of aerospace executives both sought the president's assistance, it would not be difficult to predict which of them would be more likely to win it. Witness these events of April 1971:

1. Some 80,000 to 90,000 migrant farm workers in Florida, out of work for much of the season because of crop failures and exempted from unemployment compensation, were left without means of feeding themselves and their families. Faced with the prospect of seeing their children starve, the workers demonstrated in large numbers outside President Nixon's vacation residence in Florida. The peaceful gathering was an attempt to attract public attention to their plight and to get the White House to intercede. The workers succeeded in attracting the attention only of the police, who dispersed them with swinging clubs. Eventually the Florida farm counties were declared disaster areas because of the crop losses sustained by the commercial farms. The government emergency relief money ended up in the hands of the big growers who worked with state

agencies in distributing it. Since the migrant workers had no state residence, they did not qualify for relief and were "summarily left out of the decisions."[14]

2. During the very week the farm workers were being clubbed in Florida, leaders of the aerospace industry placed a few telephone calls to Washington and were invited to meet quietly with the president to discuss their companies' problems. Later that same day the White House announced a $42 million authorization to the aerospace industry to relocate, retrain, and in other ways assist its top administrators, scientists, and technicians. The spending plan, an industry creation, was accepted by the government without prior study.[15]

Contrasting the treatment accorded the farm workers with that provided the aerospace industrialists (or big-farm owners), we might ask: is the president responding to a "national interest" or a "special interest" when helping the giant firms? Much depends upon how the labels are applied. Those who believe the national interest necessitates taking every possible measure to maintain the profits and strength of the industrial and military establishment, of which the aerospace industry is a part, might say the president is not responding to a special interest but to the needs of national security. Certainly almost every president in modern times might have acted accordingly. In contrast, a regional group of farm workers represents a marginal interest. Without making light of the suffering of the migrant families, it is enough to say that a president's first responsibility is to tend to our industrial economy. In fact, the argument goes, when workers act to disrupt and weaken the sinews of industry, as have striking coal miners, railroad operators, and steel workers, the president may see fit to deal summarily with them.[16]

Other people would argue that the national interest is not served when giant industries receive favored treatment at the expense of workers, taxpayers, and consumers and to the lasting neglect of millions like the farm workers. That the corporations have holdings that are national and often

---

14. Tom Foltz, "Florida Farmworkers Face Disaster," *Guardian*, April 3, 1971, p. 4.

15. *New York Times*, April 2, 1971.

16. When Ronald Reagan complained about the "special interests" attempting to thwart his desire to serve the national interest with his budget-cutting efforts, he was using a motif long propagated by political scientists who defined "special" and "national" interests by some abstract scope (local versus national) and not by the *class* interest involved (owners versus employees and consumers). Thus, Reagan was able to portray the social needs of working people as limited, parochial "special" interests, while the big companies had "national," indeed international, interests. (It is the same argument made by present-day apologists for the framers of the Constitution: see chapter four.) When asked whether a U.S. military foray into Bolivia, ostensibly to catch drug traffickers, was in the national interest, President Reagan said, "Anything we do is in the national interest": *Washington Post*, December 29, 1986.

multinational in scope does not mean they represent the interests of the nation's *populace*. The "national interest" or "public interest" should encompass the ordinary public rather than a handful of big commercial farm owners, corporate elites, and their well-paid technicians and managers. Contrary to an established myth, the public monies distributed to these favored few do not "trickle down" to the mass of working people at the bottom—as the hungry farm workers can testify.

Whichever position one takes, it becomes clear that there is no *neutral* way of defining the "national interest." Whichever policy the president pursues, he is helping some class interests rather than others, and it is a matter of historical record that presidents have usually chosen a definition of the national interest that serves the giant conglomerates. It is also clear, whether we consider it essential or deplorable, that the president, as the most powerful officeholder in the land, is most readily available to the most powerful interests in the land and rather inaccessible to us lesser mortals.

THE "NEW FEDERALISM" PLOY

Upon assuming office, President Reagan vowed "to curb the size and influence of the federal establishment." For fiscal year 1988, however, he offered a record trillion-dollar federal budget, almost half of which went to the military and to interest on the national debt. Three-fifths of what remained went into just three programs: Social Security, Medicare, and federal retirement—more than half of which is for military pensions. As for the smaller social spending programs, Reagan sought to hand them over to the states or abolish them outright.

This "New Federalism," as Reagan called it, represented less a shift in power than in responsibility. States and cities were given the responsibility of dealing with major social problems without getting the necessary funds. In many instances, the diminished federal monies were allocated in block grants to the state governments instead of directly to the needy urban areas, as had been previously the case. The effect was to create new bureaucracies at the state level that shortchanged the cities and doled out funds to small towns and suburban communities. These latter then became yet another and wider constituency for federal funds.[17]

The "New Federalism" sought to shift public power—at least in the area of human services—back to smaller units of government, thus reviv-

17. Howard Kurtz, "Hostility to 'New Federalism' Is Bipartisan Among Mayors," *Washington Post*, December 10, 1984; see also *Washington Post*, January 7, 1987.

ing a dream, so dear to conservatives, of a marriage between Big Business and Little Government, one that allows business to play off states and communities against each other in order to extract more tax breaks and subsidies from them. It is easier for Dupont Corporation to control the tiny state of Delaware than deal with the federal government as a whole. Hooker Chemical Corporation would prefer to see little Niagara County in New York, rather than Washington, have sole jurisdiction over the land and people poisoned in Niagara by Hooker's toxic wastes. The coal-mine companies find state safety inspectors more malleable and more easily bought off than federal inspectors. And Exxon, which is more powerful and richer than Alaska, would like to see that sparsely populated state given complete control over all federal oil and natural resources within its boundaries—which in effect would give Exxon complete control over Alaska.[18]

However, on those occasions *when corporate interests have encountered democratic regulations from the states*, Reagan discarded his states'-rights posture and acted like an early Hamiltonian federalist, using the central government to override state powers. For instance, the Reagan administration decided (a) that the Atomic Energy Act of 1954—to the satisfaction of the nuclear and utilities industries—prohibited the states from establishing nuclear-plant emission standards more stringent than those imposed by federal authorities; (b) that the Federal Home Loan Bank Board—to the satisfaction of savings and loan associations and to the dismay of home buyers—could override state laws that protected low-interest mortgages; (c) that state laws protecting companies from corporate takeovers were invalid because the matter was exclusively within the province of the federal government.[19]

Like conservatives since 1787, Ronald Reagan was for stronger or weaker central government and for stronger or weaker state powers depending on which arrangement served owning-class interests on a particular issue. This is why, for all of Reagan's talk about giving power back to the states, he often stood firmly on the side of the "overgrown" federal power. For this, some New Right ideologues accused Reagan of abandoning true conservative principles. Not true. Like any conservative he understood that abstract notions such as states' rights are not an end unto themselves but just a means of serving the propertied class, and when they fail to do so, they are quietly put aside for more effective measures. This is not a matter of being pragmatic and compromising on conservative principles but of uncompromisingly pursuing ruling-class interests by whatever means available.

---

18. Sam Marcy, *Workers World*, January 23, 1981.
19. Alan Morrison, "New Federalism Holes," *New York Times*, September 20, 1982.

THE PRESIDENT VERSUS CONGRESS: WHO HAS THE POWER?

A glance at the Constitution seems to indicate that Congress is the more powerful branch of government. Article 2 gives the president the power to appoint ambassadors, federal judges, and senior executive officers (subject to Senate confirmation) and to make treaties (subject to ratification by two-thirds of the senators present). The president can veto laws (but the veto can be overriden by a two-thirds vote in Congress), and can call Congress into special session and do a few other incidental things. The president has two other more significant functions: to see that the laws are faithfully executed and to serve as commander-in-chief of the armed forces. But Article 1 seems far more important: it gives Congress the power to declare war, make the laws of the land, raise taxes, and spend money. By all appearances, it is Congress that determines policy and lays down the law and it is the president who does Congress's bidding.

The reality is something else. In the last century or so, with the growth of industrial capitalism at home and abroad, the role of government has grown enormously at the municipal, state, and federal levels and in the executive, legislative, and judicial branches. But the tasks of serving capitalism's vast interests in war and peace and dealing with the politico-economic problems it has created have fallen disproportionately on the level of government that is national and international in scope—the federal—and on the branch most suited to carrying out the necessary technical, organizational, and military tasks—the executive. The responsibilities of the executive have so expanded that there is no such thing as a "weak" or inactive president nowadays, for even Eisenhower, who preferred to exercise little initiative, found himself proposing huge budgets and participating in decisions of far greater scope than anything handled by a "strong" president a half century before.[20]

The executive branch today is a vast conglomeration of thirteen departments and hundreds of agencies, commissions, and bureaus. Many of these government units are designed to accommodate the special interests in transportation, commerce, mining, shipping, banking, veterans affairs, education, and agriculture, to name a few. Other portions of the executive are concerned with maintaining capitalism as a system.[21] For that purpose, the Executive Office of the President, a bureaucracy unto itself, contains a number of administrative units to help the president formulate

20. On the powers of the president see Richard Pious, *The American Presidency* (New York: Basic Books, 1979).

21. Karl Marx and Frederick Engels noted 140 years ago in *The Communist Manifesto* that "the executive of the modern state" manages the common affairs of the whole capitalist class.

and coordinate overall policy. Among the most powerful of these is the Office of Management and Budget (OMB), which puts together both the president's budget and the legislative program and sometimes enforces White House policy in the bureaucracy. Another crucial unit within the Executive Office is the National Security Council (NSC), created for the purpose of overall planning and coordination of military, international, and domestic policies related to national security. The NSC is the White House's instrument (along with the Defense Department and to a lesser extent the State Department) for managing counterinsurgency in the Third World, the cold war, and U.S. global corporate hegemony. The CIA reports directly to the NSC.

The growth of presidential powers has been so great as to have occasioned a relative decline in the powers of Congress (even though legislative activity itself has increased over the years). This is especially true in international affairs. The end result is a presidency that tends to eclipse Congress—and sometimes the law itself. The president commands a number of resources that give him a decided edge over Congress:

Pork Barrel. The lawmaker who votes the way the president wants on crucial bills is more likely to get that veterans' hospital built in his or her district, or support for an emergency farm bill, or a federal contract for a shipyard back home. One representative who opposed Reagan's bill for the MX missile was informed that his district might lose an agricultural service office; others who supported the MX received political favors from the White House.[22]

Personal Lobbying. The president sometimes directly approaches members of Congress for their support, inviting them to breakfast at the White House, flattering their egos, appealing to their personal and party loyalty, promising White House support during the next election campaign. The lawmaker might come to feel he or she would not look good going against the president. The prestige of the presidency itself lends persuasion to this pressure.

Superior Media Exposure. Commanding the kind of media attention that most politicians can only dream of, the president is able to define the agenda more readily than legislative leaders. Transmitted by a dutiful press, the president's appeals shape the climate of opinion to which Congress must react. One study found that on only five of thirty-six occasions that President Reagan appeared in a formal address on evening television was the congressional opposition given an opportunity to respond directly to him on the same network. In addition, live network coverage of the

22. *New York Times*, March 26, 1985.

president's messages seems "to have had an unmistakable impact on measures being considered by Congress."[23]

Unitary Office. There being only one president but many legislators, the chief executive has the advantage of unitary initiative and action. Almost by definition, a legislature is a collection of voices and interests, not structured as a command post, and usually not productive of cohesive national policy. Today, the executive plays a greater role in shaping the legislative agenda than do the legislators. One hears of "the president's program" rather than "Congress's program." Approximately 80 percent of the major laws enacted originate in the executive branch.

Information. In just about every policy area—from weapons systems to management of timber lands—the executive controls most of the crucial information. Congress frequently goes along because it depends so heavily on what the executive departments have to say. At times, presidents place themselves and their associates above congressional interrogation by claiming "executive privilege." Although nowhere mentioned in the constitution, "executive privilege" has been used to withhold information on everything from undeclared wars to illegal campaign funds and burglaries.[24]

National Security and War. Under the guise of national defense and national security, the president removes whole policy areas from public scrutiny and from congressional oversight, making claim to an unaccountable power that circumvents congressional mandates. A report by two House subcommittees dealing with foreign affairs complained of the "unwillingness of the executive branch to acknowledge major decisions and to subject them to public scrutiny and discussion."[25] Congress unknowingly funded CIA operations in Laos and Thailand that were in violation of congressional prohibitions. The legislature ordered a halt to expansion of a naval base in the Indian Ocean, only to discover that construction was continuing. Many members of the Senate had not heard of the automated battlefield program for which they voted secret appropriations.[26] The statute that created the CIA permitted it to expend billions of dollars

23. Report on Media Access by the Library of Congress, Washington, D.C., October 3, 1984.

24. Executive privilege was given a legal peg by the Supreme Court, which decided that a "presumptive privilege" for withholding information (in noncriminal cases) belonged to the president: *United States* v. *Nixon* (1974). Most certainly "presumptive," since it has no existence in the Constitution or any law.

25. *New York Times*, January 22, 1973. By entering into "executive agreements" with foreign nations, the president can even circumvent the Senate's power to ratify treaties.

26. Paul Dickson and John Rothchild, "The Electronic Battlefield," *Monthly Review*, May 1971, pp. 6–14.

without regard to the provisions of law regulating government spending and without the knowledge of Congress.[27]

"War is the true nurse of executive aggrandizement," wrote James Madison in 1787. About two hundred years later, the executive invaded the sovereign state of Grenada and forceably overthrew its government without a declaration of war and engaged in illegal acts of war against Nicaragua, including the arming and training of a mercenary invasion force, again without a declaration from Congress. The CIA overspent its legal limits in the covert war against Nicaragua. U.S. planes and bases were used for support in the Nicaraguan war, against the expressed desire of Congress. And American flight crews were not only ferrying arms to the contra mercenaries (without congressional knowledge) but reportedly were smuggling cocaine and other drugs on their return trips to the United States. In sum, the White House undermined Congress's power to make war, make laws, appropriate funds, and exercise legislative oversight.[28]

Levers of Power. The peculiar danger of executive power is that it executes. Presidents have repeatedly engaged in acts of warfare without congressional approval because they have had at their command the military forces to do so. If the executive branch proposes, it just as often disposes, having the crucial say on how things get done, acting with the force of state, using its military and security forces and covert-action White House "secret teams" to exercise extraordinary initiatives of its own.

Some instances drawn from the Reagan years illustrate how the executive can circumvent the law at home and abroad:

1. Although price-fixing by retail business has been outlawed since 1911, Reagan's antitrust division simply refused to enforce the law.
2. The administration terminated Social Security benefits for hundreds of thousands of disabled Americans. When federal courts found the rulings to be illegal, the administration proclaimed it would neither respect nor appeal the unfavorable court decisions, but would simply ignore them.
3. The administration refused to spend some $22 billion in funds appropriated by Congress for housing and low-income programs, and impounded billions of dollars intended for improvements in mass transit and air safety.

---

27. Louis Fisher, *Presidential Spending Power* (Princeton, N.J.: Princeton University Press, 1975).

28. Jonathan Bennett, "Embargo May Violate U.S. and International Law," *Guardian*, May 15, 1985; Joel Brinley, "Contra Arms Crews Said to Smuggle Drugs," *New York Times*, January 20, 1987; Philip Brenner, "The Casualties of War," *Christian Science Monitor*, August 8, 1984.

4. In violation of a law passed by Congress prohibiting military sales to Guatemala, the Reagan administration agreed to sell several millions of dollars worth of military equipment to that government, asserting that since the sale would be a cash transaction, it would not violate the congressional ban!
5. The General Accounting Office (an investigative arm of Congress) released a report showing that the Reagan administration violated U.S. law in its preparations for increased intervention in Central America, including its training of military personnel and its overspending on military construction in Honduras without authorization by Congress.
6. The Reagan administration involved itself in secret arms sales to Iran and an illegal diversion of funds to the mercenaries waging war in Nicaragua.[29]

Congress itself has sometimes collaborated in the usurpation of its power, granting each president, and a widening list of executive agencies, confidential funds for which no detailed invoices are required. The legislators sometimes have preferred to pass on to the president the task of handling crises. The Gramm-Rudman Act of 1985, for instance, attempts to eliminate the federal deficit over a five-year period by a series of automatic reductions (should Congress be unable to make the required cuts on its own), giving the president new discretion and new leverage especially in military spending.[30]

Under the guise of limiting presidential power, Congress sometimes actually expands it. Thus, the War Powers Act of 1973, requiring the president to seek congressional approval within sixty days for any war he has launched, actually expands his war-making powers, since the Constitution does not grant the president power to engage in warfare without *prior* congressional approval.[31]

---

29. *New York Times*, January 30 and May 13, 1984, March 25, 1986; *Los Angeles Times*, November 4, 1984; *Washington Post*, December 12, 1983; "Propriety of Funding Methods Used by the Department of Defense in Combined Exercises in Honduras," General Accounting Office report B-213137, Washington, D.C., June 22, 1984. The Iran-contra story is still unfolding at the time of this writing. For more circumventions of the law by the executive branch, see the next chapter.

30. *New York Times*, December 13, 1985. It is still too early to tell how this law will work, if it works at all. The Supreme Court has already invalidated a key provision of the act that gave the Comptroller General (head of the GAO) the power to order the spending cuts needed to meet deficit targets. The Court decided this was an infringement on the president's authority to execute the laws: *Bowsher* v. *Synar* (1986).

31. The War Powers Act allows the president to engage U.S. troops only in case of an attack on the United States or its territories, possessions, or armed forces. In invading Grenada and sending troops to Lebanon and military "advisors" to El Salvador and Honduras who are engaged in combat actions, the president violated the act, for in each of these instances no attack had been made against the U.S. and Congress was not consulted.

Many of the restrictions imposed on the executive by Congress are more form than substance. Thus, despite the National Emergencies Act of 1976, which terminated all emergency powers previously granted to presidents, there exist some 470 statutes that enable the chief executive to claim potentially dictatorial powers even if only for a specified time, to seize properties and institute martial law, control transportation, and restrict travel. The Foreign Assistance Act of 1961 requires the president to give prior notice to Congress concerning CIA operations other than those exclusively for intelligence collection. However, if the president finds that the operation is important to the "national security" and extremely "sensitive," then Congress can be bypassed—which is what happened when the United States sold arms to the terrorist regime in Iran, subsequently leading to the Iran-contra scandal.[32]

It would be wrong to conclude from all this that the legislative branch has been reduced to a mere rubber stamp. From time to time Congress has attempted to check the expansive powers of the executive. Both houses now have budget committees with staffs that can more effectively review the president's budget. Along with the investigations conducted by its standing committees and subcommittees, Congress has the General Accounting Office (GAO), which, as already noted, is independent of the executive branch and which reports directly to the legislature. Probably the most worthwhile investigative agency in government, the GAO plays an important role in uncovering executive waste, wrongdoing, mismanagement, and nonenforcement of the law.

Congress has sometimes fought back on specific issues. The Democratic House resisted a number of President Reagan's proposals, voting against chemical weapons, against antisatellite weapons testing, for a year-long ban on nuclear testing, and for less military spending than the White House wanted. Congress restored a number of worthwhile items in the 1987 budget that Reagan sought to cut, including library programs, public health services, rental housing grants, student incentive grants, soil conservation programs, and emergency food and shelter funds.[33] Yet in most of these kinds of battles the high ground belongs to the president—especially if he is a conservative.

Years ago liberals who saw how Congress managed to thwart the desires of liberal presidents like Truman and Kennedy concluded that Congress had too much power and the president not enough. But having

32. For a copy of the president's "finding" in this matter see *Washington Post*, January 10, 1987. The Foreign Military Sales Act requires the president to give both houses advance notice on major arms sales to other nations, which Reagan did not do in the secret arms deal with Iran.

33. *New York Times*, June 28, 1986.

witnessed conservative presidents like Nixon and Reagan effect their will over Congress, some of these same liberals concluded that the president was too powerful and Congress too weak. Actually, there was something more to these complaints than partisan inconsistency. In the first situation liberals are talking about the president's insufficient ability to effect measures that might benefit the ordinary working populace. And in the second instance they are talking about the president's ability to make overseas military commitments and to thwart social-welfare legislation at home.

What underlies the ostensibly inconsistent liberal complaint is that the president tends to be more powerful than Congress when he assumes a conservative stance and less powerful when he wants to push in a progressive direction. This is a reflection of not only wider politico-economic forces but of the way the Constitution structures things. As the framers intended, the system of separation of powers and checks and balances is designed to give the high ground to those who would resist social change, be they presidents or legislators. Neither the executive nor the legislature can single-handedly initiate reform, which means that conservatives need to control only one or the other branch to thwart domestic actions (or in the case of Congress, key committees in one or the other house) while liberals must control both houses and both branches.

Small wonder conservative and liberal presidents have different kinds of experiences with Congress. Should Congress insist upon passing bills that incur his displeasure, the conservative president need control only one-third plus one of either the House or the Senate to sustain his vetoes. If bills are passed over his veto, he can still undermine legislative intent by delaying enforcement under various pretexts relating to timing, efficiency, and other operational contingencies.[34] The Supreme Court has long been aware that its decisions have the force of law only if other agencies of government choose to carry them out. In recent years Congress has been coming to the same realization, developing a new appreciation of the executive's power to command in a direct and palpable way the people, materials, and programs needed for carrying out decisions.

The techniques of veto, decoy, and delay used by a conservative president to dismantle or harmstring domestic programs are of little help to a liberal president who might claim an interest in social change, for the immense social problems he faces cannot be solved by executive sleight-of-hand. What efforts liberal presidents do make in the field of social reform

34. For instance, while the president supposedly cannot impound funds allocated by Congress, he has the power to defer spending or even rescind it completely on specific projects, as long as Congress passes a resolution approving the cut within forty-five days—which Congress usually does; see Norman Ornstein, "A Line-Item Veto: Who Needs It?" *Washington Post*, August 11, 1985.

legislation are frequently thwarted or greatly diluted by entrenched conservative powers in Congress. It is in these confrontations that the Congress gives every appearance of being able to frustrate presidential initiatives.

The Reagan years lent confirmation to the above analysis, albeit with a new twist, for here was a conservative president who was not obstructionist but activist, one who sought a major transition in taxing and spending policies. The obstructionist defenses that Congress uses so well against progressive measures were less successful against Reagan, as a coalition of Republicans and "boll weevil" conservative Democrats, backed by corporate and moneyed interests outside Congress, gave the president most of what he wanted, curtailing or diminishing in one session progressive programs developed over the last fifty years. So was demonstrated a new variation on an old theme: the system moves most swiftly when directed toward conservative ends.

With an activist ultraconservative president like Ronald Reagan dedicated to rolling back social services and advancing the prerogatives of the corporate class and the military, liberals developed a new appreciation of whatever democratic features Congress might have. During the New Deal and Fair Deal days of liberal dominance of the White House, liberals were satisfied with the existing presidential system and warned against turning the president into an ineffectual lame duck by restricting the number of terms he might serve. Having endured twenty years of Roosevelt and Truman, conservatives were convinced that their main task was to trim the power of the federal government and of the presidency in particular. So they fought successfully for the Twenty-second Amendment (1951) which limited White House occupancy to two terms.

Likewise in the 1950s liberals were urging that the president be given a freer hand in foreign policy, while conservatives were pushing for the Bricker amendment, a measure that would have given the states a kind of veto over the executive treaty power reminiscent of the Articles of Confederation. Liberals talked about giving the president an item veto (allowing him to veto specific items in a bill while accepting other portions of it) so that he might better resist special-interest legislation. Conservatives treated the item veto as just another example of executive usurpation.

Today we hear a different tune. Conservatives now better appreciate the uses of a strong presidency in advancing the causes of military spending and of multinational corporate capitalism at home and abroad. Furthermore, given their ability in recent times to win the presidency (four out of the last five times) and their superior ability to raise the enormous sums needed for that endeavor, conservatives, including those on the Supreme Court, now favor an expanded executive power. A conservative president, Ronald Reagan, broadened the realm of unaccountable executive initiative and secrecy. He also requested an item veto. Conservatives, beginning with President Nixon, have been talking about a one-term six-year presidency. What others may call "lame duck," they see as six years of not having to worry about reelection, six years of more independent power. Other conservatives have toyed with undoing the Twenty-second Amendment so the president might again enjoy an indefinite number of terms.

In contrast, liberals now rail against the "imperial president."[35] They talk about holding firm with the War Powers Act and making the executive more accountable to Congress. Under their breaths they are thankful for the Twenty-second Amendment. And, except for a few like Ted Kennedy who have not moved beyond the liberal conventional wisdom of the 1950s, liberals are now opposed to the item veto. They discovered that a presidency which so grew in power under their domain can be effecively used for conservative and even authoritarian goals.

Change from the Top?

The ability of reform-minded executives to generate policies for the benefit of less privileged constituents is limited. Not only presidents but mayors and governors have complained that the problems they confront are of a magnitude far greater than the resources they command. And we can suspect them of telling the truth. Most of the resources are preempted by vested interests. The executive leader who begins the term with the promise of getting things moving is less likely to change the political-corporate-class system than be absorbed by it. Once in office, he finds himself staggered by the vast array of entrenched powers working within and without government. He is confronted with a recalcitrant legislature and an intractable bureaucracy. He is constantly distracted by issues and operational problems that seem to take him from his intended course, and he finds it difficult to move in progressive directions without incurring the hostility of those who control the economy and its institutional auxiliaries. So he begins to talk about being "realistic" and working with what is at hand, now tacking against the wind, now taking one step back in the often unrealized hope of taking two steps forward, until the public begins to complain that his administration bears a dismaying resemblance to the less dynamic, less energetic ones that came before. In the hope of maintaining his efficacy, he begins to settle for the *appearance* of efficacy, until appearances are all he is left struggling with. It is this tugging and hauling and whirling about in a tight circle of options and ploys that is celebrated

---

35. Interestingly enough, some conservatives now rail against an "imperial Congress": for example, Norman Podhoretz, "The Imperial Congress," *Washington Post*, December 23, 1986.

by some as "the give-and-take of democratic interest-group politics." To less enchanted observers, the failure of reform-minded leaders to deliver on their promises demonstrates the difficulty of working for major changes within a politico-economic system structured to resist change.

The executive has grown in power and responsibility along with the increasing concentration of monopoly capital. As already noted, a centralized nationwide capitalist economy needs a centralized nationwide state power to tend to its needs. By the same token, as United States corporate interests grow to international scope and are confronted with challenges from various anti-imperialist forces, so the president's involvement in international affairs grows—and so grows the military establishment intended to defend "U.S. interests" abroad. The president can intervene in other countries in a variety of ways. He can also blow up the world with the nuclear arsenal at his command. Such powers do not advance the democratic interests of the American people, nor are they so designed. The immense military power the president commands, supposedly to make us all much safer, actually gives the chief executive a life-and-death power over the American people (and over other peoples). Ironically, then, as the executive power grows in foreign affairs, so the president's power over the American people becomes less accountable and more dangerous.

In most domestic areas, the increase in presidential powers has not kept up with the growth in presidential responsibilities, so although the president and the government are often held responsible for the economy, they do not have all that much control over it. If anything, the growing involvement of the executive in industrial matters has increased its dependence on corporate organizations for information, cooperation, and leadership in the policy process. The purpose of executive involvement in the economy is to serve the process of capital accumulation and not to control the economy in order to bring it into line with democratic, egalitarian social goals. There is, then, not likely to be much progressive change from the top, no matter who is in the White House, unless there is also a mass mobilization of the people for social change.

14

The Politics of Bureaucracy

Conservatives would have us believe that bureaucracy is a malady peculiar to the liberal welfare state or to socialism. In fact, bureaucracy can be found in just about every area of modern capitalist society; in hundreds of giant business corporations; in universities, religious establishments, and other private organizations; in the military, FBI, and CIA; as well as in national, state, and local administrations. Bureaucracy has replaced the charismatic and traditional forms of authority found in earlier societies because it is a technically superior method of organization, superior as is machine production to nonmachine production. In its model form, bureaucracy has the following characteristics: (1) the systematic mobilization of human energy and material resources for the fulfillment of explicitly defined policy goals or plans; (2) the use of trained career personnel who occupy nonhereditary offices of specified jurisdictions; (3) the specialization of skills and division of labor, coordinated by a hierarchy of command that is accountable to some authority or constituency.[1] Bureaucracy can be used to administer a national health program or run death camps. Much depends on the political and class context in which it operates.

THE MYTH AND REALITY OF INEFFICIENCY

Bureaucracies have certain bothersome characteristics that seem to inhere in the nature of the beast. For instance, the need for consistent and accountable operating procedures can create a tendency toward inertia, red tape, and a limited capacity to respond to new initiatives. The need to

1. See Max Weber's classic statement, "Bureaucracy," in Hans Gerth and C. Wright Mills (eds.), *From Max Weber: Essays in Sociology* (New York: Oxford University Press, 1958), pp. 196–244.

divide responsibilities over widely dispersed areas can cause problems of coordination and accountability. Highly centralized supervision, in turn, can create problems of congestion and poor responsiveness. And for the average citizen there is the problem of the incomprehensible forms and labyrinthian runarounds orchestrated by the petty autocrats and uncaring paper pushers who sometimes inhabit both public and private bureaucracies.

Despite these problems, bureaucracies perform crucial and complex tasks—for better or worse—that could not be accomplished without the systematic administrative capacity that is the hallmark of modern organization. "The feat of landing men on the moon," observes Duane Lockard, "was not only a scientific achievement but a bureaucratic one as well."[2] The same might be said of the Vietnam War, the Social Security system, and the farm, highway, housing, and defense programs.

According to the prevailing ideology of corporate America public bureaucracy is expensive, inefficient, a drain on the more productive private economy, and oppressive to our freedom. The conservative remedy is to hand over public programs to private contractors ("privatization") or abolish them altogether ("deregulation"). This conservative attack on government diverts attention from the realities of class privilege and class power. When things go wrong with the economy, the conservative critics blame not the corporate interests that own and control that very economy but the government that dares to tamper with the free market.

In truth, there are inefficiencies and waste in both public administrations and private businesses, but the ones in the private realm are seldom publicized or investigated. Administrative costs are generally lower in the public than the private realm. Administrators in government work longer hours for far less pay than managers in private bureaucracies. Public oversight keeps down the salaries of government officials and sometimes acts as a check on their performance, but consumer "sovereignty" has no such effect on corporate salaries.

Public administration carries out tasks that private business could not handle. Consider the much maligned post office: what private corporation would deliver a letter 3,000 miles, door to door, for twenty-two or twenty-five cents, or forward your mail to a new address at no cost for as long as you want.[3] Consider Social Security: what private companies would guar-

2. Duane Lockard, *The Perverted Priorities of American Politics* (New York: Macmillan, 1971), p. 282.

3. The deterioration of postal services has resulted from cutbacks and attempts to run things on a more "profit-motivated" basis: see my "Don't Dump on the Post Office," *The New Haven Advocate*, February 5, 1986. On the comparison of public and private management costs and the relative efficiency of public administration, see John Schwarz, *America's Hidden Success* (New York: W. W. Norton, 1983), pp. 70–73; also Charles Goodsell, *The Case for Bureaucracy* (Chatham, N.J.: Chatham House, 1983).

antee solvent pension funds administered regularly to millions of elderly citizens for decades on end with built-in cost-of-living allowances? Social Security's hidden efficiency can be measured in the millions of people helped and the social costs saved thereby.

This is not to make light of government waste. The General Accounting Office found that the federal government—under a supposedly economy-minded conservative Republican administration had lost billions of dollars in 1985 because of poor management in major agencies, the most costly being the Pentagon and the National Aeronautics and Space Administration (NASA). But business seldom complains about wasteful military and space spending—there is too much profit to be had in that kind of largesse. Nearly one-fourth of today's federal budget goes for services or alleged services rendered by private contractors. There too, one hears very little complaining from industry about excessive government expenditures.[4]

Many of our most costly government programs are designed to subsidize business, either through direct grants and services as in agriculture or indirectly through lucrative contracts as in the defense industry. Private profitability feeds from the public trough. In cities throughout the nation, working-class neighborhoods have been razed to make way for shopping malls, industrial parks, sports arenas, and convention centers, built with public funds. While business benefits from such ventures, the public monies invested are seldom recovered and the projects often become continual drains on municipal budgets. When the New York Yankees threatened to leave town unless their stadium was refurbished, the city expended $28 million on the job and granted the Yankees a lease on very favorable terms. More than a decade later the city was still servicing a multimillion dollar debt and the Yankees were enjoying handsome profits indeed.[5] These kinds of arrangements are at the heart of the urban fiscal crisis in America.

Instead of contrasting the profitability of private business with the debt-ridden costliness of government, we would do better to see the connection between the two. Government failure is built on private success. "The very governments which have continually . . . subsidize[d] business are then charged with inefficient performance by the business class."[6]

---

4. *Washington Post*, December 27, 1985; John Hanrahan, *Government by Contract* (New York: W. W. Norton, 1983). A 1986 audit found spending abuses by NASA officials and contractors in virtually every aspect of NASA's operations. The waste estimated at over $3.5 billion was "only the tip of the iceberg" according to federal auditors: *New York Times*, April 23, 1986.

5. Susan Fainstein and Norman Fainstein, "The Political Economy of American Bureaucracy," in Carol Weiss and Allen Barton (eds.), *Making Bureaucracies Work* (Beverly Hills: Sage, 1980), p. 285.

6. Ibid.

Sometimes government agencies perform inefficiently because their missions are impossible. A few agencies like the Office of Economic Opportunity are assigned the task of "eradicating" poverty, an undertaking that could be accomplished only with a major transformation of the economic system. Government in capitalist America is not allowed to make a profit, unlike in socialist countries where municipalities directly own enterprises and pocket their earnings. Surplus empty offices in a U.S. government building may not be rented, even if this benefited the public treasury, for it would put government in competition with private real estate interests.

Government is given the unprofitable "markets" that business does not want. Thus, public hospitals show none of the profits of private ones because they handle the people who cannot afford the astronomical costs of private health care. Likewise, low-income public housing provides shelter for those excluded from the private housing market. And public welfare administers to those who cannot sell their labor on the private market.

Government bureaucracies have little control over the production process, over the resources and decisions of the economy which determine what is produced, how, where, and by whom.

> Thus the public schools train children for economic success, yet have no control over the requirements of private employers. The Department of Energy is supposed to insure an adequate supply of gasoline, but it cannot even command accurate data from the oil companies, much less itself extract petroleum from the ground and process it. The Department of Housing and Urban Development (HUD) can subsidize low-income housing, but it can neither build units itself nor divert private investment from middle-class suburban development. In each case the public bureaucracy is inefficient and ineffective. But its problems are foreordained by the conditions under which public agencies operate.[7]

SECRECY AND UNACCOUNTABILITY

Business, we are told, answers to the public through the competition of the free market, but government strives for secrecy and unaccountability. In fact, as just noted, government is more the object of public scrutiny than is business. People expect government to solve problems because they have no expectation that business will. They blame government precisely because it is *more* controllable than business.[8]

This is not to deny that bureaucracies (both public and private) have a strong tendency toward secrecy. Much of the secrecy in public bureaucracy is on behalf of private business and the military. The government has suppressed information concerning health and safety problems that might prove troublesome to powerful business interests, including data on toxic waste disposal, and on the harmful features of certain medical drugs, pesticides, and nuclear reactors.[9] The government suppressed information regarding the medical problems of 30,000 American soldiers exposed to nuclear tests in the 1950s and the ill effects of defoliants upon military personnel in the Vietnam War.[10] Every year about $25 billion to $30 billion

---

7. Ibid., p. 286.
8. Ibid., p. 283.
9. See for instance *New York Times*, February 20, 1983 and March 28, 1986.
10. Howard Rosenberg, *Atomic Soldiers* (Boston: Beacon Press, 1980); Harvey Wasserman and Norman Solomon, *Killing Our Own* (New York: Delacorte, 1980).

is spent on secret programs hidden in the Pentagon budget, secret even to Congress.[11]

Presidents pledge to conduct "open administrations" that have "nothing to hide." Yet, once in office, they are inclined toward secrecy. The more secrecy, the more opportunity for them to do what they want without having to answer for it. The executive branch withholds from the public about 16 million documents a year. During his tenure in office President Reagan talked about getting government off the backs of people but he worked at getting people off the back of government. He issued a presidential directive that forced some two million government workers to take a pledge of secrecy. He required almost 300,000 past and present federal employees to agree to submit to lifetime government censorship of their writings and speeches. (In 1985, a total of 14,144 books, articles, and speeches were submitted to government censors for advance review.) Reagan instituted polygraph tests for public employees to ascertain who was leaking information to the press—but he never responded to suggestions that he himself take a lie detector test to see if he was telling the truth about his role in the Iran-contra affair. Hostile to the Freedom of Information Act, the Reagan administration sought to undercut it by expanding the restrictive classifications of documents, blocking out more and more information on the documents that were released, imposing long delays on releasing materials, and charging exorbitant copying fees. In a press conference, Reagan made clear his discomfort with the democratic process: "You can't let your people know" what the government is doing "without letting the wrong people know—those who are in opposition to what you're doing."[12]

Public servants who become "whistleblowers"—that is, who defy the code of secrecy by informing a member of Congress or a reporter or a superior about some wrongdoing—risk punishment for their efforts. One federal employee who tried to warn the government that it was wasting millions on a foreign aid program had his memorandum destroyed and his job abolished. Another who complained of illegal use of travel funds in his bureau found his work performance judged "unacceptable" and his job terminated. Another who exposed instances of patient abuse at a Veterans Administration hospital was labeled a troublemaker and fired. An auditor

---

11. *Wall Street Journal*, September 25, 1985; *Washington Post*, January 15, 1987. Secret expenditures by the executive would seem to violate Article I, section 9 of the Constitution which states that "no money shall be drawn from the Treasury" without "a regular statement and account of the receipts and expenditures."

12. Walter Karp, "Liberty Under Siege," *Harper's*, November 1985, p. 56; Steve Weinberg, "Trashing the FOIA," *Columbia Journalism Review*, January/February 1985, pp. 21–28. Eve Pell, *The Big Chill* (Boston: Beacon Press 1985); *New York Times*, October 19, 1983, and October 23 and 29, 1986.

in the Pentagon, who discovered that contractors were padding expenses and enjoying excessive payments for spare parts, was told to resign his job by Pentagon superiors. A navy petty officer said he found that millions of dollars of equipment and supplies for his aircraft carrier, the Kitty Hawk, had possibly been lost, stolen, or sold illegally. The petty officer said that his superiors were aware of the situation. He claimed that he was warned by those he had fingered that he might end up being dumped overboard if he were not quiet. These are not isolated instances. The special board created to handle whistleblower complaints had a backlog of 1,000 cases only four months after its creation. Once fired, whistleblowers find few job opportunities in government or in industries dealing with government contracts. Instead of being rewarded for their honesty, they are punished.[13]

To prevent federal employees from "committing truth," the White House has sought greater power to control and punish disclosures—even of unclassified materials. It has argued in several cases that government information is government property; therefore whistleblowers who take and release such information are guilty of theft. Erstwhile Attorney-General Bell denounced Justice Department personnel who leaked information to the press regarding FBI wrongdoings as having violated their oath to uphold the law.[14] Thus, leaking information about crimes is itself treated as a crime. Note, however, that much of this secrecy does not inhere in the bureaucratic process as such, but is imposed by the White House or by top political appointees. When it comes to secrecy, politics is in command, not bureaucracy.

BUREAUCRATIC ACTION AND INACTION

Many of the rulings of bureaucratic agencies, published daily in the *Federal Register*, are as significant as major pieces of legislation, and in the absence of precise guidelines from Congress, they often take the place of legislation. One year, for instance, without a single law being passed and without a word of public debate, the Price Commission approved more than $2 billion in rate increases for 110 telephone, gas, and electric companies, thereby imposing upon the public by administrative fiat an expenditure far greater than what is contained in most of the bills passed by Congress. In 1983, under a directive from the White House, the Social

13. Ralph Nader, Peter Petkes, and Kate Blackwell (eds.), *Whistleblowing* (New York: Bantam, 1972); *Washington Post*, October 3, 1982, December 19, 1983, January 18, 1985; *Newsweek*, August 5, 1985; Dina Rasor, *The Pentagon Underground* (New York: Times Books, 1985).

14. *New York Times*, May 18, 1977, and July 12 and August 8, 1978.

Security Administration set about to cut $3.4 billion and 265,000 disabled persons from the disability insurance program established by Congress, all done by an "intensified review" of "stricter eligibility" rules.[15]

The political process does not end with the passage of a bill but continues at the administrative level, albeit in more covert fashion, influencing how a law is administered—if at all. As of 1987, despite repeated criticism, the Environmental Protection Agency (EPA) continued to fail to enforce a program devised by Congress to ensure safe storage and disposal of industrial wastes, according to a GAO study.[16] Since its establishment in 1977, the Office of Surface Mining (OSM), has done little to regulate strip mining. At least 6,000 sites have been mined since 1977 without the legally required environmental controls, resulting in thousands of miles of landslides and polluted streams. The OSM has not collected some $200 million in fines owed by coal operators and the rate of collection is dropping. Of the 4,000 mine owners ordered to halt illegal operations from 1979 to 1983, more than half ignored the order.[17]

Often, agencies are not sufficiently staffed to handle the enormous tasks that confront them. The federal government has twenty-five inspectors to monitor the transportation of hazardous wastes over the entire country. The EPA staff can monitor but a fraction of the 1,000 new potentially toxic chemicals that industry pours into the environment each year. Representatives of a farm-workers union complained that enforcement of existing laws, not enactment of new ones, was needed to alleviate the housing, wage, and safety problems faced by farm workers. "We've got plenty of laws, beautiful laws on housing, but they're not enforced," said one union official.[18]

While some laws go unenforced, others are so transformed during implementation as to subvert the intent of the law. We have already noted how this was done to the Freedom of Information Act. A few more examples might suffice: (1) A House subcommittee charged that the Merit System Protection Board created by Congress to protect whistleblowers had been administered so as to give them even less protection than before, requiring them to carry the burden of proof in ways not authorized by

---

15. *New York Times*, February 9 and April 7 and 21, 1983.

16. *Washington Post*, January 17, 1987. On nonenforcement regarding the law to protect children from lead-based paint see *New York Times*, August 27, 1983. For an example of how EPA Administrator William Ruckelshaus protected uranium mining polluters see *Progressive*, December 1984, p. 11. For other instances of EPA and FDA nonenforcement of the law see *Washington Post*, January 26 and May 8, 1983. Of the money allocated to clean up hazardous wastes dumps, the Reagan administration budgeted only half: *In These Times*, November 10–16, 1982.

17. *Daily World*, October 16, 1985.

18. Quoted in the *Guardian*, September 17, 1980.

statute. (2) The Clean Air Act passed by Congress was gravely weakened by administrative fiat when the EPA decided to relax national smog standards by more than 50 percent. (3) Without changing a word of the federal strip-mining law, the government systematically weakened it by relaxing regulations and getting rid of conscientious enforcers, as in the following instance:

> For four years, Bruce Boyens . . . stalked the sites of strip mines, forcing coal companies to restore the natural landscape of hills and mountains they had laid bare. When operators threatened to beat up his inspectors, he called in federal marshals to subdue them. When state officials seemed too cozy with coal companies, he leaned on them to get tough.
>
> Now his days as a fearsome enforcer in the coals fields are over. . . . He was being transferred to Washington, far from Appalachia. OSM called it a salute to his expertise. Boyens, who had no choice, took it as a "get out" [order].[19]

In each of the above instances, it was not "bureaucratic usurpation" as such which undermined legislative intent, but the political will of the policymakers on top, who set about sabotaging bureaucratic enforcement of the law.

People who insist that things do not get done because that is simply the nature of the bureaucratic beast seem to forget that only certain kinds of things do not get done, while other things are accomplished all too well. The law making some 13 million children eligible for medical examination and treatment, supported by public health advocates and liberals, is legally the same as the law to develop a multibillion-dollar "Star Wars" outerspace weapon system, supported by the White House, giant industrial contractors, research institutes, Pentagon brass, and members of Congress whose patriotism is matched only by their desire to bring the defense bacon home to their districts and keep their campaign coffers filled by appreciative corporate donors. If anything, the Star Wars program is of vastly greater technical and administrative complexity. Yet it moves full steam ahead, while the children's health program hardly moves at all. Congress discovered that almost 85 percent of the youngsters have been left unexamined, causing "unnecessary crippling, retardation, or even death of thousands of children," according to a House subcommittee report.[20]

---

19. *Washington Post*, June 6, 1982. For the other examples noted above see *Federal Times* (Washington, D.C.), October 27, 1980; Frank O'Donnell, "Smog Gone," *City Paper* (Washington, D.C.), June 24, 1983.

20. UPI dispatch, October 8, 1976. On the failure to enforce the hospital-care program for the poor see Michael Balter, "The Best Kept Secret in Health Care," *Progressive*, April 1981, pp. 35–37.

Again, the important difference between the two programs is not bureaucratic but political. The effectiveness of a law or a bureaucratic program depends on the power of the groups supporting them. Laws that serve powerful clientele are likely to enjoy a vigorous life, while laws that have only the powerless to nurture them are often stillborn. Those parts of the bureaucracy that service the capitalist class are relatively free from attack and from complaints about bureaucratic meddling. Such adminstrative units are accountable, not to the citizenry but to the corporate interests they serve.

Red tape, often seen as an inevitable by-product of bureaucracy, may actually be used as a deliberate means of immobilizing programs that incur the disfavor of powerful interests in the White House or in the economy. In response to President Reagan's hostility toward school-lunch programs, the Department of Agriculture imposed extensive and complicated income-verification systems on school districts. The increased paperwork cost the districts tens of thousands of dollars and threatened to end lunch services in some districts, while turning up very few instances of fraud (i.e., children getting lunches who were not eligible for them). In this instance, the red tape was a weapon used deliberately to overburden the school-lunch program. Again, politics, not bureaucracy, was in command.[21]

The capitalist political economy is the graveyard of reform-minded administrative bodies. An agency like the Office of Economic Opportunity, which tries to represent low-income interests and invites the participation of have-nots in urban programs, runs into powerful opposition and eventually is abolished. An agency set up to regulate industry on behalf of consumers, workers, or the environment may possess a zeal for reform in its youth, but before long the business-owned news media either turn their attention to more topical events or present an unsympathetic picture of the agency's doings. The president, even if originally sympathetic to the agency's mission, is now occupied with more pressing matters, as are its few friends in Congress. But the industry that is supposed to be brought under control remains keenly interested and ready to oppose government intrusions. First, it may challenge the agency's jurisdiction or even the legality of its existence in court, thus preventing any serious regulatory actions until a legal determination is made.[22] If the agency survives this attack, the industry then hits it with a barrage of arguments

---

21. The news report on this in the *Washington Post*, December 29, 1983 was headlined: "Bureaucracy Is Upsetting Schoolchildren's Lunch." Bureaucracy was blamed even though the facts of the story indicated another culprit.

22. See the discussion in Grant McConnell, *Private Power and American Democracy* (New York: Knopf, 1966), p. 288.

and technical information, sufficiently impressive to win the attention of the agency's investigators. The investigators begin to develop a new appreciation of the problems industry faces in maintaining profitable operations.[23]

If the agency persists in making unfavorable rulings, businesspeople appeal to their elected representatives, to a higher administrative official, or, if they have the pull, to the president himself. In its youthful days after World War I, the Federal Trade Commission (FTC) moved vigorously against big business, but representatives of industry prevailed upon the president to replace "some of the commissioners by other more sympathetic with business practices: this resulted in the dismissal of many complaints which had been made against corporations."[24] Some sixty years later, the pattern was to repeat itself. Staffed by consumer advocates, the FTC began vigorous action against questionable practices by insurance companies, funeral-home operators, doctors, and others, only to find itself under fire from Congress and the business community. It was not long before the commission had its jurisdictional powers abridged and its budget cut.[25]

Frequently, members of Congress demand to know why an agency is bothering their constituents or their big contributors. Administrators who are more interested in building congressional support than in making congressional enemies are likely to apply the law in ways that satisfy influential legislators. "If the bureaucrats are to escape criticism, unfavorable publicity, or a cut in their appropriations, they must be discreet in their relations with the legislative body."[26] Some administrative bodies, like the Army Corps of Engineers, so successfully cultivate support among powerful members of Congress and their big-business clientele as to become relatively free of supervisory control from department heads or the White House. "Fierce rivalries for funds and functions go on ceaselessly among the departments and between the agencies. A cunning bureau chief learns to negotiate alliances on Capitol Hill [Congress] that bypass the

---

23. For instance, a report by the National Academy of Sciences found that the EPA "is inevitably dependent" on the industries it regulates for much of the information it uses in decision making and that such information is easily withheld or distorted to serve industry's ends: *New York Times*, March 22, 1977; also *Washington Post*, August 24, 1979.

24. Edwin Sutherland, *White Collar Crime* (New York: Holt, Rinehart and Winston, 1949), p. 232.

25. For the full story see Michael Pertshuk, *Revolt Against Regulation* (Berkeley: University of California Press, 1982).

26. E. Pendelton Herring, "The Balance of Social Forces in the Food and Drug Law," *Social Forces*, 13, March 1935, p. 364. With a limited budget of only $2 million in 1949, the Food and Drug Administration proceeded against thousands of violators. Today, with a budget a hundred times larger, the FDA rarely if ever takes court action against major food or drug companies. It has learned discretion.

central authority of the White House."[27] In the executive branch, as in Congress, the fragmentation of power is hardly indicative of its democratization.

Given a desire to survive and advance, bureaucrats tend to equivocate in the face of controversial decisions, moving away from dangerous areas and toward positions favored by the strongest of the pressures working on them. With time, the reform-minded agency loses its crusading spirit and settles down to serving the needs of the industry it is supposed to regulate. The more public-spirited staff members either grow weary of the struggle and make their peace with the corporations or leave, to be replaced by personnel who are "acceptable to, if not indeed the nominees of, the industry."[28]

Consider John O'Leary, a director of the Bureau of Mines. Encouraged by media attention and public concern over mine disasters, O'Leary ordered the bureau's inspectors to make *unannounced* spot checks of safety conditions, a step rarely tried before, although required by law. In one month, O'Leary's inspectors made 600 checks, almost four times the number for the entire previous year, and ordered workers out of more than 200 unsafe mines. O'Leary publicly charged that the coal-mining industry was "designed for production economy and not for human economy, and there's going to have to be a change of attitudes on that." The change came—but it was of a different sort. The mine companies made known to the White House their strong desire to be rid of the troublesome director. After four months, O'Leary was removed from office. His successor, a former CIA employee, reestablished close relations with the mine owners, making personal appearances at corporate gatherings and riding in company planes.[29]

Many career administrators eventually leave government service to accept higher-paying jobs in companies whose interests they favored while in office. This promise of a lucrative post with a private firm can exercise a considerable influence on the judgments of the ambitious public administrator. Those who well serve private contractors are rewarded for their efforts. During the 1970s, a total of 343 Pentagon officers and civilians and seventeen high officials of the military-oriented space agency left their government jobs to become Northrop executives (while seventeen top Northrop people went to restock these military agencies).[30]

---

27. Douglas Cater, *Power in Washington* (New York: Random House, 1964), pp. 10–11.
28. McConnell, *Private Power and American Democracy*, p. 288.
29. *New York Times*, February 17, 1969; *Christian Science Monitor*, April 8, 1970; Jack Anderson in *Washington Post*, June 17, 1973.
30. Victor Perlo, "What is the Military-Industrial Complex," *Political Affairs*, June 1983, p. 30.

SERVING THE "REGULATED"

There are administrative bodies that come directly under the president's command. And there are independent regulatory commissions that operate just outside the executive branch, making quasi-judicial rulings which can only be appealed to the courts.[31] For the reasons just discussed, both these kinds of agencies frequently become protectors of the industries they are supposed to regulate, granting monopoly privileges to big companies that cost the public billions a year. So, the Interstate Commerce Commission continues its long devotion to the railroad companies; the Federal Communications Commission serves the telephone companies and the media networks; the Federal Elections Commission safeguards the two-party monopoly; the Food and Drug Administration devotes more energy to protecting the profits of the food and drug companies than the health of people; the Securities and Exchange Commission regulates the stock market mostly for the benefit of large investors; the Federal Energy Regulatory Commission maintains a permissive policy toward energy producers.

So with other units of government: the Department of Transportation defers to the oil-highway-automotive combine; the Agriculture Department promotes giant farming corporations; the Army Corps of Engineers and the Bureau of Reclamations continue to mutilate the natural environment on behalf of utilities, agribusiness, and land developers; the Department of Interior serves the oil, gas, mining, and timber companies; and one must not forget how the Pentagon supports the defense industry with munificently generous subsidies and contracts.[32]

Congressional oversight of the hundreds of government agencies is scant and sporadic, a Senate report concluded, largely because members of Congress fear reprisals from powerful economic interests that are regu-

31. The major independent regulatory commissions are the Federal Communications Commission, Federal Energy Regulatory Commission, Federal Trade Commission, Interstate Commerce Commission, National Labor Relations Board, and Securities and Exchange Commission. The commissions report directly to Congress but their personnel are appointed by the president, with Senate confirmation; see Louis Kohlmeier, *The Regulators* (New York: Harper and Row, 1969).

32. There is an ample literature documenting how administrative bodies serve the interests of the industries they are supposed to regulate. See Kohlmeier, *The Regulators*; Anthony Lewis, "To Regulate the Regulators," *New York Times Magazine*, February 22, 1959; Bernard Schwartz, *The Professor and the Commissions* (New York: Knopf, 1958); Pertshuk, *Revolt Against Regulation*; Richard Ney, *The Wall Street Jungle* (New York: Grove Press, 1970); Robert Engler, *Politics of Oil* (Chicago: University of Chicago Press, 1976); Henning Sjorstrom and Robert Nilsson, *Thalidomide and the Power of the Drug Companies* (New York: Basic Books, 1973); Marc Reisner, *Cadillac Desert, The American West and its Disappearing Water* (New York: Viking, 1986). On the Army Corps of Engineers' lastest atrocity see: Cass Peterson, "The Fizzling of 200-Year-Old Dream," *Washington Post*, December 26, 1986.

lated, and congressional committees are often "stacked with members who share similar backgrounds and values with the agencies they are charged with overseeing."[33] This "iron triangle" of bureaucratic unit, congressional committee, and corporate interest—with the latter as the triangle's base—gets its way on most things.[34]

The political appointees who preside over the various administrative units of government are usually so tightly bound to private interests that it is often difficult to tell the regulators from the regulated. Many of them are persons who previously were employed by the "regulated" industry.[35] Eleven of the top sixteen officials appointed by President Reagan to head the Department of the Interior were linked to the five major industries regulated by the department.[36] Administrators who have supervised such things as water-development, land-use, labor, nuclear-energy, consumer-protection, occupational safety, and food and drug regulations have had a history of previously serving as lobbyists, lawyers, and managers for the business firms they were to regulate.[37]

Federal meat-inspection laws have been administered by officials with a history of opposition to federal meat inspection. Federal housing programs have been supervised by businesspeople openly hostile to low-income public housing. Conservation and environmental programs have been given over to people who have been openly antagonistic to such programs. Energy programs have been administered by former oil-company executives who want nothing to do with the development of alternative energy sources. The Arms Control and Disarmament Agency has been "dominated by military men, conservatives and Wall Street types."[38]

Once again the problem is not in the nature of bureaucracy as such but in the political use to which the bureaucracy is put—a use that is reflective of the larger political economy. It is not that anonymous and unaccountable bureaucrats have usurped power for themselves, although persons of all ideologies have been adept at advancing this view. A closer look shows that career bureaucrats pretty much do as they are told by their administrative bosses. The professional ethic of most bureaucrats is: remain neutral and wait for the policy line to be set from above. "Bureaucratic

---

33. Senate Government Operations committee report, *New York Times*, February 10, 1977.

34. Agencies that do not serve powerful interests but only powerless people, however, are much more vulnerable to White House control; see Ronald Randall, "Presidential Power versus Bureaucratic Intransigence: The Influence of the Nixon Administration on Welfare Policy," *American Political Science Review*, 73, 1979, pp. 795–810.

35. *New York Times*, October 3, 1976.

36. *In These Times*, December 16–22, 1981.

37. *New York Times*, March 26, 1981 and September 1, 1982; *Washington Post*, October 6, 1981; August 19, 1982; and January 19, 1986; *Guardian*, March 27, 1985.

38. Sidney Lens, "The Doomsday Strategy," *Progressive*, February 1976, p. 28.

failures" are usually better described as successful uses of political power to undermine regulations and laws that prove troublesome to corporate interests. Conservative administrations appoint administrators who do not think government works, at least not in the public-service areas. This puts them into conflict with careerists who believe that government *can* work if made to do so. Careerists who buck the conservative tide may be passed over for promotion, or given negative job evaluations, undesirable transfers, unpleasant tasks, or nothing to do, causing many to leave government service.[39]

It is not enough to bemoan the fact that government agencies end up serving interests they are supposed to regulate; rather we should understand how this situation results from the politico-economic realities in which the administrators operate. In a capitalist society the special interests *are the systemic interest*, controlling the economic life of the society. Hence, regulation of the capitalist economy on anything but its own terms eventually does not work, not merely because industrialists employ shrewd lobbyists who can manipulate timid and compliant bureaucrats, but because industry *is* the economic system and sooner or later government must meet that system on its own terms or change to another. And when meeting the system on its own terms, regulation becomes a way to rig prices at artificially high levels, control markets for the benefit of large producers, secure high profits, and allow private corporations more direct and covert access to public authority.

What is needed to change things is not an endless proliferation of regulatory units but a change in the conditions that demand so much regulation—that is, a different method of ownership and a different purpose for production. Until fundamental systemic changes are made in the economic order, it seems regulation will continue to fail where it is most needed.

PUBLIC AUTHORITY IN PRIVATE HANDS

The ultimate subservience of public power to private interest comes when government gives, along with its funds and services, its very *authority* to business in such areas as agriculture, medicine, industry, and trade. Control of Western federal lands and water has been handed over to local "home-rule" boards dominated by the large ranchers, who thereby successfully transform their economic power "into a working approximation

39. *Washington Post*, January 19, 1983. The United States Chamber of Commerce reportedly had a "hit list" of career burueacrats whom it wanted removed from the EPA and from the Departments of Justice, Labor, and Energy: *Washington Post*, September 6 and 7, 1984.

of publicly sanctioned authority."[40] Large agricultural producers exercise a similar authority over farm programs. "Agriculture has become neither public nor private enterprise. It is a system of self-government in which each leading farm interest controls a segment of agriculture through a delegation of national sovereignty," a condition that has prevailed through successive administrations in the White House.[41] Trade associations develop codes meant to govern the specifications of goods produced by their industry. These "private codes are often accepted by government . . . agents as minimum requirements and may sometimes be written directly into state or local statutes, thus taking on the force of law."[42]

One congressional committee, investigating relations between government and industry, complained of a "virtual abdication of administrative responsibility" on the part of officials in the Department of Commerce, their actions in many instances being "but the automatic approval of decisions already made outside the Government in business and industry."[43] In every significant line of industry, advisory committees staffed by representatives of leading firms work closely with government agencies, making most of the important recommendations. In trying to assess their roles, it is difficult to determine where the distinction between advice and policy-making lies. There are several thousand committees and boards advising the executive branch and Congress, costing the government many millions a year to finance. The most influential deal with banking, chemicals, communications, commercial farming, oil, utilities, railroads, and taxation. They meet regularly with administrative leaders to formulate policies. Their reports become the basis for administrative actions and new legislation. With the coercive power of the state backing their decisions, they secure advantages over smaller competitors, workers, and consumers of a kind less easily gained in open competition. The meetings of these business advisory committees are not open to the press or public.

In many state and municipal governments, as in the federal government, business associations, dominated by the biggest firms, are accorded the power to nominate their own personnel to licensing boards and other administrative bodies. The transfer of public authority to private hands frequently comes at the initiative of large companies. But sometimes the government will make the first overtures, organizing private associations, then handing them the powers of the state, thereby supposedly moving

40. McConnell, *Private Power and American Democracy*, p. 210.

41. Theodore Lowi, *The End of Liberalism* (New York: W. W. Norton, 1969), pp. 103–4.

42. Jack Walker, "The Origins and Maintenance of Interest Groups in America," *American Political Science Review* 77, 1983, p. 397.

43. From a congressional report cited in McConnell, *Private Power and American Democracy*, p. 275. On the special public privileges of business see also Charles Lindblom, *Politics and Markets* (New York: Basic Books, 1977).

toward "voluntaristic" and "decentralized" forms of policy-making. In fact, these measures transfer public power to favored producers without their being held democratically accountable for the sovereign authority they exercise.

There exists, then, unbeknownst to most Americans, a large number of private decision makers who exercise public authority without having to answer to the public and who determine official policy while being primarily obligated to their private businesses. They belong to what might be called the "public-private authority." Included in this category are the various quasi-public corporations, institutions, foundations, boards, councils, "authorities," and associations, one of the most powerful being the Federal Reserve Board. The "Fed," as it is called, determines the interest rate and the money supply. Although its decisions affect the entire economy, the Fed is beholden to the banks and is run mostly by bankers. Its members are appointed to staggered fourteen-year terms by the president, who can make only two appointments during his four-year term. Once appointed, the board members answer to no one (but the banking industry). The Fed operates without even the pretense of democratic accountability, working in total secrecy, refusing to have Congress or the White House audit its books. The five regional members of its most powerful policy committee are selected not by the president but by bankers from the various regions. The bankers pick their own people to sit on a public agency and make public policy that is backed by the powers of government but is not accountable to government.[44]

There are numerous "public authorities" at the federal, state, and local levels carrying out a widely varied range of activities. They all have several things in common: they are authorized by state legislatures or Congress to function outside the regular structure of government, and because of their autonomous corporate attributes, they are seldom subjected to public scrutiny and accountability. In 1972, the public authorities in New York State alone had an outstanding debt (bonds owned by banks and rich investors) of $8.9 billion, more than twice the state's debt. To meet their obligations, they float new bond issues, none of which are passed upon by the voters, and thus make demands on future tax revenues. They are creatures that have the best of both worlds, feeding off the state treasure while remaining accountable only to themselves.[45]

The public-private authority extends overseas. When the Peruvian generals nationalized the holdings of private American oil companies, the

---

44. Mark Beibart and Gerald Epstein, "The Power of the Fed," *Progressive*, April 1983, pp. 31–35. Members of Congress have introduced legislation to make the Fed more accountable: *New York Times*, February 24, 1985.
45. *New York Times*, December 27, 1972.

president sent a special envoy to protest the move and negotiate for reacquisition. When the Bangladesh government sought to ban the importation of hundreds of useless or harmful drugs, the State Department sent an official committee (composed of representatives of drug companies) to that country to argue against the ban. Agents of ITT, the CIA, and the White House jointly considered ways of preventing a democratically elected socialist from taking office in Chile and from remaining in office. The private interests do not merely benefit from public policy; they often *make* policy by selecting key officials, directing World Bank loans and foreign-aid investments, and offering recommendations that are treated as policy guidelines—in sum, using the United States government to pursue their interests abroad.[46]

The corporate interests exert an influence that cuts across particular administrative departments. Within a government whose power is highly fragmented, they form cohesive, and sometimes overlapping, blocs around major producer interests like oil, steel, banking, drugs, transportation, and armaments; these blocs are composed of high-level bureaucrats, regulatory commissioners, senior members of Congress, lobbyists, newspaper publishers, members of trade associations, and executives of business firms, operating with all the autonomy and unaccountability of princely states within the American polity.

MONOPOLY REGULATION VERSUS PUBLIC SERVICE REGULATION

If government is capitalism's provider and protector at home and abroad, and if government and business are so intermingled as to be often indistinguishable, then why are businesspeople so critical of "government meddling in the economy"? There are a number of explanations. First, as previously noted, businesspeople are not opposed to government regulation as long as it is favorable to them. The railroad owners are quite happy with regulation by the ICC; the media networks do quite well with the FCC; the nuclear industry found shelter in the NRC; and the oil industry is at home with the National Petroleum Council. However, few industries approve of any aggressive regulation on behalf of consumers as attempted by the FTC or attempts by the Justice Department's Antitrust Division to attack business mergers.

It is necessary to distinguish between monopoly regulation and public-service regulation. *Monopoly regulation* limits entry into a market, subsidizes select industries, sets production standards that only big companies

46. On how the World Bank promotes favorable conditions for private investment in the Third World see Cheryl Payer, *The World Bank* (New York: Monthly Review, 1983).

can meet, weakens smaller competitors, and encourages monopoly pricing. This kind of regulation has long been the rule in the agribusiness, telecommunications, energy, oil, drug, rail, and (until recently) trucking and airline industries. Virtually this entire regulatory edifice was constructed in response to the needs and demands of the business community.[47] Today business demands for monopolistic regulation continue unabated even with all the talk about "deregulation."

In regard to this industry-induced monopoly regulation, conflicts tend to be *within* the business community, between companies that would be advantaged and those that would not. There is another kind of regulation, however, that is class-based, targeting entire industries and pitting workers and consumers against business. The courts have even accorded legal standing to public-interest advocates who have waged campaigns for *public-service regulation*. In some instances administrative bodies have been armed with more specific laws that attempt to restrict business conduct and protect public interests. It is these public-service regulations that are anathema to business: environmental protections, antitrust laws, worker-safety and consumer-service regulations, and other safeguards that the "free" marketplace cannot provide.

Deregulation in the public service realm does not make business more productive or even more competitive, if anything it removes a set of competing interests—those of the public—and simply leaves business freer to pursue profits without incurring any obligation for the social effects of that pursuit. Deregulation has enabled banks to increase customer-service fees at a time when their own computerized processing costs have declined. The result is a substantial rise in bank profits in recent years. As one Congressional representative observed: "It is not the customers who are clamoring for more deregulation, it is the bankers."[48] Deregulation has given the strip-miners a free hand to devastate the landscape and make off with the profits without having to pay any restoration costs. Deregulation has led to a canceling of disclosure rules so that corporate executives can now pad their paychecks with fringe benefits and perquisites without having to tell stockholders or tax collectors, an arrangement that one business journalist called "a license to steal."[49]

47. Susan Tolchin and Martin Tolchin, *Dismantling America: The Rush to Deregulate* (New York: Houghton Mifflin, 1983); also Thomas McGraw (ed.), *Regulation in Perspective: Historical Essays* (Cambridge, Mass.: Harvard University Press, 1981).

48. Rep. Fernand St. Germain, chairman of the House Banking Committee quoted in *Washington Post*, April 12, 1984. On the deregulation of the airline industry see John Nance, *Blind Trust* (New York: William Morrow, 1984).

49. Jerry Knight in the *Washington Post* business section, September 26, 1983; also Mark Green and Norman Waitzman, *Business War on the Law* (Washington, D.C.: Public Citizen, 1980). A Roper poll found that people who say government is overregulated are consistently outnumbered by those who say the agencies are not doing enough in regard to consumer safety and food, drug, and environmental protection: *Washington Post*, November 10, 1981.

Business is not really committed to some abstract principle of "free enterprise." Regulations that enhance profits are supported and those that cut into profits are denounced as violations of "sound business practice." It is only in the latter case that the cry for deregulation is heard throughout America's boardrooms. Business is concerned that public-service regulations might mobilize new constituencies, or redistribute income downward instead of upward, or increase the not-for-profit public sector of the economy. From the earliest days of the Republic to today, the owning class has feared that government might become unduly responsive to popular sentiment, arousing mass expectations and eventually succumbing to demands that could seriously challenge the existing distribution of class power and wealth.

Some complaints lodged against government are from firms least favored by government policies. Business is not without its interior divisions: policies frequently benefit the wealthier firms at the expense of smaller ones. The howls of pain emanating from these weaker competitors are more likely to be heard than the quiet satisfaction of the giant victors. Small businesses usually have good cause to complain of government meddling, since most regulations are written to suit the corporate giants and are often excessively burdensome for the smaller enterprise. Government agencies more vigorously pursue their enforcement efforts against small companies because—unlike the big firms—they have less influence in Congress and can less afford to defend themselves in drawn-out litigation.[50]

Finally, I would suggest that much of the verbal opposition to government is a manifestation of the businessperson's adherence to the business ideology, the belief in the virtues of rugged individualism and private competition. That an individual might violate this creed in his or her own corporate affairs does not mean his or her devotion to it is consciously hypocritical. One should not underestimate the human capacity to indulge in selective perceptions and rationales. These rationales are no less sincerely felt because they are self-serving; quite the contrary, it is a creed's congruity with a favorable self-image and self-interest that makes it so compelling. Many businesspeople, including those who have benefited in almost every way from government contracts, subsidies, and tax laws, believe the advantages they enjoy are the result of their own self-reliance, efforts, and talents in a highly competitive "private" market. They believe that the assistance they get from the government benefits the national economy, while the assistance others get is a handout to parasites.

50. Ann Crittenden, "Big Burden for Small Business: Government Rules," *New York Times*, July 2, 1977.

15

The Supremely Political Court

Article III, Section 1 of the U.S. Constitution reads: "The judicial Power of the United States shall be vested in one supreme Court, and in such inferior Courts as the Congress may from time to time ordain and establish." The Supreme Court justices and all other federal judges are nominated by the president and subject to confirmation by the Senate. Serving for as long as they want, federal judges can be removed from office only for misconduct and only through impeachment by the Senate. The size of the Supreme Court is determined by statute, fluctuating over the years from six to ten members, and being fixed at nine since 1877.

All three branches of government are sworn to uphold the Constitution, but the Supreme Court alone has the power of reviewing the constitutionality of actions by the other two branches, at least in regard to cases brought before it. Nothing in the Constitution gives the Court this function, but the proceedings of the Constitutional Convention reveal that many delegates expected the judiciary to overturn laws it deemed inconsistent with the Constitution.[1] Of even greater significance is the Court's power to interpret the intent and scope of laws as they are applied in actual situations. This power of judicial *interpretation* is also limited to cases brought before the Court by contesting interests. Our main concern here is with trying to understand the political role the Court has played.

WHO JUDGES?

Some Americans think of the Constitution as a vital force, having an animation of its own. At the same time they expect Supreme Court justices

1. Max Farrand, *The Framing of the Constitution of the United States* (New Haven: Yale University Press, 1913), pp. 156–57. See Chief Justice John Marshall's argument for judicial review in the landmark case of *Marbury* v. *Madison* (1803).

to be above the normal prejudices of other persons. Thus, they envision "a living Constitution" and an insentient Court. But a moment's reflection should remind us that it is the other way around. If the Constitution is, as they say, an "elastic instrument," then much of the stretching has been done by the nine persons on the Court, and the directions in which they pull are largely determined by their own ideological predilections. As Chief Justice Hughes pointedly remarked, "We are under a constitution but the constitution is what the judges say it is."[2]

By its nature, the Supreme Court is something of an aristocratic branch: its members are appointed rather than popularly elected; they enjoy life tenure and are formally accountable to no one once in office; they have the final word on constitutional matters. Over the generations, the Court's members have varied from liberal to archconservative. Generally speaking, by class background, professional training, and political selection, the justices have more commonly identified with the landed interests than with the landless, the slave owners rather than the slaves, the industrialists rather than the workers, the exponents of Herbert Spencer rather than the proponents of Karl Marx, the established authority rather than the rebel. Over a century ago Justice Miller, a Lincoln appointee to the Court, made note of the class biases of the judiciary: "It is vain to contend with judges who have been at the bar, the advocates for forty years of railroad companies, and all the forms of associated capital, when they are called upon to decide cases where such interests are in contest. All their training, all their feelings are from the start in favor of those who need no such influence."[3]

Nor does the situation differ much today. Whether appointed by Democratic or Republican presidents, judges are drawn preponderantly from highly privileged backgrounds.[4] One study finds that the American Bar Association's quasiofficial Federal Judiciary Committee, whose task is to pass on the qualifications of prospective judges (at all federal levels), favors those whose orientation is conservative and supportive of corporate interests.[5]

Through most of its history the High Court has shown "a definite partiality for the rich."[6] This is due to:

---

2. Dexter Perkins, *Charles Evans Hughes* (Boston: Little, Brown, 1956), p. 16.
3. Quoted in Felix Frankfurter, *Mr. Justice Holmes and the Supreme Court* (New York: Atheneum, 1965), p. 54.
4. Sheldon Goldman, "Johnson and Nixon Appointees to the Lower Federal Courts: Some Socio-Political Perspectives," *Journal of Politics*, 34, August 1972, pp. 934–42.
5. See Joel B. Grossman, *Lawyers and Judges: The ABA and the Politics of Judicial Selection* (New York: Wiley, 1965).
6. Russell Galloway, *The Rich and the Poor in Supreme Court History 1790–1982* (Greenbrae, Calif.: Paradigm Press, 1982), p. 181.

1. The Court's systemic mandate under the Constitution—as intended by the framers—to act as a check on the democratic majority and as a protector of private contract, credit, and property. In a capitalist society it would be hard for a judicial branch—be it liberal or conservative—to function by consistently opposing the demands of the capitalist system.
2. As just noted, the process of professional education and advancement contains a built-in class bias which makes it unlikely that dissidents will be picked for the bench—and very few have. The bar associations and law schools, and the rich foundations that finance the law journals, endowed chairs, and research grants in jurisprudence are not dedicated to transforming the existing system of ownership and wealth. Whatever changes they might allow are intended to "revitalize" the law so as to stabilize better the ongoing class structure.[7]
3. The selection of jurists for the Supreme Court and the lower courts is accomplished by a political process that favors social elites. The range of acceptable political ideology is from ultraconservative to mainstream liberal. From the first years of the Republic, presidents have selected justices according to their politico-economic ideologies. These justices "have tended to vote repeatedly in tightly knit blocs on the main economic issues, so that constitutional adjudication becomes largely a matter of political head-counting similar to the decision making process in the House and Senate. . . ."[8] In most cases regarding the uses and distribution of wealth, there are well-articulated rationales supporting either a conservative or liberal viewpoint. The determining factor as to how justices decide an issue, then, has less to do with objective inquiry than with ideological preference.[9] Both conservative and liberal ideologies, of course, accept the existing economic system as an unchallengeable given.

Occasionally a president will select someone for the Court whose behavior goes contrary to his expectations, but generally presidents have been successful in matching court appointments with their own ideological preferences. President Reagan has been second to none in this endeavor, having stocked more than half of the 744 federal judgeships with ideologically committed conservatives, mostly in their thirties and forties, who will be handing down decisions and shaping the law of the land into the

7. See Joan Roelofs, "Foundation Influence on Supreme Court Decision-Making," paper presented at the annual meeting of the American Political Science Association, Chicago, 1983.
8. Galloway, *The Rich and the Poor . . .*, p. 179.
9. Ibid.

"I'm happy to say that my final judgment of a case is almost always consistent with my prejudgment of the case."

second and third decades of the next century. As compared to his predecessor, Jimmy Carter, Reagan appointed very few Blacks, Latinos, or women to the courts. He also picked many more upper-class persons: 81 percent of his appointees had incomes of over $200,000 and 23 percent admitted to being millionaires.[10]

In some instances, a conservative ideology seemed to be the *only* qualification of Reagan's candidates. Thus, the extremely conservative Daniel Manion, age 44, appointed to a lifetime position as federal appellate judge, was declared "minimally qualified" by the American Bar

10. Sheldon Goldman, "Reaganizing the Judiciary," *Judicature*, 68, April–May 1985, pp. 313–329. Philip Lacovar, "The Wrong Way to Pick Judges," *New York Times*, October 3, 1986; Tom Wicker, "Purifying the Courts," *New York Times*, April 19, 1985. Federal trials are conducted in federal district courts which decide almost 300,000 cases a year. Appeals are made to the twelve U.S Courts of Appeal which annually handle some 30,000 cases. The Supreme Court in contrast hands down about 170 decisions a year.

Association and attacked by the deans of more than forty of our most prominent law schools for his lack of "scholarship, legal acumen, professional achievement, wisdom, fidelity to the law and commitment to our Constitution."[11] To succeed Burger as chief justice of the Supreme Court, Reagan picked Justice Rehnquist, the most conservative member of the Court, who proceeded to give evasive testimony to a Senate committee during his confirmation hearings regarding his past anti-civil-rights activities and his purported violation of judicial ethics.[12]

CONSERVATIVE JUDICIAL ACTIVISM

It is said that the devil himself can quote the Bible for his own purposes. The Constitution is not unlike the Bible in this respect, and over the generations, Supreme Court justices have shown an infernal agility in finding constitutional justifications for the continuation of almost every inequity and iniquity, be it slavery or segregation, child labor or the sixteen-hour workday, state sedition laws or assaults on the First Amendment.

In its early days under Chief Justice John Marshall the Court emerged as a guardian of property, declaring that a corporation was to be considered a "person" entitled to all the rights accorded persons under the Constitution.[13] The Marshall Court supported the supremacy of federal powers over the states. In *McCulloch* v. *Maryland* (1819) the Court forbade Maryland from taxing a federal bank and affirmed Congress's right to create a bank (a power not mentioned in the Constitution). Marshall argued that Article I, Section 8, gave Congress the right "to make all laws necessary and proper" for carrying out its delegated powers. So was the

---

11. *New York Times*, July 25, 1986; Lacovar, "The Wrong Way to Pick Judges." Manion also was faulted for making many mistakes in grammar and spelling in his briefs. After intensive White House lobbying, he was confirmed 48 to 46 by a Republican-controlled Senate.

12. Rehnquist testified that he had supported desegregation of schools; when confronted with a segregationist memorandum he wrote as a law clerk in 1952, he claimed it was the opinion of the late Justice Robert Jackson (who had opposed segregation). Rehnquist never was able to refute eyewitness testimony that he harassed Black and Hispanic voters in Phoenix in the 1960s. Nor did he explain why he signed an anti-Semitic covenant for one of his homes. As a Supreme Court justice, Rehnquist cast the deciding vote in *Laird* v. *Tatum* (1972) to dismiss a probe of Army intelligence—even though he had prior knowledge of and direct involvement in that very case when serving in the Nixon administration. Thus, he protected himself from possible damage claims if the suit were upheld. When questioned about this violation of judicial ethics he said he could not remember. *New York Times*, September 11 and 17, 1986. For federal district court, Reagan picked an admitted admirer of the Ku Klux Klan, Jefferson Beauregard Sessions III. Sessions was too much even for the Senate, which refused to confirm him.

13. *Trustees of Dartmouth College* v. *Woodward* (1819).

groundwork laid for the expansion of federal power and the protection of corporate interests by judicial activists like Marshall.

Much of the debate about the Supreme Court today centers on the question of whether the Bench should exercise a liberal "judicial activism" by vigorously supporting individual rights and social needs, or a conservative "judicial restraint" by deferring to the other two branches of government and cleaving close to past traditions. Actually, through most of its history the Court has engaged in a *conservative* judicial activism—and does so today. This conservative predominance was punctuated by one liberal period (1836–1890) during which the Court assumed a *less* activist role, somewhat like that of a mediator between rich and poor, allowing government reform legislation to stand. But even then "the Court's personnel were recruited mainly from the class of corporate lawyers, so there was no shortage of empathy with the desires of expanding capitalism."[14]

Only during a relatively few years interspersed in the 1940–1969 period—and most notably during the 1960s—did the High Court become a more active supporter of individual rights and economic reform on behalf of the poor. This development convinced conservatives that judicial activism is a peculiarly liberal malady, even though throughout the Court's history the most audacious activism has been exercised in defense of economic conservatism. When the federal government wanted to establish national banks, or give away half the country to private speculators, or subsidize industries, or set up commissions that fixed prices and interest rates for manufacturers and banks, or send Marines to secure corporate investments in Central America, or imprison people who spoke out against war and capitalism, or deport immigrant radicals without a trial, or use the United States Army to shoot workers and break strikes, the Court inventively found constitutional pegs that made such activities acceptable.

But if the federal or state governments sought to limit workday hours, set minimum wage or occupational safety standards, insure the safety of consumer commodities, guarantee the right of collective bargaining, or in other ways offer protections against the powers of business, then the Court ruled that ours was a limited form of government that could not tamper with the rights of property and the "free market" by depriving owner and worker of "substantive due process" and "freedom of contract"—concepts elevated to supreme status even though the limitations claimed on their behalf exist nowhere in the Constitution.[15]

---

14. Galloway, *The Rich and the Poor . . .*, pp. 163, 180, and passim.

15. "Substantive due process," a seemingly contradiction in terms was a judicial invention that allowed the Court to judge not only the procedural matters of due process but the content of the legislation, whether it interfered with the liberty of individuals and corporations to use their property as they saw fit. On this and the sanctity of contract see *Allegeyer* v. *Louisiana* (1897), *Lochner* v. *New York* (1905), *Adair* v. *United States* (1908).

Whether the Court judged the government to be improperly interfering with the economy depended on which social class benefited. When Congress outlawed child labor, the Court found it to be an unconstitutional usurpation of the reserved powers of the states under the Tenth Amendment.[16] But when the states passed social-welfare legislation, the Court found it in violation of "substantive due process" under the Fourteenth Amendment.[17] Thus, while prohibiting Congress from supposedly encroaching on the reserved powers of the states, the Court claimed federal prerogatives to prevent the states from using their reserved powers—if these encroached upon the privileges of business. Juridically speaking, it's hard to get more activist than that.

The Fourteenth Amendment, adopted in 1868 ostensibly to establish full citizenship for Blacks, says, "No State shall make or enforce any law which shall abridge the privileges or immunities of citizens of the United States; nor shall any State deprive any person of life, liberty, or property, without due process of law; nor deny to any person within its jurisdiction the equal protection of the laws." Once again the Court decided that "person" included corporations and that the Fourteenth Amendment was intended to protect business conglomerations from the "vexatious regulations" of the states.

The Court handed down a series of decisions in the latter half of the nineteenth century and the early twentieth, most notably *Plessy* v. *Ferguson* (1896), which turned the Fourteenth Amendment on its head and denied Afro-Americans equal protection. The *Plessy* decision enunciated the "separate but equal" doctrine, which said that the forced separation of Blacks from Whites in public facilities did not impute inferiority as long as facilities were more or less equal (which they rarely were). The doctrine gave constitutional legitimation to the racist practice of segregation.

Convinced that they too were persons despite the treatment accorded them by a male-dominated society, women began to argue that the Fourteenth and Fifth Amendments applied to them and that the voting restrictions imposed on them by state and federal governments should be abolished. A test case reached the Supreme Court in 1894 and the justices decided that they could not give such a daring reading to the Constitution.[18] The Court seemingly had made up its mind that "privileges and immunities of citizens," "due process," and "equal protection of the laws"

16. *Hammer* v. *Dagenhart* (1918). The Tenth Amendment reads: "The Powers not delegated to the United States by this Constitution, nor prohibited by it to the states, are reserved to the States respectively or to the people." See also *Carter* v. *Carter Coal Co.* (1936).

17. *Morehead* v. *New York* (1936).

18. *Minor* v. *Happersett* (1894).

applied to such "persons" as business corporations but not to women and Blacks.

Well into the New Deal era, the Supreme Court was the activist bastion of laissez-faire capitalism, striking down reforms produced by the state legislatures and Congress and limiting government's ability to regulate the economy. The Court served capitalism almost too well. An increasingly centralized economy demanded a centralized regulation of business and labor. The Great Depression of the 1930s made clear to many liberal policymakers that only the federal government could revive a stagnant economy, create new investment opportunities, and subsidize business on a grand scale. At the same time the government had to implement long-overdue reforms to create some modest measure of social justice. Justice Brandeis expressed this liberal position clearly: "There will come a revolt of the people against the capitalists, unless the aspirations of the people are given some adequate legal expression. . . . Whatever and however strong our convictions against the extension of governmental function may be, we shall inevitably be swept farther toward socialism unless we can curb the excesses of our financial magnates."[19]

Capitalism had to be reformed and updated, if only to prevent socialism. As Joan Roelofs noted, robber barons and naked exploitation had to be replaced by a more covert, technocratic form of rule that made some gesture at including working-class elements.[20] From 1937 onward, under pressure from the public and the White House, the Supreme Court began to accept the constitutionality of New Deal legislation. At the same time the Court continued to hand down decisions that denied the Bill of Rights to persons who agitated and organized against capitalism.

CIRCUMVENTING THE FIRST AMENDMENT

While opposing restrictions on economic power, the Court seldom opposed restraints on free speech. The same conservatism that feared experimentation in economics also feared the radical ideas that underlay such changes. The First Amendment says, "Congress shall make no law . . . abridging the freedom of speech, or of the press." This would seem to leave little

19. Louis D. Brandeis, *Business: A Profession* (Boston: Small, Maynard, 1933), p. 330, cited in Joan Roelofs, "The Supreme Court and Corporate Capitalism: An Iconoclastic View of the Warren Court in the Shadow of Critical Theory," paper presented at the Northeastern Political Science Association meeting, November 1978.

20. Roelofs, "The Supreme Court and Corporate Capitalism. . ."

room for doubt as to the freedom of *all* speech.[21] Yet ever since the Alien and Sedition Acts of 1798, Congress and the state legislatures have found repeated occasion to penalize the expression of heretical ideas as "subversion" or "sedition."[22] During the First World War, Congress passed the Espionage Act, under which almost two thousand successful prosecutions were carried out, usually against socialists, who expressed opposition to the war. One individual, who in private conversation in a relative's home opined that it was a rich man's war, was fined $5,000 and sentenced to twenty years in prison.[23] The government imprisoned American socialist leader Eugene V. Debs for enunciating similar opinions from a public platform.

The High Court's attitude toward the First Amendment was best expressed by Justice Holmes in the famous *Schenck* case. Schenck was charged with attempting to cause insubordination among United States military forces and obstructing recruitment, both violations of the Espionage Act of 1917. What he had done was distribute a leaflet that condemned the war as a wrong perpetrated by Wall Street. The leaflet also urged people to petition for repeal of the draft law. In ordinary times, Holmes reasoned, such speech is amply protected by the First Amendment, but when a nation is at war, statements like Schenck's are not protected, for they create "a clear and present danger" of bringing about "the substantive evils that Congress has a right to prevent."[24] Free speech, Holmes argued, "does not protect a man in falsely shouting fire in a crowded theatre and causing a panic." The analogy is farfetched: Schenck was not in a theater but was seeking a forum to voice his opposition to policies that Holmes treated as beyond challenge. Holmes was summoning the same argument paraded by every ruler who has sought to abrogate a people's freedom: these are not normal times; there is a grave menace

---

21. Even the staunchest proponents of free speech allow that libel and slander might be restricted by law, although here too such speech when directed against public figures has been treated as protected under the First Amendment. See *New York Times Co.* v. *Sullivan* (1964), and *Time Inc.* v. *Hill* (1967).

22. *Sedition* is defined in Webster's Dictionary as "excitement of discontent against the government or resistance to lawful authority."

23. Hearings before a Subcommittee of the Senate Judiciary Committee, *Amnesty and Pardon for Political Prisoners* (Washington, D.C.: Government Printing Office, 1927), p. 54. See also Charles Goodell, *Political Prisoners in America* (New York: Random House, 1973), Chapter 4.

24. *Schenck* v. *United States* (1919); also Holmes's decision in *Debs* v. *United States* (1919). Holmes was considered one of the more liberal justices of his day. In subsequent cases he placed himself against the Court's majority and on the side of the First Amendment, earning the title of the "Great Dissenter." See *Abrams* v. *United States* (1919), and *Gitlow* v. *New York* (1925).

within or just outside our gates; national security necessitates a suspension of democratic rules.[25]

More than once the Court treated the allegedly pernicious quality of a radical idea as certain evidence of its lethal efficacy and as justification for its supression. When the top leadership of the Communist party was convicted in 1951 under the Smith Act (which made it a felony to teach or advocate the violent overthrow of the government) the Court upheld the act and the convictions, arguing that there was no freedom under the Constitution for those who conspired to propagate revolutionary movements. Free speech was not an absolute value but one of many competing ones. Justices Black and Douglas dissented, arguing that the defendants had not been charged with any acts nor even with saying anything about violent revolution, but were intending to publish the classic writings of Marx, Engels, and Lenin. In any case, the First Amendment was designed to protect the very heretical views we might find offensive and fearsome. Safe and orthodox ideas rarely needed constitutional protection.[26]

Six years later, fourteen more Communist leaders were convicted under the Smith Act. This time, however, some of the hysteria of the McCarthy era had subsided and the Court's political alignment had shifted with the addition of new members; so the justices virtually reversed themselves, ruling that the Smith Act prohibited only incitement to unlawful actions and not "advocacy of abstract doctrine." The convictions were overthrown. Justice Black added the opinion that the Smith Act itself should be declared unconstitutional: "I believe that the First Amendment forbids Congress to punish people for talking about public affairs, whether or not such discussion incites to action, legal or illegal."[27]

Freedom for Revolutionaries?

Opposed to Black's view are those who argue that revolutionaries and communists should not be allowed "to take advantage of the very liberties

25. At no time had Schenck obstructed anything. He was convicted of *conspiracy* to obstruct. The allegedly wrongful *intent* of his action constituted sufficient grounds for conviction. Under the law, "conspiracy" is an agreement by two or more people to commit an unlawful act, or a lawful act by unlawful means. In some cases, working for a common purpose, even without actual cooperative actions, has been treated as sufficient evidence of conspiracy. Thus, some antiwar demonstrators brought to trial for conspiracy to incite riot had not met each other until the time of the trial. Judge Learned Hand described the conspiracy doctrine as the "prosecutor's darling"; it can make a crime out of the thoughts in people's heads, even when these are expressed openly and promulgated by lawful means. See Jessica Mitford, *The Trial of Dr. Spock* (New York: Knopf, 1969); also Thomas I. Emerson, *The System of Freedom of Expression* (New York: Vintage, 1971).

26. *Dennis et al.* v. *United States* (1951).

27. *Yates et al.* v. *United States* (1957). The Smith Act was repealed in 1977.

they seek to destroy." Revolutionary advocacy constitutes an abuse of freedom, for it urges us to violate the democratic rules of the game. Hence, the argument goes, in order to preserve our political freedom, we may find it necessary to deprive some people of theirs.[28] Several rejoinders might be made to this position.

First, as a point of historical fact, the threat of revolution in the United States has never been as real or harmful to our liberties as the measures taken to "protect" us from revolutionary ideas. History repeatedly demonstrates the expansive quality of repression: first, revolutionary advocacy is suppressed, then unpopular doctrines, then "inciting" words, then "irresponsible" news reports and public utterances that allegedly undermine our foreign policy or national security, then any kind of criticism that those in power find intolerable.

Second, the suppression is conducted by political elites who, in protecting us from "harmful" thoughts, are in effect making up our minds for us by depriving us of the opportunity of hearing and debating revolutionary ideas with revolutionary advocates. An exchange is forbidden because the advocate has been silenced—which in effect silences us too.

Third, it is debatable whether socialist, communist, and other anticapitalists are dedicated to the destruction of freedom. Much of the ferment in United States history, branded as "revolutionary," actually augmented our democratic rights. The working-class agitations of the early nineteenth century widened the areas of dissent and helped extend the franchise to propertyless working people. The organized demonstrations against repressive local ordinances in the early twentieth century by the revolutionary-minded Industrial Workers of the World (the Wobblies' "free-speech fights") fortified the First Amendment against attacks by the guardians of property. The crucial role Communists played in organizing the industrial unions in the 1930s and struggling for social reforms strengthened rather than undermined democratic forces. Americans were never "given" their freedoms; they had to organize, agitate, and struggle fiercely for whatever rights they do have. As with our bodily health so with the health of our body politic: we best preserve our faculties and liberties against death and decay by vigorously exercising them.

Fourth, revolutionaries would argue that freedom is in short supply in the *present* society, where wealth and power serve mostly the interests of the few. The construction of new social and economic alternatives can

28. For samples of this thinking see the Vinson and Jackson opinions in the *Dennis* case; also Sidney Hook, *Political Power and Personal Freedom* (New York: Criterion Books, 1959); Carl A. Auerbach, "The Communist Control Act of 1954: A Proposed Legal-Political Theory of Free Speech," in Samuel Hendel (ed.), *Basic Issues of American Democracy*, 8th ed. (Englewood Cliffs, N.J.: Prentice-Hall, 1976), pp. 59–63.

bring an increase in freedom, including freedom from poverty and hunger, freedom to share in making the decisions that govern one's work and community, and freedom to experiment with new forms of production and ownership. Admittedly some freedoms enjoyed today would be lost in a revolutionary society—for instance, the freedom to exploit other people and get rich from their labor, the freedom to squander natural resources and treat the environment as a septic tank, the freedom to monopolize information and exercise unaccountable power. In many countries successful social revolutionary movements have brought a net increase in the freedom of individuals, revolutionaries argue, by advancing the conditions necessary for health and human life, by providing jobs and education for the unemployed and illiterate, by using economic resources for social development rather than for corporate profit, and by overthrowing repressive reactionary regimes and ending foreign exploitation and involving large sectors of the populace in the task of socialist reconstruction. Revolutions can extend a number of real freedoms without destroying those that never existed for the people of those countries. The argument can be debated, but not if it is suppressed. In any case, the real danger to freedom in America is from the undemocratic control exercised by those in government, the media, academia, business, and other institutions who would insulate us from "unacceptable" viewpoints. No idea is as dangerous as the force that would seek to repress it.

AS THE COURT TURNS

The Supreme Court's record in the area of personal liberties, while gravely wanting, is not totally devoid of merit. Over the years the Court has extended portions of the Bill of Rights to cover not only the federal government but state government (via the Fourteenth Amendment). Attempts by the states to censor publications, deny individuals the right to peaceful assembly, and weaken the separation between church and state were overturned.[29]

The direction the Supreme Court takes depends (a) on the pressures exerted by various advocacy groups and the political climate of the times, and (b) the political composition of the Court's majority. In the 1960s, fortified by the social activism of the wider society, especially in the civil rights area, and by a liberal majority of justices, the Court under Chief Justice Earl Warren took a pronouncedly liberal activist role. The Warren Court took steps to safeguard individual rights in criminal-justice proceed-

29. See respectively *Near* v. *Minnesota* (1931), *DeJonge* v. *Oregon* (1937), *McCollum* v. *Board of Education* (1948).

ings, including the right of a poor person to benefit of counsel in state criminal trials[30] and of an arrested person to have a lawyer at the onset of police interrogation.[31]

In some states, less than a third of the population elected more than half the legislators; the Warren Court ruled that malapportioned district lines had to be redrawn in accordance with population distribution, so that voters in the overpopulated districts were not denied equal protection under the law.[32] The Court also took the disestablishment clause in the First Amendment seriously when it ruled that prayers in the public school were a violation of the separation of church and state.[33]

The Warren Court handed down a number of decisions aimed at abolishing racial segregation. The most widely celebrated, *Brown* v. *Board of Education* (1954), unanimously ruled that "separate educational facilities are inherently unequal" because of the inescapable imputation of inferiority cast upon the segregated minority group, an imputation that is all the greater when sanctioned by law. This decision overruled the "separate but equal" doctrine enunciated in 1896 in the *Plessy* case.[34]

The law has always treated public assistance for the poor and the disabled as "privileges" which could be cut off at will. The Warren Court rejected the distinction between "rights" and "privileges" and held that persons who qualified for benefits had a protected "property" interest that could not be taken away without due process of law. Instead of just allowing the other branches of government to act on behalf of the needy as did earlier liberal justices, "for the first time in the nation's history, the Court majority began to exercise initiative on behalf of the poor."[35]

While opening up new opportunities for democratic gains in civil liberties, civil rights, and protections for the poor, the Warren Court did not stray very far from the basic capitalist ideology shared by both liberal and conservative jurists, to wit:

1. Capital mobility is a primary value; firms may invest or disinvest at will and move elsewhere regardless of the hardship wreaked upon the surrounding community and work force.

---

30. See *Gideon* v. *Wainwright* (1963).
31. *Escobedo* v. *Illinois* (1964) and *Miranda* v. *Arizona* (1966).
32. See *Baker* v. *Carr* (1962) and *Reynolds* v. *Sims* (1964). A similar decision was made in regard to congressional districts in *Wesberry* v. *Sanders* (1964).
33. See *Engles* v. *Vitale* (1962) and *School District of Abington* v. *Schempp* (1963). The First Amendment reads: "Congress shall make no law respecting an establishment of religion, or prohibiting the free exercise thereof."
34. See also the decision nullifying state prohibitions against interracial marriage: *Loving* v. *Virginia* (1967). (Loving was the plaintiff's name.)
35. See the discussion in Galloway, *The Rich and The Poor. . .*, pp. 160–3; the quotation is from p. 163; also *King* v. *Smith* (1968); *Sniadich* v. *Family Finance Corporation* (1969); *Shapiro* v. *Thompson* (1969); *Hunter* v. *Erickson* (1969).

2. Employees make no "investment," therefore they acquire no legal say in the direction of their company or the products of their labor.
3. Employees must obey the decisions of owners, including arbitrary directives that violate the labor contract—pending completion of an often inadequate grievance process. Most forms of employee self-protection, including wildcat strikes (work-stoppages that occur during the terms of a contract) and secondary boycotts are outlawed or heavily restricted.
4. It is assumed that the law provides a peaceful resolution of class conflict through collective bargaining and arbitration between "equal partners." In fact, it provides no such thing. The ability of labor to win a contract is determined by the relative bargaining stengths of management and labor in open struggle, with most of the legal restrictions stacked against unions.[36]

Refurbished with Nixon, Ford, and Reagan appointees, the Court under Chief Justice Warren Burger and more recently Chief Justice William Rehnquist took a decidedly rightward turn on a variety of crucial issues:

Labor, Business, and Class Inequality. In decisions involving disputes between workers and owners, the Burger Court sided with the owners even more decisively than the Warren Court, resuscitating the contract clause as a barrier to reform legislation and weakening labor's ability to organize and bargain collectively.[37] The Court ruled that workers do not have the right to strike over safety issues if their contract provides a grievance procedure. This decision denied miners the right to walk off the job in the face of serious safety violations covered up by management.[38] The Court decided that employers can in effect penalize workers for unionizing by closing down operations and denying them jobs, without having to negotiate the matter with them.[39] And companies can now unilaterally terminate a labor contract and drastically cut employees' wages by filing for "reorganization" under the bankruptcy law.[40] In a 5 to 4 decision the Burger conservatives held that unions have no power to prevent members from quitting the union and crossing picket lines during a strike or when a strike seemed imminent.[41] In general, labor unions have been hit hard by the conservative-dominated Supreme Court.

---

36. Karl Klare, "Critical Theory and Labor Relations Law," in David Kairys (ed.), *The Politics of Law* (New York: Pantheon, 1982), pp. 65–88; Klare treats *Boys Market, Inc.* v. *Retail Clerks Local 770* (1970).
37. On the contract clause see *Allied Structural Steel Co.* v. *Spannaus* (1978).
38. *Gateway Coal Co.* v. *United Mine Workers* (1974).
39. *First National Maintenance Corp.* v. *National Labor Relations Board* (1981).
40. *Washington Post*, February 23,1984.
41. *Pattern Makers' League of North America, AFL-CIO* v. *NLRB* (1985).

Despite a law passed by Congress limiting water subsidies to farms of 160 acres or less and only for farmers who "live on or near the land," the Burger Court held that large commercial farms, including ones owned by Southern Pacific and Standard Oil, were entitled to the subsidies.[42] In seeming violation of the Clean Air Act, the Court said industries could expand in regions with the dirtiest air even if it results in an increase in pollution.[43] In seeming violation of the equal-protection clause of the Fourteenth Amendment, the justices decided that a state may vary the quality of education in accordance with the amount of taxable wealth located in its school districts, thus allowing just about any degree of inequality short of absolute deprivation.[44] Finally, by upholding laws that reduced welfare assistance, the conservative jurists rejected the idea that aid to the poor was protected by due process.[45]

Individual Rights. In the area of criminal justice the Burger Court decided it was no longer necessary for states to require a unanimous jury verdict, thus making it easier for the prosecution to obtain convictions that were not beyond a reasonable doubt.[46] The *Miranda* decision, which forbade the use of police torture in obtaining confessions, also was weakened.[47] The justices decided the death penalty was not a violation of the Eighth Amendment's prohibition against "cruel and unusual punishment," nor was a life sentence given to a man for three minor frauds totalling $230.[48] And it was held that the prohibition against cruel and unusual punishment did not protect schoolchildren from corporal punishment even though the children had been severely injured by school officials.[49]

In First Amendment cases the Burger Court usually favored government authority over dissent. Thus, reporters were denied a right to confidential news sources.[50] The Bench allowed the U.S. Army to spy secretly on lawful civilian political activity,[51] but prohibited civilians from bringing political ideas openly to the Army.[52] In the latter instance the justices ruled that military posts can ban political literature and demonstrations—

42. Eric Nadler, "Supreme Court Backs Agribusiness," *Guardian*, July 2, 1980.
43. *Chevron USA Inc.* v. *National Resources Defense Council Inc. et al* (1984).
44. *San Antonio Independent School District* v. *Rodriguez* (1973).
45. *Dandridge* v. *Williams* (1970); *Rosado* v. *Wyman* (1970).
46. *Johnson* v. *Louisiana* (1972) and *Apodaca* v. *Oregon* (1972).
47. *Michigan* v. *Mosely* (1975) and *Ristaino* v. *Ross* (1976).
48. *Gregg* v. *Georgia* (1976); *Rummel* v. *Estelle* (1976). Rehnquist argued in *Rummel* that cruel and unusual punishment might be when someone is given a life sentence for "overtime parking." Such an example leaves room for nearly any kind of unjust sentence and reduces the Eighth Amendment protection to almost nothing.
49. *Ingraham* v. *Wright* (1977).
50. *United States* v. *Caldwell* (1972); also *Zurcher* v. *Stanford Daily* (1978).
51. *Laird* v. *Tatum* (1972).
52. *Greer* v. *Spock* (1976).

thus denying American soldiers the First Amendment rights they supposedly were to defend with their lives. The Court said that bans on the posting of political signs in public places are not a restriction of free speech.[53] The justices upheld a law requiring male college students to register with the Selective Service System if they want federal financial aid—a requirement that can be more successfully evaded by students who do not need aid.[54]

Executive Power. A prominent Harvard law professor commented on the Burger Court: "In one sphere after another, the court has affirmed the almost boundless authority of government over the individual and of the executive over the other branches."[55] In regard to the executive branch's power, the Burger Court ruled that the State Department could deny a passport to a former CIA employee who had written books exposing illegal CIA covert overseas operations. Neither Congress nor the Constitution granted this power to the executive but the Bench declared that in matters of "foreign policy and national security" the absence of an empowering law is not to be taken as a sign of congressional disapproval. The president now had unlimited power—by judicial fiat—to do what he wanted unless Congress specifically legislated prohibitions. This decision inverted the lawmaking process and gave federal authorities the power to deny the constitutional freedom of travel to critics whom the government thought might "damage" U.S. foreign policy by word or action.[56]

As part of a continuing pattern of deferring to presidential power in military and foreign affairs, the federal courts refused to hear cases challenging the president on such things as the undeclared war in Vietnam, the unprovoked invasion of Grenada and the imposition of embargoes on Nicaragua.[57] In a landmark decision the Supreme Court overturned the "legislative veto," a device used in over 200 laws that allowed Congress to give the president authority to do something while retaining the right to negate his action by a simple majority decision. The Court ruled this was an infringement on executive power and that Congress could limit the president's actions only the usual way, by passing a law and overriding an executive veto if necessary.[58]

---

53. *Members of the City Council of Los Angeles et al.* v. *Taxpayers for Vincent et al.* (1984). The Court has passed several decisions restricting demonstrations and leafleting at shopping malls, for instance: *Clark* v. *Community for Creative Non-Violence* (1984).

54. *Selective Service* v. *Minnesota Public Interest Research Group* (1984). In order to apply for aid any nonregistrant would be forced to incriminate himself.

55. Laurence Tribe quoted in *Washington Post*, July 8, 1984.

56. *Haig* v. *Agee* (1981); also the more recent restrictions on Americans' right to travel to Cuba: *Regan* v. *Wald* (1984).

57. For instance, *John Conyers et al.* v. *Ronald Reagan*, denied January 20, 1984: U.S. District Court for District of Columbia.

58. *Immigration and Naturalization Service* v. *Chadha* (1983).

The Electoral System. While unable to contravene earlier reapportionment cases, the Burger Court nibbled away at them, ruling that the "one-person, one-vote" rule should be applied less rigorously to state legislative districts than to congressional ones because state districts have "indigenous" qualities that ought sometimes be preserved.[59] The Court later held that partisan gerrymandering of legislative districts violated the Constitution but only if it were so severe as to "consistently degrade" a political group's influence.[60] The Burger Court decided that states could not prohibit corporations from spending unlimited amounts of their funds to influence the outcome of public referenda or other elections because the Constitution guarantees freedom of speech to business firms just as to human beings, and spending money on campaigns is a form of "speech."[61]

Gender and Race. Cases that do not directly challenge corporate power or executive authority, including such issues as abortion, race and sex discrimination, affirmative action, and separation of church and state, have received mixed treatment by the conservative Burger Court. On occasion the moderate conservatives sided with the two remaining liberals on the Bench to defeat the ultraconservatives.[62] The Court ruled that affirmative action programs as a general remedy for past discrimination could benefit racial minorities—including persons who were not necessarily actual victims of discrimination,[63] but the Court also ruled that seniority systems had priority over affirmative action.[64] The justices upheld the denial of tax-exempt treatment for schools that discriminate on the basis of race,[65] but they also supported a Minnesota statute providing state income tax relief for private schools, thus providing a public subsidy to the "White flight" to private institutions.[66]

---

59. *Mahan* v. *Howell* (1973).

60. *Davis* v. *Bandemer* (1986).

61. *First National Bank of Boston* v. *Bellotti* (1978); *Citizens Against Rent Control et al.* v. *City of Berkeley et al.* (1981). Rich individuals also are allowed to spend any amount in an "independent" effort to elect or defeat any candidate, and candidates may spend as much as they desire of their personal fortunes on their own campaigns, a decision that greatly favors the wealthy: *Buckley* v. *Valeo* (1976).

62. Note, for instance, two positive decisions on women's rights: *California Federal Savings and Loan Association* v. *Guerra* (1987) and *Roberts* v. *U.S. Jaycees* (1984). On the struggle over abortion see Eva Rubin, *Abortion, Politics and the Courts* (Westport, Conn.: Greenwood Press, 1983). Occasionally, even the ultraconservatives join in a liberal decision as when the Court ruled unanimously in *Meritor Savings Bank, FSB* v. *Vinson* (1986) that sexual harassment on the job violated a person's civil rights, and in *Palmore* v. *Sidoti* (1984) that a divorced woman cannot be denied custody of her children because of her remarriage to a man of another race.

63. *Wygant* v. *Jackson (Michigan) Board of Education* (1986).

64. *Firefighters Local Union No. 1784* v. *Stotts et al.* (1984).

65. *Bob Jones University* v. *United States* (1983). But see the subsequent narrowing decision in *Allen* v. *Wright* (1984).

66. *Mueller* v. *Allen* (1983).

While particular cases may go either way, the majority of victories in discrimination cases have been won not by poor Blacks or women but by White men.[67]

The Supreme Court's conservative bias is reflected not only in the decisions it hands down but in the kinds of cases it selects or refuses to review. During the last two decades of conservative domination of the Court, review access has been sharply curtailed for plaintiffs representing labor, minorities, consumers, and individual rights. Powerless and disfranchised individuals have had a diminishing chance of getting their cases reviewed by the Supreme Court unlike powerful and prestigious petitioners such as the government and the giant corporations.[68] The Court's ideological prejudgments determine which cases it will pick as vehicles for its judge-made law.[69]

Consider the area of criminal justice: under the Burger Court, state and federal prosecutors were able to gain a hearing by the Bench at a rate fifty times greater than defendants; pauper's petitions were accepted at one-sixth the rate of the later Warren Court years; criminal defendants who could afford the legal filing fee were twice as likely to be granted review as were indigent defendants.[70] In choosing cases the way it does, the Court sends out a clear message to lower courts: if you uphold a conviction you are less likely to suffer the embarrassment of being reviewed and reversed by the Supreme Court than if you rule in favor of defendants. With its power to review or not review, the High Court exercises an influence over lower-court rulings.

It has been argued that because its work load has so increased, the Court must perforce turn down greater numbers of cases. The truth is, while the number of lower-court appeals have indeed multiplied (numbering about five thousand a year), the amount of time the Burger Court spent on deliberations and the number of cases it heard diminished by 25 percent as compared to the Warren Court and 40 percent as compared to the earlier Hughes Court.[71] It is hard to argue that the Court is in-

---

67. For a good study of the failure of federal and state courts to fulfill the constitutional and common law promise of equality see Charles Haar and Daniel Fessler, *The Wrong Side of the Tracks* (New York: Simon and Schuster, 1986).

68. Janis Judson, *The Hidden Agenda: Non-Decision-Making on the U.S. Supreme Court* (University of Maryland, Ph.D. dissertation, 1986); Ralph Nader, "The Justices Slam the Door," *Nation*, November 12, 1977, pp. 496–98.

69. The Court's liberals, Marshall and Brennan, were far less likely to deny certiorari (review) than the conservative majority; see the statistical breakdowns in Judson, *The Hidden Agenda*, pp. 36, 43,71.

70. Steven Duke and Patrick Malone, "An Overzealous Supreme Court," *Washington Post*, October 21, 1984.

71. See Justice Douglas's calculations in William O. Douglas, *The Court Years 1939–1975* (New York: Random House, 1980), p. 384, cited in Judson, *The Hidden Agenda*, p. 63.

creasingly overworked when in fact its conservative majority has been reducing the time spent on cases. In any case, even if it were true that the Court is overburdened, this does not explain the evident class bias as to which cases are selected for review and which are refused certiorari.

INFLUENCE OF THE COURT

A few generalizations can be drawn about the Supreme Court's political influence. More often than not, the Court has been a conservative force. For over half a century it wielded a pro-business minority veto on the kind of reform legislation enacted in European countries decades before. It prevented Congress from instituting progressive income taxes, a decision that took eighteen years and a constitutional amendment to circumvent. It accepted racist segregation for more than fifty years. It delayed female suffrage for some twenty-five years and has denied women equal protection under the Fourteenth Amendment since 1894 (which is why women have been struggling to get an Equal Rights Amendment added to the Constitution). And it has now prevented Congress from placing limitations on personal campaign spending by the rich.

But the High Court's ability to impose its will on the nation is far from boundless. Presidents usually get the opportunity to appoint two or so members to the Court and so exert an influence on its political makeup. The Court cannot make rulings at will but must wait until a case is brought to it either on appeal from a lower court or, less frequently, as a case of original jurisdiction (as in a dispute between two states). And the Court is always operating in a climate of opinion shaped by political forces larger than itself. Thus, its willingness to depart from the casuistry of *Plessy* v. *Ferguson* and take the Fourteenth Amendment seriously in *Brown* v. *Board of Education* depended in part on the changing climate of opinion and the growing political struggle against segregation.

At the same time, the Court is not purely a dependent entity. The Court's decisions can have an important feedback effect.[72] By playing a crucial role in defining what is constitutional, the Court gives encouraging cues to large sectors of the public, including the Congress itself. Unable to pass a civil-rights act for seventy years, Congress enacted three in the decade after the *Brown* case. And civil-rights advocates throughout the nation pressed all the harder to make desegregation a reality. Likewise, the Warren Court's decisions protecting the rights of the poor opened a whole

72. Theodore Becker (ed.), *The Impact of Supreme Court Decisions: Empirical Studies* (New York: Oxford University Press, 1969).

new field of welfare reform litigation, helped eliminate deficiencies in public assistance programs, and was an inducement to various poor people's movements.

Most discussions of the Supreme Court's power focuses on its ability to move in a progressive direction against entrenched conservative interests (as in the 1960s), or resist progressive change in times of popular agitation (as in the 1930s). Thus the Court is seen as challenged by strong countervailing forces and is therefore deemed the "least dangerous branch."[73] But the Reagan years offer another paradigm: a militantly conservative Court bolstered by a militantly conservative executive. Here the Court's impact can be far-reaching indeed, for it can "rewrite" much of the Constitution, inventing concepts and arguments that feed an authoritarian executive power, rigging the rules of the game so as not only to roll back substantive political and economic gains but undermine the democratic process itself (such as it is).

In reaction to the liberal activism of the Warren Court, conservatives today argue that the Court must cease its intrusive role and defer to the policy-making branches of government.[74] But this "judicial restraint" is applied in selective ways and exists more in appearance than in actuality. When conservatives in Congress, the White House, and certain state and local governments launched attacks against freedom to travel, labor rights, the right to counsel, and free speech, the conservative Court deferred to these other branches of government. But while professing deference to the other branches, the Court's conservative majority showed a willingness to almost casually overturn major legislative initiatives, including protections for the poor, the limitation placed on campaign spending, the legislative veto, and the farm-acreage limitations for water subsidies.

Like the Courts of earlier days, the Burger Court played federal power against state power to defend owning class interests. Thus it limited the federal government's ability to protect hour-and-wage conditions of workers, claiming an infringement of states rights under the Tenth Amendment, and then restricted the ability of states to limit business's spending power in referenda, claiming federal prerogatives under the First Amendment. Despite the absence of judicial restraint manifested in such cases, one hears little complaint from conservatives about the Court's

73. Alexander Bickel, *The Least Dangerous Branch* (New York: Bobbs-Merrill, 1959).

74. For a statement supporting liberal activism see Justice William Brennan, "The Constitution of the United States: Contemporary Ratification," text of an address at Georgetown University, Washington, D.C., October 12, 1985. For "anti-activist" conservative responses see President Reagan's remarks reported in *New York Times*, October 22, 1985, and Raoul Berger, "Justice Brennan Is Wrong," *Washington Post*, October 28, 1985. For critical discussions see Stephen Halpern and Charles Lamb (eds.), *Supreme Court Activism and Restraint* (Lexington, Mass.: D. C. Heath, 1982).

usurpation of policy-making powers. Judicial activism that strengthens authoritarian and corporate class interests is acceptable. Judicial activism that defends democratic working-class rights and social equality invites attack. This double standard should remind us of the underlying and inescapable nature of class politics—even for those who claim to represent more elevated principles.

16

Democracy for the Few

A glance at the social map of this country reveals a vast agglomeration of groups and governing agencies. If by pluralism we mean this multiplicity of private and public groups, then the United States is a pluralistic society. But then so is any society of size and complexity, including allegedly totalitarian ones like the Soviet Union with its multiplicity of regional, occupational, and ethnic groups and its party, administrative, and military factions all competing over policies.[1]

But the proponents of pluralism presume to be saying something about how *power* is distributed and how *democracy* works. Supposedly the desirable feature of a pluralistic society is that it works through democratic means and produces democratic outputs. Policies not only are shaped by competing groups but also benefit the human needs of the populace. Thus Ralf Dahrendorf writes: "Instead of a battlefield, the scene of group conflict has become a kind of market in which relatively autonomous forces contend according to certain rules of the game, by virtue of which nobody is a permanent winner or loser."[2] If there are elites in our society, the pluralists say, they are numerous and specialized, and they are checked in their demands by other elites. No group can press its advantages too far and any group that is interested in an issue can find a way within the

---

1. See, for instance, Donald R. Kelly, "Interest Groups in the USSR: The Impact of Political Sensitivity on Group Influence," *Journal of Politics*, 34, August 1972, pp. 860–88; also H. Gordon Skilling and Franklyn Griffiths (eds.), *Interest Groups in Soviet Politics* (Princeton, N.J.: Princeton University Press, 1971). By the simple definition of pluralism offered above, even Nazi Germany might qualify as pluralistic. The Nazi state was a loose, often chaotic composite of fiercely competing groups. See Heinz Höne, *The Order of the Death's Head* (New York: Coward, McCann, and Geoghegan, 1970).

2. Ralf Dahrendorf, *Class and Class Conflict in Industrial Society* (Stanford, Calif.: Stanford University Press, 1959), p. 67.

political system to make its influence felt.[3] Business elites have the capacity to utilize the services of the government to further their interests, but, the pluralists argue, such interests are themselves varied and conflicting. The government is not controlled by a monolithic corporate elite that gets what it wants on every question. Government stands above any one particular influence but responds to many. So say the pluralists.

PLURALISM FOR THE FEW

The evidence offered in the preceding chapters leaves us with sufficient reason to doubt that the United States is a pluralistic democracy as conceived by the pluralists. To summarize and expand upon what has been said:

1. Public policies favor the large investor interests at a substantial cost to the rest of the populace. Democratic struggles have won some real benefits for the public, yet assistance has not reached millions who are most in need, and no solution is in sight for the problems of unemployment, substandard housing, economic immiseration, environmental devastation, pollution, and deficiencies in our educational, medical, and transportational systems. There is glut in the private commodity market and scarcity in public services. While the rich get ever richer, possessed with more money than they know what to do with, the majority of the populace lives under a condition of economic insecurity, fearing retirement and the loss of earning power. While federal, state, and local governments go deeper into debt, military dictatorships throughout the world batten on the largesse of the Pentagon, as do defense contractors at home.

2. To think of government as nothing more than a referee amidst a vast array of competing groups (which presumably represent all the important and "countervailing" interests within the society) is to forget that government best serves those who can serve themselves, granting hundreds of billions of dollars in tax cuts to the rich in recent years while cutting back on social services for the rest of us. There are reasons why important public programs fail to measure up to their promise. Often the allocations are

---

3. One of the earliest pluralist statements is in Earl Latham, *The Group Basis of Politics* (Ithaca: Cornell University Press, 1952). See also Arnold M. Rose, *The Power Structure* (New York: Oxford University Press, 1967); Robert Dahl, *Who Governs?* (New Haven: Yale University Press, 1961); Edward Banfield, *Political Influence* (New York: Free Press, 1961); Nelson Polsby, *Community Power and Political Theory*, Rev. ed. (New Haven: Yale University Press, 1980). The criticisms of pluralism are many: the best collection of critiques can be found in Charles A. McCoy and John Playford (eds.), *Apolitical Politics* (New York: Crowell, 1967); see also Marvin Surkin and Alan Wolfe (eds.), *An End to Political Science: The Caucus Papers* (New York: Basic Books, 1970).

meager while the problem is immense, as with programs relating to poverty and unemployment. Other times the expenditures may be substantial but the problem is deeply ingrained in the economic system itself and is not solved by merely having public money thrown at it, for example, job training for which there are no jobs. And sometimes immense sums are channeled through the private sector to enrich the suppliers without any commensurate output in the service. In this way, public funds augment the capital-accumulation process and do not compete with the private market. Neither do they significantly answer to the needs for which they were ostensibly allocated. To pour more money into a service without a change in the market relations enjoyed by the suppliers is merely to make more public funds available to the private suppliers without guaranteeing an improvement in the service.[4]

3. Power in America "is plural and fluid," claims Max Lerner.[5] In reality, power is distributed among heavily entrenched, well-organized, well-financed politico-economic conglomerates that can reproduce the social conditions needed for continued elite hegemony. Of the various resources of power, wealth is the most crucial, and its distribution is neither "plural" nor "fluid." Not everyone with money chooses to use it to exert political influence, and not everyone with money need bother to do so. But when they so desire, those who control the wealth of society enjoy a persistent and pervasive political advantage.

4. The political advantage enjoyed by the moneyed class is fortified by a variety of institutional and governmental arrangements. The pluralists have not a word to say about the pervasive role of political repression in American society, the purging and exclusion of anticapitalist dissidents from government, the labor movement, the media, academia, and the entertainment world, along with the surveillance and harassment of protest groups and sometimes even mild critics. Nor do the pluralists give any recognition to the way that the moneyed power controls the communication industry and most other institutions of society, setting the terms for the socialization, indoctrination, and recruitment of governmental and nongovernmental elites. Pluralists seem never to allude to the near-monopoly control of ideas and information which is the daily fare of the news and entertainment sectors of the mass media, creating a climate of opinion favorable to the owning-class ideology at home and abroad. Nor are the pluralists much troubled by the rigged monopoly rules under which the two major political parties operate, and an electoral system that treats

---

4. For instance, the cost of Medicaid and Medicare rose from $4.8 billion in 1967 to $57 billion in 1980 to $81.7 billion in 1982. The billions have enriched the "prestigious inhabitants of Country Club America": Carl Rowan, *Washington Post*, September 15, 1982.

5. Max Lerner, *America as a Civilization* (New York: Simon and Schuster, 1957), p.398.

private money as a form of free speech, and vast sums of it as a prerequisite for office.

5. The pluralists make much of the fact that wealthy interests do not always operate with clear and deliberate purpose.[6] To be sure, elites, like everyone else, make mistakes and suffer confusions as to what might be the most advantageous tactics in any particular situation. But if they are not omniscient and infallible, neither are they habitual laggards and imbeciles. If they do not always calculate rationally in the pursuit of their class interests, they do so often and successfully enough. It is also true that the business community is not unanimous on all issues.

6. Is then the American polity ruled by a secretive, conspiratorial, omnipotent, monolithic power elite? No, the plutocracy, or ruling class, does not fit that easily refuted caricature. First of all, it cannot get its way on all things at all times. No ruling class in history, no matter how autocratic, has ever achieved omnipotence. All have had to make concessions and allow for unexpected and undesired developments. In addition, the ruling elites are not always secretive. They rule from legitimized institutions. The moneyed influence they exercise over governing bodies is sometimes overt—as with reported campaign contributions and control of investments, and sometimes covert—as with unreported bribes and deals. The ruling class controls most of the institutions and jobs of this society through corporate ownership and by control of management positions, interlocking directorates, and trusteeships, the elite membership of which, while not widely advertised, is well-documented public knowledge. However, these elites do often find it desirable to plan in secret, to minimize or distort the flow of information, to deny the truth, to develop policies that sometimes violate the law they profess to uphold. Instances of this have been treated in this book.

7. American government is not ruled by a monolithic elite. There are serious differences in tactics, differences in how best to mute class conflict and maintain the existing system at home and abroad. Differences can arise between moderately conservative and extremely conservative capitalists, between large and not-as-large investor interests, and between domestic and international corporations—all of which lends an element of conflict and indeterminacy to policies. But these conflicts seldom take into account the interests of the public. Given the wide-ranging interests of the corporate class, policy is dictated by a variety of elites that cut across various financial circles and governing agencies. When push comes to shove, what holds them together is their common interest in preserving a

6. Dahl, *Who Governs?*, p. 272. Also see Robert A. Dahl, *Modern Political Analysis* (Englewood Cliffs, N.J.: Prentice Hall, 1970).

system that assures their continued accumulation of wealth and enjoyment of social privilege.

Does this amount to a "conspiracy theory" of society? First, it should be noted that conspiracies do exist. A common view is that conspiracy is only the imaginings of kooks. But just because some people have fantasies of conspiracies does not mean that all conspiracies are fantasies. There is ample evidence of real ones. The early planning of the Vietnam War as revealed in the *Pentagon Papers*, the ITT-CIA-White House Policy of destabilizing Chile, the Watergate break-in and the Watergate cover-up, the FBI COINTELPRO disruption of dissident groups, the several well-orchestrated energy crises that sharply boosted oil prices in the 1970s, the Iran-contra arms deals, and the Wall Street "insiders" stock trading scandals of 1986–87 are some important conspiracies that are a matter of public record. Webster's dictionary defines conspiracy as "a planning and acting together secretly, especially for an unlawful or harmful purpose." All the above examples fit the definition.

Ruling elites admit to a conscious and constant need to plan in secret, resorting to sometimes drastic measures, often without being held accountable to anyone: they call it "national security." But when one suggests that their plans (whether covert or overt) benefit the interests of their class and are intended to do so, one is dismissed as a "conspiracy theorist." It is allowed that farmers, steelworkers, and even welfare mothers may plan concerted actions and try to use political means to help themselves, but it may not be suggested that moneyed elites do as much—even when they actually occupy the decision-making posts. Instead we are asked to believe that financial elites and political rulers walk through life in an innocent, disinterested state. Or if they do consciously respond to and pursue certain interests, it is never their own, or only accidentally their own, for presumably they are indifferent to the fate of their vast holdings.

Although there is no one grand power elite, there is continual cooperation between various corporate and governmental elites in every area of the political economy. Many of the stronger corporate elites tend to predominate in their particular spheres of interest more or less unmolested by other elites.[7] In any case, the conflicts between plutocratic elites seldom work to the advantage of the mass of people. They are conflicts of haves versus haves. Often they are resolved not by compromise but by logrolling and involve more *collusion* than competition. These mutually satisfying arrangements among "competitors" usually come at the expense of public interest—as when the costs of collusion are passed on to the public in the

7. Peter Bachrach, *The Theory of Democratic Elitism* (Boston: Little, Brown, 1967), p. 37.

form of higher prices, higher taxes, environmental devastation, and inflation. The demands of the have-nots may be heard occasionally as a clamor outside the gate, and now and then something is tossed to the unfortunates. But generally speaking, pluralist group politics engages the interests of extremely limited portions of the population, within a field of political options largely shaped by the interests of corporate capitalism.

One might better think of ours as a dual political system. First, there is the *symbolic* political system centering around electoral and representative activities including campaign conflicts, voter turnout, political personalities, public pronouncements, official role-playing, and certain ambiguous presentations of some of the public issues that bestir presidents, governors, mayors, and their respective legislatures. Then there is the *substantive* political system, involving multibillion-dollar contracts, tax write-offs, protections, rebates, grants, loss compensations, subsidies, leases, giveaways, and the whole vast process of budgeting, legislating, advising, regulating, protecting, and servicing major producer interests, now bending or ignoring the law on behalf of the powerful, now applying it with full punitive vigor against heretics and "troublemakers." The symbolic system is highly visible, taught in the schools, dissected by academicians, gossiped about by news commentators. The substantive system is seldom heard of or accounted for.

Interest-group politics is tiered according to the power of the contenders. Big interests, like the oil, banking, and defense industries, operate in the most important arena, extracting hundreds of billions of dollars from the labor of others and from the public treasure, affecting the well-being of whole communities and regions, and exercising control over the most important units of the federal government. In contrast, consumer groups, labor unions, and public-interest advocates move in a more limited space, registering their complaints against some of the worst, or more visible, symptoms of the corporate system and occasionally winning a new law or regulation. Finally, the weakest interests, like welfare mothers and slum dwellers, are shunted to the margins of political life, where they remind us of their existence with an occasional demonstration in front of city hall as they attempt to make a claim on the human-services budget.

It is worth repeating that this diversity of groups does not represent a democratization of power. A wide array of politico-economic power formations does not indicate a wide sharing of power in any democratic sense, for the sharing occurs largely among moneyed interests that are becoming increasingly less competitive and more concentrated and collusive in economic ownership. Decision-making power is "divided" in that it is parceled out to special public-private interest groups—quasiautonomous, entrenched coteries that use public authority for private purposes of low visibility. The fragmentation of power is the pocketing of power, a way of insulating portions of the political process from the tides of popular sentiment. This purpose was embodied in the constitutional structure by the framers in 1787 and has prevailed ever since in more elaborate forms.

Along with the special interests of business firms, there is the overall influence exerted by *business as a system*. More than just an abstraction, business as a system of power, a way of organizing property, capital, and labor, is a pervasive social force. Corporate business is not just another of many interests in the influence system. It occupies a strategic position within the economic system; in a sense, it *is* the economic system. On the major issues of the political economy, business gets its way with government because there exists no alternative way of organizing the economy within the existing capitalist structure. Because business controls the very economy of the nation, government perforce enters into a unique and intimate relationship with it. The health of the capitalist economy is treated by policymakers as a necessary condition for the health of the nation, and since it happens that the economy is in the hands of large investors, then presumably government's service to the public is best accomplished by service to these investors. The goals of business (rapid growth, high profits, and secure markets) become the goals of government, and the "national interest" becomes identified with the dominant capitalist interest.

Since policymakers must operate in and through the private economy, it is not long before they are operating *for* it. In order to keep the peace, business may occasionally accept reforms and regulations it does not like, but government cannot ignore business's own reason for being, i.e., the accumulation of capital. In a capitalist system, public policies cannot persistently violate the central imperative of capital accumulation. Sooner or later, business as a system must be met on its own terms or be replaced by another system.

REFORM AND THE "MIXED ECONOMY"

Observing the growth of government involvement in the economy, some writers mistakenly conclude that we have become a "post-capitalist" society with a "mixed economy" that is neither capitalist nor socialist.[8] Proponents of this view avoid any consideration of whom government benefits when mixing itself with the economy. They assume that government operates in a class vacuum with neutral intent and socially beneficent effect. Business elites know otherwise. They are capable of making

8. For instance, Dahrendorf, *Class and Class Conflict in Industrial Society*.

class distinctions in public policy. So they support government services and regulations that benefit corporate interests, and they oppose government services and regulations that benefit workers, consumers, the needy, and the environment but are potentially costly to business.

Government involvement in the economy represents not a growth in socialism (as that term is normally understood by socialists) but a growth in state-supported capitalism, *not the communization of private wealth but the privatization of the commonwealth*. This development has brought a great deal of government planning, but it is not of the kind intended by socialism, which emphasizes the social ownership of productive forces and the reallocation of resources for democratic purposes. As several English socialists pointed out, in criticism of the policies of the British Labour party:

> Planning now means better forecasting, better coordination of investment and expansion decisions, a more purposeful control over demand. This enables the more technologically equipped and organized units in the private sector to pursue their goals more efficiently, more "rationally." It also means more control over unions and over labor's power to bargain freely about wages. This involves another important transition. For in the course of this rationalization of capitalism, the gap between private industry and the State is narrowed.[9]

In Western industrial nations, including the United States, government economic planning revolves around regulating and preserving capitalism, not ending it. The outcome is a more centralized blend of capitalist public-private powers. Under the guise of insulating decision making from selfish interest groups and corrupt politicians, corporate-political elites will push for tighter control over the political economy while bypassing the public, the unions, and Congress. This is state planning *for* and *by* the owning class. Its function is not social welfare or reform but the maintenance of capital profitability at home and abroad.

Given the monopoly they enjoy over society's productive capacity, the giant corporations remain the sole conduit for most public expenditures. Whether it be for schools or school lunches, sewers or space ships, submarines or airplanes, harbors or highways, government relies almost exclusively on private contractors and suppliers. These suppliers may be heavily subsidized or entirely funded from the public treasure, but they remain "private" in that a profit—usually a most generous risk-free one—

9. Stuart Hall, Raymond Williams, and Edward Thompson, "The May Day Manifesto," excerpted in Carl Oglesby (ed.), *The New Left Reader* (New York: Grove Press, 1969), p. 115. Also S. M. Miller, "Planning: Can It Make a Difference in Capitalist America?" *Social Policy*, September/October 1975, pp. 12–22.

accrues to them for whatever services they perform. The government is not a *producer* in competition with business, such rivalry not being appreciated in a capitalist economy, but a titanic *purchaser* or *consumer* of business products.

Sometimes the government will exercise direct ownership of a particular service, either to assist private industry—as with certain port facilities and research institutions—or to perform services that private capital no longer finds profitable to provide on its own—as with the nationalized companies in Great Britain and the bus and subway lines in many American cities. Public ownership in this context is often only on paper, representing nothing more than a change from private stocks to public bonds—owned by the same wealthy interests that had held the stocks. Instead of collecting dividends on their stock, investors collect interest on their government bonds, which offer a high rate and a safe investment. So private capital readily sells its franchise to the government for a nice price, while "ownership" in the form of a huge debt, with all the risks and losses and none of the profits are passed on to the public.[10] Public ownership is not socialism unless it breaks the moneyed power of the investor class, so that the wealth of the enterprise as well as nominal ownership is in public hands. In sum, the U.S. "mixed economy" has little to do with socialism. The merging of the public and private sectors is not merely a result of the growing complexity of technological society nor is it a transition toward socialism. It is in large part a necessary development for the preservation of propertied class interests.

The Limits of Reform

Defenders of the existing system assert with pride that "democratic capitalism" provides the institutional means for peaceful change and that the history of capitalism has been one of gradual reform. To be sure, important reforms have been won by working people. To the extent that the present economic order has anything humane and civil about it, it is because of the struggles of millions of people engaged in the defense of their standard of living and their rights as citizens, a struggle that began well before the Constitutional Convention and continues to this day.

It is somewhat ironic, though, to credit capitalism with the genius of

10. Note how the bond issue for nationalized firms in France offered by the "socialist" government in France in 1981 attracted big investors: *Washington Post*, September 10, 1981. The "socialist" government in Spain nationalized vast private holdings to avert their collapse. After bringing them back to health with generous nourishment from the public treasure, they were sold back to private companies, just as Reagan did with Conrail: *New York Times*, January 6, 1986.

gradual reform when (a) most reforms through history have been vehemently resisted by the capitalist class and were won only after prolonged, bitter, and sometimes bloody popular struggle and (b) most of the problems needing reform have been caused or intensified by capitalism.

We might ask: Why doesn't the future arrive? Why is fundamental change so difficult to effect? Why is social justice so hard to achieve? The answer is twofold: First, because the realities of power militate against fundamental reform, and second, because the present politico-economic system could not sustain itself if such reforms were initiated. Let us take each of these in turn:

1. Quite simply, those who have the interest in fundamental change have not yet the power, while those who have the power have not the interest, being disinclined to commit class suicide. It is not that decision makers have been unable to figure out the steps for change; it is that they oppose the things that change entails. The first intent of most officeholders is not to fight for social change but to survive and prosper. Given this, they are inclined to respond positively not to group *needs* but to group *demands*, to those who have the resources to command their attention. In political life as in economic life, needs do not become marketable demands until they are backed by "buying power" or "exchange power," for only then is it in the "producer's" interest to respond. The problem for many unorganized citizens and workers is that they have few political resources of their own to exchange. For the politician, the compelling quality of any argument is determined less by its logic and evidence than by the strength of its advocates. The wants of the unorganized public seldom become marketable political demands—that is, they seldom become imperatives to which officials find it in their own interest to respond, especially if the changes would put the official on a collision course with those who control the resources of the society and who see little wrong with the world as it is.

2. Most of the demands for fundamental change in our priorities are impossible to effect within the present system if that system is to maintain itself. The reason our labor, skills, technology, and natural resources are not used for social needs and egalitarian purposes is that they are used for corporate gain. The corporations cannot build low-rent houses and feed the poor because their interest is not in social reconstruction but in private profit. For the state to maintain a "healthy" economy within the present capitalist structure, it must maintain conditions that are favorable to investment, that is, it must guarantee high-profit yields. Were the state instead to decide to make fundamental changes in our economic priorities, it would have to redistribute income, end deficit spending by taxing the financial class from whom it now borrows, stop bribing the rich to get still richer with investment subsidies and other guarantees, and redirect capital investments toward not-for-profit public goals. But if the state did all this,

investment incentives would be greatly diminished, the risks for private capital would be too high, many companies could not survive, and unemployment would reach disastrous heights. State-supported capitalism cannot exist without state support, without passing its immense costs and inefficiencies on to the public. The only way the state could redirect the overall wealth of society toward egalitarian goals would be to exercise democratic control over capital investments and capital return, but that would mean, in effect, public ownership of the means of production—a giant step toward *socialism*.

What is being argued here is that, contrary to the view of liberal critics, the nation's immense social problems are not irrational offshoots of a basically rational system, to be solved by replacing the existing corporate and political decision makers with persons who would be better intentioned and more socially aware. Rather, the problems are rational outcomes of a basically irrational system, a system structured not for the satisfaction of human need but the multiplication of human greed, one that is grossly inequitable, exploitative, and destructive of human and natural resources at home and abroad.[11]

How then can we speak of most government policies as being products of the democratic will? What democratic will demanded that Washington be honeycombed with high-paid corporate lobbyists who would regularly raid the public treasure on behalf of rich clients? What democratic mandate directed the government to give away more monies every year to the creditor class, the top 1 percent of the population, in interest payments on public bonds than are spent on services to the bottom 20 percent? When was the public consulted on Alaskan oil leases, bloated defense contracts, and agribusiness subsidies? When did the American people insist on having unsafe, overpriced drugs and foods circulate unrestricted and an FDA that protects rather than punishes the companies marketing such products? When did the public urge the government to go easy on polluters and allow the utility companies to overcharge consumers? When did the voice of the people clamor for unsafe work conditions in mines, factories, and on farms? And how often have they demonstrated for multibillion-dollar tax breaks for the super-rich and a multibillion-dollar space program that will put missiles in the sky while leaving the rest of us more burdened by taxes and deprived of necessary services here on earth? What democratic will

11. It is not that state-supported capitalism is the cause of every social ill in modern society but that capitalism has no fundamental commitment to remedying social ills, despite its command over vast resources that might be directed toward such ends. And capitalism does much to create and intensify the profoundly irrational economic and social arrangements that breed ills and injustices at home and abroad.

decreed that we destroy the Cambodian countryside between 1969 and 1971 in a bombing campaign conducted without the consent or even the knowledge of Congress and the public? When did public opinion demand that we send the Marines into Lebanon, wage a mercenary war of attrition against Nicaragua, violate the SALT II arms limitations, support wars against popular forces in El Salvador, Guatemala, the Western Sahara, and East Timor, or subvert progressive governments in Chile, Indonesia, and a dozen other countries?

Far from giving their assent, ordinary people have had to struggle to find out what is going on. And when public opinion has been registered, it has been demonstrated in the opposite direction, against the worst abuses and most blatant privileges of plutocracy, against the spoliation of the environment and the use of government power to serve corporations, and against bigger military budgets and military intervention in other lands.

DEMOCRACY AS CLASS STRUGGLE

The ruling class has several ways of expropriating the earnings of the people. First and foremost, as *workers*, people receive only a portion of the value their labor power creates. The rest goes to the owners of capital. On behalf of the owners, managers continually devise methods—including speed-ups, lay-offs, the threat of plant closings, and union busting—to tame labor and secure the process of capital accumulation.

Second, as *consumers*, people are victimized by monopoly practices that force them to spend more on less. They also are confronted with increasingly exploitative forms of *involuntary* consumption, as when relatively inexpensive mass-transit systems are neglected or eliminated, creating a greater dependency on automobiles; or when low-rental apartments are converted into high-priced condominiums; or when local farm products are replaced by expensive processed foods transported long distances by agribusiness.

Third, over the last thirty years or so, with each successive "tax reform" bill, working people as *taxpayers* have had to shoulder an ever larger portion of the tax burden, while business pays less and less. Indeed, the dramatic decline in business taxes has been a major cause of the growth in the federal deficit.[12] As we have seen, the deficit itself is a source of profit to the moneyed class and an additional burden to taxpayers. This regressive system of taxation and deficit spending represents a major upward redistribution of income from labor to capital.

12. John McDermott, "The Secret History of the Deficit," *Nation*, August 21–28, 1981, pp. 129, 144–46.

Fourth, as *citizens*, the people get less than they pay for in government services. The lion's share of federal spending goes to large firms, defense contractors, banks, and other creditors. As citizens, the people also endure the hidden "diseconomies" shifted onto them by private business, as when a chemical company contaminates a community's groundwater with its toxic wastes.

These various means serve the process of capital accumulation, which is the essence of capitalism—the investment of money to extract still more money from the populace, from their labor, their consumption, their taxes, and their environment. But this process of extraction and accumulation, with all its related abuses and injustices, instigates a reactive resistance from workers, consumers, community groups, and taxpayers—who are usually one and the same people, those whom I have been calling "the democratic forces." There exists, then, not only class oppression but class struggle, not only plutocratic dominance but popular opposition to the policies and social conditions created by state-supported capitalism. The ruling class predominates but it must continually strive to recreate the conditions of its dominance.

Plutocratic culture would have us think that the "American heritage" consists of a series of heroic military vignettes: George Washington at Valley Forge, the battle of the Alamo, the winning of the West, and U.S. Marines hoisting the flag on Iwo Jima. But there is also a tradition of *people*'s struggle in the United States that has been downplayed or ignored by the dominant elites and their representatives. This democratic struggle ebbs and flows but it has never ceased. Forced to react to the exploitative conditions imposed upon them and moved by a combination of anger and hope, ordinary people in America have organized, agitated, demonstrated, and engaged in electoral challenges, civil disobedience, strikes, sit-ins, takeovers, boycotts, and sometimes violent clashes with the authorities—for better wages and work conditions, for a fairer allocation of taxes and public services, for political and economic equality, and for peace and nonintervention abroad. Against the heaviest odds, against courts and laws, against the clubs and guns of police and army, against the calumny and slander of well-paid propagandists—the working people, racial minorities, and women of the United States have suffered many defeats but won some important victories, forceably extracting concessions and imposing reforms upon resistant rulers.

To the extent they have sought to equalize social, legal, and economic conditions, the democratic forces are the major limitation on capitalism's relentless exploitation of labor and on the mistreatment of the people and the environment; they are the major democratic bulwark against plutocracy.

If we think of democracy as something more than a set of political procedures and as a system that also must produce *substantive* outcomes that sustain and advance the health, well-being, and living standards of the people (the *demos*) rather than serving the privileges of the few, then those who fight for these substantive benefits are engaged in not just "economic issues" but in advancing democracy. Through history the democratic forces have come to consider their class demands for such things as jobs and old-age security to be as much a part of their birthright as more formal political rights. Indeed many of the struggles for *political* democracy, the right to vote, assemble, petition, and dissent, have been largely propelled by the *class* struggle, by a desire to democratize the rules of the political game so as to be in a better position to fight for one's economic interests. The battle for democratic rights has not occurred in a class vacuum but has been much fortified by the fight against the moneyed interests. In a word, *the struggle for democracy has been part of the class struggle.*

Throughout the history of the United States, as noted earlier, the propertied elites have resisted the expansion of democracy. At the Philadelphia convention in 1787, the delegates showed an undisguised hostility toward the popular forces of that day and only reluctantly agreed to democratic concessions in order to assure ratification of their elitist Constitution. For the next 40 or 50 years in many states, the propertied classes resisted universal male suffrage, and for 140 years they opposed female suffrage. Through the nineteenth century and into the twentieth, they resisted emancipation, the expansion of civil rights and civil liberties, the legalization of labor unions, and a whole array of social legislation. They knew that the growth of popular rights would only strengthen popular forces and put limits on the elites' ability to pursue their interests. They instinctively understood, even if they seldom publicly articulated it, that *it is not socialism that subverts democracy, but democracy that subverts capitalism.*

Today, as the capitalists reduce the earning power of working people in order to maintain profits, they diminish both the buying power of consumers and their own markets. So they need more subsidies, tax breaks, and monopolistic protections from government to maintain capital accumulation. Stagnation, underconsumption, and other economic distortions are recurrent features of this crisis. The Keynesian solution (relied upon by liberals and conservatives alike) of borrowing from the future through a system of deficit spending, so government might maintain business profits, social programs, and huge military budgets, proves increasingly difficult as fiscal resources—especially wages—decline.

The conservative solution is to return to the days before the New Deal.

To maintain profit rates, the tax burden is shifted downward, government support of business is increased, and consumers are made to spend still more for less—all of which leads to a diminution of people's living standards.[13] To bolster profits, government programs that cut into business earnings must be abolished regardless of their social and human value; so ruling elites attack occupational, consumer, and environmental protections under the pretense that such programs "cost jobs."

To maintain profits, wages must be held down: one way is to increase the supply of workers in relation to jobs, forcing people to compete more intensely for work on terms more favorable to employers. Historically, this is done by eliminating jobs through mechanization, by bringing immigrant labor into the country, and by investing capital in countries that offer cheaper labor markets. More recently, the administration in Washington sought to increase the labor supply by easing child-labor laws, lowering the employable age for some jobs, and raising the retirement age, so putting millions of additional workers onto an already overcrowded job market.

Another way to hold down wages is to eliminate alternative sources of support so that people become exclusively reliant on wages and more compliant as wage earners. Wage workers are made, not born. Historically the process of creating people willing to work for subsistence wages entailed driving them off the land and into the factories, denying them access to farms and to the game, fuel, and fruits of the commons. Divorced from these means of subsistence, the peasant became the proletarian. Today, unemployment benefits and other forms of public assistance are reduced in order to deny alternative sources of sustenance. Public jobs are eliminated so that still more workers will compete for employment in the private sector. Conservatives seek to lower the minium wage for youths and resist attempts to equalize wages and job opportunities for women and minorities, so keeping women, youth, and minorities as the traditional underpaid "reserve army of labor" used throughout history to depress wages.

Still another way to hold down wages and maximize profits is to keep the work force divided and poorly organized. There is today in the United States a $500 million industry specializing in union busting. In addition, racism has played an important divisive role, as the economic fears and anger of Whites are channeled away from employers and toward minority fellow workers who are also competitors for jobs, education, and housing.

---

13. As Paul Volcker, chairman of the Federal Reserve Board said: "The standard of living of the average American has to decline." *Washington Post*, March 9, 1980.

Racism also has a deflationary effect on wages similar to sexism: when a large minority of the work force are underpaid because they are Black, Latino, or female, this increases profit margins for the owners and holds down the price of labor in general.

Rulers have often sought to mute popular grievances by conjuring up domestic radical enemies and foreign foes. In these times of economic recession, plutocratic representatives fill the air with alarming tales of terrorists and KGB infiltration at home and of a "Soviet Menance" that is out to destroy us and ensiave the world. In truth, the existing system is threatened not from without but from within, from the crisis of capitalism itself. But the cold warriors direct public attention to irrelevant foes, calling for still more sacrifices by the people in order to strengthen the repressive capacity of the state and bolster a highly expensive, dangerous—but highly profitable—military-industrial establishment. The cold warriors also use the "Soviet Menace" to justify intervention against liberation movements that threaten the reactionary Third World social order, which multinational capitalism finds so compliant and profitable.

Before long, the democratic forces mobilize to protect their standard of living from conservative attack and to oppose such dangerous and destructive manifestations of the cold war as the draft, the nuclear-arms race, and U.S. intervention in places like El Salvador. Once again democracy proves troublesome to capital in its war against labor at home and abroad. *So the ruling class must attack not only the people's standard of living but the very democratic rights that help them defend that standard.* Thus, the right to strike is under ever more persistent attack by both the courts and legislatures. With more injunctions, fines, and jail sentences, and more restrictive "right to work" and "open shop" laws, union organizing becomes increasingly difficult—all in an era when collective bargaining was assumed to be an established right. The laws against progressive minor parties are tightened after successive third-party challenges, and public funding of the two-party monopoly is expanded.

Federal security agencies and local police violate constitutional protections in order to stifle progressive activists. The Supreme Court, packed with conservative appointees, moves to overturn or weaken many of the civil liberties and civil rights won in the past, including protections against forced confessions, arrest without warrant, invasion of privacy, and affirmative action. Even the right to demonstrate and distribute handbills and newspapers is under attack in some locales. In contrast, the Court decides that spending ceilings on campaign contributions place an unconstitutional limit on free speech; thus the Court gives the rich a greater capacity for speech than the rest of us and a still greater opportunity for the power of money to prevail over the power of numbers.

THE TWO FACES OF THE STATE

Some critics of capitalism believe that as the problems of the economy deepen, modern capitalism will succumb to its own internal contradictions; as the economic "substructure" gives way, the "superstructure" of the capitalist state will be carried down with it and the opportunity for a better society will be at hand. One difficulty with this position is that it underestimates the extent to which the state can act with independent effect to preserve the capitalist class. The state is more than a front for the economic interests it serves; it is the single most important force that corporate America has at its command. The power to use force, the power of eminent domain, the power to tax, spend, and legislate, to use public funds for private profit, the power of limitless credit, the power to mobilize highly emotive symbols of loyalty and legitimacy—such resources of the state give corporate America a durability it could never provide for itself. Behind capitalism there stands the organized power of the state. "The stability and future of the economy is grounded, in the last analysis, on the power of the state to act to preserve it."[14] The corporations can call on the resources of the state to rationalize and subsidize their performance, maintain their profit levels, socialize costs by taxing the many, and keep dissidents under control through generous applications of official violence.

The state, however, is not merely a puppet of the capitalist class. As already noted, to fulfill its task of bolstering the capitalist system as a whole, the state must sometimes resist particular corporate interests. The state is also the place where liberal and conservative ruling-class factions struggle over how best to keep the system afloat. The more liberal elements see that democratic concessions sometimes can be functional to the existing politico-economic system—by keeping capitalism from devouring those who make and buy its products. If conservative goals are *too* successful, as with the upward income redistribution achieved by the Reagan administration, then the contradictions of capitalism intensify and so do the instabilities of the system. Profits may be maintained and even increased for a time through various financial contrivances, but unemployment grows, markets shrink, discontent deepens, and small and not so small businesses perish. As the pyramid begins to tremble from conservative victories, some of the less myopic occupants of the apex develop a new appreciation for the base that sustains them and a sudden dislike for the suicidal excesses of "trickle-*up*" economics. These kinds of elite differences are fought over within the state.

---

14. Gabriel Kolko, *The Triumph of Conservatism* (Chicago: Quadrangle Books, 1967), p. 302.

The state's ability to act in the interests of the capitalist class is limited by several factors. First, government officials cannot always know what are the best policies for the corporate system, especially since particular industrial interests conflict with each other or need contradictory things—such as immediate tariff protections *and* long-range free-trade agreements, or cutbacts in wages *and* growing consumer markets. Confusions and conflicts arise within the state that reflect the irrationalities of capitalism itself.

Second, the capitalist state is limited by the historic emergence and competing appeal of socialist states and anti-imperialist forces in various parts of the world. The specter of socialism continues to haunt the bourgeois world both as a direct challenge and as an embarrassing reminder that capitalism is not the immutable, natural condition of all human society.

Third, just as troublesome in the immediate future are the competing interests of other capitalist nations. The Soviet Union may remain the ideological enemy, but serious market conflicts are likely to arise with economic competitors like Japan and Germany. As stagnation and unemployment become chronic conditions throughout the capitalist world, the competition between capitalist nations will intensify, posing problems for which the capitalist nation-state is not likely to find easy answers.

Fourth, state action on behalf of capitalism is limited by the underlying structures of capitalism itself. So the state must deal with capitalism's contradictions on capitalism's own terms—which is itself something of a contradiction, for the state rarely can get to systemic causes. It attends to toxic waste rather than to the modes of production and profit of the chemical and oil industries; it comes up with offers of job programs and poverty programs rather than resolving the modes of investment that create unemployment and the highly inequitable distribution of income, wealth, and taxes. The crises periods of U.S. capitalism are longer and deeper and the recovery periods shorter and more shallow with greater indebtedness and higher rates of inflation and unemployment becoming a permanent feature.[15]

The lopsided, massive accumulation of capital which is *the* measure of success under capitalism is also a danger to the system when carried beyond a certain point. The loan portfolios of American banks include more than $500 billion in farm and Third World debt, which carries a high risk of default. With major banks going under because of bad loans, sinking real-

15. Thus, twenty years ago a $20 billion deficit was considered serious; today it would be considered a healthy victory to get the annual deficit to below $100 billion. Twenty years ago, 5 percent unemployment and 4 percent inflation were thought to be real problems; today such unemployment and inflation levels are treated as quite acceptable and normal.

estate values, and widespread banking fraud, the banking system today is as fragile as it was before the Great Depression.[16]

The lopsidedness shows up in other ways: the rich are getting richer than ever, while the populace works harder for less.[17] The country entered 1986 with $100 billion in international debt—that is, money owed by the government (and ultimately by the workers and taxpayers) to foreign investors. By 1989, the United States will owe more than $600 billion to the rest of the world and will have to pay over $60 billion in interest payments, a sum requiring the annual output of 1.5 million workers.[18] And within the United States itself, the more than $2 trillion debt incurred by the government will have to be paid by the working populace to rich creditors. What will happen to the stock market with its fitful leaps upward and dangerous slumps, and to the banks, the wage structure, the international credit system, and the enormous debt structure? It is hard to see any solutions to these vast problems.

Finally, the greatest restraint on the capitalist state comes in having to deal with the populace. The state cannot fulfill its role of protecting the plutocratic class and legitimating exploitative social relations unless it maintains its own legitimacy in the eyes of the people. And it cannot do that without keeping an appearance of popular rule and an appearance of neutrality in regard to class interests. More important than the constraints of appearances are the actual power restraints imposed by democratic forces. There is just so much the people will take before they begin to resist. Marx anticipated that class struggle would bring the overthrow of capitalism. Short of revolution, class struggle constrains and alters the capitalist state, so that the state itself, or portions of it, become an arena of struggle that reflects the conflict going on in the wider society. Having correctly discerned that "American democracy" as professed by establishment opinion makers is something of a sham, some people incorrectly dismiss the democratic rights and gains won by popular forces as of little account. But these democratic rights and the organized resistant strength of democratic forces are, at present, all we have to keep some ruling elites from doing what in their heart of hearts they would like to do to make this nation perfectly safe for capitalism.

The vast inequality in economic power as exists in our capitalist society translates into a great inequality of social power. Capitalism constricts not only people's material conditions but their freedom too, their ability to act

---

16. So concludes the economist Lester Thurow in his "The 20's and 30's Can Happen Again," *New York Times*, January 22, 1986.

17. Over 40 percent of the eight million new jobs created between 1979 and 1985 paid poverty wages, compared to 20 percent of the new jobs created the previous six years: *Washington Post*, February 19, 1987.

18. Thurow, "The 20's and 30's . . ."

in accordance with their own interests—whatever their formal freedoms. They are not even free to feed and shelter themselves unless someone above makes a profit from such productive efforts. How far, then, does democracy go under capitalism? The state plays a fundamentally contradictory role. It is the contradiction between democracy and capitalism. More than half a century ago the great sociologist Max Weber wrote: "The question is: How are freedom and democracy in the long run at all possible under the domination of highly developed capitalism?"[19] That question is still with us. As the crisis of capitalism deepens, as surplus resources disappear and more austerity is needed, as the contradiction between the egalitarian expectations of democracy and the dominating thievery of capitalism sharpens, the state must act more repressively to hold together the existing class system. In some countries, rulers have resorted to a dictatorial final solution, smashing all democratic organizations so better to impose a draconian economy on the people and maintain the dominance of capital over labor, using fascism to protect capitalism while claiming they were saving democracy from communism.

Why doesn't the capitalist class in the United States resort to fascist rule? It would make things easier: no criticisms from the press, no organized dissent, no environmental or occupational protections, no elections or labor unions to worry about. As of now, there is no need for such drastic measures since the dominant class is getting much of what it wants behind a democratic facade. Better to break unions and hold down wages by using court injunctions, and by refusing to negotiate contracts, rather than having to put union leaders before a firing squad. Better to drown out and isolate radical opponents with a moneyed media monopoly rather than having to silence them with assassination squads. "A state based solely on the continuous resort to compulsion is revealed as an obvious instrument of class domination."[20] And a state revealed as an obvious instrument of class dominance loses popular support, generates resistance rather than compliance, and activates a revolutionary class consciousness.

Representative government is a very serviceable form of governance for capitalism, even if often a troublesome one, for it offers a modicum of liberty and self-rule while hiding the class nature of the state. Rather than relying exclusively on the club and the gun, bourgeois democracy employs a cooptive, legitimating power—which is ruling-class power at its most hypocritical and most effective. By playing these contradictory roles of

19. H. H. Gerth and C. Wright Mills (eds.), *From Max Weber: Essays in Sociology* (New York: Oxford University Press, 1958).

20. Bruce Berman, "Class Struggle and the Origins of the Relative Autonomy of the Capitalist State," paper presented at the American Political Science Association, New York, September 1981. Berman offers a good discussion of the contradictory class role of the state.

ALIVE AND WELL

protector of capital and "protector of the people," the state best fulfills its fundamental class role. What is said of the state is true of the law, the bureaucracy, the political parties, the legislators, the universities, the professions, and the media. In order to best fulfill their class-control and class-dominating functions yet keep their social legitimacy, these institutions must maintain the appearance of neutrality and autonomy. To foster that appearance, they must occasionally actually exercise some critical independence and autonomy from the state and from capitalism. They must save a few decisions for the people, attempt to soothe or blunt intense popular agitations, and take minimally corrective measures to counter the more egregious transgressions against democratic appearances—as when "reining in" the CIA and investigating the Watergate and Iran-contra scandals.

In a country like the United States, the success of a dictatorial solution to the crisis of capitalism would depend on whether the ruling class could stuff the democratic genie back into the bottle. Ruling elites are restrained in their autocratic impulses by the fear that they could not get away with it, that the people and the enlisted ranks of the armed forces would not go along. More likely, an American ruling-class-in-crisis will prefer something short of an all-out military dictatorship, a "democracy for the fewer still." This would entail keeping certain accoutrements of democracy such as a money-dominated two-party monopoly, an electoral system that focuses on relatively meaningless issues, a shift of policy-making power to nonelective and unaccountable public-private groups, a limited and tepid verbal dissent that leads to no serious organized opposition, politically monopolized mass media that embrace existing arrangements at face value, a few tame and ineffectual labor unions, the activation and financing of organized bigotry and right-wing religionists, and an all-imposing national-security state that claims to defend the citizenry from external enemies while actually protecting capitalism from its own people. This book has tried to demonstrate that we are much closer to that democracy for the few than we might have imagined.

WHAT IS TO BE DONE?

Those who seek fundamental progressive changes would do well not to dilute their demands as did too many liberals during the Reagan era, who hoped thereby to preserve their credibility. The democratic agenda for the coming decade should be truly democratic in its content and direction. Here is a partial listing of things needed for a more just and desirable social order:

1. A bilateral, mutually verifiable nuclear and nonnuclear arms reduction agreement with the Soviet Union, to ease international tensions and minimize the likelihood of war.
2. Elimination of the Strategic Defense Initiative ("Star Wars"), a horrendously costly weapon that will only instigate a new and greater escalation of the arms race.
3. With an arms reduction, the United States (as with the USSR) would be able to drastically cut its huge military expenditures and redirect billions of dollars into social programs for the most needy, exactly reversing the spending trend of the Reagan era.
4. There are a variety of reforms needed in the political system. A few of the most immediate ones would be (1) a standard federal electoral law allowing easy ballot access for third parties; (2) a strict cap on electoral spending and free media access for all candidates; (3) an end to life tenure for judges and Supreme Court justices; all jurists should serve for limited and fixed terms.
5. Reintroduce the progressive income tax (eliminated during the Reagan years) for rich individuals and corporations—without the many

loopholes and deductions that still exist. Also reintroduce the inheritance tax for the rich, which has practically been abolished.

6. Increase the minimum wage, and legislate a guaranteed minimum income above the poverty level.

7. Abolish antilabor laws like Taft-Hartley which make union organizing so hazardous for workers. Provide government protections that give workers the right to unionize without the harassment and firings they now face.

8. Distribute to almost two million needy farmers the billions of federal dollars now received by rich agribusiness firms. Encourage organic commercial farming and phase out the use of pesticides and chemical fertilizers.

9. Engage in a concerted effort at conservation and ecological restoration, including a massive clean-up of the land, air, and water.

10. Develop rapid mass transit systems within and between cities for safe, economical transportation and to minimize the ecologically disastrous effects of vehicular traffic.

11. Phase out nuclear plants and develop a crash program to develop alternate thermal, hydro, tidal, and solar energy sources.

12. Cancel the national debt, with compensation to small bondholders and only minimal and partial compensation to large ones. The national debt is a transfer program from taxpayers to bondholders, from labor to capital, from average people to the wealthy. Like Latin American peasants, U.S. taxpayers will be sacrificing their standard of living for generations to come to pay off wealthy creditors—as they are doing today.[21]

13. Initiate a massive federal job program, putting people to work on the various undertakings mentioned above. There are many important vital services that are needed, and many people in need of work. And there is money available to put them all to work doing the things needed. A Works Project Administration (WPA), more encompassing than the New Deal one, could put people to work reclaiming the environment, building needed industries, housing, and transportation, providing services for the aged and infirm and for the public in general. And people could be put to work producing goods and services in competition with, and finally to replace, the private market. The New Deal's WPA engaged in the production of goods, including manufacturing clothes and mattresses for relief clients, surgical gowns for hospitals, and canned meat, fruits, and vegetables for the jobless poor.[22] This kind of not-for-profit direct production to meet human

---

21. Michael Kinsley, "A Debt We'll Never Repay," *Washington Post*, November 27, 1986.
22. Kim Moody, "Going Public," *Progressive*, July 1983, p.20.

needs brings in revenues to the government both in the sales of the goods and in taxes on the incomes of the new jobs created. Eliminated from the picture are those who live off the labor of others, which explains their fierce hostility toward government programs that engage in direct production.

14. End the U.S.-sponsored war against the poor of the world. Eliminate all foreign aid to regimes engaged in oppression of their own peoples. The billions of U.S.-tax dollars that flow each year into the Swiss bank accounts of foreign autocrats and militarists could be better spent on human services at home.

Those who insist that government is parasitic and business is productive nevertheless keep relying on public funds to bolster private investments. As the evidence accumulated in this book indicates, it is the privileged element of the private sector that parasitically feeds off the commonweal and not vice versa. The policy changes listed above reverse that flow, transfering wealth from the private to the public realm, for public needs. But none of these measures will prevail unless the structural problems of capitalism are themselves resolved. For as social goals and investment targets are transformed to not-for-profit direct production to meet human needs, private capital will go on strike, so to speak; investors will refuse to invest and will close down production. What is needed then is public ownership of all the major means of production and public ownership of the wealth, the moneyed power itself, in a word, socialism.

But can socialism work? Is it not just a dream in theory and a nightmare in practice? Can the government produce anything of note? As mentioned in an earlier chapter, various private industries (defense, railroads, satellite communication, aeronautics, and nuclear power, to name some) exist today only because the government funded the research and development and provided most of the risk capital. We already have some socialized services and they work quite well if given sufficient funds. Our roads and water supplies are socialized as are our bridges and ports, and in some states so are our liquor stores, which yearly generate hundreds of millions of dollars in state revenues. And there are the examples of "lemon socialism" in which governments in this and other countries have taken over industries ailing from being bled for profits, and nursed them back to health, testimony to the comparative capacities of private and public capital.

The publicly owned railroads in France and Italy work much better than the privately owned ones in the United States (which work as well as they do only because of public subsidies). State and municipal uinversities in the United States are public and therefore "socialist" (shocking news to some of the students who attend them) and some of them are among the very best institutions of higher learning in the country. A 1981 Department of Energy study found that publicly owned utilites are better managed than investor-owned ones. And because they do not have to produce a profit for stockholders, their rates are lower and their surplus earnings go back into the public budget to pay for maintenance and technical improvement.[23] The Minitel videotext system, a state-owned monopoly, provides communication and information services to millions of people in France far in advance of anything offered by AT&T or any other private company in the United States.

How do we get to socialism? Only time will tell. Better to know where we want to go and not yet be able to get there, than to go full speed ahead without knowing where we are going—which is the modus operandi of capitalism. Capitalism is a system without a soul and without a direction. It has nowhere to go, for it has nothing it wants to accomplish except the reproduction and expansion of its own capital accumulation process.

Whether socialism can be brought about within the framework of the existing modern capitalist state or by a revolutionary overthrow of that state is a question unresolved by history. So far there have been no examples of either road to socialism in modern industrial society. But because something has never occurred in the past does not mean it cannot happen in the future. In the late nineteenth century, knowing persons, relying on the fact that a successful workers' revolution had never taken place, concluded that one never would. Yet early in the next century the Bolshevik revolution exploded upon the world. And bourgeois pundits scoffed at the idea that "native" peoples could overthrow modern colonial powers and achieve self-rule, yet such things have happened.

The question of what kind of socialism we should struggle for deserves more extensive treatment than can be given here. American socialism cannot be modeled on the Soviet Union, China, Cuba, or other countries with different historical, economic, and cultural developments. But these countries ought to be examined so that we might learn from their accomplishments and problems. Whatever else one wants to say about existing socialist societies, they have achieved what capitalism cannot and has no intention of accomplishing: adequate food, housing, and clothing for all; economic security in old age; free medical care; free education at all levels; and the right to a job—in countries that are not as rich as ours but which use productive resources in more rational ways than can be done under capitalism.[24]

---

23. MacNeil-Leher News Hour, PBS television, January 26, 1984.

24. See, for instance, Albert Szymanski, *Is the Red Flag Flying? The Political Economy of the Soviet Union Today* (London: Zed, 1979); Mike Davidow, *Cities Without Crisis* (New York: International Publishers, 1976).

The destructive and unjust effects of capitalism upon our nation, the pressures of competition between capitalist nations, the growing discontent and oppression of the populace, the continual productive growth within socialist nations, the new revolutionary victories against Western imperialism in the Third World, all these things make objective conditions increasingly unfavorable for capitalism. Yet people will not discard the system that oppresses them until they see the feasibility of an alternative one. It is not that they think society *should* be this way, but that it *must* be. It is not that they don't want things to change, but they don't believe things *can* change—or they fear that whatever changes might occur would more likely be for the worse.

What is needed is widespread organizing not only around particular issues but for a socialist movement that can project both the desirability of an alternative system and the *possibility* and indeed the great *necessity* for democratic change. Throughout the world and at home, forces for change are being unleashed. There is much evidence—some of it presented in this book—indicating that Americans are well ahead of the existing political elites in their willingness to embrace new alternatives, including public ownership of the major corporations and worker control of production. With time and struggle, as the possibility for progressive change becomes more evident and the longing for a better social life grows stronger, people will become increasingly intolerant of the monumental injustices of the existing capitalist system and will move toward a profoundly democratic solution. We can be hopeful the day will come, as it came in social orders of the past, when those who seem invincible will be shaken from their pinnacles.

There is nothing sacred about the existing system. All economic and political institutions are contrivances that should serve the interests of the people. When they fail to do so, they should be replaced by something more responsive, more just, and more democratic. Marx said this, and so did Jefferson. It is a revolutionary doctrine, and very much an American one.

About the Author

Michael Parenti received his Ph.D. from Yale University and has taught political and social science at various colleges and universities. In addition, he has been a guest lecturer on campuses throughout the country. His writing has also appeared in the *Journal of Politics*, *Political Science Quarterly*, *American Political Science Review*, *Politics and Society*, *Political Affairs*, *the Nation*, *Monthly Review*, *New York Times*, *Los Angeles Times*, and numerous other publications. His books include *The Anti-Communist Impulse*, *Ethnic and Political Attitudes*, *Trends and Tragedies in American Foreign Policy* (a book of edited readings), *Power and the Powerless*, and *Inventing Reality: The Politics of the Mass Media* (the latter two are published by St. Martin's Press). He is currently completing a book entitled *The Sword and the Dollar: Imperialism, Revolution, and the Cold War.* Dr. Parenti can be contacted directly at: 2801 Adams Mill Rd. NW, Washington, DC 20009.

Index